M000099249

Making Milton

Making Milton

Print, Authorship, Afterlives

Edited by

EMMA DEPLEDGE, JOHN S. GARRISON,
AND MARISSA NICOSIA

OXFORD

UNIVERSITY PRESS

OXFORD
UNIVERSITY PRESS

Great Clarendon Street, Oxford, OX2 6DP,
United Kingdom

Oxford University Press is a department of the University of Oxford.
It furthers the University's objective of excellence in research, scholarship,
and education by publishing worldwide. Oxford is a registered trade mark of
Oxford University Press in the UK and in certain other countries

© the several contributors 2021

The moral rights of the authors have been asserted

First Edition published in 2021

Impression: 1

All rights reserved. No part of this publication may be reproduced, stored in
a retrieval system, or transmitted, in any form or by any means, without the
prior permission in writing of Oxford University Press, or as expressly permitted
by law, by licence or under terms agreed with the appropriate reprographics
rights organization. Enquiries concerning reproduction outside the scope of the
above should be sent to the Rights Department, Oxford University Press, at the
address above

You must not circulate this work in any other form
and you must impose this same condition on any acquirer

Published in the United States of America by Oxford University Press
198 Madison Avenue, New York, NY 10016, United States of America

British Library Cataloguing in Publication Data
Data available

Library of Congress Control Number: 2020943348

ISBN 978–0–19–882189–2

DOI: 10.1093/oso/9780198821892.001.0001

Printed and bound in the UK by
TJ Books Limited

Links to third party websites are provided by Oxford in good faith and
for information only. Oxford disclaims any responsibility for the materials
contained in any third party website referenced in this work.

Acknowledgements

Making Milton began when all three co-editors were in residence at the Folger Shakespeare Library in Washington, DC. Anyone who has conducted research at the Folger knows that discoveries occur not only in the reading room but also at daily teatime, during informal play readings, and over meals when scholars come together for discussion and recreation. We hope this volume replicates the sense of community and generous conversation that accompanied its beginnings. Even in our earliest conversations about what this volume might look like, we discussed how each of our different methodological approaches informs how we see Milton: as a brand in the book trade, as an authorial persona, as a canonized poet whose works were deemed ripe for appropriation and adaptation. Our warm thanks go to the Folger and all of their friendly, helpful staff.

We are grateful to all of the contributors for their enthusiasm and hard work. Thanks also go to Angelica Duran, Lukas Erne, and David Loewenstein for their precious advice and feedback during the early stages of this project. Honor Jackson, Joseph Malcomson, and Nicole Polglaze were instrumental in helping this project come to life by providing invaluable administrative and editorial support. Eleanor Collins and Jacqueline Baker of Oxford University Press have guided this project elegantly to fruition. We also wish to heartily thank the Press's anonymous readers for their insightful comments and feedback. This book is much improved as a result of their suggestions.

Emma would like to thank the English Departments at the Universities of Fribourg and Neuchâtel, Switzerland, especially Indira Ghose and Kilian Schindler, and Martin Hilpert and Patrick Vincent. She is also grateful to the Swiss National Science Foundation for funding her research at the Folger Shakespeare Library. John thanks his colleagues at Grinnell College, whose insight and enthusiasm has continually invigorated him in this project. The Center for the Humanities at Grinnell College also provided funding towards the completion of this book. Marissa thanks her colleagues at the Pennsylvania State University–Abington College for supporting her research and her scholarly community in Philadelphia, especially Claire Falck, Glenda Goodman, Carissa Harris, Melissa E. Sanchez, and Thomas Ward, for helpful readings and fruitful conversations.

Contents

List of Illustrations

Notes on Contributors

Editors

Emma Depledge is Assistant Professor of English Literature, 1500–1790, at the Université de Neuchâtel. She is the author of *Shakespeare's Rise to Cultural Prominence: Print, Politics and Alteration, 1642–1700* (Cambridge University Press, 2018) and co-editor of *Canonising Shakespeare: Stationers and the Book Trade, 1640–1740* (Cambridge University Press, 2017). She writes the annual review of editions and textual studies for *Shakespeare Survey* and is an associate editor for *English Studies*.

John S. Garrison is Professor of English at Grinnell College, where he teaches courses on early modern literature and culture. His recent books include *Shakespeare at Peace* (with Kyle Pivetti, Routledge, 2018) and *Shakespeare and the Afterlife* (Oxford University Press, 2019).

Marissa Nicosia is Assistant Professor of Renaissance Literature at the Pennsylvania State University–Abington College. She is co-editor of *Renaissance Futures,* a special volume of *Explorations in Renaissance Culture* (2019), and she has published articles on early modern literature in journals such as *Modern Philology, Milton Studies,* and *The Papers of the Bibliographical Society of America.*

Contributors

Antoinina Bevan Zlatar is an Academic Associate at the University of Zurich. She is the author of *Reformation Fictions: Polemical Protestant Dialogues in Elizabethan England* (Oxford University Press, 2011), *What is an Image in Medieval and Early Modern England?* (co-edited with Olga Timofeeva, Narr Verlag, 2017), and articles on seventeenth-century cultures of reading. Her current book project, generously funded by a Swiss National Science Foundation award, is entitled *Making and Breaking Images in John Milton's Paradise Lost.*

Thomas N. Corns is Emeritus Professor of English Literature at Bangor University. His many publications include *Milton's Language* (Blackwell, 1990), (with Gordon Campbell) *John Milton: Life, Work, and Thought* (Oxford University Press, 2008), *The Milton Encyclopedia* (Yale University Press, 2012), and *A New Companion to Milton* (Wiley-Blackwell, 2016). He is also editor (with David Loewenstein) of the forthcoming *Paradise Lost, Complete Works of John Milton,* vol. I (Oxford University Press) and general editor (with Gordon Campbell) of the *Complete Works of John Milton,* 11 vols. (Oxford University Press).

Stephen B. Dobranski is editor of *Milton Studies* and Distinguished University Professor in the Department of English at Georgia State University. He is the author of several books, including *Milton's Visual Imagination: Imagery in 'Paradise Lost'* (Cambridge University Press, 2015); *Readers and Authorship in Early Modern England* (Cambridge University Press, 2005); and *The Cambridge Introduction to John Milton* (Cambridge University Press, 2012). He has also edited *Milton in Context* (Cambridge University Press, 2010) and co-edited *Milton and Heresy* (Cambridge University Press, 1998). Most recently, he served as general editor of the three-volume series *Early Modern British Literature in Transition, 1557–1714* (Cambridge University Press, 2019).

Lara A. Dodds is Professor of English at Mississippi State University. She is the author of *The Literary Invention of Margaret Cavendish* (Duquesne University Press, 2013). Her work has appeared in the journals *Milton Studies, Milton Quarterly, Early Modern Studies Journal, English Literary Renaissance,* and *Restoration,* and, most recently, in *Queer Milton* (Palgrave Macmillan, 2018, edited by David Orvis).

Angelica Duran is Professor of English, Comparative Literature, and Religious Studies at Purdue University, where she has been since earning her PhD in English Literature from Stanford in 2000. She is the author of *Milton among Spaniards* (University of Delaware Press, 2020), *The Age of Milton and The Scientific Revolution* (Duquesne University Press, 2007), and over forty chapters and articles; editor of *The King James Bible across Borders and Centuries* (Duquesne University Press, 2014) and *A Concise Companion to Milton* (Wiley-Blackwell, rev. 2011); and co-editor of *Milton in Translation* (Oxford University Press, 2017) and *Mo Yan in Context* (Purdue University Press, 2014). She is on the Executive Committee of the Milton Society of America (2012–21) and the editorial board of *Milton Quarterly* (2005–).

Neil Forsyth is Honorary Professor at the University of Lausanne, Switzerland. He is the author of numerous chapters, articles, and book-length studies, including *John Milton: A Biography* (Lion Hudson, 2008), *The Satanic Epic* (Princeton University Press, 2003), and *Shakespeare the Illusionist: Magic, Dreams and the Supernatural on Film* (Ohio University Press, 2019). He also co-edited (with C. Tournu) *Milton: Rights and Liberties* (Peter Lang, 2007) and has written a narrative history of the devil entitled *The Old Enemy: Satan and the Combat Myth* (Princeton University Press, 1989).

Blaine Greteman is Associate Professor of English at the University of Iowa. He is the author of *The Poetics and Politics of Youth in Milton's England* (Cambridge University Press, 2013). His work has also appeared in the journals *Renaissance Quarterly* and *English Literary History,* as well as in the collection *Young Milton* (edited by Edward Jones, Oxford University Press, 2015).

John K. Hale is Professor of English at the University of Otago. He is the author of *Milton as Multilingual: Selected Essays 1982–2004* (Otago Studies in English, 2005), *Milton's Cambridge Latin: Performing in the Genres 1625–1632* (Medieval and Renaissance Texts and Studies, 2005), *John Milton Latin Writings: A Selection* (MRTS, 1999), and *Milton's Languages: The Impact of Multilingualism on Style* (Cambridge University Press, 1997).

He co-authored *Milton and the Manuscript of De Doctrina Christiana* (with Gordon Campbell, Thomas Corns, and Fiona Tweedie, Oxford University Press, 2007) and *John Milton, De Doctrina Christiana*, edited and translated for the *Complete Works of John Milton*, vol. 8 (with J. Donald Cullington, Oxford University Press, 2012). His *Milton's Scriptural Theology: Confronting De Doctrina Christiana* (Arc Humanities Press) appeared in 2019. He is the Milton Society of America Honoured Scholar for 2021.

David Loewenstein is Edwin Erle Sparks Professor of English and the Humanities at Penn State–University Park. His publications include *Representing Revolution in Milton and His Contemporaries: Religion, Politics, and Polemics in Radical Puritanism* (Cambridge University Press, 2001); *Heresy, Literature, and Politics in Early Modern English Culture* co-editor (Cambridge University Press, 2006); *Early Modern Nationalism and Milton's England* co-editor (University of Toronto Press, 2008); *John Milton, Prose: Major Writings on Liberty, Politics, Religion, and Education* editor (Wiley-Blackwell, 2013); and *Treacherous Faith: The Specter of Heresy in Early Modern English Literature and Culture* (Oxford University Press, 2013). He is currently editing *Paradise Lost* (the first modern edition to include both the 1667 and 1674 editions of the poem) for the new Oxford University Press edition of *The Complete Works of John Milton*.

Kyle Pivetti is Associate Professor of English at Norwich University. His first book is titled *Of Memory and Literary Form: The Making of Nationhood in Early Modern England* (University of Delaware Press, 2015). He is also the co-author of *Shakespeare at Peace* (Routledge, 2018) and *Shakespeare's Shame: Emotion and Memory in the Plays and Poems* (Northwestern University Press, forthcoming), and co-editor of *Sexuality and Memory in Early Modern England: Literature and the Erotics of Recollection* (Routledge, 2015). His research in memory and the formation of political identity has been featured in *Queer Milton* (Palgrave Macmillan, 2018) and the journals *Shakespeare, Studies in Ethnicity and Nationalism, Modern Philology*, and *Explorations in Renaissance Culture*.

Noam Reisner is Associate Professor in the Department of English and American Studies at Tel Aviv University. He is the author of *Milton and the Ineffable* (Oxford University Press, 2009) and *John Milton's Paradise Lost: A Reading Guide* (Edinburgh University Press, 2011). His work has appeared in the journals *The Cambridge Quarterly, Philological Quarterly, Renaissance Studies,* and *Milton Quarterly*, as well as in the collection *Young Milton* (edited by Edward Jones, Oxford University Press, 2015).

Elizabeth Sauer FRSC, is Professor of English at Brock University and past President of the Milton Society of America. Publications include *Emergent Nation: Early Modern British Literature in Transition*, editor (Cambridge University Press, 2019); *Women's Bookscapes*, co-editor (Michigan University Press, 2018); *Milton, Toleration, and Nationhood* (Cambridge University Press, 2014); *Reading the Nation in English Literature*, co-editor (Routledge, 2010); *Milton and Toleration*, co-editor (Oxford University Press, 2007); *'Paper-contestations' and Textual Communities in England* (University of Toronto Press, 2005); *Reading Early Modern Women*, co-editor (Routledge, 2004); *Books and Readers in Early Modern England*, co-editor (University of Pennsylvania Press, 2002); and *Milton and the Imperial Vision*, co-editor (Duquesne University Press, 1999).

Nigel Smith is the William and Annie S. Paton Foundation Professor of Ancient and Modern Literature and Chair of the Committee for Renaissance and Early Modern Studies at Princeton University. His major works are *Andrew Marvell: The Chameleon* (Yale University Press, 2010; pb 2012), *Is Milton better than Shakespeare?* (Harvard University Press, 2008), the Longman Annotated English Poets edition of Andrew Marvell's *Poems* (2003, 2007), *Literature and Revolution in England, 1640–1660* (Yale University Press, 1994), and *Perfection Proclaimed: Language and Literature in English Radical Religion 1640–1660* (Oxford University Press, 1989). He has also co-edited, with Nicholas McDowell, *The Oxford Handbook of Milton* (Oxford University Press, 2009, pb 2011). *Polyglot Poetics: Transnational Early Modern Literature* is forthcoming.

Rachel Willie is Reader in Early Modern Literary Studies at Liverpool John Moores University. Her monograph *Staging the Revolution: Drama, Reinvention and History 1647–1672* (Manchester University Press, 2015; pb 2019) was shortlisted for the University English Early Career Book Prize in 2016. With Kevin Killeen and Helen Smith, she has co-edited *The Oxford Handbook of the Bible in Early Modern England, c. 1530–1700* (Oxford University Press, 2015; pb 2018; winner of the Roland H. Bainton Prize, Reference Works, 2016). With Gábor Gelléri, she is co-editor of *Travel and Conflict in the Early Modern World* (Routledge, 2020). She is currently principal investigator on the AHRC-funded project 'Soundscapes in the Early Modern World'.

1

What Made Milton?

Emma Depledge, John S. Garrison, and Marissa Nicosia

When readers opened John Milton's *Poems* (1645), they encountered a unique vision of the poet in his early career (see Figure 1.1). On the verso, a stylized engraved portrait by William Márshall in which the author is framed by the four muses, and a 'literary joke' is inscribed in Greek.[1] On the recto, statements about the poet's Latinity and evidence of his collaboration with the composer Henry Lawes.[2] This is not the pamphleteering Milton of the *Divorce Tracts*, the Latin Secretary writing *Eikonoklastes*, or the blind, embattled republican dictating *Paradise Lost* to his amanuensis. Instead, this is a young Cambridge poet entering the marketplace of print with a volume of poetry published by a stationer who would go on to become the premier literary publisher of his day: Humphrey Moseley.

We begin with this particular construction of Milton in a volume of poetry published early in his writing life and political career because it encapsulates vectors of influence addressed by the essays in *Making Milton: Print, Authorship, Afterlives*. Milton's *Poems* abides by what would emerge as Moseley's house style; this is a slim octavo publication with an author portrait, an erudite title page, and a series of paratexts in which Milton's authorship is praised. As Stephen B. Dobranski notes in the next chapter (p. 19), Moseley writes in a preface to *Poems* of Milton's 'peculiar excellency' and of his desire to 'solicit' Milton's manuscript from him. By preparing the 'true Copies' and accepting Moseley's request to publish his texts,[3] Milton, like Moseley, may have been seeking to establish himself in what was then still an emerging literary

---

[1] On the inscription, see Gordon Campbell and Thomas Corns, *John Milton: Life, Work, and Thought*, 182, and below.

[2] Lawes is believed to have been Milton's collaborator on *A Maske Presented at Ludlow Castle*, and the poet celebrates his friendship with the musician in his Sonnet 13, 'To Mr. H. Lawes, on his Aires'. For Lawes's relationship with the playwrights and poets of his day, see Ian Spink, *Henry Lawes: Cavalier Songwriter*, 23–72.

[3] One assumes that Moseley was the instigator because, after hinting at the success he enjoyed with Spenser, he explains his decision to publish Milton's poems: 'The Author's more peculiar excellency in these studies, was too well known, to conceal his Papers, or *to keep me from attempting to sollicit them from him*' (emphasis ours, see 'The Stationer to the Reader' in Milton, *Poems*, a4r). However, as Campbell and Corns rightly note, 'only Milton himself can have pulled together the contents of *Poems*' (*John Milton: Life, Work, and Thought*, 182).

Emma Depledge, John S. Garrison, and Marissa Nicosia, *What Made Milton?* In: *Making Milton: Print, Authorship, Afterlives*. Edited by: Emma Depledge, John S. Garrison, and Marissa Nicosia, Oxford University Press (2021). © Emma Depledge, John S. Garrison, and Marissa Nicosia. DOI: 10.1093/oso/9780198821892.003.0001

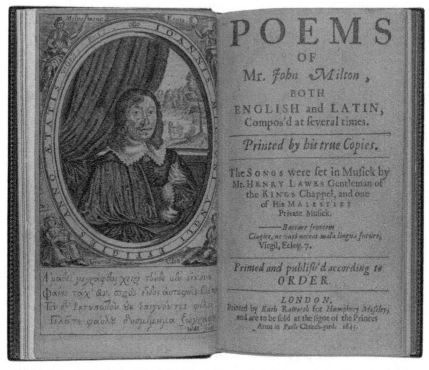

Figure 1.1 *Poems of Mr. John Milton, Both English and Latin, Compos'd at several times* (London, 1645), frontispiece and title page. Folger Shakespeare Library, Shelfmark: M2160 copy 1. Used by permission of the Folger Shakespeare Library.

marketplace.[4] Moseley had just published an edition of Edmund Waller when he issued Milton's *Poems*. Between 1645 and 1656, Moseley positioned Milton in a literary canon of poets and playwrights that he described as 'the best Wits of our, and Foreign Nations'.[5] In addition to plays by the likes of Francis Beaumont and John Fletcher, Ben Jonson, Thomas Middleton, and John Webster, Moseley produced editions of poems by Thomas Carew, William Cartwright, Abraham Cowley, Richard Crashaw, William Davenant, John Denham, John Quarles, James Shirley, Thomas Stanley, John Suckling, and Henry Vaughan. It is thus noteworthy that Milton and Moseley chose to include *A Maske Presented at*

---

[4] See David Kastan, who claims that what enabled 'an idea of English literature to form and be generally recognized was largely the work of one publisher and bookseller in the middle of the seventeenth century, Humphrey Moseley', before going on to discuss Moseley's poetry collections and subsequent play collections of the 1640s and 1650s ('Humphrey Moseley and the Invention of English Literature', 111); see also, John Barnard, 'London Publishing', 8–9; Paulina Kewes, 'Give Me the Sociable Pocket-books...'; Ann Baynes Coiro, 'Milton and Class Identity', 277; Timothy Raylor, 'Moseley, Walkley, and the 1645 Editions of Waller'.

[5] See 'The Stationer to the Reader', in *The Last Remains of Sr John Suckling* (London, 1659), A3r.

Ludlow Castle in this collection of lyric poetry, marking Milton as an author of different genres. The volume also included letters in which the masque was praised, and it combined both Latin and English verse. Milton thereby projected his authorial identity into the world alongside an ambitious stationer who likewise sought to fashion himself through the book trade.

Milton's collaboration with Moseley also resulted in an author portrait Milton did not appreciate, but it seems he was able to score a discreet victory over Marshall, the engraver of the collection's portrait frontispiece.[6] Marshall had 'produced illustrations for several attacks on radical puritans...including [an attack on] *The Doctrine and Discipline*'; as Gordon Campbell and Thomas Corns note, the Greek inscription Milton prepared for Marshall to engrave onto his intaglio plate, just underneath the illustration, reads, 'You would say, perhaps, that this picture was drawn by an ignorant hand, when you looked at the form that nature made. Since you do not recognize the man portrayed, my friends, laugh at this rotten picture of a rotten artist.'[7] The fact that Marshall engraved these lines confirms that he had no Greek, and the cheeky move is suggestive of how Milton worked with and against stationers in order to promote both his authorial status and his personal politics.

While Milton's political allegiance will have been well known, his poems were not especially polemical.[8] Likewise, while Moseley may have been known to sympathize with the King's supporters, when he published Milton's works he was at the earliest stages of building his reputation as a stationer. Milton's poems went on to appear in Moseley's catalogues next to royalist writers such as Carew (1651), with almost identical titles given to their collections. Warren Chernaik has suggested that Moseley's book list, his reputation as a supporter of episcopacy and Charles I, and the prefaces he added to his (subsequent) publications combined in ways that turned 'physical book[s]' into 'statement[s] of allegiance'.[9] For Chernaik, the material form of *Poems of John Milton* (1645) sees Milton 'virtually kidnapped by Moseley and transformed against his will into a royalist'.[10] In more chronologically nuanced language, Michael J. Braddick suggests that Moseley's house style and his emergence as a publisher of not just royalist poets but the best poets and dramatists of his age 'may have cast a certain *after-the-fact* social or cultural aura over Milton's book and perhaps underscored—or helped to fashion—the poet's and the book's complex identity'.[11]

---

[6] For more on Milton's response to the portrait, see the next chapter in this volume.
[7] *John Milton: Life, Work, and Thought*, 182.
[8] Campbell and Corns note that 'Milton's poems contained nothing indicative of his current fierce anti-prelatism, save for "Lycidas"; he made [almost] no allusion to the current civil war...and much of the early verse celebrated figures that the most die-hard royalist would have been happy to acknowledge as at least sound and in some cases saintly' (*John Milton: Life, Work, and Thought*, 182–3).
[9] 'Books as Memorials: The Politics of Consolation', 210.   [10] Ibid.
[11] Emphasis ours. See *The Oxford Handbook of the English Revolution*, 473. See also Steven N. Zwicker, 'On First Looking into Revisionism', 799–800.

David Scott Kastan makes a similar point about how the size and format of Moseley's poetry collections encouraged consumers to 'buy more than one volume, perhaps even the entire series'; in other words, to potentially collect Milton alongside Waller, Carew, and others.[12] Indeed, auction catalogues for the sale of private libraries in the late seventeenth and early eighteenth century suggest that a number of collectors did just that.[13] Moseley's volume(s) may have impacted perceptions of Milton's political allegiance, but they also helped to earn him a place amongst the 'Most Vendible books in England' when they appeared in William London's *Most Vendible Books* catalogue of 1658.[14] Collaborations with the book trade were therefore liable to both undermine and cement the authorial persona Milton wished to project.

The unusual positioning of Milton's entrance onto the literary scene is underscored by the full title of the 1645 volume: *Poems of Mr. John Milton, Both English and Latin, Compos'd at several times.* The title calls attention to the heterogeneity of the volume. It collects writings not only in two languages but also composed at different moments in Milton's maturation. As his first volume of published work, the collection invites us to see an evolving poet moving through adolescence into adulthood. We see Milton and his publisher making his authorial persona in this carefully ordered volume, but readers also surely found themselves asking what to make of this emergent author.

The aforementioned engraving has a place in this 'making' as well. Louis Martz posits that the portrait of the young Milton on the frontispiece intentionally depicts 'the harsh and crabbed image of a man who might be forty or fifty', an act of 'deliberate sabotage' by the skilled engraver.[15] But this rendering of the author does not necessarily constitute 'sabotage'. Instead, it may render visible the complexity of even Milton's earliest construction as an authorial persona. The portrait of a prematurely senior Milton is characterized nicely by Carolyn Dinshaw's description of the Rip Van Winkle figure: 'he is the very somatization of temporal asynchrony, his flesh in one temporal framework and his mind in another.'[16] Marshall's engraving reflects Milton's own perception of himself as ageing more quickly on the surface than in reality. In 'How Soon Hath Time', the

---

[12] See 'Humphrey Moseley and the Invention of English Literature', 114.

[13] See, for example, *A Choice Catalogue of the Library of John Parsons* (London, 1682), which shows that Parsons collected copies of Milton's *Poems* (lot 294, p. 18) and 'Carew's Poems' (lot 388, p. 20).

[14] Milton's and Carew's volumes, with their similar titles, appeared on the same page of London's catalogue. See 2E4v for 'Mr Milton's Poems with a Mask' and 'Mr Curew's Poems, with a Masque'.

[15] Louis Martz, *Milton: Poet of Exile*, 33. For an extended discussion of the possible intentions behind the engraving, see R. M. Jonson, 'The Politics of Publication: Misrepresentation in Milton's 1645 *Poems*. Peter Lindenbaum has observed how Marshall made James Shirley look like his Milton portrait in Moseley's 1646 volume of Shirley's poems, thus suggesting that both Milton's book and his face could be made to resemble those of royalist writers, and vice versa ('Milton's Contract', 187).

[16] Carolyn Dinshaw, *How Soon is Now?*, 135.

young poet reflects that, at the age of 23, 'my semblance might deceive the truth, / that I to manhood am arrived so near, / and inward ripeness doth much less appear' (5–7). Marshall's portrait conveys the peculiar status of being simultaneously mature and immature about which this poem complains.

The expanded 1673 edition of *Poems* nearly doubled the number of sonnets in the volume and included Milton's translations of Horace's fifth ode and fifteen psalms. The revised edition thus reinforces his perceived command of both poetic form and the classical and Christian traditions that intermingle in works such as *Paradise Lost*. The 1673 volume also included '*Ad Joannem Rousium*', a Latin verse letter to John Rouse, Oxford University Librarian, dated 23 January 1646. Though the poet laments his 'poor talents' in that letter, the verse itself deftly displays his command of Latin, while he nods to his travels on the Continent and his education at Cambridge. And the inclusion of the letter itself gestures towards the republic of letters within which Milton participated as a humanist. This example, like the 1645 *Poems* more generally, demonstrates why it is important to distinguish between different editions of Milton's works while analysing both the content of Milton's texts and the material forms in which they circulated.

Making Milton

Making Milton embraces the idea that Milton's reception did not follow a linear trajectory, rather that it was characterized by contradictions and inconsistencies. Milton's rise to cultural prominence is, we claim, best understood within the rich, complex system in which he emerged as an author, including the workings of the book trade; social networks that first received his writing in academies, universities, and urban settings; and the adaptation and appropriation of Milton in literary circles. The chapters therefore expose the specific ways in which Milton's status was concretized, be it through the work of individual agents of the book trade, through his own efforts to shape his reputation, or through the responses of communities of writers who reinterpreted his work. During the period in which he was writing, and in the years that directly followed, humanist discourse shifted between Latin and English, pamphlet publication spiked and declined, stage plays were banned and theatres were reopened, new modes of literary publishing emerged, and heated debates broke out about censorship and the state. Ultimately, what emerges from the volume's chapters is a robust sense of John Milton as an author both shaping his public reception and shaped by the mechanisms of public dissemination.[17]

[17] In his study of commercially motivated constructions of Shakespeare's authorial identity, Adam G. Hooks remarks, 'Instead of asking only what the book trade did for Shakespeare, I ask what Shakespeare did for members of the book trade.' The essays gathered in Part I of *Making Milton*,

The narrative presented in *Making Milton* is threefold. Contributors to Part I recognize the importance of the London book trade, which had the potential to both establish authorial reputation and confirm authorial achievement, with books made available for consumers to purchase and read. This made Milton both more and, at times, less visible as an author. Essays in Part II note that, in addition to the work of publishers and booksellers, Milton himself actively participated in the construction of his authorial profile within his own works. Our contributors demonstrate important ways in which Milton contributed to and supplemented the creation of his authorial reputation that was being established in print. Essays in the final part of the volume address Milton's legacy and reputation, with contributors analysing key instances of how readers and fellow writers have responded to Milton. This too is a form of 'making', but one with which Milton had less to do, one over which he had less control. Rather than accept the image—handed down to us by Romantic writers—of Milton the solitary genius, *Making Milton* therefore argues that Milton's authorial persona needs to be understood in the context of the multifarious, mutually beneficial relationships he enjoyed—and continues to enjoy—with stationers, writers, and readers.

In *Making Milton* we ask: what is lost when studies of the publication history of *Paradise Lost* are not attuned to the epic's early readers? What do we miss when we focus on Milton's self-fashioning in his English writings, but not in his Latin texts, or, alternatively, his revolutionary prose, without considering how those works were published within England and beyond its borders? How might the methods of critical bibliography, new historicism, formalism, biography, and literary history answer the question of how the Milton we know was made? *Making Milton* offers a number of answers to these questions, but we hope to also inspire fresh inquiry by bringing often disparate threads of scholarly conversation into productive dialogue.

Making Milton comes at a time of renewed interest in the author and when new discoveries and developments allow for a more nuanced understanding of Milton's place in literary history. Major publications of the past few years have expanded our knowledge of the Milton canon while insisting that scholars pay attention to the whole body of Milton's work, as opposed to simply addressing well-known texts such as *Paradise Lost*. For example, Oxford University Press is in the process of publishing a new eleven-volume edition of Milton's *Complete Works*.[18] The edition includes manuscript versions of key texts as well as marginalia and other notes supplied by several early modern readers.

'Milton and the Book Trade', share a spirit with this approach to inquiry. See Hooks, *Selling Shakespeare*, 3.

[18] The following have been published to date: *Volume II: The 1671 Poems: Paradise Regain'd and Samson Agonistes*, ed. Laura Lunger Knoppers (2008); *Volume III: The Shorter Poems*, ed. Barbara Kiefer Lewalski and Estelle Haan (2012); *Volume VI: Vernacular Regicide and Republican Writings*, ed.

Making Milton is in productive dialogue with a range of ongoing conversations about the writing, publication, and reception of Milton's work and of early modern literature more broadly. Our inquiry asks new questions about Milton's own life, as well as about the habits and contexts of his early readers.[19] It also opens new avenues for considering the author's political and religious convictions, especially in the context of how his works were disseminated.[20] Such questions must take into account how Milton's works were published, revised, and recontextualized.[21] Any investigation of Milton's emergence as a writer necessitates exploration of his education and his early exposure to other writers.[22] Equally,

---

N. H. Keeble and Nicholas McDowell (2013); *Volume VIII: De Doctrina Christiana*, ed. John K. Hale, J. Donald Cullington, Gordon Campbell, and Thomas N. Corns (2012); and *Volume XI: Manuscript Writings*, ed. William Poole (2019).

[19] Four biographies have been published recently, reflecting renewed interest in Milton's life and authorial afterlife. These include Anna Beer's *Milton: Poet, Pamphleteer, and Patriot*; Campbell and Corn's *John Milton: Life, Work, and Thought*; Neil Forsyth's *John Milton: A Biography*; and Nicholas McDowell's *Poet of Revolution: The Making of John Milton*, which appeared after this project was completed. Our volume also builds on crucial work that has explored readers of Milton's work and the changing nature of readership in early modern England more broadly. Key volumes include Sharon Achinstein's *Milton and the Revolutionary Reader* and *Literature and Dissent in Milton's England*, which have provided insight into how literature was not only informed by, but also involved in, the shaping of political debates in the public sphere. The recent collection *John Milton: Life, Writing, Reputation* (Paul Hammond and Blair Worden, eds.) has urged scholars to reassess questions of how Milton's life experience and personal beliefs shaped his writing and our volume responds to that call.
[20] Stephen B. Dobranski's *Readers and Authorship in Early Modern England* has been crucial in encouraging scholars to pay attention to the active role readers and consumers play in shaping the meaning of texts. Previous studies have also rendered visible the religious aspects of Milton's reception. For example, Catherine Gimelli Martin's *Milton Among the Puritans* argues that the poet's reputation as puritanical is largely based on reader reception and one that obfuscates the many secular influences to which his writing points. Stephen Fallon's *Milton's Peculiar Grace* evocatively argues that Milton was not a religious writer but rather one deeply invested in assuring his own literary immortality. What has emerged from these and similar studies is a sense that Milton's reputation has been anything but fixed. Rather, it emerges from vexed publication contexts that he himself actively attempted to influence.
[21] Major studies in book history and bibliography have enabled critics to shed important light on the role collaborative practices played in the canonization of authors such as Shakespeare, Dryden, Richardson, and Wordsworth. However, with the exception of highly specialized descriptive bibliographies and the production of scholarly editions, the methodologies of new bibliography and authorship studies have seldom been unified in the interpretation of Milton's works and his reification as an authorial figure. We build on Dobranski's groundbreaking example in *Milton, Authorship and the Book Trade*, extending his discussion into a later period and expanding his case studies into a more detailed narrative of how Milton helped to shape, while himself being shaped by, the English book trade.
[22] See, for example, Claire M. L. Bourne and Jason Scott-Warren's identification of what may be Milton's annotated copy of Shakespeare's 1623 folio (Bourne, 'Vide Supplementum: Early Modern Collation as Play-Reading in the First Folio', and Scott-Warren, 'Milton's Shakespeare?'). Other recent volumes testify to increased interest in the content and contexts of Milton's early writing, including Blaine Greteman, *The Poetics and Politics of Milton's Youth*, and *Young Milton: The Emerging Author, 1620–1642*, ed. Edward Jones. Greteman's book touches upon the importance of Milton's early work and the political context in and for which he was writing. Jones's collection has been recognized as a much-needed volume on the early Milton and won the Irene Samuel Award (which recognizes a distinguished multi-author collection on Milton). It contains commentary on the political writings and on his life. Indeed, only three of the twelve articles have literary criticism as their primary focus. Especially important to our volume are Milton's early Latin writings, studies of which include Estelle Haan's *From Academia to Amicitia* and *Both English and Latin*, as well as John K. Hale's *Milton's Cambridge Latin*. These studies lay helpful groundwork in setting the historical context that influenced

study of Milton's afterlives needs to consider the circulation, translation, and appropriation of his texts by later authors.[23]

Each of our volume's three parts—'Milton and the Book Trade', 'Milton's Construction of an Authorial Identity', and 'Milton's Afterlives'—foregrounds the different ways through which to investigate the evolution of Milton's authorial persona during his lifetime and long after his death. Although distributed into three groupings, the essays in this volume are not meant to be read in isolation but, rather, in conversation with each other. For example, readers with an interest in Milton's relationship to drama will find discussion of how John Dryden's operatic adaptation of *Paradise Lost* may have impacted new editions of Milton's poem in Part I; analysis of how Milton's *A Maske Presented at Ludlow Castle* enabled him to engage with nationalism in the part on Milton's construction of an authorial persona; and, within the part dedicated to Milton's afterlives, an account of recent performances of *Paradise Lost* and *A Maske* in London and beyond. As Elizabeth Sauer notes in her Afterword (Chapter 16), what emerges from the volume as a whole is a renewed vision of not only how Milton was made but also why Milton continues to matter.

The part entitled 'Milton and the Book Trade' examines Milton's attempts to guide his works through the press, but ultimately argues that editors and individual stationers—from typesetters and illustrators to publishers and printers—had a more profound impact on Milton's authorial afterlife than he could possibly have envisaged. Milton often enjoyed a metonymic relationship with his books. For example, when Milton's 'treasonable' writings prompted calls for his arrest after the Restoration of the monarchy in 1660, physical copies of *Eikonoklastes* (1649) and *Pro Populo Anglicano Defensio* (1651) were called upon to answer for his absent authorial body. Milton evaded officers of the law, prompting Charles II—in his proclamation of 13 August 1660—to urge private citizens to deliver copies of these texts to the relevant authorities, much as one might denounce a fugitive hiding on one's own property.[24] The failed manhunt was replaced by a book hunt. What is more, material copies of *Eikonoklastes* and *Pro Populo Anglicano Defensio*

Milton's early writing, and open opportunities now to examine his early efforts to shape that historical context.

[23] Our volume's interest in reception thus complements the recent *Milton in the Long Restoration* (ed. Blair Hoxby and Ann Baynes Coiro, 2016), which focuses on diverse receptions and includes consideration of writers as late as Jane Austen. *Making Milton*'s focus on specific questions about the shifting evolution of his authorial persona also places it in dialogue with recent volumes such as *Milton in the Americas* (a special issue of *Milton Studies*, ed. Angelica Duran and Elizabeth Sauer, 2017), *Milton in Popular Culture* (ed. Laura Knoppers and Gregory Colón Semenza, 2006), *Milton's Modernities: Poetry, Philosophy, and History from the Seventeenth Century to the Present* (ed. Feisal G. Mohamed and Patrick Fadely, 2017), and *Milton in Translation* (ed. Angelica Duran, Islam Issa, and Jonathan R. Olson, 2017).
[24] This is Wing C3323, published as two sheets with blank versos. Charles II, *Proclamation, for calling in and suppressing of two books written by John Milton*, sheet 1.

were not just to be 'publicly burned' but specifically burned 'by the hand of the common Hangman', thus suggesting the extent to which material books could stand in for Milton's absent authorial body.[25] Milton's writings may have earned him the wrath of the King, but it was his books, his 'progeny', that suffered public execution in lieu of his authorial body.[26] The essays contained in this part of *Making Milton* argue for the need to interrogate Milton's books for the important insight they offer into his attempts to fashion himself as an author, the collaborations he enjoyed with agents of the book trade, and the ways in which Milton's books and reputation were shaped by—and helped to shape—the careers of stationers.

Milton's relationship with the English book trade was increasingly complex, and it changed over the course of his life.[27] Milton befriended and defended stationers, particularly in his writings against state licensers, but he also worked (from 1649) as a licenser for the Commonwealth government.[28] He helped to form print culture while his writing career and authorial reputation were sculpted by the agents who oversaw the London book trade. Milton also sought to fashion his authorship through careful negotiations within the book trade, just as stationers, such as Moseley and Jacob Tonson, used Milton and the profits his work generated for them as a platform to shape their own careers and the reputation of their publishing houses. Milton's views on print publication developed over the course of his lifetime, as did both the perceived market for his works and the kind of Milton offered in bookshops—be it a radical republican, a royalist, a prestigious literary author sold to elite subscribers, or an intellectually and financially accessible author available in less expensive editions.

In 'Milton and Transcendent Authorship', Stephen B. Dobranski explores the careful ways in which Milton exploited the respective benefits of oral transmission, manuscript, and print in order to memorialize friends and family and to live on through his works. Blaine Greteman focuses on the material history of *Epitaphium Damonis* in order to provide a corrective to the view of Milton as a solitary writer. Indeed, as Greteman argues, 'the poem carefully affirms, reconstitutes, and expands the social, poetic, and political networks that Milton established' in England and abroad, particularly during the 1630s (p. 32). Emma Depledge and Tom Corns focus on two very different, but equally significant, editions of *Paradise Lost*. Depledge outlines how material features of Tonson and Richard

---

[25] Ibid., sheet 2.

[26] On the relationship between publication, authorship, and procreation, see Douglas Brooks, *Printing and Parenting in Early Modern England*.

[27] On Milton's changing attitude to print publication, see Saunders, *The Profession of English Letters*. On Milton's self-fashioning in print and his collaborations with the book trade, see Dobranski, *Milton, Authorship, and the Book Trade*; Hale, 'Milton's Self-Presentation in Poems'; and Revard, *Milton and the Tangles of Neaera's Hair*.

[28] For an insightful discussion of Milton's work as a licenser, see Dobranski, *Milton, Authorship, and the Book Trade*, ch. 6.

Bentley's folio edition of 1688 helped to canonize Milton as a prestigious literary author but claims that the publication history of *Paradise Lost* was shaped not so much by the work's perceived 'genius' as by a successful adaptation and commercial rivalry between stationers. Corns takes as his focus the 1711 edition, also published by Tonson but in a smaller and less costly format. He indicates how Joseph Addison and Richard Steele's account of the poem in *The Spectator*—a publication that featured both characters discussing the text and a paratextual advert for the Tonson edition—helped to promote Tonson's publication and Milton's authorship. As he argues, this was a wonderful example of 'product placement', with the *Spectator* character 'Sir Roger ... shown pocketing Tonson's 1711 *Paradise Lost* with the premeditation of James Bond sipping Heineken in *Skyfall*' (p. 55). Equally, as Corns demonstrates, Tonson and the authors of *The Spectator* helped to make Milton accessible to a wider readership, with the stationer issuing inexpensive copies that made Milton affordable and Addison providing the kind of analysis and explanation needed to make Milton comprehensible for a less scholarly audience. Cumulatively, the chapters in Part I demonstrate the complex and contradictory image of Milton the author that emerges from his sometimes deliberate and sometimes inadvertent collaborations with agents of the book trade.

The essays gathered within Part II, 'Milton's Construction of an Authorial Identity', reveal how Milton asserted his status as an author—and encouraged others to assess his status—not just by displaying knowledge of previous writers but also by innovating the work of those authors in ways that speak to vexed issues in his contemporaneous culture. As the essays in this part make clear, Milton's authorial persona emerges from his careful interplay with past and present concerns over authorial humility and appropriate sources of inspiration, as well as active polemics surrounding iconoclasm, nationalism, drama, Latin, Protestantism, and republicanism. For this second part of *Making Milton*, *translatio* offers a particularly helpful analytic keyword, given its function to move elements across (*trans*) from one side (*latio*) of early modern culture (its classical underpinnings) to the other side of that culture (its contemporary Christian context). That is, Milton is as much making sense of the world's operations through pagan allegory as he is making sense of his own poetic process. As we will see in this part's case studies, this conflation of ancient and early modern elements at the heart of humanist *poesis* becomes even more evocative as the poet's work appears in reception contexts after his lifetime.

Challenging ourselves to view Milton's writing anew allows us to ask new questions about his efforts at self-fashioning. How did he seek to resuscitate debates or discourses in order to sustain the genealogies in which he wanted to be placed? Where did he see the limits in his own orthodoxy or radicalism? Who did he perceive to be his desired readers in his lifetime and what readers did he foresee in generations to come? What did he want to say about himself as a writer and about the act of writing itself? Across his work, Milton actively informs his readers about his own process of writing, all the while emphasizing that his writing is in active dialogue with authors from the past, ideas circulating in the present, and readers and writers in the world to come. Renaissance writers, especially ones with such grand ambitions as Milton's, carefully balanced a deeply humanist reverence for the past with an awareness of how their writing might be influenced by—and ultimately be remembered within—an era of highly contested political and religious change.[29]

Scholars contributing to Part II of the volume help us see Milton's efforts to defend his reputation in print and to shape how his reputation would be received by future generations. John K. Hale, for example, examines the Latin of the *Defensio Secunda* (*Second Defence*) in order to argue that this text not only defends Milton's reputation but also offers a candid expression of the author's sense of self-worth. This lively essay helps us 'hear' Milton's Latin voice as never before and, in turn, obtain a more robust sense of Milton's style. Revisiting *A Maske*, David Loewenstein further contributes to this part's shared project of hearing new subtleties in Milton's writing when we seek traces of self-fashioning. What emerges is a nuanced sense of the experimental masque exploring how England might reshape its national identity and what role the energies of literary imagination might have in such a project. Although Milton's relationship to the theatre was notoriously vexed, Rachel Willie builds on Loewenstein's chapter to suggest that Milton's complex ideas about drama were developed in dialogue with his contemporaries such as Sir William Davenant.

Turning our attention to the creative possibilities that Milton imbued in his muse, Kyle Pivetti moves from *Paradise Lost* to the early Latin poems in order to consider Milton's alignment of poetic inspiration with both states of crisis and opportunities for erotic expression. Antoinina Bevan Zlatar considers how Milton positioned himself and his theodicy within ongoing debates about visual depiction and iconoclasm in the seventeenth century. Noam Reisner, on the other hand, moves from *Paradise Regained* into the earliest writing in order to reveal how Milton engages directly with Pauline texts, complicating recent arguments about the extent to which Milton's canonization as a religious writer relies upon reader reception rather than the intention of his own writings. Taken as a whole, the essays in Part II build on previous studies of Milton's early writings to suggest that the author was actively attempting numerous authorial personae as he fashioned his identity in print.

---

[29] For the foundational text on authorial self-fashioning in the Renaissance, see Stephen Greenblatt, *Renaissance Self-Fashioning*. Some interesting starting points on Milton's self-fashioning are Jacob Blevins's *Humanism and Classical Crisis*, 85–154; Stephen M. Fallon's *Milton's Peculiar Grace*; and Reuben Sánchez's *Typology and Iconography*, 137–212.

It is widely known that Milton's contemporaries read and remarked on his works. Just as Milton's reputation was forged by his own writings and the efforts of stationers, it was also shaped by his early readers and interlocutors.[30] The final part of *Making Milton*, essays collected under the heading 'Milton's Afterlives', shows the various ways Milton's early readers engaged with his poetic forms, themes, and image, to shape both his reputation and their own careers and works. Likewise, the study of Milton's reception is neither especially new nor old.[31] As Rachel Trubowitz writes in her introduction to a recent special issue on 'Milton and the Politics of Periodization', the contextualist historicism that has dominated Milton studies for the last generation has ensured that Milton's early readers are rarely ignored.[32]

In an era of shifting ideas about authorship, reading, and literary ownership, Milton was made and remade by his younger peers. The 1674 edition of *Paradise Lost* included a poem by Andrew Marvell celebrating Milton's epic, and mocking John Dryden's recent attempt to dramatize the poem as an opera for the public stage entitled *The State of Innocence*.[33] The essays in this part consider how writers, publishers, directors, and performers remade Milton and how these acts of reception inflect how we understand Milton's works today. What have writers and thinkers done with Milton over the last 350 years? Where in the world have Milton's works travelled? How has Milton's authorial legacy excluded or included voices in the canon? Like Marvell and Dryden, writers, thinkers, and performers have forged contentious and mutually beneficial connections with Milton. Cumulatively, the authors in this part demonstrate the ways in which a variety of 'John Miltons' were made, remade, received, and refashioned by a range of writers across historical and geographical boundaries.

From discussions of women's authorship to imperial endeavours, Milton was a touchstone. Nigel Smith turns our attention to Milton's prose and calls into question both recent discussions of Milton as a supposedly radical writer and the nature and degree of Milton's own radicality in dialogue with his contemporaries. Lara Dodds rethinks Milton's status as an enabling or disabling 'bogey' in women's literary history by examining Anne Finch's engagement with *Paradise Lost*. She shows that Finch's appropriation of Milton and his canonical authority enabled claims for her own inclusion and laid a path for other female poets. Taking inspiration from a twenty-first-century performance of *A Maske* at the Sam Wanamaker Playhouse, London, Neil Forsyth reconsiders the erotic energies in Milton's masque. Angelica Duran examines how the presence of Milton's works

---

[30] For a recent account of Milton's early reception, see David Harper 'The First Annotator of *Paradise Lost* and the Makings of English Literary Criticism'.

[31] The recent volume *Milton in the Long Restoration* (ed. Blair Hoxby and Ann Baynes Coiro) shows the range of Milton's reception in the century or so after his death through translation, adaptation, appropriation, commentary, and even intensive editing for publication.

[32] Trubowitz, 'Introduction'.   [33] Andrew Marvell, 'On Mr Milton's *Paradise Lost*'.

on the Inquisition lists circulating in Mexico inflected his reception in the Americas.[34] Duran offers a comprehensive account of Milton's literary history in Mexico and tracks French, Spanish, Italian, and later, English, books throughout Spanish colonial territories. Her essay, like the others in this part, points to complex moments of reception and revision that will prove to be fruitful avenues for continued research on Milton's afterlives. From Milton's reception in the Americas to women writers responding to *Paradise Lost*, writers, political activists, and artists are remaking Milton, and reception studies are alive and well in Milton studies.[35]

Readers of *Making Milton* may take different pathways through the volume guided by particular lines of inquiry. For example, those interested in Milton and genre might begin with David Loewenstein's new reading of *A Maske* and then turn to Rachel Willie's discussion of Milton's relationship with the dramatic genre and the dramatic theory of playwright William Davenant. Another trajectory that would take an interest in contexts for reading Milton might move from Angelica Duran's exploration of 'Mexican Miltons' to Nigel Smith's essay on radicalism. We have deliberately avoided a chronological structure in order to reflect the flux of Milton's journey from reviled regicide to revered national poet, but those wishing to trace his life and works sequentially may wish to start with Stephen B. Dobranski's and Blaine Greteman's discussions of Milton's earliest writings and their circulation. Other courses through the volume will reveal robust discussions of Milton's Latinity, his significance in Restoration culture, his fraught intersections with women writers, and his often inextricable stances on politics and theology. *Making Milton* demonstrates how the author was made by communities and continues to make community. We hope readers will find their own connections both between and within the essays collected here.

Today, Milton survives as one of the most studied and respected of all early modern writers, but in 1687 William Winstanley announced that Milton's 'Fame is gone out like a Candle in a Snuff', adding that his 'Memory will always stink'.[36] Winstanley's prediction points out the ways in which canon formation and the ascendency of certain authors over others are not a matter of happenstance. That Milton was remembered and that we continue to teach, analyse, and celebrate his work testify to the often invisible operations by which authors are made by a

---

[34] Duran's essay in this volume is linked to her recent work on Milton's reception in Spanish— Duran, *Milton among Spaniards*.

[35] Significant recent work in this field includes varioum studies such as Miner, Moeck, and Jablonski's *Paradise Lost, 1668–1968* and Leonard's *Faithful Labourers*; accounts of Milton's reception in the Americas and beyond such as Wilburn's *Preaching the Gospel of Black Revolt*, Stevens and Simmons, eds., 'Milton in America', Duran and Sauer, eds., 'Milton in the Americas', and Rajan and Sauer's volume *Milton and the Imperial Vision*; feminist works such as Miller's *Engendering the Fall*, which looks at the seventeenth-century women writers who influenced and were inspired by Milton's writings; and studies of Milton and popular culture, such as Knoppers and Semenza's volume *Milton in Popular Culture* and Brown's *Milton on Film*.

[36] Winstanley, *The Lives of the Most Famous English Poets*, 95.

variety of factors, including the force of their own writing, the dynamic energy between those who champion and those who detract from an author's work, the historical circumstances present when texts are written or later received, the work of the publishing field, and the remaking of the author's works by later adapters. The contributors to this volume address when, how, and why Milton rose to cultural prominence, and why he continues to matter today. Focusing on Milton's lifetime and the years after his death, the essays tell a new story of Milton's rise from the smoke of Winstanley's metaphoric candle.

PART I

MILTON AND THE BOOK TRADE

2

Milton and Transcendent Authorship

Stephen B. Dobranski

Writing a tribute to Shakespeare in 1630, Milton lingered on the playwright's prophetic lines, 'easy numbers', and the 'deep impression' that his works continue to make on the imagination of readers.[1] He describes Shakespeare's poetry as having an almost Medusa-like effect, overwhelming readers' hearts and fancy, and leaving them astonished and transfixed—a 'live-long monument' to the 'Dear son of memory, great heir of fame' (8, 5).[2] Surprisingly, Milton says nothing about the theatre in his poem, an omission which might reflect an early Puritan sensibility or may have occurred because he wished to stress instead Shakespeare's natural poetic forms, what he praises as the 'flow' of his rhythmic verses (10).

Also striking is that Milton in 'On Shakespeare' emphasizes the esteemed author's 'leaves' and 'book' as part of his lasting achievement (11). Shakespeare, Milton writes, needs no 'hallowed relics' (3) or pyramid pointing to the stars because he remains alive not just through his readers but also in print. Notwithstanding Lukas Erne's recent argument that Shakespeare cared about the popularity of his publications and even envisioned some of his plays as printed texts, Milton's diction may reveal more about himself than it does about Shakespeare.[3] Admittedly, the decision to highlight the playwright's material book fits the poem's original bibliographical context: it was first printed along with six other encomia at the start of Shakespeare's second folio. But that Milton composed his verse in 1630 suggests his language was not occasioned by the poem's inclusion in Shakespeare's volume. Two years before the second folio, Milton was already thinking of the playwright's fame more in terms of the page than the stage.[4] He specifically refers to Shakespeare's book as 'unvalued' (11), which surely means that he thought the publication was 'invaluable' but also

---

[1] Milton, 'On Shakespeare', in Orgel and Goldberg, eds., *The Major Works*, 20, ll. 10 and 12. All subsequent quotations of Milton's poetry in this chapter, unless otherwise indicated, are taken from this edition and cited parenthetically by line number.

[2] For the possible negative connotations of such quasi-paralysis—which may evoke the Lady's frozen state in *A Maske*—see John Guillory, *Poetic Authority: Spenser, Milton and Literary History*, 19.

[3] See Lukas Erne, *Shakespeare and the Book Trade* and *Shakespeare as Literary Dramatist*.

[4] The date 1630 appeared after the title of the poem when it was reprinted, with some revisions, in Milton's own first collection of verse, *Poems of Mr. John Milton, Both English and Latin* (London, 1645), B6r. In the second folio of 1632, the title is 'An Epitaph on the Admirable Dramaticke Poet, W. Shakespeare'; a similar long title was used when the poem was published eight years later in *Poems: Written by Wil. Shake-speare* (London, 1640), K8r-v.

Stephen B. Dobranski, *Milton and Transcendent Authorship* In: *Making Milton: Print, Authorship, Afterlives*. Edited by: Emma Depledge, John S. Garrison, and Marissa Nicosia, Oxford University Press (2021). © Stephen B. Dobranski.
DOI: 10.1093/oso/9780198821892.003.0002

implies Milton's sense that the poet-playwright's achievement in print—his value as a writer worth reading—had not yet been fully appreciated.[5]

This chapter examines Milton's ideas of authorship as well as his own practices of writing and publishing over the first half of his career. As in his encomium to Shakespeare, Milton conceives of the best poetry as continuing to live after an author's death. But even while he embraces such an idealistic notion of a poem's ongoing power—an ideal that Shakespeare himself pursued in several of his sonnets—Milton repeatedly connects that capacity to a tangible, and thus vulnerable, form. Milton did not understand publication as the final step in his authorship: he continued to revise many of his works after they were printed—most notably *Paradise Lost,* but also *A Maske,* the Nativity Ode, *The Tenure of Kings and Magistrates, Eikonoklastes, The Readie and Easie Way to Establish a Free Commonwealth, The History of Britain,* and the first of his divorce tracts.[6] But, whereas Shakespeare contrasted the enduring life of his 'powerful rhyme' with the limitations of 'marble' and 'gilded monuments', Milton often associated poetic transcendence with a necessarily material form, especially in print.[7] Even early on, he understood writing as both letter and spirit: his words needed an appropriate physical presence if they were to have a lasting spiritual life.

Milton must have come to appreciate the impact of print at a young age. Growing up in London in the early 1600s, he witnessed firsthand the rapid expansion of the English book trade and its growing cultural, religious, and political relevance. By the time of the Restoration, there were at least fifty-three printing houses in England, and scholars have estimated that by the end of the century London alone had over 175 bookshops, with some contemporary accounts putting the number closer to 600.[8] Both types of businesses clustered around St Paul's Churchyard—an area that Thomas Nashe called the 'Exchange of All Authors'—a short walk from Milton's family home in All Hallows parish.[9] When Milton began attending St Paul's grammar school, probably at age 10, he would have walked daily past the yard's many bookshops or 'stations' to get to his classes at its east end.

Yet manuscript and oral transmission remained important throughout the seventeenth century, and Milton naturally had recourse to both of these other

---

[5] All references to word definitions and etymologies in this chapter draw from the *Oxford English Dictionary Online,* http://www.oed.com.

[6] When *The History of Britain* was published a second time, in 1698, as part of *A Complete Collection of the Historical, Political, and Miscellaneous Works of John Milton,* it bore a new title page announcing, '*Publish'd from a Copy corrected by the Author himself*'. See Wolfe, ed., *Complete Prose Works of John Milton,* III: l–lix, for a list of the changes and corrections made in this edition.

[7] Shakespeare, Sonnet 55, in Duncan-Jones, ed., *Shakespeare's Sonnets,* 221.

[8] Pollard and Redgrave, *The Short-Title Catalogue, 1475–1640,* III: 232–59. See also Plant, *The English Book Trade,* 64; and Johns, *The Nature of the Book,* 66, 72. The contemporary estimate comes from Atkyns, *Original and Growth of Printing,* D4v.

[9] Nashe, *Strange Newes,* D3r.

modes.[10] The musician Henry Lawes claimed to have tired out his hand making so many copies of Milton's *A Maske Presented at Ludlow Castle*, and the versions of Milton's two poems about Thomas Hobson that appear in the miscellanies *Banquet of Jests* (1640) and *Wit Restor'd* (1658) seem to have been based on alternative scribal copies.[11] When in 1645 the bookseller Humphrey Moseley decided to finance Milton's first printed collection of verse, he explained that he had previously come across some of the poet's works in manuscript.[12] Moseley writes in his preface to *Poems of Mr. John Milton* that the author's 'peculiar excellency in these studies, was too well known to conceal his Papers, or to keep me from attempting to sollicit them from him [*sic*]'.[13] Milton seems to have more often shared his poetry orally; travelling in Italy in 1638 and 1639, he visited Italian academies in Rome and Naples, and recited several of his poems—what he modestly described as 'some trifles which I had in memory, composed at under twenty or thereabout'.[14] Also, while a student at Cambridge, in addition to the regular debates and declamatory exercises held at Christ's College, Milton was invited to perform at a few university events.[15] A fellow of Christ's asked him in 1628 to recite publicly one of his Latin poems, and later that same year he gave a rousing oration at an annual university ceremony called a salting.[16]

Oral delivery was also part of Milton's method of composition long before he went blind. His nephew, Edward Philips, recalled that he and his brother were asked to write 'from [Milton's] own dictation, some part, from time to time, of a Tractate which he thought fit to collect from the ablest of Divines'. Philips adds that Milton 'set out several Treatises' about the clergy, a description that invites us

[10] On the three modes' complementary relation, see McKenzie, 'Speech–Manuscript–Print'.

[11] Milton, 'Upon old Hobson the Carrier of Cambridge', F11r–F12r; and 'Another on the Same' and 'Another', G2v–G3v. A second edition of *Banquet of Jests*, including Milton's poem, was published in 1657. Other versions of Milton's poems that were published separately—in, for example, the miscellanies *The Compleat Courtier* (1683) and *Cupids Cabinet Unlockt*—might have circulated in manuscript or, more likely, were adapted from the versions in his 1645 *Poems*. For a discussion of the latter miscellany, see Erne, '*Cupids Cabinet Unlockt* (1662), Ostensibly "By W. Shakespeare", in Fact Partly by John Milton'.

[12] Lawes, 'To the Right Honorable John Lord Vicount Bracly', A2r. See Chapter 1 in the present volume for more on the 1645 poetry collection.

[13] Milton, *Poems of Mr. John Milton*, A4r.

[14] Milton, *The Reason of Church-Government*, in Orgel and Goldberg, eds., *The Major Works*, 165–73, 169. All subsequent quotations of Milton's prose in this chapter are taken from this edition, unless otherwise noted.

[15] For a discussion of the emphasis placed on oral disputation, see Ong, 'Introduction'.

[16] The Latin poem that Milton recited might have been '*Naturam non Pati Senium*' ('That nature does not suffer from old age'). A salting was a ceremony in which freshmen were formally inducted to the ranks of upperclassmen. Inductees were expected to perform for their fellow students; if their wit was found to be wanting—if it were deemed to be insufficiently 'salty'—the punishment was having to drink beer that had literally been salted. See Roslyn Richek, 'Thomas Randolph's Salting (1627), its Text, and John Milton's Sixth Prolusion as Another Salting'; Sarah Knight, 'Milton's Student Verses of 1629' and 'Royal Milton'; and Robert Dulgarian, 'Milton's "Naturam non pati senium" and "De Idea Platonica" as Cambridge Act Verses: A Reconsideration in Light of Manuscript Evidence'.

to imagine Milton pacing back and forth and composing aloud, as his nephews took dictation.[17]

Yet, as Philips's recollection suggests, Milton's recitations and oral performances were almost always precursors to print publication. In the case of his highly successful trip to Italy, Milton included in his 1645 *Poems* the 'trifles' that he had recited on the Continent. He was also delighted to have been given written (as opposed to merely spoken) words of praise from members of Italian academies. He basks in the knowledge that 'written Encomiums' are not something 'the Italian is...forward to bestow on men of this side the Alps', as if the physical copies gave the compliments added significance.[18] A few years after his return, he handed them over to Moseley to have them printed and preserved in his first collection of poetry.

Milton also converted his oral performances from Cambridge into printed texts. He had the Latin poem that he recited published separately, most likely so that he could give copies as gifts to friends and acquaintances.[19] Similarly, he followed up his spirited oration from the university salting by having it printed; the lines of English pentameter were included in his 1673 *Poems, &c.* under the title 'At a Vacation Exercise', and he gave a copy of the longer sections in Latin prose to the bookseller Brabazon Aylmer. They were published in 1674 with several of Milton's other college exercises and a selection of his private correspondence.[20]

Even the intensely personal *Epitaphium Damonis*, in which Milton mourns the death of his dear friend Charles Diodati, was printed separately in either 1639 or 1640, another indication of Milton's early appreciation of the capability of publication. Presumably, he wished to give away copies as gift-texts.[21] In the poem, he explains that he had hoped to share with his late friend his future plans for writing an epic as they rested 'in the murmuring shade' near the River Colne (*et arguta paulum recubamus in umbra*, 148). Now, since his friend has died, the poet turns away from pastoral and accepts that he himself (*Ipse ego*, 162) must announce publicly his ideas about writing a British heroic poem. Milton appears to have thought that print would best memorialize his friend and best serve this ancillary function of declaring his intention of becoming a national poet.

It was twelve years earlier at the salting ceremony at Cambridge that Milton apparently made his first public pronouncement of his poetic aspirations, interrupting his jocular, often bawdy Latin speech to break into English couplets and

---

[17] Phillips, 'The Life of Mr. John Milton', 62.
[18] Milton, *The Reason of Church-Government*, 169.
[19] Wolfe, ed., *Complete Prose Works of John Milton*, I:314. This was Milton's first printed poem; no copies survive.
[20] See Milton, 'At a Vacation Exercise', D8v–E2v; and Prolusion VI, H1r–I3v.
[21] For a discussion of this poem and the significance of its material form for Milton's poetic ambition, see Blaine Greteman's chapter in this volume and Cedric C. Brown, *Friendship and its Discourses in the Seventeenth Century*.

meditate in earnest on his larger goals. But even here, at a young age and in the midst of a raucous assembly, he was already thinking about the form of his future works. Milton announced that he hoped one day to write about 'some graver subject' (30)—heaven, the sea, secrets of creation, or heroes of old—a much more serious topic, which would earn him greater renown than performing at a light-hearted college entertainment. He specifically uses a clothing metaphor to describe how his 'naked thoughts' need appropriate words (23), calling on his native language to 'bring thy chiefest treasure' from 'thy wardrobe' (18) and to deck his ideas 'in thy best array' (line 26). That he lingers on this sartorial vehicle suggests that he will require decorative expressions to build his lofty rhyme; Milton is emphasizing that the English language is capable of great poetry. But his clothing metaphor also implies that early on he envisioned his thoughts and imagination as depending on some kind of tangible embodiment to move his audience and have a lasting effect. His synaesthetic wish to 'clothe my fancy in fit sound' (32) conflates the oral delivery of the salting ('sound') with his aspiration that his ideas need ultimately to find an appropriate exterior form ('clothe').

Two years later, around the same time that Milton composed 'On Shakespeare', he explored more fully the essential physical expression of his writing in 'The Passion'. Here he underscores the connection between his poem's form and content. Focusing on the hypostatic union and the condescension of 'our dearest Lord' (10) to enter a 'Poor fleshly tabernacle' (17), Milton similarly searches for a fit corporeal shape for his spiritual anguish: 'The leaves should all be black whereon I write, / And letters where my tears have washed a wannish white' (34–5). This ideal of matching the intensity of his grief with the material form of his verse leads him to imagine that he might even score his 'plaining verse' on 'the softened quarry' of the 'sad sepulchral rock' that blocked the cave where Jesus was buried (46–7, 43). As in 'At a Vacation Exercise', Milton conceives of a complementary relation between his thoughts and their expression, but now he has moved from metaphor to a more literal description of his ideas' physical appearance. Like George Herbert, who crafted a series of unique poetic structures that enact the spiritual discoveries that his poems describe, Milton searches for an appropriate form that will enhance his work's poetic meaning. But whereas Herbert in *The Temple* focused on his versification's visual impact and the sequence of his lyrics, Milton instead emphasizes the physical means of transmission as contributing to his poetry's sense and significance.[22]

Such a concept of authorship, implying an inseparable relation between material form and poetic meaning, anticipates the philosophy of matter that will animate the story of creation and the war in heaven in *Paradise Lost*. When Raphael in the epic explains to Adam and Eve that angels can eat the same food as

---

[22] On the visual qualities of *The Temple* and the structure of its poetic sequence, see Wilcox, in *The English Poems of George Herbert*.

humans, he describes 'one first matter all' that is 'Indued with various forms, various degrees / Of substance, and in things that live, of life' (5.472-4).[23] Raphael can thus 'convert.../ To proper substance' Adam and Eve's 'earthly fruits' (5.492-3, 464)—and the couple can transform their own material 'nourishment' into 'vital spirits' that enable motion and thought (5.484, 485)—because all created things are made of the same dynamic substance that takes on different forms depending on how rarefied it is.[24] Raphael focuses on the implications of this conjunction and distinction for created beings—for angels and humans—but, given Milton's aspiration that his poems will continue to live through their material transmission, a similarly monist conception of existence seems to apply to his writing. He does not understand his poems as composed of discrete elements—of meaning and matter—but instead sees them as inseparably material and spiritual.

Here we might also think of the Anglo-Catholic emphasis on ritual and ecclesiastical adornment that had been revived under William Laud, appointed Archbishop of Canterbury in 1633 and thus the effective head of the English Church. Laud attempted to establish a more rigid Church hierarchy and to enforce uniform religious practices across all four nations. But he also, in an effort to downplay the importance of sermonizing, revived a pre-Reformation emphasis on the sensual and ceremonial that to his opponents seemed regressively Catholic. The underlying principle in Laud's ecclesiology was what he called the 'Beauty of Holiness', an allusion to 1 Chronicles 16:29, and Psalms 29:2 and 96:9. He believed that external worship should connect intimately with a believer's inner faith: 'I found that with the Contempt of the Outward Worship of God, the Inward fell away apace, and Profanness began boldly to shew it self.'[25]

In this context, early modern writers may have strived, consciously or unconsciously, for an aesthetic that similarly matched poetic meaning and literary form. The sometimes harsh prosodic irregularities in John Donne's *Songs and Sonnets*, for example, dramatize the passion and candour of his lyrics' speakers, while shape poems by Herbert and Robert Herrick use typography to amplify, subvert,

---

[23] Milton expounds on his theory of matter in *De Doctrina Christiana*, where he develops the material and spiritual implications of creation *ex deo*. Humankind, Milton writes, 'is not double or separable: not, as is commonly thought, produced from and composed of two different and distinct elements, soul and body. On the contrary, the whole man is the soul, and the soul the man: a body, in other words, or individual substance, animated, sensitive, and rational' (Wolfe, ed., *Complete Prose Works of John Milton*, VI:318).

[24] I discuss Milton's monist philosophy and its specific implications for his visual descriptions in Dobranski, *Milton's Visual Imagination*. See also the still definitive study of Milton's philosophy of matter in Fallon, *Milton among the Philosophers*, esp. 80, 102, 145.

[25] Laud, *The History of the Trouble and Tryal of the Most Reverend Father in God and Blessed Martyr, William Laud*, X3v.

or comment on the poets' imagery and diction.[26] Milton, of course, was no Laudian, and he reacted with repugnance to the extravagance and luxury of the English Church under the imperious archbishop.[27] But the Puritan rejection of ritual and ceremony—of outward or physical manifestations of meaning—points up the question that he seems to be raising about poetic form in works such as 'The Passion' and 'At a Vacation Exercise'. What is the appropriate appearance for poetry that opposes a Laudian emphasis on symbolism? If Milton spurned the spiritual significance that episcopacy attached to ornamentation in worship, what should his religious verse look like?

Behind such questions also lies Milton's vaunting ambition. Already as a young writer, he wished to create something grand, something that would continue to be read long after he died, like the 'easy numbers' and prophetic lines in Shakespeare's 'unvalued book'. Milton wanted, as he tentatively put it in one of his early tracts on church government, to 'leave something so written to aftertimes as they should not willingly let it die'.[28] Thus, when he concludes 'On Shakespeare' with the pronouncement that 'kings for such a tomb would wish to die' (16), he sounds almost envious. If even kings covet the 'pomp' (15) of Shakespeare's monument, so must Milton.

The idea of continuing to live through writing extends back at least to 480 BCE and the Greek poet Simonides, to whom is traditionally attributed an epitaph memorializing the Spartan soldiers who died at the Battle of Thermopylae. More well known, though, would have been the development of this idea in the writings of Ovid and Horace. Concluding *Metamorphoses* with the doctrines of Pythagoras, Ovid reinforces his poem's overarching theme of mutability by cataloguing how everything exists in a state of flux—desire, language, love, myth, nations, and all aspects of nature and humanity. In the subsequent, brief epilogue, he then singles out his art and fame as exceptions: 'my better Part transcend the skie; / And my immortal name shall never die'.[29] Transcendence comes through constancy, and constancy does not come easy: it derives from the greatness of the author's poetic achievement.

Horace also celebrates poetry's life-saving power, but he focuses on the subject— not the writer—who is made immortal. In his *Odes*, he attributes a hero's renown to both deeds and the Muse: 'What would Romulus be today if a churlish silence stood in the way of his just desserts? . . . If a man is worthy of praise, the Muse does not let

---

[26] On the influence of theology on Donne's poetic style, see Anderson, 'Internal Images'; and Cruickshank, *Verse and Poetics in George Herbert and John Donne*. On the 'rough' quality of Donne's verse, see Patrides, 'John Donne Methodized'.

[27] See, for example, 'Milton's Anti-Laudian Masque' in Marcus, *The Politics of Mirth*, 169–212.

[28] Milton, *The Reason of Church-Government*, 169.

[29] Sandys, trans., *Ovid's Metamorphosis*, Ss3v. A similar sentiment occurs in *Amores*: 'I, too, when the final fires have eaten up my frame, shall still live on, and the great part of me survive my death' (*ergo etiam cum me supremus adederit ignis, / vivam, parsque mei multa superstes erit*). See Showerman, trans., *'Heroides' and 'Amores'*, I.15.39–42 (pp. 378–9).

him die; the Muse bestows the bliss of heaven'.[30] Horace goes on to assure his friend
Lollius that time will not erase his remarkable achievements because he will
continue to be honoured in verse.[31] Helen and Hector were famous because they
had been the subjects of great poems; other, comparable Helen and Hector figures
have been utterly forgotten because they lacked a sacred poet, such as Horace, to
preserve their deeds. Here he provocatively attributes his transcendent power to
chartis (30), a word that can signify a poem or paper—that is, either the figurative
work or its material incarnation that will honour and keep alive Lollius.

This theme of immortality through verse continued to interest poets throughout the early modern period, as they sought both to memorialize their patrons'
and beloveds' virtues and to fulfil their own laureate ambitions.[32] But when, for
example, Edmund Spenser in his *Amoretti* promises his Elizabeth to 'let baser
things devize / To dy in dust, but you shall live by fame: / My verse your vertues
rare shall eternize', he contrasts the fame that his poetry offers with the limitations
of the sordid, material world.[33] Twice he attempts to write his beloved's name on
the shore, but Elizabeth chides his futile efforts: she points out that, like the words
in the sand, she also must 'decay' and perish (7). Spenser's solution ultimately
evokes the end of Ovid's *Metamorphoses* as the author writes her into his sonnet,
thus preserving her name 'in the hevens' (12), a poetic destination that seems to
defy and stand in opposition to the lovers' ephemeral physical experience.

Ben Jonson also looks to the stars, but he instead adapts Horace's pledge to
Lollius. In a verse epistle addressed to Philip Sidney's daughter, the Countess of
Rutland, Jonson recounts that other people were as heroic as Achilles or as
beautiful as Helen, but they did not have effective press agents: 'none so live, /
Because they lacked the sacred pen could give / Like life unto them'.[34] While
Jonson's choice of 'pen' suggests the material act of writing, the modifier 'sacred'
echoes Spenser's ethereal diction in *Amoretti*, emphasizing the spiritual nature of
the lady's promised afterlife. 'It is the Muse alone can raise to heaven' (41), Jonson
insists, listing various classical deities who survive as constellations—Hercules,
Castor and Pollux, Jason, and Ariadne.[35] In contrast to such heavenly immortality,
he disdains pompous attempts to preserve souls in material things, 'in touch or
marble, or the coats / Painted or carved upon our great men's tombs, / Or in their
windows' (44–6). Through Jonson's poetry, the countess can achieve a glorious

---

[30] Rudd, ed. and trans., *Odes and Epodes*, book IV, ode 8, ll. 20–9 (pp. 242–3).

[31] Ibid., book IV, ode 9 (pp. 245–7).

[32] For the influence of Ovid on early modern expressions of art's transcendence, see Kilgour, *Milton and the Metamorphosis of Ovid*, esp. 68–9, 325.

[33] Spenser, 'Sonnet 75', 9–11. Subsequent quotations are taken from this edition (Larson, ed., *'Amoretti' and 'Epithalamion'*) and cited parenthetically.

[34] Jonson, 'An Epistle to Elizabeth, Countess of Rutland', 55–7. Subsequent quotations are taken from this edition (Maclean, ed., *Ben Jonson and the Cavalier Poets*) and cited parenthetically.

[35] Jonson potentially includes himself as author through the surrogate artist figure Ariadne. For a discussion of this epistle as an incomplete text, see Dobranski, *Readers and Authorship in Early Modern England*, 97–118.

transcendence, whereas physical things will always have a limited preservative power; they 'do but prove . . . / . . . graves; when they were born, they died' (46–7).

Like the poems by Spenser and Jonson, some of Milton's meditations on fame and the endurance of verse are also not materially minded. In *Ad Patrem*, for example, which Milton probably composed in the 1630s, he aspires to commemorate his father. Here he directly addresses the 'youthful verses'—what he modestly calls 'pastime[s]' (*iuvenilia carmina, lusus*, 115)—and asks them to keep alive his father's name:

> Si modo perpetuos sperare audebitis annos,
> Et domini superesse rogo, lucemque tueri,
> Nec spisso rapient oblivia nigra sub Orco,
> Forsitan has laudes, decantatumque parentis
> Nomen, ad exemplum, sero servabitis aevo.

(ll. 116–20)

[If only you dare hope for endless years—dare think to survive your master's pyre and look upon the light—and if dark oblivion does not drag you down to crowned Orcus, perchance you will treasure these praises and a father's name rehearsed in song as an example of a distant age.]

The passing reference to a destructive pyre may still hint at his poetry's physical existence as either a book or manuscript. But the emphasis falls on his writing's aural quality. Perhaps because Milton was striving to relate to his musician father, he repeatedly calls his creations 'song[s]' and describes himself as singing (*decantatumque parentis*)—as opposed to writing or printing—his father's name for future generations.

Milton again echoes Ovid as well as Spenser and Jonson in positing a heavenly reward in another Latin poem, *Mansus*, probably written in 1638 or 1639 during his Continental journey. He praises the esteemed Italian patron Giovanni Battista Manso, assuring him that his support for the poets Torquato Tasso and Giambattista Marino will earn him a lasting reputation:

> quacunque per orbem
> Torquati decus et nomen celebrabitur ingens,
> Claraque perpetui succrescet fama Marini,
> Tu quoque in ora frequens venies plausumque virorum,
> Et parili carpes iter immortale volatu.

(49–53)

[wherever Torquato's glory and great name shall be celebrated throughout the world, wherever the brilliant fame of enduring Marino increases, your praises too will frequently be on men's lips, and flying by their side you shall enjoy their immortal flight.]

If this account of poetic immortality has a tangible quality, it is the lips and hands of future readers who, Milton imagines, will physically express their appreciation for Manso's patronage—an image that recalls how Shakespeare will also be kept alive in the hearts and minds of his astonished readers.[36]

But even in *Mansus*, as Milton develops the poem's somatic ideal so as to address his own lasting achievement, his concept of poetic afterlife starts to solidify into something more physical. He hopes for 'such a friend' as Manso, 'who knows so well how to honour the sons of Phoebus' (78–9) and who might 'draw my features from marble' (*Forsitan et nostros ducat de marmore vultus*, 91). Milton's other imagery also glances at the material transmission of the texts that Manso sponsored: 'Happy friendship once joined you with great Tasso, and inscribed your names on everlasting pages' (*et aeternis inscripsit nomina chartis*, 8). In these lines, as in Horace's *Odes*, the author's literal, physical pages (*chartis*) play a crucial role: they bind and preserve the patron and poet, enabling their names to appear together for all time.

Lycidas, too, if we take one final example, subtly interests itself in the material process of defying death and keeping alive its subject. Milton wrote the ode to mourn Edward King, a learned friend from Christ's College who had died the previous year in a shipwreck on the Irish Sea. As the ode's uncouth swain calls on nature to sympathize with his grief, he briefly becomes consumed with the idea of adorning his friend's hearse with 'every flower that sad embroidery wears' (148). He launches into a floral catalogue—'The tufted crow-toe', 'the pale jessamine', 'The glowing violet' (143, 145)—until he suddenly remembers that Lycidas was lost at sea and so there is no hearse to decorate. This acknowledgement, in part a recognition of the limits of the pastoral mode, also marks a subtle shift in the poem's material transmission. The poet at last realizes that he cannot 'strew the laureate hearse' (151), an allusion to the early modern tradition of affixing handwritten memorial poems to the hearse as a funeral procession made its way to the burial site.[37] In place of this scribal tradition, Milton turns to the printed memorial book *Justa Edouardo King* (1638), in which his ode was originally published; it is here that he finally finds reassurance and consolation: 'Now Lycidas the shepherds weep no more; / Henceforth thou art the genius of the shore' (182–3). The specific choices of 'Now' and 'Henceforth' point both to the ode itself and to its immediate context as the closing poem in the 1638 collection.[38] Following the book's thirty-five other English, Latin, and Greek commemorative verses, the speaker can directly address King's other classmates with a hard-earned confidence. He tells them that their combined efforts have been successful: 'Weep

---

[36] The image also recalls the epilogues to *A Midsummer Night's Dream* and *The Tempest*. On Milton's broader attempt to locate 'literary commemoration' in readers, see Menges, 'Books and Readers in Milton's Early Poetry and Prose'.

[37] For this tradition, see Brooks and Hardy, '*Poems of Mr. John Milton*', 183.

[38] Milton, *Justa Edouardo King*, H3v–I2r.

no more, woeful shepherds, weep no more, / For Lycidas your sorrow is not dead' (165–6). This latter clause may initially sound strange—why should they stop crying if their sorrow is not dead?—but the poet is referring to the power of *Justa Edouardo King*; the printed volume will continue to preserve both Lycidas and the poet-shepherds' grief.

Understanding that Milton conceived of his writing as having both a spiritual and material presence underlines the audacity of Sonnet 8. According to a note in the author's hand in a surviving manuscript copy, he composed the poem 'When the assault was intended to the Citty', a reference to the autumn of 1642 when Londoners feared an attack by the king's forces near the start of the civil wars. A note in another hand in the same copy (which has been struck through) adds that the poem was hung 'On his dore'.[39] But, even without these explanations, the sonnet's opening lines clearly establish the poem's intent. Milton begins by beseeching a 'Captain or colonel, or knights in arms' (1) to spare his home from violence and plunder, and in exchange he offers to spread the would-be marauder's 'name o'er lands and seas' (7).

In this case, the material circumstances of the sonnet's original publication gently undercut its audacious boast. On the one hand, Milton was claiming that his writing had transcendent power and could broadcast the military leader's fame to 'Whatever clime the sun's bright circle warms' (8); on the other hand, the handwritten slip of paper that Milton fastened to his door in St Botolph's parish must have seemed especially slight to passers-by as the capital braced for an imminent military assault. The brazenness of Milton's proffer of fame would have been amplified not only by his choice of English, a language whose value in the 1640s was limited outside of the British Isles, but also by the poem's flimsy material form. Milton seems to be upping the stakes: he is suggesting that he is such a great poet that he can make the captain or colonel famous in a sonnet, even an English sonnet, even a handwritten English sonnet that, exposed to wind and rain, he left on his door.

Milton's faith in a monist authorship—of a close relation between a work's physical embodiment and spiritual afterlife—would have been more sorely tested just one year later when his pamphlet defending divorce was repeatedly attacked, including calls for its destruction. Milton published *The Doctrine and Disciple of Divorce* on 1 August 1643, and within six months he had written and published a revised and greatly expanded second edition, trying to clarify and bolster his earlier argument. First, an anonymous critic complained of Milton's 'intolerable abuse of Scripture'; then a Presbyterian divine, Herbert Palmer, went before Parliament to ask that Milton's 'wicked booke' be publicly burnt.[40] The

---

[39] Trinity College Manuscript, in Fletcher, ed., *John Milton's Complete Poetical*, I:396–7.
[40] *An Answer to a Book. Intituled, 'The Doctrine and Discipline of Divorce'*, E2v; and Palmer, *The Glasse of Gods Providence towards His Faithfull Ones*, I1r.

Commons agreed to have the Committee for Printing begin an investigation.[41] One month later, on 16 September, William Prynne called for the suppression of Milton's tract, which Prynne unfairly characterized as an argument for permitting 'divorce at pleasure'.[42]

Milton responded to all of these criticisms and threats with *Areopagitica*, an eloquent defence of free speech and an affirmation of books as both letter and spirit. Good books, he insists, are not another ware that Parliament can regulate, like flax or tobacco; instead, they possess the essence of their creator, 'the precious life blood of a master-spirit, embalmed and treasured up on purpose to a life beyond life' (240).[43] Throughout the tract, Milton repeatedly treats books as alive and lively, describing them as, among other examples, a 'streaming fountain' (260), a 'flowery crop' (267), and a lovely virgin (263). He also compares books to 'those fabulous dragons teeth' that Cadmus sowed to create the magic soldiers who sprang from the ground and founded Thebes (240). This allusion recalls the ideal of a readerly legacy from 'On Shakespeare' and *Mansus*: books are 'vigorously productive', like Cadmus's seeds, because they will 'spring up' informed readers who keep alive an author's writings (240).

But simultaneously, in *Areopagitica*, Milton stresses that a writer's 'precious life blood' also exists as a tangible product. The allusion to the dragon's teeth, for example, has another, more physical implication: Cadmus, traditionally credited with inventing letters, represents a material agent on whom authors depend to create and preserve their works.[44] When in the same passage Milton claims that 'books are not absolutely dead things' (239), he highlights the ongoing potency of printed material, but his understatement implies that books are also not entirely alive. Thus, 'as good *almost* kill a man as kill a good book' (240, emphasis added). Milton repeatedly reminds readers of the material process of book production by incorporating expressions such as 'impression', 'gathering', and 'fill up the measure', subtle allusions to what the seventeenth-century Stationer Joseph Moxon described as a special '*Printers* Language'.[45] This diction points up the essential role of printing in transmitting and preserving an author's labours. As Milton more forcefully declares near the end of *Areopagitica*, 'learning is indebted' to the 'honest profession' of bookmaking (273).

The following year, in 1645, the publication of *Poems of Mr. John Milton* must have reinforced and deepened Milton's appreciation for the importance of the

---

[41] *Journal of the House of Commons: Volume 3: 1643–1644*, 606.

[42] Prynne, *Twelve Considerable Serious Questions touching Church Government*.

[43] Milton, *Areopagitica*, in Orgel and Goldberg, eds., *The Major Works*, 236–73. The page numbers of further references to *Areopagitica* will be cited in text.

[44] According to other traditions, Cadmus introduced letters into Greece. See Hulley and Vandersall, eds., *Ovid's Metamorphosis*, 148–9.

[45] 240, 263, 243; and Moxon, *Mechanick Exercises of the Whole Art of Printing (1683–4)*, 16. I make this argument in 'Principle and Politics in Milton's *Areopagitica*'. See also Dobranski, *Milton, Authorship, and the Book Trade*, 116–24.

material form in his aspiration to achieve poetic immortality. Fifteen years after 'On Shakespeare', he at last had his own 'unvalued book' that could appeal to his readers' hearts and minds (11). But while Milton's identity represents the chief organizing principle for the diverse occasional poems collected in the 1645 volume, he discovered during the book's creation that no author is an island, that—contrary to his earlier praise of Shakespeare—no author could 'buil[d] thyself a live-long monument' (8). Milton would need to collaborate if his writings were to have a transcendent afterlife. According to his brief account of the book's printing, he had little control over the layout and physical design; for example, referring to the unflattering frontispiece portrait by William Marshall discussed in Chapter 1 of this volume, he states that 'at the suggestion and solicitation of a bookseller, [he] suffered [him]self to be crudely engraved by an unskillful engraver'.[46] In addition to essential contributions from the publisher Moseley and the frontispiece's engraver, Milton depended on Ruth Raworth, the printer, as well as the musician Lawes, who composed the music for *A Maske Presented at Ludlow Castle* and whose name appears on the title page, presumably to entice possible readers. As Milton argues against censorship of the book trade in *Areopagitica*, he compares the pursuit of knowledge—and, by extension, authorship—with the constructing of 'the house of God' in that both require various, differently skilled, people, 'some cutting, some squaring the marble, others hewing the cedars' (266). He opposed prepublication licensing in part because it threatened to undo this collective enterprise that includes authors, readers, and Stationers.

When later that same year Milton sent inscribed copies of eleven of his prose tracts along with *Poems of Mr. John Milton* as gifts to the Bodleian's librarian John Rouse, the volume of verse went missing. Milton sent Rouse a replacement copy of *Poems* and included a handwritten ode, *Ad Joannem Rousium*. Here he beseeches the librarian to preserve his publications among the library's 'eternal works' and 'famous monuments of men' ('*Aeternorum operum*', '*virum monumenta*, 54, 51). Following his recent bad luck—first with the uproar that his divorce tract had caused, then with the loss of the book that he sent Rouse—Milton acknowledges that the material embodiment of his works allows them to survive and paradoxically makes them vulnerable. Copies go missing or get stolen (40–1), and he adds that the 'accursed upheaval' (*civium tumultus*, 29) of the ongoing civil war was threatening to quash interest in such 'nourishing studies' (*studia sanctus*, 30).

But Milton sounds sanguine about the fate of his books. His works can endure because of caretakers such as Rouse and institutions such as the Bodleian. As a testament to Milton's confidence in the librarian, the manuscript copy of the poem he sent Rouse is still today, almost four centuries later, housed in the

---

[46] Wolfe, ed., *Complete Prose Works of John Milton*, IV:750–1.

Bodleian Library, along with what seems to be the replacement copy of the 1645 *Poems* that he sent Rouse. But that Milton in 1673 later had his ode printed—in addition to, for the first time, his verses from the salting ceremony—further suggests his commitment to print and his ongoing belief in its value for achieving immortality. A year before he died, Milton was still actively pursuing what he believed to be the fittest material means for preserving his work and striving to ensure his authorial transcendence.

3

Making Connections with Milton's
Epitaphium Damonis

Blaine Greteman

The pastoral elegy *Epitaphium Damonis*, which was written and printed in
*c.*1639–40, is not one of Milton's most loved or discussed poems, but it has
major implications for understanding his later career, announcing his epic ambitions more explicitly than any other work before *Paradise Lost*. 'Give place then,
O forests' (*Vos cedite, silvae*), sings the narrator Thyrsis, as he abandons his
pastoral pipe and projects a poetic career in which he will sing the history of his
nation instead (160).[1] This future epic will tell of Trojan conquest, of Igraine,
Arthur, and Merlin, as the poet's pipe, 'transformed by my native muses, sounds
out a British tune' (*patriis mutata camœnis / Brittonicum strides*) (170–1). Epic
achievement will not come without sacrifice and loss, however, and Thyrsis admits
that 'one man cannot do all things, cannot hope to do all things' (*omnia non licet
uni, / Non sperasse uni licet omnia*) (171–2). To become a new poet, he will need to
leave his pastoral preoccupations behind, and most critics have believed Milton
himself does this by shrinking his social world.

Although Milton's defenders have protested that, 'in person [Milton] could be
gregarious, fun-loving, and sociable', they have tended to see his poetry as a more
lonely pursuit, since 'the writing of poetry inclined one toward being solitary,
moody, introspective, thoughtful, serious, and deep'.[2] And no poem exemplifies
this more that the *Epitaphium Damonis*. Milton's 'most autobiographical poem',
as Barbara Lewalski describes it, is 'filled with anguish for the loss of his oldest, and
perhaps only, truly intimate friend'.[3] In the poem, Milton, in the pastoral persona
of Thyrsis, not only bids farewell to Charles Diodati, who died a year earlier in
1638, but also to the Italian poets and poetry he encountered on his Continental
tour. As it depicts 'the unbridgeable gap between the protagonist of the poem and
the society in which he finds himself', Milton turns inward 'to fulfil his destiny in
England'.[4] In what might be seen as an early, more nationalistic version of

---

[1] Milton, *Epitaphium Damonis,* in Orgel and Goldberg, eds., *The Major Works,* 149–61. Hereafter in
this chapter cited parenthetically from this edition.
[2] Roy C. Flannagan, *John Milton: A Short Introduction*, 36.
[3] Barbara Lewalski, *The Life of John Milton*, 109.
[4] Stephen Guy-Bray, *Homoerotic Space*, 121, 125.

Blaine Greteman, *Making Connections with Milton's* Epitaphium Damonis In: *Making Milton: Print, Authorship, Afterlives.*
Edited by: Emma Depledge, John S. Garrison, and Marissa Nicosia, Oxford University Press (2021). © Blaine Greteman.
DOI: 10.1093/oso/9780198821892.003.0003

Milton's "fit audience...though few", the narrator Thyrsis claims, with little ambiguity, that he does not care if his epic finds readers in the outside world ('*externo*...*orbi*', 174). If we think of Milton as an asocial or antisocial author—producing poetry the way a silkworm produces silk, as Karl Marx described him—then this critical understanding of the *Epitaphium Damonis* as a lonely and isolated work is the most obvious beginning of that thread.

But the epitaph was not merely the product of private grief, and by drawing on the work's material history we can demonstrate the ways the poem carefully affirms, reconstitutes, and expands the social, poetic, and political networks that Milton established during his schooling in England and his travels abroad during the 1630s. Recent work on Milton and print has begun to challenge long-held views of him as a singular and somewhat antisocial genius. Chief among this work is Stephen B. Dobranski's *Milton, Authorship, and the Book Trade*, which argues that the 'persona of the independent author that Milton implies in many of his texts paradoxically required a collaboration among' amanuenses, acquaintances, printers, distributors, and retailers.[5] Ann Baynes Coiro has likewise argued that 'Milton's success in constructing himself as English literature's great, solitary author' obscures an important story about 'collaborative, theatrical, and historically and culturally embedded work', such as *A Maske Presented at Ludlow Castle*.[6] But we need to rebalance the agencies implied when Coiro suggests that Milton 'was clearly not yet ready to be a public writer' when *A Maske* was published in 1637.[7] To understand the emergence of Milton the author, it is important to consider not just when Milton was ready to be a public writer but also the conditions that made stationers receptive to printing his attacks on licensing, monopolies, and overreaching church authorities in works like *Areopagitica* and the Smectymnuus tracts. By the same token, Dobranski's book understandably focused most of its attention on the named works that establish Milton's persona, such as *Areopagitica* and the 1645 *Poems*. It had less to say about the period before Milton became 'Mr John Milton', author, and about the network of printers, publishers, and booksellers who produced his anonymous early works, although in his essay for the current volume Dobranski makes it clear that Milton thought about the materiality of his poems early and often. Even in the 'intensely personal *Epitaphium Damonis*', Dobranski notes, we find an 'indication of Milton's early appreciation of the capability of publication' to preserve the memory of author and subject in tangible form—a monist conception of authorship that echoes Milton's monist conception of God's creation itself (p. 20). My method here is to look at print as a networked technology and ask what connections a text like *Epitaphium Damonis* facilitates between Milton and a wider world. Considered as an instrument of connection, it quickly becomes apparent that the *Epitaphium*

---

[5] Dobranski, *Milton, Authorship and the Book Trade*, 9.
[6] Coiro, 'Anonymous Milton, or *A Maske* Masked', 609.   [7] Ibid., 612.

Damonis is less a lonely cry than a bridge between richly social worlds of cosmopolitan poetic achievement and oppositional print.

Milton's *Epitaphium Damonis* was first printed in quarto, on a single sheet, without imprint or title page. Survival rates for single-sheet publications are generally low, and this was likely a limited edition, with only one known surviving copy, held by the British Library, where it was not discovered until the twentieth century.[8] John Shawcross convincingly dates the publication to 1639–40, less than a year after Milton's return from Italy.[9] This apparently makes the *Epitaphium Damonis* the first work Milton had printed, although Henry Lawes had helped bring an edition of *A Maske* into print in 1637 without Milton's name attached. Indeed, based on a thorough comparison of fonts, Shawcross also proposes that the two works shared the same printer, Augustine Mathewes.[10] 'It seems natural', as Shawcross notes, that Milton 'would have sought out his "recent" printer' for this new work,[11] and examination of these and other texts printed by Mathewes around this time confirms that attribution. We find an unusual double-cuspated 'A', for example, not only on the title pages of *A Maske* and the *Epitaphium*, but also on Peter Heylyn's *A Coale from the Altar,* all of which Mathewes printed between 1636 and 1637. The type is worn in all instances, and it is especially clear that the type used in the 1637 impression of *Coale* derives from the same type fount as *A Maske*. They share a battered question mark and a misplaced italic question mark that may have resulted from foul case, while the ornaments shared by the *Epitaphium* (A1v) and *A Maske* (A2r) also appear in other works Mathewes printed, including *The Wits,* by William Davenant, and *A Collection of Such Sermons and Treatises,* by Samuel Ward.[12] Mathewes's work on the *Epitaphium Damonis* connects Milton to a rich field of literary publications and to a growing oppositional print network at a crucial moment in his career.

---

[8] Bradner, 'Milton's *Epitaphium Damonis*'.

[9] Shawcross, 'The Date of the Separate'. Shawcross writes contra Fletcher, 'The Seventeenth-Century Separate Printing of Milton's *Epitaphium Damonis*'.

[10] Shawcross, 'The Date of the Separate', 263–4.   [11] Ibid., 264.

[12] I have inspected these works at the British Library and the University of Illinois Special Collections. The italic question mark mentioned by Shawcross also appears throughout *Coale from the Altar*; the battered question mark appears on B3v., D1v, E2r, and elsewhere. The ornaments at the top of A2r in the 1637 *A Maske* and A1v in *Epitaphium* appear identical, with only slight variants in the pattern. If we represent the patterns alphabetically, they are ABCDEABCDFABCDE (*A Maske*) and ABCDABCDABCDABCE (*Epitaphium*). That is, Shawcross explains, 'A Maske is headed by five ornaments printed one after the other in a row three times except that what would have been the fifth ornament in the second grouping is a different (or sixth) ornament, probably as a result of foul case; and the elegy is headed by the identical first four ornaments printed one after the other in a row four times, except that what would have been the fourth ornament in the fourth grouping is the identical fifth ornament used in the *A Maske* row' ('The Date of the Separate', 264). This is a characteristic pattern for Mathewes—it is not included, for example, on the 1626 edition of Samuel Ward's sermons printed by Miles Flesher, but it appears in the familiar pattern (ABCDABCDBA) in Mathewes's 1636 reprint (A3r) and Edward Norris's 1636 'Treatise Maintaining that Corporeal Blessings are to be Sought' (ABCDABC, B1r).

Literary scholars often speak anecdotally of 'networks'. Before quantifying and mapping them it is therefore worth defining the term more specifically. Bruno Latour usefully clarifies that to speak of a social or actor network 'does not designate a thing out there that would have roughly the shape of interconnected points, much like a telephone, a sewage, or a freeway "network"'.[13] Rather, it is a way of tracing 'a set of relations'.[14] For the quantitative analysis below, I have followed the traces of those connections left by publication co-occurrence; each time a publisher's, printer's, bookseller's, or author's name appears in the same bibliographic record for a given text, I establish a connection, or 'edge', between them. Those connections can then be mapped or analysed to understand which people are most connected or which collaborations form bridges between figures who might otherwise lack any path between them. The visualization in Figure 3.1, for example, maps this article's discussion of people connected to the production and circulation of the *Epitaphium Damonis*.

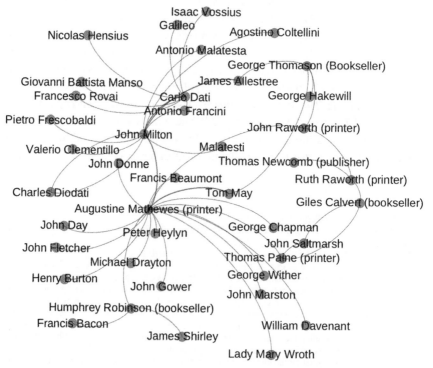

Figure 3.1 *Epitaphium Damonis*, printing and circulation diagram. Created by, and used with the permission of, Blaine Greteman.

---

[13] Latour, *Reassembling the Social*, 129.   [14] Ibid.

Such mapping and analysis can be useful even when its details are not entirely legible (as is the case with so many network 'hairballs') because at a glance we can begin to understand the poem as a technology of connection rather than a product of isolation. Aside from mapping, they can be useful for determining which figures are most connected or serve as bridges between communities.

One might object, however, that network models like this over-represent textual exchanges, such as Milton's printing a poem or sending it to his correspondents, which leave a tangible trace, in comparison with daily, consistent, intimate interactions that do not. But while close familial and peer connections are no doubt important, they have traditionally been privileged by literary scholarship in a way that may also distort our understandings of sociality and influence. As Michel Callon, John Law, and Arie Rip note, 'the production and distribution of texts...constitutes a vital method for building worlds', and network analysis gives us a useful set of tools for exploring those worlds.[15] Moreover, as Mark Granovetter explains in a seminal article, 'weak ties' in social networks, such as the ones formed by occasional correspondence or business dealings, are paradoxically far more powerful in communicating new information than strong ties such as the ones formed within nuclear families:

> Whatever is to be diffused can reach a larger number of people, and traverse greater social distance (i.e., path length), when passed through weak ties rather than strong. If one tells a rumor to all his close friends, and they do likewise, many will hear the rumor a second and third time, since those linked by strong ties tend to share friends. If the motivation to spread the rumor is dampened a bit on each wave of retelling, then the rumor moving through strong ties is much more likely to be limited to a few cliques than that going via weak ones; bridges will not be crossed.   (1366)

On a practical level, this means we are more likely to learn about new ideas, or communicate our own ideas more broadly, if our social network includes many weak ties.

Counter-intuitively, as recent statistical analysis has confirmed, we can remove strong ties from a network without much impact, but removing only a few weak ties will cause a network to collapse.[16] If a writer like Milton wants his voice to carry a long way, in other words, he needs an abundance of weak ties at least as much as he needs close personal attachments. A materialist approach to the *Epitaphium Damonis* reminds us that, for Milton, the physical form of this work was essential to its function in cultivating those ties. In 1639 this anonymous Latin poem, by a still-obscure poet for his obscure friend, would not have had a great market and, as we will

---

[15] Callon, Law, and Rip, 'How to Study the Force of Science', 14.
[16] Onela et al., 'Structure and Tie Strengths in Mobile Communications Networks'.

see, it was not made to sell. Its value was as a material object that could be circulated as a token of a budding author's deep affections and high ambitions. It connected him to a world of cosmopolitan intellectuals who would lend his voice authority when their commendations were published in his 1645 *Poems* and to a world of stationers who held the expertise to promote that voice for a broader public.

Milton seemed to recognize the value of such connections, writing to the Italian scholar Carlo Dati that he cherishes their distant tie more than those who are 'closely bound' to him 'by the chance of proximity of neighborhood or some other tie of no real importance' (*vicinae aut aliqua nullius usus necessitudo mecum . . . conglutinavit*).[17] We have Milton's letter, written nearly ten years after his Italian journey, because Milton had just belatedly learned that Dati received a copy of the *Epitaphium Damonis* that was sent at some much earlier date. He makes it clear that he had not sent the poem as a private act but, instead, because 'I thought in this way, that I would either allure you or some of the others to write' (*Existimabam etiam fore hoc modo, ut vel te vel alium ab scribendum allicerem*) (C 12.48). Estelle Haan notes that, when Milton writes of sending the poem 'to you', he uses the plural (*ad vos*), which shows 'that it was to the academy as a whole rather than to Dati personally, as has generally been assumed hitherto, that Milton sent the separate *Epitaphium Damonis*'.[18] In short, although the poem depicts a desolate universe in which men are strangers to one another (*aliena animis*), Milton printed and circulated his poem to alleviate that condition. The gesture worked, prompting Dati's reply, as well as his own request that Milton contribute to a collection of poems on the recently deceased member of the Academy, Francesco Rovai. He attempts to persuade Milton by telling him that the Dutch scholars Nicolas Heinsius and Isaac Vossius have agreed to produce such verses and, although we have no evidence that Milton complied, we can already see Milton's *Epitaphium Damonis* opening up a wider social network rather than confirming its collapse.[19]

Understood in the context of its dissemination, the poem itself makes this obvious. In the poem, Milton/Thyrsis says he still has the gifts ('*munera*') he received from the Tuscan shepherds, specifically naming Dati and Antonio Francini, another of the Florentine intellectuals Milton befriended on his Italian journey (134). The gifts he names—reed baskets, bowls, and pipes—are all prizes traditionally given to pastoral poets, and Milton elsewhere says that these gifts include the verses Dati and Francini exchanged with him in the Florentine academies during his visit.[20]

[17] Milton, *Familiar Letters*, in Patterson, ed., *The Works of John Milton*, 12:44.
[18] Haan, *From Academia to Amicitia*, 55.   [19] See also Green, 'Reaching a European Audience'.
[20] Milton related his success reading his poems at the Florentine academies, where they 'were received with written encomiums', in *The Reason of Church Government*, Orgel and Goldberg, eds., *The Major Works*, 165–73, 169. See Cedric C. Brown, 'Milton, the Attentive Mr Skinner, and the Acts and Discourses of Friendship' and *Friendship and its Discourses in the Seventeenth Century*.

The *Epitaphium* continues and extends this social world. The poem invokes the poet Giovani Battista Manso, the subject of Milton's *Mansus*, in even more elaborate terms (he is '*mirandus*'), praising the 'wonderful artwork' (*mirum artis opus*) of two cups he has given to Milton (183). These cups ('*pocula*', 181) are likely an allusion to Manso's books, *Poesie Nomiche* and *Erocallia*, which contain the Neoplatonic imagery of Cupid and the Phoenix that Milton uses in his own poem to describe their elaborate engraving and to set the scene for Damon's final apotheosis among the gods.[21] In his 1647 letter Milton is delighted to learn that all these men, through Dati, have received his poetic missive, and he promises to send the 1645 *Poems*, which prominently featured testimonials by each of them. Understood as an intermediary in this exchange, Milton's initial foray into print authorship reads as an explicit effort to maintain and cultivate social connections.

The work of Harold Love and others has accustomed us to thinking about manuscript circulation in terms of gift exchange, community formation, and prestige.[22] So why did Milton go to the trouble of having the poem printed for such limited distribution? Milton similarly circulated copies of the 1637 *Maske* by sending them as gift-texts to people who were not close intimates but whose association he clearly valued, like Sir Henry Wotton, whose acknowledgement of the gift was printed in the 1645 *Poems*.[23] But Henry Lawes, in the dedication of the 1637 *A Maske*, explains that he undertook its printing in response to a clear demand, as the 'often copying of it hath tir'd my pen to give my severall friends satisfaction' (A2r–v). Lawes was at this point a far more renowned name than Milton—his name even appears next to Milton's on the title page of the 1645 *Poems*—and the publisher obviously agreed that demand for his work would recoup the cost of printing. By contrast, Milton does not seem to have been struggling to keep up with demand with the *Epitaphium Damonis*, and there are no indications that it was published as a commercial venture.

Instead, print publication was part of Milton's own gesture of commemoration and his strategy of cultivating distant relationships. In his letter to Dati, Milton draws on the metaphor of texts as funerary monuments, which was familiar from commemorative editions like the 1632 folio of Shakespeare's plays where, as noted in the previous chapter, Milton's own work first appeared in print. The *Epitaphium Damonis* is the 'tomb of Damon' [*Damonis tumulum*], which he has worked to adorn.[24] Milton says he took 'care' to send it as a 'proof of talent, however small, and love to you', and its material form matters both as

---

[21] See de Filippis, 'Milton and Manso'.

[22] See Love, *Scribal Publication in Seventh-Century England*; Marotti, *Manuscript, Print, and the English Renaissance Lyric*; and Scott-Warren, 'Reconstructing Manuscript Networks'.

[23] When Milton sent a gift-copy of *A Maske* to Henry Wotton, it turned out the elder man had already received another copy of the work, anonymously bound with Thomas Randolph's works, as discussed by Coiro, 'Anonymous Milton, or *A Maske* Masked', 609–29.

[24] Milton, *Familiar Letters*, in Patterson, ed., *The Works of John Milton*, 12:48.

commemoration and as announcement of poetic ambition.[25] Private printing like this was probably more common than we realize and, while it was not exactly cheap, it would have likely been possible to print one hundred pages of a single-sheet publication like this for just under 8s. As Ian Gadd notes, this was less than half the purchase price of Shakespeare's first folio, and, for a relatively affluent young man like Milton, it would have provided an avenue into print without the need to persuade a publisher to take it.[26]

The printer of Milton's poem, Augustine Mathewes, was himself an opportune connection for an aspiring author who had an interest in the commemorative and social powers of print. Mathewes worked regularly with Humphrey Robinson, the influential publisher of *A Maske* (1637).[27] He had printed important works of drama and literature by writers including John Donne, George Wither, William Davenant, Michael Drayton, Francis Beaumont, Tom May, William Rowley, and John Marston. He was a careful printer of Latin verse, such as the miscellany *Parentalia,* which included poems by various Oxford and Cambridge wits, including William Cartwright and Thomas Randolph, and *Parerga* by Milton's friend and former instructor at St Paul's, Alexander Gill. As William Riley Parker observes, 'In the eight years 1630–7, if we may judge from surviving books with his name or initials on the imprint, he was, although unlicensed, one of the most important and active of London printers. Only Thomas Cotes, Thomas Harper, and Miles Flescher can be compared with him in quantity of output.'[28]

But Parker's observation points to a paradox: although Mathewes produced a fairly high volume of titles, when we analyse a graph of the English print network during the years 1630–7, he appears to be neither central nor strongly connected to leading members of the book trade.[29] In network analysis, 'degree' is the number of connections a person has to others, and when we use title page attributions to see which printers, publishers, booksellers, and authors are connected to one another in this way, Mathewes's degree ranking is 146 out of 150. This is extraordinarily low for a printer, especially considering his prodigious output. Further analysis of the records attributed to him in the *English Short Title Catalogue* explain his apparently anomalous position: Mathewes was a master of

[25] Ibid.

[26] Private communication, 4 September 2017. Gadd extrapolates his estimate of private printing costs from Blayney, 'The Publication of Playbooks'.

[27] See Parker, 'Contributions Toward a Milton Bibliography', and Dobranski, *Milton, Authorship and the Book Trade*, 77–8.

[28] Parker, 'Contributions Toward a Milton Bibliography', 427.

[29] This analysis is drawn from the Shakeosphere database at https://shakeosphere.lib.uiowa.edu/networkAnalytics.jsp/. The project uses natural language-processing tools to mine the names of printers, publishers, booksellers, and authors from the *English Short Title Catalogue*. Those names are stored back to a relational database, from which we project the bipartite network (people and records) onto a graph in which people are connected through their co-occurrence in bibliographical records. We use the NetworkX Python library to analyse this graph. For more on this process see the Shakeosphere website and ch. 2 of Barabási, *Network Science*, 42–71.

what Sabrina A. Cohen has called 'the underinformed title page', which can be used as 'a smoke screen behind which to conduct political and religious battles'.[30] Mathewes's publications were more than twice as likely to be missing information (about his own name, or that of the authors, booksellers, or publishers involved) than those by Miles Flesher. They are four times more likely to be missing such information than the other printers Parker mentions as comparable in terms of output, Thomas Cotes and Thomas Harper.[31]

If on the one hand Mathewes was connected to a respectable field of authors and publishers, on the other he was associated with the world of unlicensed and increasingly oppositional print. As one study put it, he seems to have avoided asking 'awkward questions' about licensing or ownership when authors or publishers brought him material.[32] And he began to find himself at odds with both the state and authorities in his own trade as early as 1621, when he was fined for printing George Wither's *Motto,* an unlicensed political satire that in 1621 violated the royal proclamation 'Against excesse of lavish and licentious speech of matters of state'.[33] Wither worked with Mathewes more consistently than any other member of the book trade during his war with the Stationers' Company during the 1620s and 1630s and must have had him in mind when he argued that an 'honest Stationer is he, that exercizeth his Mystery (whether it be in printing, bynding, or selling of Bookes) with more respect to the glory of God, & the publike advantage, then to his owne commodity', taking care with controversial works 'like a discreet Apothecary in selling poysnous druggs'.[34] Mathewes's discretion sometimes extended to printing under pseudonyms—'Jan Maast', for example, when producing Middleton's controversial *Game at Chess* with the false imprint 'Ghedruckt in Lydden by Ian Masse'.[35] But joining Wither in his fight against the company's monopolies and licensing practices ultimately cost Mathewes professionally. He was censored early in his career for illegally operating multiple presses, and after the 'great error' of printing a forbidden book brought down the wrath of the Star Chamber, he was called in again in 1637, ultimately losing his status as master printer.[36]

That book was *The Holy Table, Name and Thing, More Anciently, Properly and Literally Used, Under the New Testament, then That of an Altar,* published anonymously by John Williams, Bishop of Lincoln. It openly challenged Laud's controversial directives to standardize the placement of communion altars on the east wall of the church, surrounded by rails. Although it was a more diplomatic

[30] Baron, 'Licensing Readers, Licensing Authorities in Seventeenth-Century England', 224.

[31] Fifty-one per cent of the 260 records attributed to Augustine Mathewes (and variants of his name) in the *ESTC* lack identifying information. This compares with 25% of 514 for Miles Flesher, 12.5% of 327 for Thomas Cotes, and 14% of 390 for Thomas Harper.

[32] Witten-Hannah, 'Lady Mary Wroth's *Urania*', 73.

[33] James I, *A Proclamation Against Excesse.*   [34] Wither, *The Schollers Purgatory,* H2v–H3r.

[35] See Weiss, 'Casting Compositors, Foul Cases, and Skeletons', 209.

[36] 'Petition of Augustine Matthews', Vol. CCCLXIV, 345.

and ambivalent salvo than those launched by William Prynne, Henry Burton, or John Bastwick, Laud attacked the book in his speech, censuring them before the Star Chamber, saying, 'I am fully of opinion, this Booke was thrust now to the Presse, both to countenance these Libellers, and as much in him lay, to fire both Church and State.'[37] Indeed, Mathewes may have slyly stoked the coals of this controversy in ways that have not been noticed. Just before printing *The Holy Table*, Mathewes printed the book to which it was replying, *A Coale From the Altar*, by Peter Heylyn, the Laudian apologist. Heylyn himself was responding to a letter that Williams had circulated in manuscript, and Mathewes prefaces Heylyn's work with an unusual note from the 'Printer to the Reader', in which he explains that 'howsoever the Letter by him here replyed unto, be scattered up and downe, and in divers hands; Yet because possiblie, the Copie of the same hath not hitherto been seen of all, who may chance cast their eyes upon this Treatise ... the very Letter it selfe is herewith Printed, and bound together with it.'[38] Printing the letter has the effect of giving Laud's opponents the final word even in a text ostensibly meant to defend his position.

Considering Mathewes's subsequent punishment for printing Williams's work, it is hard to read this as an entirely innocent gesture, and it is certainly clear that printing Heylyn's work did not ingratiate Mathewes with the Laudian establishment. When the Dean of the Arches, John Lambe, surveyed the printing trade in preparation for the new 1637 Star Chamber Decree to regulate printing, he recommended that Mathewes should be excluded from the list of licensed printers thanks to his role in the controversy, with Marmaduke Parsons 'in his room'.[39] Mathewes petitioned the commissioners to intercede with Laud later that year, describing himself as 'poor' and 'destitute of any other calling whereby he may mainteyne his wife and familie' and begging to be reinstated and admitted as a master printer.[40] But his petition was not granted, and in fact when Williams was forced to recant his book he cast the blame squarely on Mathewes and the others involved who produced it. A document from 1638 in the Lambeth Palace library, endorsed with an order from King Charles that it be delivered to the High Commission, begins with Williams's admission that his first offence was 'permitting the Coppie thereof to fall into the hands of a Stationer, who caused the same to be printed in London without full and Lawfull Authoritie'.[41]

The episode drove Mathewes into the shadows, where it would seem he continued working with his own or others' equipment until at least June 1653,

---

[37] Laud, *A Speech Delivered in the Starr-Chamber*, I3v. See also Fincham and Tyacke, *Altars Restored*, 158–9.

[38] Heylyn, *A Coale from the Altar*, A3r–v.

[39] Transcribed in Arber, *The Term Catalogues*, IV.528.

[40] Gardiner, *Documents relating to the proceedings against William Prynne*, PRO, SP 16/363, ff.-217.

[41] Lambeth MS. 1030/92, transcribed in Blethen, 'Bishop John Williams's Recantation'.

when he entered a text in the Stationers' Register.[42] He may have worked briefly with Parsons until that man's death in 1639/40, and shortly after the printing of the *Epitaphium Damonis* he reappears briefly in the Stationer's Register in 1641 to transfer his 'estate, right, title and interest' in various texts to other printers, always with the proviso that 'the said Mr Mathewes is to have the workemanship of printing them (if hereafter he shall keepe a printing house) and shall doe them as reasonably as any other printer will doe the same'.[43] These contracts included one with John Raworth, whose widow Ruth would be responsible for printing Milton's 1645 *Poems* and, with her second husband Thomas Newcomb, seven of his prose tracts between 1650 and 1660.[44] But the shop where the fonts and ornaments used in the *Epitaphium Damonis* show up most frequently in the 1640s is that of Thomas Paine. Paine worked with Matthew Simmons on Milton's *Doctrine and Discipline of Divorce* and *Tetrachordon,* as well as on other Simmons publications. He often worked with the radical bookseller Giles Calvert (as did Raworth), and we find the fonts, ornamental borders, and crowned national emblems from *Epitaphium Damonis* used in his printing of the Leveller William Walwyn's defence of religious freedom, *A Parable.*

It is impossible to know whether Mathewes was working as a journeyman under Paine or whether Paine had simply acquired his materials. It is clear, however, that Mathewes's clash with Church, state, and company authorities thrust him into the midst of a growing oppositional print network just as Milton was seeking a printer for the *Epitaphium Damonis.* Milton's publications to this point—an unnamed appreciation for Shakespeare in the second folio, an anonymous masque with music by the royal musician Henry Lawes, and a poem in a genteel Cambridge memorial volume—showed few signs that he would soon emerge, with the name 'Mr. John Milton' splashed prominently across his title page, as a critic of the unholy alliance between an overweening Church and 'old patentees and monopolizers in the trade of bookselling'.[45] But even as *The Epitaphium Damonis* announced Milton's grand poetic ambitions and affirmed a cosmopolitan intellectual community, it was a link to a constellation of book producers who had their own reasons for helping him make that case. Milton needed printers to establish his name; printers like Augustine Mathewes and Matthew Simmons needed authors with established names as allies in their own extended war against print licensing and monopolies. The wider context of the *Epitaphium Damonis's* production makes it clear that the circumstances of Milton's stationers cannot be disentangled from the arc of his own career. His emerging authorial identity was not solitary but social, and print was an essential strategy for constructing, promoting, and preserving it.

[42] Plomer, *A Transcript of the Registers of the Worshipful Company of Stationers,* 419.
[43] Ibid., 29.   [44] See Dobranski, *Milton, Authorship and the Book Trade,* 128.
[45] Milton, *Areopagitica,* in Orgel and Goldberg, eds., *The Major Works,* 236–73, 273.

4

Repackaging Milton for the Late Seventeenth-Century Book Trade

Jacob Tonson, *Paradise Lost*, and John Dryden's *The State of Innocence*

Emma Depledge

The 1688 folio edition of *Paradise Lost*, published by Jacob Tonson the Elder (1655/6–1736) and his fellow bookseller Richard Bentley (1645–97), had a profound impact both on Milton's authorial afterlife and on Tonson's career as a stationer.[1] Milton may have been dead by 1688, but this volume was nonetheless an act of mutual promotion: Tonson made Milton into an elite book-trade product as Milton made Tonson the fortune and reputation that enabled him to transform his fledgling company into the eighteenth century's most formidable literary publishing house. I contrast the material features of this expensive publication with previous editions of *Paradise Lost* to suggest how the 1688 folio helped to revive interest in Milton's work and canonize him as a prestigious literary author. I also explore the reasons why Bentley and Tonson chose to publish Milton at this time and posit that Tonson's motivation for investing in *Paradise Lost* may have had more to do with the success enjoyed by an operatic alteration, John Dryden's *The State of Innocence*, than it did with the perceived marketability of Milton's poem.

Early Editions of *Paradise Lost*

An examination of earlier editions of *Paradise Lost* helps to make clear the influence that Bentley and Tonson's 1688 folio had on Milton's authorial

---

[1] I emphasize the impact the 1688 folio had on Tonson's career, but in doing so I do not wish to diminish Bentley's role in the project. It seems that Bentley owned a quarter share (see Mandelbrote, 'Richard Bentley's Copies'). The 1688 edition was issued with three different imprints: one listing Bentley, one listing Tonson, and one listing both men together. It would thus be incorrect to refer to the 1688 edition as Tonson's alone, but Bentley died in 1697, less than a decade after the folio's publication, whereas Tonson lived until 1736 and went on to become the most influential stationer of the early eighteenth century.

Emma Depledge, *Repackaging Milton for the Late Seventeenth-Century Book Trade: Jacob Tonson,* Paradise Lost, *and John Dryden's* The State of Innocence In: *Making Milton: Print, Authorship, Afterlives.* Edited by: Emma Depledge, John S. Garrison, and Marissa Nicosia, Oxford University Press (2021). © Emma Depledge.
DOI: 10.1093/oso/9780198821892.003.0004

reputation. These were issued by Samuel Simmons, a printer-publisher.[2] Simmons published Milton's poem early in his career as a stationer, and he does not appear to have had great confidence in the poem's ability to sell.[3] *Paradise Lost* was first published in 1667 and sold by a handful of booksellers. Robert Boulter, Peter Parker, Matthias Walker, S. Thomson, H. Mortlack, and T. Helder were all named in imprints as stocking the first edition of *Paradise Lost*, thus suggesting caution as each would have been responsible for selling a small number of copies. That said, the large number of stationers stocking *Paradise Lost* at shops operating from locations as far apart as 'Fleet-Street' and 'Bishopgate-Street' will have had the positive side effect of making Milton's poem available from a range of locations across London. The more diverse the shops selling a book, the more likely consumers were to stumble upon it, whether they were actively looking to acquire a copy or not. Simmons's caution may thus have been to Milton's advantage, with his sales strategy inadvertently helping to promote Milton to a wider readership.

Simmons's 1667 quarto edition of *Paradise Lost* was reissued a number of times, with the paratextual material added to later issues suggesting that he (and his fellow booksellers and their customers) thought it necessary to augment and improve on the first.[4] The first issue did not contain any paratextual framework, meaning that readers went straight from title page to poem. The poem was divided into ten books, with line numbers helpfully inserted (perhaps for the first time in an English poem) to mark every tenth line of verse,[5] but there was no pagination and the text appears cramped, with little spacing and double-rule lines around—at times poorly set—type. The lines of verse sit snug against claustrophobic text boxes. Later issues of the first edition were furnished with fourteen pages of paratexts that prefaced the poem with arguments detailing the main action of each book, with a note from the printer, an errata list, and justification from Milton himself explaining why the poem, contrary to most of the heroic works circulating in the late 1660s, did not rhyme. The addition of arguments aligned

---

[2] Simmons's name did not appear on a copy of *Paradise Lost* until 1668; explanations offered for Milton's choice of printer include the location of Simmons's print shop; the fact that Simmons, unlike most members of the book trade, was not badly impacted by the Great Fire of London in 1666; fidelity, as Simmons's relatives had printed some of Milton's earlier work; and the fact that Simmons was known as a dissenter (Lindenbaum, 'Milton's Contract'; MacLennan, 'John Milton's Contract for *Paradise Lost*'; Dobranski, *Milton, Authorship, and the Book Trade*, 35–6; and Moyles, *The Text of Paradise Lost*).

[3] As Campbell and Corns observe, *Paradise Lost* was the first title Simmons entered into the Stationers' Register alone. See *John Milton: Life, Works, and Thought*, 333.

[4] As Moyles shows, there were five issues of the first edition of *Paradise Lost* and, as Dobranski has demonstrated, there were six variant title pages of the first edition, but 'there is no relationship' between the different title pages and internal variants within the issues. In seeing the added paratexts as improvements, I do not wish to suggest that internal changes and corrections within the different issues necessarily show improvement. See Dobranski, 'Simmons's Shell Game', 64–5, 65; and Moyles, *The Text of Paradise Lost*, 4, 16.

[5] William Poole states that the addition of line numbers was 'a practice unwitnessed outside the editions of the Greek and Latin classics prepared for schoolboys and scholars' (*Milton and the Making of Paradise Lost*, 10).

Milton's poem with the classical epics he sought to emulate, but this was a case of reissuing rather than generating a new edition (the text was not reset), so it was not possible to situate the arguments before each book. Instead, they are grouped together before the poem begins. The arguments are not afforded a new page each—something which would have been possible with reissuing, had Simmons deemed it worth the cost in extra paper—and are instead clumped together, divided only by rule lines. Rather than prepare the reader for the content of the book that follows, the combined and continuous arguments therefore offer a summary of the entire plot of Milton's epic. Thus, the reissued copies of the first edition of *Paradise Lost* augmented the number of paratexts and, in doing so, arguably aided readers, but the overall quality of the edition remained low.

Sales of Milton's *Paradise Lost* may have been somewhat slow when it was first published in 1667. The author's contract with Simmons has survived, and it stipulates that Milton was to receive five pounds on receipt of the manuscript and a further five pounds once Simmons had sold 1,300 copies of the poem. Milton did not receive the second sum until April 1669, suggesting that it took almost two years to sell 1,300 copies.[6] It would seem that *Paradise Lost* made but a modest impact when it was first released onto the market.

A second edition of *Paradise Lost* was published in octavo format in 1674, seven years after the first. It was advertised on its title page as 'Revised and Augmented' by Milton, divided into twelve books, and supplemented by commendatory poems by 'S.[amuel] B.[arrow]' (in Latin) and Andrew Marvell (in English). The poem's arguments were now helpfully positioned before each book. The edition also featured a portrait of Milton, but, as Don-John Dugas has observed, this edition is 'much less attractive than the first edition because of the poor quality of its type'.[7] Equally, the line numbers of the first edition are no longer present, meaning that part of the helpful apparatus disappeared even as the poem's arguments moved to greater usability and prominence. The second edition was reissued a year later, possibly suggesting poor sales. A third edition of *Paradise Lost*, released in 1678, retained the octavo format and the division of the poem into twelve books but did little to improve on the quality of the previous two editions. It was also printed on cheap paper, with a great deal of bleed-through. As Moyles notes, it also introduced 'fresh … compositorial errors, chiefly foul case and omission'.[8] Simmons did not publish any further editions of *Paradise Lost* as he sold the rights in copy (that is, the copyright) to Brabazon Aylmer shortly after.

Confusion over the transactions between Simmons, Aylmer, and Tonson might have unnecessarily complicated our understanding of when *Paradise Lost* was and

---

[6] See MacLennan, 'John Milton's Contract for *Paradise Lost*', and French, *The Life Records of John Milton*, 4: 429–31. Moyles suggests that copies of the first edition went on sale soon after the poem's entry in the Stationers' Register in August 1667, thus about twenty months before Milton received payment on 26 April 1669. Like me, Moyles suspects that sales were 'lagging' (*The Text of Paradise Lost*, 4, 14–15).

[7] Dugas, *Marketing the Bard*, 77.   [8] Moyles, *The Text of Paradise Lost*, 32.

was not deemed to be a valuable investment. Aylmer purchased the rights in copy in 1680 and is reported to have paid twenty-five pounds for it, but he never published *Paradise Lost*.[9] It may be that Aylmer, a friend of Milton's, purchased the rights to prevent the poem from falling into the hands of the wrong publisher.[10] Aylmer then sold the rights to Tonson, and it is at this point that confusion seems to have crept into the story. Dugas writes that 'Milton scholars agree that Tonson bought the half-copyright to *Paradise Lost* from Aylmer in 1683 and that he paid more for that half than the £25 Aylmer had paid Simmons for the whole copyright in 1680', but adds that 'the original source of this story remains obscure'.[11] These transactions are not recorded in the Stationers' Register, but we do have a reliable early witness in the form of Thomas Newton.[12] In his account of 'The Life of John Milton', which precedes his 1749 edition of *Paradise Lost*, Newton reports that Aylmer sold the rights in copy 'to Jacob Tonson at two different times, one half on the 17th of August 1683, and the other half on the 24th of March 1690, with a considerable advance of the price'.[13] Thus, rather than suggest that Aylmer made a profit in 1683, Newton's account states that Tonson paid more for the *second* half of Aylmer's copy in 1690/1 than he did for the *first* half in 1683. This makes far more sense when we consider that the first three editions of *Paradise Lost* were by no means bestsellers and that Aylmer did not deem the poem profitable enough to produce his own edition.

Newton's account of the transaction history also makes more sense in the context of Tonson's career because it is unlikely that he would have been able to afford to pay a great deal for the rights in copy to *Paradise Lost* in 1683. Indeed, I suspect that half was all he could afford at that stage and that he likely co-financed the purchase with his regular business partner, Bentley, with whom he went on to co-publish the 1688 folio.[14] In 1683, Tonson was but a junior stationer. He was apprenticed to Thomas Basset in June 1670, but he did not complete his apprenticeship or set up his own publishing firm until 1678.[15] Tonson began his career with joint publishing ventures with other stationers, particularly with his elder brother Richard and with Bentley, who was then working alongside

---

[9] He did, however, publish *Epistolarum familiarum liber* (1674) and *Brief History of Muscovia* (1682), but was refused a licence to publish Milton's *Letters of State*. See Marja Smolenaars, 'Aylmer, Brabazon (*bap.* 1645, *d.* in or after 1719), bookseller'.

[10] On their friendship, Lindenbaum notes that Aylmer is reported to have occupied a role as pall bearer at Milton's funeral. See 'Authors and Publishers in the Late Seventeenth Century'.

[11] Dugas, *Marketing the Bard*, 77, n. 9.

[12] As Lindenbaum states, 'there is good reason to believe' Newton's account as 'Newton's edition of *Paradise Lost* was prepared for the Tonson firm and Newton had access to Tonson's records' ('Authors and Publishers in the Late Seventeenth Century', 33, n. 4).

[13] xxxviii.

[14] According to the list of stock transferred from Bentley to Richard Wellington after the former's death in 1697, Bentley at some point owned a one-quarter share in *Paradise Lost*. See Mandelbrote, 'Richard Bentley's Copies'.

[15] On Tonson's early career, see MacKenzie, 'Tonson, Jacob, the elder (1655/6–1736), bookseller'.

James Magnes (d.1678). Tonson's early releases predominantly involved quarto playbooks and poems, particularly those by John Dryden. In the 1680s Tonson had by no means attained the formidable reputation which he was to acquire in the eighteenth century. He was, however, already engaging in shrewd, at times illegal, publishing projects, such as the pirate edition of Shakespeare's *Hamlet* that he brought out with Bentley in 1683/4.[16]

Tonson was clearly planning ahead as we know that he had heard of and developed an interest in Milton before the end of his apprenticeship.[17] Aylmer may not have wished to publish *Paradise Lost*, but one assumes that, if he could have owned the complete copyright, then Tonson would have purchased it in its entirety in 1683. Tonson's ambition despite low funds is also reflected in the fact that the 1688 *Paradise Lost* was financed by subscription. As John Barnard notes, subscription publication, which first emerged in the mid-seventeenth century, was designed to enable the publication of 'large, learned books that were commercially unviable'.[18] It seems that it was only by pre-selling copies of the folio and by negotiating with Aylmer, who may have retained a 50 per cent share in the poem,[19] that Tonson could bring out a luxurious publication that was to transform both the reputation of Milton's *Paradise Lost* and his own career. Indeed, Aylmer is included in the subscribers list, suggesting either that his name was published out of recognition for letting Bentley and Tonson publish the poem to which he owned half the copyright, or else that he just purchased an advance copy of the 1688 folio. In the latter case, this may again be due to the friendship Aylmer enjoyed with his late friend Milton.

Milton, Tonson, and the 1688 *Paradise Lost*

The material form of the fourth edition represented a radical departure from those discussed above. The 1688 edition smacked of quality. It was the first edition of *Paradise Lost* to be published in folio format, with its 'monumental stature [seen to] symbolize big or important ideas'; indeed, it has been suggested that books in this format 'proclaimed their own merit, whether or not public opinion had yet deemed them worthy of such celebration'.[20] The 1688 folio was furnished with wide margins that offered readers plenty of room to add their own annotations to Milton's poem. The type was clear, and the volume featured an engraved portrait of Milton over an epigram in which Dryden helped to canonize him as the

---

[16] This edition, Wing S2951, was deliberately misdated '1676'. See Depledge, 'False Dating'.
[17] Tonson wrote of how he ' "had a mind to have seen Miltons Books" and of how, having failed to gain any during his first trip to see Milton, he would gaze in the direction of Milton's home whenever he went to Moorfields'. See Lynch, *Jacob Tonson: Kit-Cat Publisher*, 13.
[18] Barnard, 'London Publishing, 1640–1660', 11.
[19] The absence of Aylmer's name on the 1688 folio imprints suggests that he was a silent partner.
[20] Robert B. Hamm, Jr, 'Rowe's "Shakespeare"'.

national poet by depicting Milton as an English heir to the two most revered classical writers. Dryden claims that Milton possessed both Homer's 'loftiness of thought' and the 'Majesty' of Virgil. The 1688 folio was also printed on quality paper to match the elite company in which Dryden's epigram placed Milton, and the volume even featured twelve detailed engravings—one for each book—by John Baptist Medina and others (see Figure 4.1). Concerning the illustrations, Robert B. Hamm, Jr acknowledges that the 1688 *Paradise Lost* was remarkable in that it 'helped to introduce the Franco-Flemish style of book illustration to England', but he rightly adds that these illustrations are yet more exceptional in the context of Tonson's career as a stationer and 'should not be seen as indicative of the general quality of Tonson's books' until that point.[21] Thus, the 1688 folio marked a radical

Figure 4.1 John Milton, *Paradise Lost. A poem in twelve books* (1688). Illustration to and argument of Book IX. Folger Shelfmark M2147. Gg[1] (p. 219) and facing plate. Used by permission of the Folger Shakespeare Library.

---

[21] Ibid., 181. On innovations associated with Tonson and Dryden's earlier translation projects, see Gillespie, 'The Early Years of the Dryden-Tonson Partnership'.

departure not just for Milton's poem but also for Tonson's house style as the publisher pulled out all the stops for Milton.

Perhaps most significantly, though, the 1688 folio edition included a list of 'The | NAMES | OF THE | Nobility and Gentry' that 'Encourag'd' the volume's publication through their subscriptions, a list that transformed Milton's reputation from that of a dissenting king killer to one appreciated by men across the political spectrum. The list included the likes of Dryden, as well as a series of earls, lords, even bishops, some of whom prepaid for one copy, others of whom paid for as many as three copies of Milton's poem. Some subscribers were Whigs and others were Tories; it was not a partisan list. Instead, the list suggests that Milton's poem was aimed at and approved by a great variety of readers. Surprisingly, even Sir Roger L'Estrange subscribed to the 1688 edition of *Paradise Lost*.[22] This was the first time that a work of imaginative English literature had been published by subscription, and the financial aid Bentley and Tonson enlisted had positive implications for Milton. Readers perusing the list included at the end of the volume would have seen the names of 538 influential figures who not only supported the publication of *Paradise Lost* but also by implication endorsed the poem and its author. The ranks and reputations of the subscribers added status to the publication and helped to promote Milton and his poem as belonging to elite, high culture, much as Tonson's later subscription edition of Shakespeare (1723–5), which featured a list headed by the King, helped to canonize Shakespeare.

As is often noted, Tonson stated that the 1688 *Paradise Lost* turned out to be the most lucrative of his publishing ventures,[23] but this venture also looks to have transformed *Paradise Lost* into an elite book-trade product. The 1667, 1674, and 1678 editions of the poem cost approximately 3s each.[24] Tonson claimed that 'the Price of [the 1688 edition of *Paradise Lost*] was Four times greater than before'; this indicates a retail price of around 12s for the 1688 folio, but Barnard, who used paper counts to calculate his figures, suggests that 'even 15s. is a reasonable estimate for the price of a copy of the 1688 *Paradise Lost*'.[25] As a point of comparison, Milton's single poem was in 1688 retailing for around the same price as a copy of the Fourth Folio (1685) of Shakespeare's collected plays.[26] The subscribers to this volume were not only promoting Milton but also self-fashioning, as the list announced them as people capable of spending up to 15s

[22] On the relationship between the two, see von Maltzahn, 'L'Estrange's Milton'.

[23] Osborn, ed., *Joseph Spence: Observations, Anecdotes, and Characters*, 333.

[24] Robert Clavell lists the price of *Paradise Lost* bound as costing 3s in 1669, and a Term Catalogue entry for Trinity 1674 lists 'Paradise Lost. A Poem, in Twelve Books; Revised and Augmented by the Author, John Milton' (i.e. the second edition) as costing the same, 3s. The prices for *Paradise Regained* are taken from the *Term Catalogues* (I. 56 and I. 453).

[25] This calculation is based on the number of sheets used to print the 1688 edition in comparison with those used to print the related publication *Paradise Regained*, which used a tenth fewer sheets and which retailed (bound) for 4s in 1671 and for 1s 6d in 1680. See Barnard, 'Large- and Small-Paper Copies', 270.

[26] On the price of the Fourth Folio see Hansen and Rasmussen 'Shakespeare Without Rules'.

on a single poetry book. Thus, in contrast to earlier editions of *Paradise Lost*, the 1688 folio edition was a magisterial publication and one that functioned as a material witness attesting to the quality of Milton's work, Tonson's (and Bentley's) house style, and the financial worth of its subscribers.

The 1688 folio marked the beginning of Tonson's promotion of Milton and was Tonson's first major publishing venture. Thus, the project played a highly significant role not just in Milton's authorial afterlife but also in Tonson's career. As Peter Lindenbaum states, 'Tonson was the leading publisher and bookseller of literary works of his generation and it was John Milton who made him.'[27] Even the most famous portrait of Tonson depicts him as proudly holding his folio edition of *Paradise Lost*. According to Newton, Tonson acquired the last of Aylmer's copy in 1690/1, presumably with profits from 1688, and (with Bentley) brought out a second folio edition of *Paradise Lost* in 1691. Tonson also acquired the rights to a substantial number of other Milton texts and in 1695 published alone both a third folio edition of *Paradise Lost* and *The Poetical Works of John Milton*. The 1695 edition of *Paradise Lost* then arguably took Tonson's project to canonize Milton via the book trade a step further by also including critical commentary by the scholar Patrick Hume. Indeed, this was the first critical edition of a work of English poetry.[28] Profits from the 1688 edition enabled Tonson to not only acquire and publish Milton's other works but also bring out similarly prestigious editions of Virgil, Homer, and Shakespeare.[29] As Barnard writes, Tonson's 'willingness to advance copy money [£200 to Dryden for his Virgil] was undoubtedly based on his earlier experience of jointly publishing...*Paradise Lost* (1688)'.[30] Thus, I would argue that this project was mutually beneficial: Tonson shaped Milton's authorship, while his later publishing career was shaped by the profits earned from the 1688 edition of *Paradise Lost*.

Conclusion: the Influence of Dryden's *The State of Innocence*

To anyone who observed the fortunes of the first three editions of *Paradise Lost*, Tonson's decision to invest in Milton's poem may have seemed an unusual, unwise business move. I wish to conclude by suggesting that the 1688 *Paradise*

[27] Lindenbaum also suggests that Tonson 'unmade John Milton' by dividing Milton's literary from his non-literary works, but I would instead emphasize the greater visibility Milton as literary author gained in the wake of the 1688 folio edition of *Paradise Lost*. On Milton and Tonson and the division between Milton's literary and non-literary works, see Lindenbaum, 'Rematerializing Milton', 5.

[28] See Moyles, *The Text of Paradise Lost*, and David Harper, 'The First Annotator of *Paradise Lost* and the Makings of English Literary Criticism'.

[29] On the Virgil, see especially Barnard, 'Dryden, Tonson, and Subscriptions for the 1697 Virgil'. On Alexander Pope's translations of the *Iliad* and the *Odyssey*, see Mack, *Alexander Pope: A Biography*, 268, 416.

[30] Barnard, 'The Large- and Small-Paper Copies', 269.

Lost had less to do with the perceived vendibility of the poem and more to do with Tonson's own ambitions and frustrations as a stationer, particularly as Dryden's stationer. Dryden, who we know admired the poem, probably helped to persuade Tonson—his friend and collaborator on numerous projects—to bring out an edition of *Paradise Lost*,[31] but Tonson may also have seen *Paradise Lost* as a consolation prize for Dryden's *The State of Innocence*. Dryden's operatic alteration of *Paradise Lost* had proven to be an exceptionally profitable print commodity. *The State of Innocence* was first entered in the Stationers' Register on 17 April 1674. It was entered by Henry Herringman under the title '*The Fall of Angells and man in innocence, An heroic opera*' and attributed to 'John Dreyden' [*sic*].[32] It is sometimes misstated that Tonson and not Herringman entered the copy for *The State of Innocence* in 1674.[33] It is a logical mistake to make as we tend to think of Tonson as always having been Dryden's publisher, but their literary-commercial relationship was not confirmed until 1679. That it was Herringman and not Tonson who entered the copy for Dryden's adaptation is, I argue, precisely the point. Tonson lost out to Herringman because *The State of Innocence* came too early in Tonson's career as a stationer.

Dryden's alleged conversation with Milton in 1674, during which he is said to have asked permission to put Milton's 'Paradise Lost into Rhime for the Stage',[34] is now infamous. However, the anecdote and the critical fortunes of Dryden's *The State of Innocence* and Milton's *Paradise Lost* may, I believe, have masked our appreciation of the role Dryden's alteration played in the promotion of Milton's poem at the end of the seventeenth century.[35] The relationship between Milton's and Dryden's texts goes beyond the mere act of adaptation, or 'alteration'. Dryden asked permission to 'tagg [Milton's] Points' in 1674, and his opera was not published until February 1677, but it still looks to have impacted on the second edition of *Paradise Lost* when it was released in summer 1674. A piece of commendatory verse, composed by Milton's friend Marvell, was added to the second edition, and it is hard not to read Marvell's lines as a response to Dryden's alteration. It is generally assumed that Marvell, and perhaps Milton too, read the

---

[31] Dryden and Tonson collaborated on translations and collections in the early 1680s, and Dryden's influence over Tonson is demonstrated in Tonson's acceptance of Dryden's advice to reprint 1,000 copies of Lord Roscommon's *Essay on Translated Verse*. See Ward, *Letters of John Dryden*, 22–3. Tonson also credited John Somers with persuading him to publish Milton in 1688 and again in 1711. See Gillespie, 'The Early Years of the Dryden-Tonson Partnership'.

[32] Eyre and Rivington, *A Transcript of the Registers of the Worshipful Company of Stationers of London*, 1.479.

[33] See, for example, Zwicker, 'John Dryden Meets, Rhymes, and Says Farewell to John Milton', 184.

[34] See Darbishire, ed., *The Early Lives of Milton*, 335, and, for a recent discussion of the important relationship between Dryden, Milton, and Andrew Marvel, see Zwicker, 'John Dryden Meets, Rhymes, and Says Farewell to John Milton'.

[35] On *The State of Innocence*, see Marcie Frank's chapter 'Staging Criticism, Staging Milton: John Dryden's The State of Innocence' in her monograph *Gender, Theatre, and the Origins of Criticism from Dryden to Manley*; and Zwicker, 'John Dryden Meets, Rhymes, and says Farewell to John Milton'.

opera shortly after it was composed. Indeed, in the preface to the first edition Dryden claimed that the opera had also enjoyed extended manuscript circulation, complaining that 'many hundred Copies of it [were] dispers'd abroad without my knowledge or consent'.[36] This suggests that the opera will have been easy to access despite the delay between completion and print publication. Marvell speaks of how others ought not 'dare' to pretend to share in Milton's labours, and refers to 'town-Bayes', Dryden's nickname. The second edition of Dryden's opera appeared in 1678, within twelve months of the first edition. The third edition of *Paradise Lost* also appeared in 1678, after a hiatus of four years, suggesting that it could have been released in response to the interest generated by Dryden's piece. Thus, even before the first edition of *The State of Innocence* was published, Dryden's alteration looks to have impacted on the timing of and paratexts to the second edition of *Paradise Lost*, and it may also have influenced the timing of the release of the third edition of *Paradise Lost*.

I suspect that Dryden and his opera also influenced the publication of the fourth edition of *Paradise Lost*. Tonson did not become Dryden's publisher until 1679, but he soon after sought to obtain the exclusive rights to publish Dryden's earlier works.[37] Tonson did not manage to secure the rights to *The State of Innocence*; one imagines that Herringman would have been loath to relinquish the rights to such a popular print commodity. Dryden's opera went through an impressive nine editions between its first release in 1677 and the turn of the century. A second edition was published in 1678, a third and fourth followed in 1685, a fifth in 1690, a sixth in 1692, and a seventh and eighth in 1695. A pirated ninth edition, falsely dated '1684', was also published.[38] The closest Tonson came to publishing *The State of Innocence* during the seventeenth century was to include the title within *The Dramatic Works of Mr John Dryden in Three Volumes*, which was issued from 1691, but this was but a Sammelband of previously published Dryden quartos, stitched together and furnished with new title pages.[39] Tonson's interest in the title is also reflected in his appearance in the imprint to the 1695 edition of *The State of Innocence*, but he merely stocked the play in his shop; it is printed for Herringman and to be sold by others, as Herringman was by then a wholesale publisher.[40] Tonson finally obtained the rights in copy from Herringman around the turn of the century: he is named in

---

[36] For more on manuscript copies of Dryden's opera, see Hamilton, 'The Manuscripts of Dryden's *The State of Innocence* and the Relation of the Harvard Ms to the First Quarto'.

[37] As Raymond N. MacKenzie has stated, Tonson 'began to buy up the rights to Dryden's earlier works during the 1680s' ('Tonson, Jacob, the elder (1655/6–1736), bookseller').

[38] See Hamilton, 'The Early Editions of Dryden's *The State of Innocence*'. This edition is listed as MacDonald 81c. See Macdonald, *John Dryden: A Bibliography of Early Editions and of Drydeniana*.

[39] See Macdonald, *John Dryden: A Bibliography of Early Editions and of Drydeniana*.

[40] The imprint states that the edition was printed for Herringman but 'sold by J. Tonson, F. Saunders, and T. Bennet'. Herringman was by then a wholesale publisher and had turned his shop, the Blue Anchor, over to Saunders and Bennet. On Herringman's career, see Francis X. Connor, 'Henry Herringman, Richard Bentley and Shakespeare's Fourth Folio (1685)'.

the imprint as the publisher of the opera in 1703. Thus, he clearly wanted to profit from *The State of Innocence*, but the rights to publish it remained beyond his reach during the seventeenth century.

The publication history of Milton's most famous poem could therefore have been shaped less by the work's perceived 'genius' and more by Tonson's frustrations after failing to obtain the rights to a successful Dryden adaptation. We may never know for sure what made Tonson and Bentley decide to publish the 1688 folio edition of *Paradise Lost*, but we do know that it proved to be a wise decision: the venture was a huge success. It marked the beginnings of Jacob Tonson's rise to commercial prominence and his long career as a shaper of the literary canon. But, of yet more importance to this volume, the 1688 folio edition of *Paradise Lost* also helped to canonize Milton as a prestigious author and *Paradise Lost* as an elite book-trade product.

5

Joseph Addison and the Domestication of *Paradise Lost*

Thomas N. Corns

As WILL [Honeycomb]'s Transitions [from one topic to another] are extreamly quick, he turned from Sir ROGER [de Coverley], and applying himself to me, told me, there was a Passage in the Book I had considered last *Saturday*, which deserved to be writ in Letters of Gold; and taking out a Pocket *Milton*, read the following Lines, which are part of one of *Adam*'s Speeches to *Eve* after the Fall....[1]

Sir ROGER listened to this Passage with great Attention, and desiring Mr. HONEYCOMB to fold down a Leaf at the Place, and lend him his Book, the Knight put it up in his Pocket, and told us that he would read over those Verses again before he went to Bed.[2]

Thus, on the Tuesday following Joseph Addison's Saturday examination of the tenth book of *Paradise Lost*,[3] Richard Steele ingeniously loops back to engage with that essay. There used to be a commonplace observation in media studies that the characters in television drama were never depicted watching television. Steele, boldly, shows the characters of Mr Spectator's club actually discussing a copy of *The Spectator*. The characters primarily engaged in that exchange are surprising, and Steele's choice indicates how readership and styles of reading had apparently changed since Milton had envisaged a 'fit audience', presumably of ideologically sympathetic readers, appreciating his epic in the 'evil days' of the mid-1660s (7.25–31).[4] We do not hear from Sir Andrew Freeport, though he is present as the discussion starts. As a Whig merchant he is perhaps the heir to the London puritans Milton may have anticipated as his readership. Instead, the advocate of Milton's poem is Will Honeycomb, something of a womanizer (at least in his youth): 'To conclude his Character, where Women are not concerned, he is an

---

[1] Here Steele inserts *Paradise Lost*, 10.888–908. The passage had been briefly discussed but not quoted in Addison's essay.

[2] Bond, ed., *The Spectator*, 3:345.   [3] Ibid., 3:329–39.

[4] All quotations from *Paradise Lost* in this chapter are drawn from Orgel and Goldberg, eds., *The Major Works*, 355–618; subsequent references are cited in my text.

Thomas N. Corns, *Joseph Addison and the Domestication of* Paradise Lost In: *Making Milton: Print, Authorship, Afterlives.* Edited by: Emma Depledge, John S. Garrison, and Marissa Nicosia, Oxford University Press (2021). © Thomas N. Corns. DOI: 10.1093/oso/9780198821892.003.0005

honest worthy Man.'[5] His interlocutor, Sir Roger de Coverley, is a superannuated rake, though by now he has mellowed into a genial old country gentleman (and by implication a Tory backwoodsman); he was 'what you call a fine Gentleman, had often supped with my Lord *Rochester* and Sir *George Etherege*, fought a Duel upon his first coming to Town, and kick'd Bully *Dawson* in a publick Coffee-house for calling him Youngster'.[6] Dawson seems to have been a legendarily dissolute gambler. The other two associates of young de Coverley would have been rather better known to early readers. Etherege, a libertine poet and then Restoration dramatist, had spent the 1660s in 'womanizing, gambling, and drinking'.[7] John Wilmot, the second Earl of Rochester, though he had reputedly died a penitent, was a byword for the obscenity and profanity of some aspects of Restoration culture. His works, or at least a selection of those poems attributed to him, remained in print in the age of Addison and Steele. Edmund Curll had published very recently a third edition of *The Works of the Right Honourable Earls of Rochester and Roscommon* (London, 1709), and Steele and Addison each cite approvingly two of Rochester's less obscene poems in *Spectator* papers.[8] But the collection manifests ample evidence both of the obscenity of Rochester's wit and of the depravity of the milieu he depicts. The relatively anodyne prefatory life notes that 'Temperance . . . was . . . laid aside, and a Loose given to all the Pleasure of the Court and Town, of Love and Wine'.[9] Rather than fit audience, Etherege, Rochester, and the youthful Sir Roger were more likely to have joined with the 'tigers of Bacchus, these new fanatics of not the preaching but the sweating-tub [apparatus used in the treatment of sexually transmitted diseases], inspired by nothing holier than the venereal pox', whose terrorizing of Restoration London Milton had accurately prophesied.[10]

Plainly, a narrative, albeit fictional, that has figures like de Coverley and Honeycomb discussing *Paradise Lost* suggests a taste for his writing stripped of an awareness of how ideologically repellent his views and values were to their own. Admittedly, this *Spectator* paper perhaps functions by depicting a cultural realignment it is really seeking to promote. But the mode of reading and responding is also that encouraged in Addison's essays on *Paradise Lost*. Steele is writing somewhat whimsically, in that his account of de Coverley and Honeycomb relates their difficulties in securing rich wives, and Adam's speech is a lament to the misfortune of his marriage to Eve and the 'Innumberable / Disturbances on earth through female snares' (10.896–7).[11] De Coverley is invited to reflect on the passage as an

---

[5] Bond, ed., *The Spectator*, 1:13.   [6] Ibid., 1.8 and n. 4.
[7] Barnard, 'Etherege, Sir George (1636–1691/2), playwright and diplomat'.
[8] Bond, ed., *The Spectator*, 1:386–7, 3:100.
[9] Rochester, *The Works of the Right Honourable Earls of Rochester and Roscommon*, a7v.
[10] Milton, *The Ready and Easy Way to Establish a Free Commonwealth*, in Orgel and Goldberg, eds., *The Major Works*, 347–8.
[11] Quoted in Bond, ed., *The Spectator*, 3:345.

antidote to reflection of his failure to secure a bride. He is invited to use the text, or rather a tiny sample of the whole, as an emotional corrective.

The passage is also a wonderful piece of early product placement (a term not coined until 1982).[12] In the issue of *The Spectator* that carried the fourth essay on *Paradise Lost*,[13] and subsequently repeated, there appeared an advertisement placed by Jacob Tonson as 'just published' a 'very neat Pocket Edition... of Paradise Lost, a Poem, in twelve Books'.[14] This was the ninth edition of 1711 and the first genuinely small-format version to be made available. Tonson's economy editions of 1705 and 1711 were bulky octavos. This is a duodecimo measuring about 9 by 14 centimetres, smaller than a modern Penguin paperback, which is 11 by 18 centimetres, and neat enough to fit in a gentleman's pocket as a readily available source of interest and solace. As R. G. Moyles, on whose account I here draw, concludes, 'In spite of its cramped text... its size and price combined to make it one of Tonson's best-selling editions.'[15] Addison and Steele had long known Tonson. They were all members of the Kit-Cat Club, a gathering of leading Whig thinkers, activists, and apologists. Tonson had frequently published Addison in a professional relationship going back to the 1690s. Steele was the father of Tonson's illegitimate niece.[16] Moreover, Tonson was a regular advertiser.[17] So a pleasing reciprocity is marked by Steele's little manoeuvre; Sir Roger is shown pocketing Tonson's 1711 *Paradise Lost* with the premeditation of James Bond sipping Heineken in *Skyfall*.

But how does Addison go about the eighteen core essays on *Paradise Lost*, and what does it disclose about his expectations of his readers and his own cultural agenda? Dr Johnson, as dominant an arbiter of taste in his own age as Addison had been in the 1710s, took a long and generous view in a way that showed appreciation of the kind of cultural transformation *The Spectator* papers were promoting:

> That general knowledge which now circulates in common talk, was in his time rarely to be found. Men not professing learning were not ashamed of ignorance; and in the female world, any acquaintance with books was distinguished only to be censured. His purpose was to infuse literary curiosity, by gentle and unsuspected conveyance, into the gay, the idle, and the wealthy; he therefore presented knowledge in the most alluring form, not lofty and austere, but accessible and familiar.... Had he presented *Paradise Lost* to the publick with all the pomp of

---

[12] All references to word definitions and etymologies in this chapter draw from the *Oxford English Dictionary Online*, http://www.oed.com.

[13] For Saturday, 26 January 1712; Bond, ed., *The Spectator*, 3:9–15.

[14] Bond, ed., *The Spectator*, 3:345 n. 2.   [15] Moyles, *The Text of* Paradise Lost, 43.

[16] Carter, 'Kit-Cat Club (*act.* 1696–1720)'; Rogers, 'Addison, Joseph (1672–1719), writer and politician'; Winton, 'Steele, Sir Richard (*bap.* 1672, *d.* 1729), writer and politician'.

[17] Bond, ed., *The Spectator*, 1:xxiii.

system and severity of science, the criticism would perhaps have been admired, and the poem still have been neglected; but by the blandishments of gentleness and facility, he has made Milton an universal favourite, with whom readers of every class think it necessary to be pleased.[18]

Johnson shrewdly recognizes that Addison operated in the period in which high-culture literature started to attract a wider and less educated readership, who required reassurance as well as guidance.

The direction had been set almost twenty years earlier when Tonson had published in uniform with the sixth edition of *Paradise Lost* Patrick Hume's *Annotations on Milton's* Paradise Lost. *Wherein The Texts of Sacred Writ, Relating to the Poem, are Quoted; the Parallel Places and Imitations of the Most Excellent* Homer *and* Virgil, *Cited and Compared; All the Obscure Parts Render'd in Phrases More Familiar; the Old and Obsolete Words, with the Originals, Explain'd and Made Easie to the English Reader* (London, 1695). As mentioned in the previous chapter, the publication has the distinction of being the first sustained and detailed scholarly annotation of an English vernacular poem. The title adumbrates the intended readerships. These are people too little steeped in the Bible to pick up the references, too unfamiliar with the major texts of classical literature to grasp the allusions, and so unlatined as to be unable to guess the meaning of obscure vocabulary. But herein rests something of a rare flaw in Tonson's business model, in that the edition Hume's text accompanies and with which it was often (though not always) bound was an expensive de luxe folio. The *Annotations* is now a relatively rare book, and while its commissioning and publication show Tonson was thinking about serving a wider readership, this was not the publication to do that. It was used by later editors of Milton, and, as Marcus Walsh observes, 'Much of the original spadework of identifying Milton's use of the Bible was carried out by Hume, and much was exploited by later editors of *Paradise* Lost';[19] but I doubt those who paid a premium price for the sixth edition often reached for its rather pedantic companion.

Addison published his work on Milton after the significant publishing development of Tonson's provision of two fairly cheap octavos of 1705 and 1707 and the pocket edition of 1711. The term 'pocket edition' dates from 1640, though early examples were usually prayer books and other devotional publications. The publishing phenomenon and the critical essays enjoyed a particular synergy: plentiful copies of cheap versions supplied the readers and the essays stimulated the market. The Tonson–Addison collaboration arguably made Milton more accessible—both financially and intellectually—than the expensive and cumbersome 1695 edition often credited with making him accessible.

---

[18] Johnson, *Lives of the English Poets*, 1: 446–7.
[19] Walsh, *Shakespeare, Milton, and Eighteenth-Century Literary Editing,* 59.

Johnson speaks of the idle and the ignorant as potential new readers of Milton, and postulates a time when women were just entering in numbers on high-culture reading and when men perhaps began to feel an obligation to feign familiarity with it. Addison is helpful to both groups. His six general essays rehearse some of the larger arguments about Milton's achievement in terms that render them tractable to easy appropriation and incorporation into polite conversation. But better still for the timid or incompetent reader, the twelve essays on the twelve books of the poem render it unnecessary to read *Paradise Lost* itself. His quotations are extensive, and he outlines the content of each book as, of course, Milton himself had done in the arguments he was constrained by his first publisher to supply. Moreover, Addison guides his readers to an appropriate response, judging the qualities of each of his extracts. Thus, in his account of Book I, the observation that 'There are several other Strokes ... wonderfully poetical, and Instances of that Sublime Genius so peculiar to the Author' ushers in the quotation of lines 181–3, 541–3, 567–73, 663–6, 710–12, and 726–30, each with scarcely an observation from Addison.[20] Thus equipped, the reader of *The Spectator* could at the least communicate a semblance of familiarity with and appreciation of Milton's poem.

By the time Addison's work had percolated through English society and, in Johnson's phrase, 'readers of every class think it necessary to be pleased' with *Paradise Lost*, recourse to the *Spectator* essays would at least have obviated the need actually to read the poem through. Addison plainly knows Hume's annotations but steers his own approach away from anything smacking of pedantry (much as Johnson recognized). He wears his own (very real) erudition lightly:

> I might, in the course of these Criticisms, have taken notice of many particular Lines and Expressions which are translated from the *Greek* Poet, but as I thought this would have appeared too minute and over-curious, I have purposely omitted them. The greater Incidents, however, are not only set off by being shown in the same Light, with several of the same Nature as *Homer*, but by that means may be also guarded against the Cavils of the Tasteless and Ignorant.[21]

Addison's care for his reader's attention span precludes Hume's kind of engagement with the text.

But Addison's critical agenda extended much further than merely facilitating the cultural simulation of the idle. The papers on *Paradise Lost* mark the ascendancy of literary neoclassicism in the English context. The tussle between writers who privileged classical models and those resistant to such influences extended far back into the Elizabethan and Jacobean periods and the resilient adoption of the former particularly by Ben Jonson. His plays, of course, were

---

[20] Bond, ed., *The Spectator*, 3:89–90.   [21] Ibid., 3:312.

largely structured on Aristotelian principles, and Martial's epigrams, among other classical forms, were imitated by him and by his closer followers, pre-eminently Robert Herrick. But there remained something gloriously eclectic about early-Stuart neoclassicism. Jonson could structure a play like Sophocles but populate it with figures who would have been at home in a coney-catching pamphlet. Herrick's appropriation of Martial is leavened by a healthy slice of bucolic England. Milton's most neoclassical vernacular poem before *Paradise Lost*, 'Lycidas', though shaped by Virgil and Theocritus, is textured with Spenserianisms.

Addison likes his neoclassicism in a purer form. Unrelentingly, the touchstone of the status of Milton's epic is its conformity with the practices of Virgil and Homer. He announces his project thus: 'I shall ... examine it by the Rules of Epic Poetry, and see whether it falls short of the *Iliad* or *Æneid* in the Features which are essential to that kind of Writing.'[22] I suspect to nobody's surprise, he does indeed see it not to fall short of the classical models. Homer and Virgil recur as carefully observed patterns for Milton's practice. Thus, for example, he notes that '*Adam*'s Converse with *Eve*, after having eaten the forbidden Fruit, is an exact Copy of that between *Jupiter* and *Juno*, in the Fourteenth *Iliad*'.[23] But Addison manifests a pronounced anxiety when Milton apparently strays off-message. There are allegorical passages in Virgil's epic but nothing as extended as the roles of Sin and Death. Addison responds with an explanation that here, regrettably, earlier and perhaps inferior notions of vernacular epic are breaking through the classical perfection towards which Milton otherwise, successfully, aspires: 'Such Allegories rather savour of the Spirit of *Spencer* and *Ariosto*, than of *Homer* and *Virgil*.'[24] Milton writes within a mature tradition of hexameral poetry and palpably draws, sometimes quite extensively, on the *Divine Weekes and Workes*, Joshua Sylvester's translation of *La Semaine* and *La Seconde Semaine* of Guillaume de Saluste, Sieur du Bartas.[25] Addison certainly had some familiarity with this work, because he alludes disparagingly, if a trifle tentatively, to it in an account of 'false Wit'.[26] However, he nowhere connects Milton's epic with this non-classical influence and model in his essays on *Paradise Lost*. Homer and Virgil, not the homespun Sylvester, are the company his Milton keeps.

But Addison, perhaps purposefully, rather misses the point of Milton's relationship with the writers of classical epic, though in this he follows John Dryden's lead, articulated in the epigraph he supplied to the 1688 fourth edition, which was subsequently repeated:

---

[22] Ibid., 2:539.   [23] Ibid., 3:311.   [24] Ibid., 3:60.

[25] The fullest account, though perhaps overstating the case, remains Taylor, *Milton's Use of Du Bartas*.

[26] Bond, ed., *The Spectator*, 1:247.

Three Poets, *in three distant* Ages *born,*
Greece, Italy, and England *did adorn.*
The First *in loftiness of thought surpass'd;*
The Next *in Majesty; in both the* Last.
The force of Nature *could no further goe:*
To make a Third *she joined the former two.*[27]

Dryden represents Milton as the peer of Virgil and Homer, combining the strengths of both, a line Addison assiduously follows. Milton, however, represents his role not as equal to theirs but superior by reason of its subject matter. His narrative of the fall is:

> sad task, yet argument
> Not less but more heroic than the wrath
> Of stern Achilles on his foe pursued
> Thrice fugitive about Troy wall; or rage
> Of Turnus for Lavinia disespoused,
> Or Neptune's ire or Juno's, that so long
> Perplexed the Greek and Cytherea's son[.]
>
> (9.13–19)

Ancient heroes chasing each other around legendary battlefields plainly fall short in terms of epic decorum once compared with Milton's subject. His muse, his 'celestial patroness' (9.21), outranks the fictive muses of Helicon because she is a Christian muse, imparting Christian truth, not classical fable.

Occasionally Addison does observe his Christian duty of asseverating the superiority of Milton's subject. He observes, for example, that the vision of futurity that Michael vouchsafes to Adam is superior to the equivalent prolepsis in Virgil's poem in that '*Adam*'s Vision is not confined to any particular Tribe of Mankind, but extends to the whole Species'.[28] But Addison's principal concerns in his engagement with Milton's theology have a rather different focus, on the assertion of his Protestant orthodoxy. He is not a close reader, or at least a close critic, of theological nuance, and his tendency is to incorporate Milton into the mainstream of Protestant thinking. Of course, he writes without the advantage of having Milton's highly heterodox treatise, *De Doctrina Christiana*, at his elbow, unlike modern critics.[29] The most doctrinally rich section of the poem is the discussion between the Father and the Son in Book 3. Here, a generally Arminian soteriology

---

[27] Dryden, 'Portrait Frontispiece'.   [28] Bond, ed., *The Spectator*, 3:361.
[29] The work, unpublished in Milton's lifetime, was rediscovered only in 1823. For a history of the manuscript, see Campbell, Corns, Hale, and Tweedie, *Milton and the Manuscript of De Doctrina Christiana*.

is explicitly developed, in itself unremarkable to Addison's age in that it was the then dominant position among theologians of the Church of England. But there is implicit within that discourse a vision of the relationship between the Father and the Son and of the marginalization of the Holy Spirit that could cause at least some disquiet among Trinitarians. Addison affirms that Milton 'chuses to confine himself to such Thoughts as are drawn from the Books of the most Orthodox Divines, and to such Expressions as may be met with in Scripture.... He has represented all the abstruse Doctrines ... with great Energy of Expression, and in a clearer and stronger Light than I ever met with in any other Writer.'[30] The conversation of the Father and the Son is followed by the long, rather digressive, account of the Paradise of Fools (3.440–97), which I have elsewhere argued functions as a component in a complex rhetorical strategy on Milton's part, an attempt to re-engage with disappointed theological radicals after the apparent passive orthodoxy of the soteriological account.[31] The passage is, of course, unmistakably and fiercely anti-Catholic. Addison likes his poetry decorous and his religion cool. He finds the passage aesthetically awkward. As in the case of the allegorical figures of Sin and Death, he identifies the inappropriateness of the passage in terms of the rules of epic in that they are 'astonishing. But not credible... they are the Description of Dreams and Shadows, not of Things or Persons.'[32] But on the polemical vigour of the passage he makes no comment. Addison was, in Pat Rogers's phrase, 'a Hanoverian of unquestioned fidelity',[33] and for him and for other Whigs the exclusion of a Jacobite succession depended primarily on the inadmissibility of a Catholic monarch. But anti-Catholic sentiment is rare in *The Spectator*. Addison's most patient exploration of religious differences comes in paper 201, where he plays a patient Anglican game:

> As Enthusiasm is a kind of Excess in Devotion, Superstition is the Excess not only of Devotion, but of Religion in general.... An Enthusiast in Religion is like an obstinate Clown, a Superstitious Man like an insipid Courtier. Enthusiasm has something in it of Madness, Superstition of Folly. Most of the Sects that fall short of the Church of *England*, have in them strong Tinctures of Enthusiasm, as the *Roman* Catholick Religion is one huge overgrown Body of childish and idle Superstitions.[34]

Where would Milton figure on this spectrum? Purely on the basis of Addison's essays on *Paradise Lost* one would think 'a solid Anglican', and an Anglican too polite to say much about the evil of Catholicism. Addison does not pursue the

[30] Bond, ed., *The Spectator*, 3:141–2.
[31] Corns, 'Roman Catholicism, *De Doctrina Christiana*, and the Paradise of Fools'.
[32] Bond, ed., *The Spectator*, 3:145–6.
[33] Rogers, 'Addison, Joseph (1672–1719), writer and politician'.
[34] Bond, ed., *The Spectator*, 2:289.

campaign against superstition very far. Yet Milton's 'Enthusiasm', at least in the mid-century decades, was plain and unequivocal, and it had been restated in the age of Addison through the publication in 1698 of *A Complete Collection of the Historical, Political and Miscellaneous Works of John Milton* (London). Published in three substantial folio volumes, it came prefaced with a biography of Milton by John Toland, the *enfant terrible* of English radical thought. Just a glance at the title pages of Milton's anti-prelatical tracts of 1641–2 would have disclosed that here we have an enthusiast, not an Addisonian Anglican.

In a wide-ranging review of the cultural shifts between 1688 and 1714, Christopher Hill speculates that 'Milton's political writings were more influential in this period than in his lifetime'.[35] That is a difficult proposition either to confute or confirm. *Eikonoklastes* had been the official justification for the regicide, and his Latin *Defences* had repeated that role across Europe. Apart from the three-volume folio associated with Toland, his prose works were scarcely in print after 1688. On the other hand, his influence on radical Whig thought had done something to fashion the arguments for the Williamite revolution, and in due course his influence would surely be felt among the founding fathers of the American republic. What is certain, however, is that the readership for his poetry, and particularly for *Paradise Lost*, grew remarkably quickly, a growth both stimulated and facilitated by the availability of economy editions after the turn of the century. Addison reflected and stimulated that trend, and in so doing he deflected interest in Milton's writings away from what was radical either politically or theologically. Hill is on less controversial grounds when he observes, 'Addison and Steele [in *The Spectator*] sought...to civilise the nonconformist *bourgeoisie*, to pietise the backwoods gentry—and their wives and daughters.'[36] Addison's version of Milton, domesticated and now fit for the fireside or breakfast table of that readership, functioned as a major component in that agenda, and functioned, too, to build the necessary bridges between high-culture vernacular literature and a less expert audience. Milton's Samson had preferred to 'drudge and earn [his] bread' than 'to sit idle on the household hearth'.[37] I wonder what Milton would have made of Addison's presentation of his long epic. What we do know is that Milton went to great lengths to construct, or make, his own authorial identity. Milton's construction of his authorial identity is the focus of the chapters in Part II.

---

[35] Hill, *The Century of Revolution*, 257.   [36] Ibid.
[37] Milton, *Samson Agonistes*, in Orgel and Goldberg, eds., *The Major Works*, 671–715, ll. 573 and 566.

PART II

MILTON'S CONSTRUCTION OF AN AUTHORIAL IDENTITY

6

Young Milton's Pauline Temper

Noam Reisner

The opening invocation to *Paradise Regained*, written late in Milton's life, offers a stunning claim to direct apostolic authority, intensifying the more traditional prophetic stance of *Paradise Lost* and much of Milton's earlier poetry. Rather than invoking the 'heavenly muse', Milton invokes the direct inspiration of the 'spirit who led'st this glorious eremite / Into the desert',[1] and goes on to assert that the interpolated narrative elements he is about to introduce into the Gospel temptation scene of Luke were 'unrecorded left through many an age, / Worthy t'have not remained so long unsung' (I. 17–18). Regardless of whether one wishes to identify Milton's 'spirit' with the Holy Ghost or, more abstractly, with the Godhead,[2] it is clear that Milton is presuming here to give an account of true events as if he were recalling a memory, indeed as if he were there as one of the Apostles. This is partly anticipated by the opening lines of the poem which identify Milton as the poet of *Paradise Lost*, the entire narrative of which is abstracted into two lines taken from Romans 5:19:

> I who erewhile the happy garden sung,
>> By one man's disobedience lost, now sing
>> Recovered Paradise to all mankind,
>> By one man's firm obedience fully tried.

(I. 1–4)

The echo of Romans 5:19—'For as by one man's disobedience many were made sinners, / so by the obedience of one shall many be made righteous'—is perhaps theologically predictable and unremarkable,[3] but, given the overall apostolic tone of the invocation, the borrowing of Pauline phraseology (filtered through the familiar English translation of the Geneva and King James Bibles) functions as a latent form of authorial identification. Milton is not laying claim to abstract apostolic authority but instead drawing inspiration from his favourite Apostle and author, Paul.

---

[1] *The Complete Works of John Milton: Volume II*, I.8–9. Subsequent quotations in this chapter are taken from this edition and are cited parenthetically.
[2] See John Carey's note on this line, *Milton: The Complete Shorter Poems*, 424.
[3] All quotations from the Bible in this chapter are from the Authorized Version.

Noam Reisner, *Young Milton's Pauline Temper* In: *Making Milton: Print, Authorship, Afterlives*. Edited by: Emma Depledge, John S. Garrison, and Marissa Nicosia, Oxford University Press (2021). © Noam Reisner.
DOI: 10.1093/oso/9780198821892.003.0006

It is hard to overestimate the importance of Pauline theology to Milton's evolving ideas and spiritual-ideological commitments throughout his life. The term 'Pauline theology', however, is too vast and imprecise when it comes to Milton, and requires continual qualification.[4] Beyond tracing Milton's well-documented commitment, for example, to the tenets of Pauline liberation theology, it is very difficult to determine to what extent the *literary* character of Paul as an Apostle and writer impacted on Milton's evolving view of himself as a uniquely elected prophetic, if not apostolic, poet and polemicist. Milton was a devout student of Pauline theology and even a radical Pauline thinker in his own right, but can we also say that he was deeply Pauline in his literary temper? I use the word 'temper' in the sense of 'character' or 'mental quality' (*Oxford English Dictionary* II.4b), but also in the sense of 'temperament' or mental attitude. It is important to assess both how Milton draws on the theology of the Pauline Epistles and the various ways in which Milton identified with the rhetorical and evangelical moods of their apostolic author.

Milton's productive and highly imaginative process of identification with the apostolic persona of Paul took different forms throughout his life but can be traced ultimately to his formative education with his private tutor, Thomas Young, and later under Alexander Gill at St Paul's School.[5] As biographers tell us, young Milton began reading in the Bible early, first in English while attending All Hallows for catechism as a young boy of 5 or 6.[6] Soon after, under the guidance of Young and other private tutors, Milton most likely began to read the Bible also in Latin. Milton would later tell us in a Latin verse letter addressed to Young that it was he, 'a pastor famed for his respect for the primitive faith and skilled in feeding the Christian sheep' ('antiquæ clarus pietatis honore / Præsul Christicolas pascere doctus oves', 17–18), who first introduced him to the classics: 'It was with him leading the way that I first traversed the Aonian retreats and the hallowed greenery of the twin-peaked summit' ('Primus ego Aonios illo præeunte recessus / Lustrabam, & bifidi sacra vireta jugi', 29–30).[7] We will return to *Elegia quarta* later on, but for now it is safe to assume that Young's 'Aonian' retreats also

---

[4] See, for example, Timothy O'Keeffe, *Milton and the Pauline Tradition*. O'Keeffe surveys the influence of various Pauline themes on Milton's major poetry and prose while placing Milton's Pauline belief system in a dialectic between Thomist and Reformed theological traditions. For the important place of Pauline theology in *Paradise Lost*, particularly in the final 'lapsarian' books of the epic, see also Jason Rosenblatt, *Torah and Law in* Paradise Lost; for *Paradise Regained*, see Ken Simpson, *Spiritual Architecture and Paradise Regained: Milton's Literary Ecclesiology*. For Milton's translation of Pauline liberation theology into secular political theory, see Joan S. Bennett, *Reviving Liberty: Radical Christian Humanism in Milton's Great Epics*; Benjamin Myers, *Milton's Theology of Freedom*; and Filippo Falcone, *Milton's Inward Liberty: A Reading of Christian Liberty from the Prose to* Paradise Lost. Falcone's is one of the most detailed and thought-provoking analyses of Milton's deep spiritual commitments to Pauline liberation theology within the wider Reformed tradition.

[5] For recent work on the Gills, see William Poole, 'The Literary Remains of Alexander Gil the Elder (1565–1635) and Younger (1596/7–1642?),' 163–91.

[6] See Barbara K. Lewalski, *The Life of John Milton*, 4.

[7] *The Complete Works of John Milton: Volume III*, 129–31. Translation from the Latin by Haan.

included the New Testament (if not in Greek, then certainly in Latin) alongside other 'profane' classics, with a clear emphasis on what Milton metaphorically describes later on in the elegy as Young's great facility in introducing him to the 'celestial dew, the mighty task of religion's saving power' ('Cælestive...rore.../ Grande salutiferæ religionis opus', 45–6).[8] Certainly, when Milton himself later became tutor to his nephews, as Edward Phillips recounts, he dedicated 'Sunday's work...for the most part the Reading each day a Chapter of the Greek Testament, and hearing his Learned Exposition upon the same'.[9]

Once Milton entered St Paul's School, probably at age 12, he evidently continued his studies in divinity alongside the classics in both Latin and Greek, while mastering some Hebrew as well.[10] Here, however, the influence of Milton's headmaster, Alexander Gill senior, must be noted as a likely source for shaping young Milton's early identification with Paul in the direction of pious rationalism and away from mystical enthusiasm and an obsession with sinfulness. While Milton clearly drew immense inspiration from the 'Lutheran' Paul and the Augustinian tradition underpinning it, especially in matters pertaining to the authority of Scripture and the primacy of faith over works, he also dissented from these traditions in significant ways even before his eventual embracing of something like Arminian theology.[11] As Stephen Fallon has shown, even as a youth Milton showed no apparent interest in the despairing, predestinarian obsession of some Puritans within the Calvinist tradition with the autobiographical persona of Paul as the 'chief of sinners'.[12] The Milton of the 1630s and 1640s, taking his lead from Gill, rather saw in Paul first and foremost a model pastor and teacher committed to a rational, and above all *reasonable*, interpretation of the one true spiritual sense of the Gospel in all matters pertaining to salvation.

A useful index for Gill's pedagogic approach, which must have influenced young Milton, can be found in Gill's treatise *The sacred philosophie of the Holy Scripture* (1635), in which he sets out to defend the use of reason and 'common sense' in expounding articles of faith. Revealingly, Gill's prime model for the use of reason in teaching religion, especially when having to defend Christian belief against Jews, Turks, Catholics, and other heretics and 'Idolaters', is the mission of Paul to the Gentiles:

[8] Ibid., 131.   [9] Helen Darbishire, ed., *The Early Lives of Milton*, 61.
[10] See Gordon Campbell and Thomas N. Corns, *John Milton: Life, Works, and Thought*, 21. On Milton's Latin, see John K. Hale's essay in the present volume.
[11] For the 'Lutheran' Paul and the many contested interpretations of Pauline theology within the Reformed tradition see Stephen Westerholm, *Perspectives Old and New on Paul*, especially 88–100.
[12] See Stephen M. Fallon, *Milton's Peculiar Grace*: 'Unlike Bunyan, Milton does not treat himself as the chief of sinners. Far from expressing bouts of despair, Milton's autobiographical excursions are marked by an apparently serene confidence in his righteousness, an attitude starkly at odds with the religious culture surrounding him' (29).

For no man makes due account of the Holy Scripture, whose heart God hath not touched, and so is already won. But there is none so brutish, which doth not willingly hearken to reason. And did S. *Paul* at *Athens*, or elsewhere among Idolaters, perswade the worship of the true God, and Christ the Saviour of the world by the authority of Scripture, or by common reason, and their own poets? beside *Aratus* whose words he cites, you shall finde that his speech is in their own phrase and stile, and much of the matter in *Plato*, and in speciall his *Phaedon*, of the soules immortality.[13]

If *Areopagitica* and the preface written many years later to *Samson Agonistes* are any indication, the famous anecdote about Paul quoting Aratus, Epimenides, Euripides, and other pagan Greek writers was important to Milton.[14] While Paul's facility with the Greek classics is a proverbial *topos* in much Reformation discourse seeking to defend the use of profane classics in sacred teaching, for Milton this evidently mattered personally. It mattered because it offered him a way to identify intellectually with Paul as a deeply educated Apostle, able to apply his wide reading in the pagan classics to his religious beliefs and spiritual commitments. As Gill points out, Paul was a master of 'common reason' who was able to adapt his style, as all great rhetoricians must, to his target audience. The ability to find common ground between the Gospel teachings of Christ and, say, a given passage in Plato speaks directly to Paul's charismatic ability as a man of learning *as well as* of faith.

For young Milton, then, Paul was first and foremost a radical reformer, a teacher, and a gifted polemicist who could always be invoked to support whatever Milton believed was the one 'true' sense of the Gospel as he understood it. Milton's early identification with Paul's apostolic temper found its fullest expression, therefore, in his polemical prose, where the otherwise predictable marshalling of quotations from the Pauline Epistles to defend a given argument often sounds like an act of pious ventriloquism. In the anti-prelatical tracts, for example, Milton identifies with Paul not just as the presumed author of the three Pastoral Epistles (1 and 2 Timothy and Titus) but also as a fierce defender of Presbyterianism who is allied with Milton personally as 'an examiner, and discoverer of this

---

[13] Alexander Gill, *The sacred philosophie of the Holy Scripture* (1635), 'The Preface'.

[14] In *Areopagitica* Milton writes: 'Not to insist upon the examples of *Moses, Daniel & Paul*, who were skilfull in all the learning of the Ægyptians, Caldeans, and Greeks, which could not probably be without reading their Books of all sorts, in *Paul* especially, who thought it no defilement to insert into holy Scripture the sentences of three Greek Poets' (*John Milton: Complete Prose Works of John Milton*, vol. 2, 507–8; henceforth in this chapter all quotations from Milton's prose are from this edition, designated as *CPW*). Milton later repeats this sentiment in the preface to *Samson*, where he defends his choice of writing a Greek tragedy on biblical subject matter precisely on this ground: 'The Apostle Paul himself thought it not unworthy to insert a verse of Euripides into the Text of Holy Scripture, I *Cor.* 15.22' (*The Complete Works of John Milton: Volume II*, 66). The use of 'himself' here intensifies the emphasis that, if this was acceptable to Paul, all other Christians must find it equally acceptable.

impostorship' of the bishops who,[15] as Milton writes elsewhere, in wanting to 'maintine their domineering...seeke thus to rout, and disaray the wise and well-couch't order of Saint *Pauls* owne words'.[16] In the divorce tracts, meanwhile, Milton frequently cites and invokes Paul as a like-minded interpreter of the Mosaic law whose teaching on marriage in 1 Corinthians 7 emerges as the only rational yardstick of Christian 'charity'. Paul, for Milton, is the ultimate 'Author' (*auctor*) in the literal sense of being the first and final authority on interpreting Christ's teachings in the Gospel. At the same time, however, Milton also saw in Paul a revered *literary* author who employs his judgement and reason in interpreting Christ's words by adducing or inferring its 'hidden' meanings.[17] In fact, Milton lays claim in the divorce tracts to such degrees of intimacy with Paul, that those who would oppose Milton's idiosyncratic interpretation of Christ's and Paul's injunctions on marriage do not 'expound St *Paul*, but out-face him'.[18] Milton's reading, on the other hand, is that which is genuinely Pauline for being directly inspired by the Spirit of God to construe a commandment that is in fact never explicitly uttered: 'Neither is the Scripture hereby lesse inspir'd because St *Paul* confesses to have writt'n therein what he had not of command; for we grant the Spirit of God led him thus to express himself to Christian prudence in a matter which God thought best to leave uncommanded.'[19]

In the divorce tracts, Milton develops the novel idea that Christ's injunctions on marriage, echoed and interpreted by Paul in Corinthians, must be submitted to an overall measure of Christian charity. This bold theological manoeuvre effectively allows Milton to turn the question of marriage from a matter of doctrinal law into the cornerstone of a new Christian ethics of community. While the application of the ethics of charity to the question of marriage is indeed novel, the ethical outlook at its heart is thoroughly Pauline. It rests at the affective centre of Paul's apostolic message to the Corinthians and in Paul's so-called 'hymn of charity' in 1 Corinthians 13, which Milton cites extensively. Ultimately, however, Milton's Pauline stance on charity finds its first and most definitive political expression in *Areopagitica*, where Milton expounds at length the ethical implications of an inward 'Christian liberty which *Paul* so often boasts of'.[20] In what would later become a defining feature of Milton's political thought, Milton aligns in *Areopagitica* Paul's dialectic of Gospel and Law with his evolving attack on various earthly manifestations of tyranny, which he then aligns broadly with Paul's attack on the legalism of the Pharisees, and specifically with Paul's invective in Acts 17:16–22 against the idolatry and superstition of the Athenians. Stephen Burt, building on Le Comte, has shown how, in naming his pamphlet against licensing

---

[15] *Of Prelatical Episcopacy* (1641), *CPW*, vol. 1, 651.
[16] *Animadversions* (1641), *CPW*, vol. 1, 709.
[17] 'I prove also by no lesse an Author then St *Paul* himself, 1 Cor. 7. 10, 11', *Doctrine and Discipline of Divorce* (1643), *CPW*, vol. 2, 332.
[18] Ibid, 332.   [19] Ibid., 266.   [20] *CPW*, vol. 2, 563.

Areopagitica: A Speech, Milton identifies less with Isocrates, who invented the genre in which Milton is writing, and more with Paul's sermon to the Athenians on the Areopagus in whose spirit Milton conducts his appeal to England's Parliament. As Burt argues, the parallels with Paul extend well beyond the pamphlet's broad thematic concerns and go to the very heart of Milton's polemic, where 'Paul's speech at Athens becomes Milton's demonstration of the necessity of argument, of the deep connection between true faith and inquiry'.[21] This is the adversarial Milton we have come to know from much of his prose and later poetry, for whom Pauline Christian liberty insists that all Reformed Christians who care for their soul's salvation must always treat any received orthodoxy as a contested set of ideas subject to error and misunderstanding. 'Charity' thus becomes a broadly ethical as well as hermeneutical Pauline principle, where, based on a rather curious reading of Romans 14:1–13, Milton can invoke Paul and claim 'that many other things might be tolerated in peace, and left to conscience, had we but charity, and were it not the chief strong hold of our hypocrisie to be ever juging one another'.[22]

These ideas, however, evolved hand in hand with a stylistic self-awareness that is often strikingly Pauline in its rhetorical *ethos*. Milton's tone and prose style, as well as his many autobiographical digressions, carry over the hermeneutical practice of reading within Paul into a practice of writing *as* Paul. In *Of Reformation*, for example, Milton assumes Paul's character in warning away the bishops from relying even on the ancient authorities of church fathers such as Origen or Tertullian in making claims for episcopacy. Channelling (quite out of context) Paul's rebuking of Peter in Antioch recounted in Galatians 2:11, Milton takes offence at Tertullian's criticism of Paul noted in *Adversus Marcionem* in calling him 'a novice and raw in grace' (I.xx), as Milton translates it. Although this episode has nothing to do with Tertullian's teachings on Church hierarchy, Milton uses the apparent conflict between Paul and Peter about circumcision recounted in Galatians to reflect on the wider conflict in his own day between the heart-circumcised Reformed Church and Peter's papacy, here caricatured in the Jesuits' alleged rejection of Pauline theology. This implies therefore that the Jesuits are bound, like the Jews, to the letter of the Law and its works:

> But more indignation would it move to any Christian that shall read *Tertullian* terming *S. Paul* a novice and raw in grace, for reproving *S. Peter* at *Antioch*, worthy to be blam'd if we beleeve the Epistle to the *Galatians*: perhaps from this hint the blasphemous Jesuits presum'd in *Italy* to give their judgement of *S. Paul*, as of a hot headed person, as *Sandys* in his Relations tells us.[23]

[21] Stephen Burt, '"To The Unknown God:" St Paul and Athens in Milton's *Areopagitica*', 26. See also, more broadly, Edward Le Comte, '*Areopagitica* as Scenario for *Paradise Lost*'.
[22] *CPW*, vol. 2, 563.   [23] *CPW*, vol. 1, 552–3.

What is striking here is Milton's palpable 'indignation', as if the injury were levelled at him personally, especially because of his young age. Milton felt acutely that he had to defend himself with Paul, quite rightly, against the charge that he was, as Gordon Campbell and Thomas Corns put it, 'a novice, with no pertinent publication record, holding neither church or university office'.[24] The long, much-quoted autobiographical digression in the opening of the second book of *Reason of Church-Government* is the logical climax of this anxiety. Earlier in the pamphlet, Milton had characterized the Pauline Epistles specifically as the 'heavenly structure of evangelick discipline so diffusive of knowledge and charity', which require a 'spiritual eye' in interpreting them according to their one true evangelical (and in this case Presbyterian) sense.[25] This same 'heavenly structure' and 'spiritual' hermeneutic then becomes the frame, or metaphorical structure, within which Milton finds cause to 'divulge' of himself in the hope that he may gain an equal measure of Pauline 'charity' against the charge 'that some self-pleasing humor of vain-glory hath incited me to contest with men of high estimation, now while green yeers are upon my head'.[26] In other words, Milton's long digression about himself here and elsewhere is decidedly Pauline in temper, notwithstanding its clear aversion to the Lutheran Paul's narrative of sin. The avowedly Ciceronian process of displaying what Fallon rightly labels as a process of 'ethical proof' is handled in a Pauline manner whereby Milton aligns his own sense of spiritual and evangelical merit and virtue in assuming the mantle of Paul, not as a 'novice raw in grace', but instead as one who teaches, instructs, admonishes, and interprets the Gospel on behalf of others.

Indeed, Milton's early attempts to invoke Paul as his polemical alter ego in the prose offers a tantalizing link between his prose and early poetry. The equally famous autobiographical digression at the heart of *An Apology against a Pamphlet* (1642), for example, shows how at the root of Milton's self-conception as a 'true Poem, that is, a composition, and patterne of the best and honourablest things' lies his equally familiar youthful obsession with Pauline chastity.[27] Milton was 33 years old by this point (itself an age of biblical and typological significance), but in his mind he appears still to have been that 'lady of Christ', a delicate youth late to mature who took the 'Confutant's' absurd charge that he was a frequenter of brothels as a deep and wounding insult.[28] Again, Fallon is correct in noticing that Milton's desperate attempt to prove his spiritual chastity 'unearths no sin', but he is too quick to insist that Milton 'articulates his ethic of chastity and literary excellence ... in secular terms'.[29] After all, and quite unsurprisingly by now,

---

[24] Campbell and Corns, *John Milton*, 146.
[25] *Reason of Church-Government* (1642), *CPW*, vol. 1, 758.   [26] Ibid., 806.
[27] *CPW*, vol. 1, 890.
[28] The identity of the 'Confutant', the author of *A Modest Confutation of a Slanderous and Scurrilous Libell, Entituled, Animadversions*, remains unknown. It was evidently unknown to Milton.
[29] Fallon, *Peculiar Grace*, 106.

Milton's prime model for chastity is Paul's celibacy, which Milton interpreted in spiritual and intellectual terms:

> This that I have hitherto related, hath bin to shew, that though Christianity had bin but slightly taught me, yet a certain reserv'dnesse of naturall disposition, and morall discipline learnt out of the noblest Philosophy was anough to keep me in disdain of farre lesse incontinences then this of the Burdello. But having had the doctrine of holy Scripture unfolding those chaste and high mysteries with timeliest care infus'd, that *the body is for the Lord and the Lord for the body*, thus also I argu'd to my selfe; that if unchastity in a woman whom Saint *Paul* termes the glory of man, be such a scandall and dishonour, then certainly in a man who is both the image and glory of God, it must, though commonly not so thought, be much more deflouring and dishonourable.[30]

Milton will, of course, soon rehearse these and many other ideas taken from Galatians and 1 Corinthians (and especially 1 Corinthians 7) in his divorce tracts. However, what is striking here is the way in which Milton aligns his 'naturall disposition, and morall discipline', which he apparently learnt from pagan philosophers and literary classics, with the properly Hebraic understanding of Paul's injunction to marry for those 'who cannot contain' (1 Cor. 7:7: 'For I would that all men were even as I myself. But every man hath his proper gift of God, one after this manner, and another after that'). That is, Milton does not lay claim to virginity or celibacy but instead to a mode of spiritual chastity given to him as a gift of God, which is, moreover, particular in conferring upon him something like Pauline apostolic authority when speaking about matters of the Spirit.

Milton's aligning of this mode of chastity with the poetic composition, as it were, of his virtuous character, allows the metaphor of life-as-poetry to play in several directions: Milton in this sense is both the maker (poet) of his own virtuous destiny *as* a poet, as well as a sublime poem of God, the ultimate poet or maker. Young Milton often recognized, after all, that his true gift was his poetic talent, as filtered through his favoured appropriation of Christ's parable of the talents. What I have thus far discussed with regard to Milton's Pauline temper in his prose also serves to bind many of Milton's classical and pagan allusions in the early English and Latin poetry within a metaphorical evangelical structure. While Milton rarely cites the Pauline Epistles in his early secular poetry, no doubt for reasons of decorum, his Pauline temper often shines through in the frequent interjections of an authorial persona hoping to chasten the erotically charged pagan source materials which Milton usually adapts from his other favourite alter ego, the Roman poet Ovid. One can suggest many examples, perhaps most notably from the overtly Pauline exploration of chastity in relation to language and

---

[30] *CPW*, vol. 1, 892.

rapture in *A Maske Presented at Ludlow Castle* or 'Il Penseroso',[31] but in conclusion I would like to return to Milton's fourth Latin elegy with which I began, written when Milton was a student at Cambridge in 1627.

The poem, a verse letter in the Ovidian elegiac style addressed to Thomas Young, is no less formulaic and experimental than some of Milton's other Latin verses from this time, but its subject—Milton's beloved childhood tutor—marks this as a distinctly personal poem. Thomas Young, who was serving at the time as pastor to the English merchants in Hamburg, was not an unwilling exile from England, but Milton's poem, framed within echoes from Ovid's *Tristia*, bewails and laments Young's absence as a cruel separation: 'Hei mihi quot pelagi, quot montes interjecti / Me faciunt alia parte carere mei' (21-2) ('Alas how many oceans, how many mountains have been interposed, causing me to be separated from the other part of myself!').[32] Moreover, as Maggie Kilgour rightly claims, in mapping his own sense of nostalgia and longing to his beloved tutor onto that of Perilla, Ovid's protégée in the *Tristia*, Milton imaginatively positions Young in the elegy as Ovid, his creative *fons et origo*.[33] Milton goes on in the elegy further to identify Young, hyperbolically, with Socrates to his Alcibiades, or with Aristotle to his Alexander the Great. Interestingly, however, the Ovidian frame brackets these allusions to revered pagan philosophers with a final reference to Elijah and Paul, prophet and Apostle, both of whom suffered rejection and exile at the hand of faithless kings or magistrates while on their sacred missions:

> Haud aliter vates terræ Thesbitidis olim
> Pressit inassueto devia tesqua pede,
> Desertasque Arabum salebras, dum regis Achabi
> Effugit atque tuas, Sidoni dira, manus.
> Talis & horrisono laceratus membra flagello,
> Paulus ab Æmathia pellitur urbe Cilix.
>
> (97–102)

[No different was that prophet of the land of the Tishbites when long ago with unaccustomed foot he trampled on pathless wastelands and the rough Arabian deserts as he fled from the hands of King Ahab and from your hands too, awful woman of Sidon. And such was Paul, the Cilician, when he was driven from the Emathian city, his limbs torn by a dreadfully sounding scourge.][34]

The reference to Elijah's flight from Ahab and Jezebel (1 Kings 19:1–18), and especially Paul's scourging in Philippi (Acts 16:9–40), is intriguing because of its

---

[31] See David Gay, '"Rapt Spirits": 2 Corinthians 12.2–5 and the Language of Milton's *Comus*'. For the overall play of 'rapture' in Milton's Latin poetry see Noam Reisner, 'Obituary and Rapture in Milton's Memorial Latin Poems'.
[32] *The Shorter Poems*, 129.   [33] Kilgour, *Milton and the Metamorphosis of Ovid*, 51.
[34] *The Shorter Poems*, 133–5.

revealing manipulation of context. Although one can follow Milton's polemical imagination in likening Charles I and Henrietta Maria to Ahab and Jezebel or England's High Church leaders to the magistrates of Philippi, the implication that Young was an apostolic saint banished into exile for his evangelical purity is wildly extravagant, to say the least. The biblical context is also wrong. Paul and Silas were not exiled from Philippi but, rather, fearfully told to leave once the magistrates realized they had scourged and imprisoned two Roman citizens.

As is often the case in Milton's early vocational poetry, however, both exilic images of Ovid and Paul reflect not on Young but instead on his forlorn protégé, Milton the Cambridge student, struggling to make a name for himself as an emerging poet. The underlying theme which drives the concluding allusion to Elijah, Paul, and finally Christ is the trope of true as opposed to false prophetic vocation, which then comes full circle to merge with the classical *topos* of the Roman poet as *vates*, or seer, implied in the Ovid–Virgil genealogy Milton alludes to in the opening of the elegy.[35] Elijah and Paul, both of whom are the prototypical true prophets who experienced an unmediated encounter with the divine presence (1 Kings 19:11–12 and 2 Corinthians 12:2–4 respectively), suffered exile and rejection precisely because of their unique election as the bearers of God's unadulterated truth. Indeed, the main point of the Philippi episode at the back of Milton's mind is that Paul angered the local magistrates when he drove out a 'spirit' which possessed a woman revered by the locals as a seer, exposing her as a false prophetess (even though she had proclaimed Paul and Silas as the true servants of God). In this elaborate periphrastic manner, Milton merges the sacred vocation of Paul with the poetic vocation of Ovid as a unified form of divine inspiration which Milton received, as it were, at the hands of Young and now fashions into his own sacred vocation as a poet protected by God. Line 112, which seeks to console Young in his exile by claiming God as his 'protector' and 'champion' ('Ille tibi custos, & pugil ille tibi') amid many dangers and temptations is thus, again, reflexive in its prayerful intensity. It speaks directly to Milton's personal sense of vocational anxiety and separateness as a young man uniquely elected by God to achieve great things.

In what is a recurring motif in the early poetry, Milton first draws an image of the type of man he aspires to be, in this case in the image of his former tutor, and then looks through the image to scrutinize himself. While Ovid dominates this early portrait in terms of the poetic materials and authorial personae that Milton adapts to his own emerging narrative, the vatic temper he finally reaches for is peculiarly and uniquely Pauline. Such poetic temper drives and organizes Milton's wider adversarial outlook of himself, especially at this young age, as a wayfaring

---

[35] As Haan notes, Milton embeds two allusions to Virgil's *Aeneid* and *Georgics* in lines 2 and 3 within the overall motif taken from Ovid's *Tristia* which governs the opening four lines of the elegy (see *The Shorter Poems*, 430).

Christian battling to reform and restore to God's glory a world riven by error, tyranny, and apostasy. The exilic trope of *Elegia Quarta* is finally inverted and internalized, as is the final consolation wishing Young happier days:

> Et tu (quod superest miseris) sperare memento,
>   Et tua magnanimo pectore vince mala.
> Nec dubites quandoque frui melioribus annis,
>   Atque iterum patrios posse videre lares.
>
> (122–6)

[As for you, remember to have hope (something which still remains for the wretched), and conquer your misfortunes with the bravery in your heart. And do not doubt that some day you will be able to enjoy better times and see your native home once more.][36]

It is hard to judge, of course, whether Milton himself ever felt he enjoyed better times in his native home. Milton certainly never gives the impression that he is numbered among the '*miseris*' ('wretched'), so that the 'hope' he invokes here and elsewhere is more an abstract category of ideological resolve than a religious idea of Christian consolation. The bitter experiences and disappointments of later years, culminating in the grand exilic narrative of *Paradise Lost*, indeed suggest that for the older Milton hope was replaced, rather, with indignation and angry millenarian patience. Both modes of creativity—whether of a young idealistic Milton contemplating possible futures, or of a retrospective older Milton reflecting on the futures that never were—are quintessentially Pauline in attitude. They feed on Milton's quasi-apostolic sense of unerring conviction, as well as on his burning need to educate, reform, teach, and admonish in God's name. At the same time, however, as this chapter has argued, Milton's Pauline temper shines through, perhaps even more brightly, in his searching anxiety about being able to prove worthy of assuming such a mantle to begin with.

---

[36] *The Shorter Poems*, 134–5.

7

Milton's Ludlow *Maske* and Remaking English Nationhood

David Loewenstein

Introduction: Reformed Nationhood and the Young Milton

Recent scholarship has devoted greater critical attention to the complexities and ambiguities of Milton's expressions of nationalism and national identity.[1] As a political and religious writer, Milton articulated a close identification with England as a chosen and vibrant nation—'this great and Warlike Nation', 'a Nation so pliant and so prone to seek after knowledge' (*CPW* 1:616, 2:554)[2]— capable of remaking or inventing itself anew as it faced fresh political and religious challenges, crises, and opportunities in the seventeenth century, including during the upheavals of the English Revolution. Milton regarded himself as an English patriot: thus, when travelling abroad in 1639 he signed his name as 'Joannes Miltonius, Anglus' after writing the final lines from his *A Maske Presented at Ludlow Castle* in an album book belonging to a European colleague; and he presented himself as 'Englishman' on the title pages of his Latin *Defences* of the English people.[3] Yet his writings often express his acute struggles with the English nation, including a sense of revulsion and anguish at a nation whose people too readily allow themselves to become servile to ecclesiastical and political authorities, finally 'chusing . . . a captain back for *Egypt*' (*CPW* 7:463) at the Restoration since 'sometimes Nations will decline so low / From virtue', having lost both 'inward' and 'outward liberty' (*Paradise Lost* 12.97–8, 100–1). Likewise, he struggles with his sense of England's exceptionalism: his vision of her as a 'puissant

---

[1] See especially the studies in *Early Modern Nationalism and Milton's England*, ed. David Loewenstein and Paul Stevens. See also Giuseppina Iacono Lobo, *Writing Conscience in Revolutionary England*, ch. 6 (on Milton's revolutionary prose and *Paradise Lost*); Elizabeth Sauer, *Milton, Toleration, and Nationhood*; Andrew Escobedo, *Nationalism and Historical Loss in Renaissance England: Foxe, Dee, Spenser, Milton*; Willy Maley, *Nation, State and Empire in English Renaissance Literature: Shakespeare to Milton*; Paul Stevens, 'Milton's Janus-faced Nationalism: Soliloquy, Subject, and the Modern Nation-State' and 'Milton's Nationalism and the Rights of Memory'.

[2] Milton's prose is quoted from *The Complete Prose Works of John Milton*, ed. Don M. Wolfe et al., abbreviated as *CPW*.

[3] *The Life Records of John Milton*, ed. J. M. French, 1:419; Milton signed his name thus on 10 June 1639 in Camillo Cardoyn's album at Geneva. The lines from *A Maske* are: 'If Vertue feeble were / Heaven it self would stoope to her'.

David Loewenstein, *Milton's Ludlow* Maske *and Remaking English Nationhood* In: *Making Milton: Print, Authorship, Afterlives*. Edited by: Emma Depledge, John S. Garrison, and Marissa Nicosia, Oxford University Press (2021). © David Loewenstein. DOI: 10.1093/oso/9780198821892.003.0007

Nation', set apart and singled out by God with a special role to play in history and a 'precedence of teaching nations how to live' (*CPW* 2:558, 232).

Consequently, during the English Revolution Milton's relation to the English nation was deeply conflicted, so that his 'rhetorical responses to it often vacillate between expressions of patriotic fervour and bitter lamentation, between national pride and disappointment, between national hope and doubt'.[4] After the disappointment he felt at the failure of the English Revolution and after his strenuous efforts to prompt the English people to rethink the meanings of civic, religious, and domestic liberty, Milton could poignantly and wryly observe in 1666 that '[o]ne's *Patria* is wherever it is well with him'.[5] In the cold political climate of Restoration England, Milton, having been 'allured' for so many years by the 'lovely name' of '*Patriotism*', now felt himself 'almost *expatriated*' (*CPW* 8:4) by and within his own country.[6] By then, as I have argued elsewhere, Milton was more of a dissenting and conflicted patriot than a fervent nationalist.[7]

Milton's revolutionary prose and his later poems, and to a lesser extent *Lycidas*, have provided most of the evidence for assessments of Milton's volatile relation to the English nation and for understanding the complexities of his nationalism in terms of his vocation as a poet-polemicist who yearned to use his 'native tongue' (*CPW* 1:811) to contribute to the remaking of the English nation. Yet, surprisingly little has been said about early modern nationhood in Milton's 1634 *Maske*, despite valuable work on the politics of the Ludlow *Maske* in terms of Laudian ritual, Cavalier licentiousness, and Milton's reform of the Stuart masque genre. Indeed, except for perceptive comments by Laura Knoppers on luxury and national issues, little is said about *A Maske* in *Early Modern Nationalism and Milton's England*, the book I edited with Paul Stevens.[8] In this chapter I argue that there are significant national issues dramatized in the Ludlow *Maske* and reconfigured uniquely by Milton at a moment when the Caroline masque was giving national exceptionalism spectacular representation.

Stuart nationalism in the masque was interwoven with political theory, especially since James VI and I articulated in his published political writings a theory of divine-right monarchy, and his son, Charles, agreed with his father about the national implications of that political theory. As Richard Cust and Kevin Sharpe

---

[4] David Loewenstein and Paul Stevens, 'Introduction', *Early Modern Nationalism and Milton's England*, 4.

[5] This is his last known letter to any correspondent: it was addressed to the state-councillor to the Elector of Brandenburg.

[6] Milton's letter is addressed to Peter Heimbach and dated 15 August 1666.

[7] See Loewenstein, 'Late Milton: Early Modern Nationalist or Patriot?'

[8] See the observations about luxury, licentiousness, and national vulnerability in *A Maske* in Laura Lunger Knoppers, 'Consuming Nations: Milton and Luxury', 335, 345, 350. Nor does Sauer's valuable study, *Milton, Toleration, and Nationhood*, consider *A Maske*, since she focuses on the revolutionary prose and later poems and on nationhood in Milton in relation to the struggle over toleration. Cedric Brown, *John Milton's Aristocratic Entertainments*, does note that Milton in *A Maske* is 'conscious of his role as shepherd to the nation' (151), a point I explore more fully in this chapter.

have reminded us, Charles, with his elevated sense of kingship, understood very well the ideas about kingship and national-paternal leadership articulated in James's *Basilikon Doron*, although he differed from his father in political style and temperament and preferred, as a way of projecting his authority, even more extravagant visual symbolism, ritual, and display.[9] James I had asserted that kings were 'called Gods, as being his [i.e. God's] Lieutenants and Vicegerents on earth, and so adorned and furnished with some sparkles of the Divinitie', and Charles took quite literally his status as God's lieutenant on earth, the agent of His providence.[10] In the most lavish of Caroline court masques, Thomas Carew and Inigo Jones's *Coelum Britannicum*, the symbolism of divinely ordained monarchy and aesthetic expression were not only fused but also enriched by the masque's chivalric and mythopoeic representation of nationhood: performed on 18 February 1634—seven months before Milton's Ludlow *Maske* (29 September 1634)—*Coelum Britannicum*, 'the British Heaven', celebrated in spectacular alle-gorical fashion the ancient glories and heroes of Great Britain and also, 'by implication, the feat of James and Charles in uniting the three kingdoms'.[11] It was itself an imagined construction of the king and nation in extravagant Caroline terms, and below I consider its striking blend of political and national themes: God-given kingly power, chivalric self-representation, the king's regulation of disordered political impulses, courtly chastity, and national myth-making.

But first I want to ask: how might Milton's *Maske* itself be situated in relation to the literary making of early modern English nationhood, and what does the Ludlow *Maske* tell us about the younger Milton's imaginative investment in the nation, his sense of England's exceptionalism, his yearning for national renewal, and his ambition, expressed in *The Reason of Church-Government*, to write in his 'native tongue' poetic works 'doctrinal and exemplary to a Nation' (*CPW* 1:811, 815)?[12] Moreover, how might we see this experimental entertainment in terms of the young Milton's efforts to establish himself as a writer engaged in debates about the nation and its aristocratic leadership? From the opening of the Ludlow *Maske*, as we will see below, Milton clearly signals that he too is engaging in the sort of national myth-making associated with the Stuart masque. Milton likewise invokes a poetic vision of English nationhood in those rich mythological passages near the end of the Ludlow *Maske* where he highlights the crucial role played by the local

---

[9] See Richard Cust, *Charles I: A Political Life*, 10–30. For the influence of James's text on Charles (to whom James rededicated the work), see Kevin Sharpe, *Image Wars: Promoting Kings and Commonwealths in England, 1603–1660*, 24; and James I, *A Meditation Upon the Lords Prayer, Written by the Kings Maiestie* (London, 1619), A4.

[10] James I, *A Speech in the Parliament House* (1605), in *The Workes of the Most High and Mighty Prince, James* (London, 1616), 500. On Charles's sense of his status as God's lieutenant on earth, see Kenneth Fincham and Peter Lake, 'The Ecclesiastical Policies of James I and Charles I', 44.

[11] Cust, *Charles I*, 155–6.

[12] For the full account of Milton's ambitious national cultural program of reform and his poetic aspirations in *Church-Government*, see *CPW* 1:810–23'.

goddess Sabrina, including her national historical significance. Milton is not only reforming the masque as a particular 'form of English nationhood':[13] he is also, at this moment in his early career, rethinking, in dramatic poetry, the ethics, politics, and myth-making of English nationhood to a degree that has not been fully appreciated.

Of all of Milton's major early works—and even more than *Lycidas*—Milton's Ludlow *Maske* concerns itself, as both an aristocratic household and political entertainment, with the potential for remaking England's national image and identity. Lawrence Lipking has argued that we find notable evidence of Milton's early nationalism in 1637, in *Lycidas*, where the poet expresses his anxieties about Ireland and articulates a sense of the nation not as 'an imagined community united in bonds of sympathy and interest' (a reference to Benedict Anderson's influential work on nationalism) but instead as a 'people bound together by bitter memories and common hatreds'.[14] Yet the problem with Lipking's argument is that Milton never explicitly mentions Ireland in *Lycidas* (though he refers to English Protestants crossing the Irish seas); moreover, it was not until after the Irish Rebellion broke out in autumn 1641, with its terrifying apocalyptic resonances for English Protestants, that Milton's anxieties about English national identity, his Protestant militancy, and his fears about Ireland's monstrous anti-Christian threat to the godly nation converged. In any case, Milton's nationalism already found distinctive, more explicit, and more elaborate expression in 1634 in his Ludlow *Maske*. Milton's reformed Caroline masque begins to dramatize some of the issues of national identity that would later characterize Milton's agonized nationalism. However, by this I do not mean to suggest that *A Maske* already fully expresses Milton's anguished sense of national identity. That would find notable expression in the controversial prose of the 1640s and 1650s where Milton's highly volatile relation to the English nation and his ambivalence towards it become pronounced: works in which the visionary writer vacillates between expressions of patriotic fervour and bitter lamentation, and in which he is torn between his intense identification with a mighty Protestant 'Nation chos'n before any other' (*CPW* 2:552), like a new Israel, and his revulsion at the English people's vulnerability to ecclesiastical and political servility and idolatry and to the temptations of Cavalier luxury and royalist spectacle.[15]

Nonetheless, in his *Maske* Milton is already devoting his imaginative energies to reconceiving the symbolism of familial and national representation. Milton's

---

[13] Richard Helgerson, *Forms of Nationhood*.

[14] Lawrence Lipking, 'The Genius of the Shore: Lycidas, Adamastor, and the Poetics of Nationalism'.

[15] See my essay 'Milton's Nationalism and the English Revolution: Strains and Contradictions'. On the politics of England as a new Israel, see Achsah Guibbory, *Christian Identity, Jews, and Israel in Seventeenth-Century England*. On Milton's complex attitudes towards the English people, see Paul Hammond, *Milton and the People*.

enormously high expectations for the nation and its aristocratic leaders remain central to the entertainment's political meaning. The Ludlow *Maske* also concerns itself with the process of national trial and the potential for national renewal. At the same time, it is a work in which youthful idealism is tempered by a more sober sense of the seductive powers of an attractive but menacing manifestation of evil whose 'might of hellish charms' (613),[16] displayed by Comus, ensnares his victims and has the capacity to reduce them, and by implication the nation's nobility, to bestial servility. Milton especially puts the three Egerton children—the young ruling class and progeny of John Egerton, the newly installed Lord President of the Council of Wales—prominently on display in this political entertainment, as they undergo '*hard assays*' (972), with Lady Alice deceived and tempted by Comus and with her two younger brothers, John (Lord Brackley) and Thomas, trying to discover and save her in the perilous and dark woods near Ludlow Castle.[17] However young and vulnerable they may be (they ranged in age from 9 to 15), the Egerton children, 'fair off-spring nurs't in Princely lore [i.e. behaviour, education]' (34), represent the future leadership of the English nation. Symbolically, they endure the '*hard assays*' that must strenuously test the nation, its claims to exceptionalism, and its youthful aristocratic leaders, 'our noble and our gentle youth' (*CPW* 2:406), as Milton would characterize them in *Of Education* (1644). The promise and character of England's aristocratic leaders cannot therefore simply be taken for granted.

The Ludlow *Maske*, as we shall see below, not only dramatizes a vision of reformed English national identity during the Caroline years but also redefines its implications in significant ways and reveals the young Milton as a writer already engaged in a contest for national representation. The distinctive ways *A Maske* addresses national issues become clearer, moreover, when we consider how the Caroline court masque could serve as a major imaginative vehicle for national self-representation and construction forged by its words, symbols, and rituals. Celebrating the court of Charles I and Henrietta Maria, *Coelum Britannicum* offers the most spectacular representation of nationhood in a Caroline masque.

The Spectacle of Caroline Nationhood: *Coelum Britannicum*

Performed in the Banqueting House in London before the king and queen in February 1634, *Coelum Britannicum* offers a striking comparison with the Ludlow *Maske* in terms of the way Caroline aristocratic culture was attempting, by means

---

[16] References to Milton's *A Maske* (the text that appears in the 1645 *Poems*) are taken from *The Complete Works of John Milton*, Volume 3: *The Shorter Poems*, ed. Barbara K. Lewalski and Estelle Haan.

[17] For a perceptive account of childhood on trial, as well as the political implications of that process in *A Maske*, see Blaine Greteman, *The Poetics and Politics of Youth in Milton's England*, ch. 4.

of visual and verbal representation, to aestheticize political theory and project a vision of imperial nationhood and unity during Charles I's Personal Rule of the 1630s. *Coelum* offers a mythological representation and ceremony of order, hierarchy, reverence, and loyalty, values crucial to the political image-making of Charles I and his court.[18] It celebrates the ancient glories of Great Britain, as well as the achievement of James and Charles in uniting '*the three kingdoms of England, Scotland, and Ireland*' (836–7), 'three warlike nations' now bending 'their willing knees' before Charles's throne (39–40), as Jove's ambassador Mercury, sent down from 'the high senate of the gods' (37), proclaims at the beginning of the entertainment.[19] The gods themselves strain to model themselves on chaste ideals projected by the court of Charles and Henrietta Maria as *Coelum Britannicum* extravagantly depicts nothing less than the Briticization of the heavens which, marred by the depravity and licentious behaviour of the gods, require plenty of reform.

To be sure, there is antimasque critique within this most sumptuous of Caroline entertainments, but to what extent does it ultimately challenge the masque's robust vision of Caroline national representation? *Coelum Britannicum* includes the intrusive and prickly voice of Momus, the god of ridicule and satire, who parodies and perverts the king's style of government and reformation of morals at court by mocking Jove's newly excessive regulations and decrees in heaven: 'Monopolies are called in . . . rates imposed on commodities . . . Bacchus hath commanded all taverns to be shut . . . Cupid must go no more so scandalously naked . . . Ganymede is forbidden in the bed chamber, and must only minister in public' (210 ff.).[20] Yet the image of the chivalric British king and his court constructed by *Coelum Britannicum* is never seriously undermined or dislodged—indeed, Momus departs abruptly before the masque proper begins. Momus may be 'The Supreme Theomastix', the scourge of gods (an allusion to William Prynne's 1633 attack on the court in *Histriomastix*); however, the exuberant and vibrant prosaic parody, much of it directed at 'the politic state of heaven' (169), occurs during the entertainment's antimasques. By contrast, the main masque, in its lavish culminating scenes, invites its courtly audience to wonder at a new, more perfect order of early modern chivalric British heroes and knights as the king, who himself appeared as a richly attired 'ancient hero' (895), is stellified, along with his attendant lords, in the masque's final apotheosis.[21]

---

[18] On these values in relation to Charles I's court, see Fincham and Lake, 'The Ecclesiastical Policies of James I and Charles I', 24, 42, 48.

[19] Quotations from *Coelum Britannicum* are taken from *Court Masques: Jacobean and Caroline Entertainments, 1605–1640*, ed. David Lindley.

[20] On this parody of the court and the king's style of government, see Kevin Sharpe, *Criticism and Compliment: The Politics of Literature in the England of Charles I*, 232–43.

[21] Stellification was, of course, a common feature in seventeenth-century poetry of praise: see Alastair Fowler, *Time's Purpled Masquers: Stars and the Afterlife in Renaissance English*, ch. 2.

These culminating scenes are marked by a strong symbolic and visual break with previous antimasque scenes: a huge mount appears displaying figures representing the three kingdoms of England, Scotland, and Ireland that constitute Stuart Britain and above sits the Genius of Britain as the three kingdoms invoke the holy Druids, thereby reinforcing the poetics and visual representation essential to the masque's national myth-making. At the climax, the king, queen, and court are invited to view '*a princely villa*' (959) and a garden with parterres, fountains, and grottoes, symbolic of the new civilization that coexists with and evokes the revitalized Caroline nation and culture, replacing the image of a decayed civilization that appears at the opening of the masque: '*old palaces, decayed walls . . . parts of temples, [and] theatres . . . confused heaps of broken columns . . . altogether resembling the ruins of some great city of the ancient Romans or civilized Britons*' (26–30). As the masque reaches its climax, it also represents the chivalric Charles as 'Prince Arthur, or the brave / St George himself' (967–8). This national and chivalric representation of the king exists in striking contrast to Milton's Ludlow *Maske*, where chivalric ideals, dear to the young Milton, an avid reader of chivalric romances,[22] are represented not by the Caroline monarch or primarily by the Earl of Bridgewater—that 'noble Peer of mickle trust, and power' (*Maske* 31)—but are instead dramatized by the two Egerton boys as they wander through a romance landscape, assert their courage like antique heroes, and valiantly try to save their sister Alice, 'a single helpless maiden' (*Maske* 402), from the menacing enchanter Comus.

In addition, political theory, personal ideals, and a vigorous sense of Caroline nationhood are further embodied in the extravagant allegory of *Coelum Britannicum*: at the very end, masquing figures representing Wisdom, Truth, Pure Adoration, Concord, Rule, and Clear Reputation all crown 'this king, this queen, [and] this nation', the Chorus proclaims (1038–40). In the extravagant fiction of the masque, illicit passions threatening to disrupt court and nation are expelled. Fertility and marital chastity—the 'ripe fruits' of the royal couple's 'chaste bed' promising 'Endless succession' (1057, 1061)—underpin the king's power and glorious reputation upon which the revitalized image of British chivalry and Caroline exceptionalism depends. The chaste but fertile royal love represented in the masque, which combines the king's personal ideals with his public image, has implications beyond the court and extends to the nation and its subjects. Homonoia (Greek for unity or concord) proclaims: 'And as their own pure souls entwined, / So are their subjects' hearts combined' (1132–3). The royal couple and the nation of their subjects have become inseparable in the political fiction of this most opulent Caroline masque.

---

[22] See *An Apology against a Pamphlet*, CPW 1:890–1: 'I may tell ye whether my younger feet wander'd; I betook me among those Lofty Fables and Romances . . .'.

Some sense of the sumptuous, dazzling spectacle, with its ideological and national significance expressed visually, can be gleaned from the description of the aftermath of the revels in which three clouds appeared. The abstract concepts underpinning Charles's monarchy were conveyed by the first two: on one sat the allegorical figures of Religion, Truth, and Wisdom; on the second sat Concord, Government, and Reputation. And then there was a third '*great cloud*':

> *These being come down in an equal distance to the middle part of the air, the great cloud began to break open, out of which struck beams of light; in the midst suspended in the air sat Eternity on a globe... In the firmament about him was a troop of fifteen stars, expressing the stellifying of our British heroes; but one more great and eminent than the rest, which over his head, figured his Majesty. And in the lower part was seen afar off the prospect of Windsor Castle, the famous seat of the honourable Order of the Garter.*   (1005–14)

Inigo Jones's visual extravaganza evoked the Caroline ideology of chivalric national identity and royal power in this new age of Personal Rule: it represented the deified King Charles surrounded by an order of British heroes—presented as stars which illuminate anew 'the darkened sphere' (863) of the British heavens—as the aristocratic London audience viewed Windsor Castle, symbol of the monarch's power in the country and '*seat*' of a chivalric St George whose '*Order of the Garter*' symbolizes the sacred loyalty between the sovereign and his knights.

Coelum Britannicum thus dramatizes the idea that Charles, divinely ordained and deified, along with Queen Henrietta Maria, refuses to play the part of a limited monarch and not only assumes 'the stile of Gods', as his father James characterized a king in *Basilikon Doron*,[23] but—more boldly and actively—defines the very pattern of that style, inspiring the ruling gods to reform themselves with zeal. As Mercury proclaims to Charles and Henrietta Maria at the outset, 'Th' immortal bosoms burn with emulous fires, / Jove rivals your great virtues, royal sir, / And Juno, madam, your attractive graces' (59–60). Reform is therefore central to *Coelum Britannicum*, though hardly in the sense that Milton would envision later in the year in *A Maske Presented at Ludlow Castle*. Rather, the extravagant wit and fiction of the Caroline masque suggest that Jove will renounce his 'riotous enormities' and 'licentious life' (181) and Juno her 'raging jealousies' (61) after seeing the 'bright blaze' and 'great example' (55, 63) set by Charles's court and palace, 'The envied pattern of this underworld' (56). Thus, in the hyperbolic fiction-making of *Coelum* heaven promises to become more like the exceptional British model on earth generated by the divine dyad 'CARLOMARIA' (248): a model exemplifying a new age of British potency and virtue.

---

[23] James I, *The Workes*, 137 (James's sonnet announcing the 'Argument' to *Basilikon Doron*).

A *Maske* and the Threat of National Servility

In the Ludlow *Maske*, Milton responds to the kind of national myth-making and national self-representation that *Coelum Britannicum* constructs in such an extravagant fashion. As he experiments with the genre of the masque, he interrogates, challenges, and revises its national symbolism and meanings. If in Caroline court culture personal ideals and public image fused and were expressed in a lavish entertainment like *Coelum Britannicum*,[24] so in *A Maske* Milton fuses the personal and the public as he projects personal values (such as his vision of chastity) in a reformed aristocratic entertainment that combines familial with national issues. Milton in his experimental masque is already engaged, in this pre-civil war period, in a contest of national representation in which he envisions the nation and one of its aristocratic families tested by alluring temptation and threatened by courtly servility.

A Maske begins by highlighting, in a daring way, the tension between heaven and 'the smoak and stirr of this dim spot, / Which men call Earth' (5–6)—a contrast with other masques (as Leah Marcus has observed)[25] and certainly a striking contrast with *Coelum Britannicum*, which, in its extravagant fiction, makes the Caroline British court the 'envied pattern' (*Coelum* 56) for Jove's court. By calling earth 'this dim spot', Milton's Ludlow *Maske* signals that earth is more of a fallen realm than a kingdom or nation inhabited by aristocratic men and women who are like gods and goddesses and 'those immortal shapes / Of bright aëreal Spirits' enhancing 'Joves court' (1–3). Nonetheless, *A Maske* also begins by the Attendant Spirit announcing that it is a household entertainment with significant national and imperial implications that are interconnected; at the outset, the Attendant Spirit presents Neptune in relation to Britain—'The greatest, and the best of all the main [i.e. the high seas]'—and its relation to its most visible representative on this particular political occasion, the Earl of Bridgewater, the new Lord President of Wales and the Marches. The Attendant Spirit's allegorical and mythic language conveys a sense of English hegemony and judicial authority over Wales invested in the Lord President:

> ... but this Ile
> The greatest, and the best of all the main
> He quarters to his blu-hair'd deities,
> And all this tract that fronts the falling Sun
> A noble Peer of mickle trust, and power
> Has in his charge, with temper'd awe to guide
> An old, and haughty Nation proud in Arms.
>
> (27–33)

---

[24] On Charles's symbiosis of the public and the private, see Sharpe, *Image Wars*, 247, 259–60.
[25] Leah S. Marcus, *The Politics of Mirth: Jonson, Herrick, Milton, Marvell and the Defense of Old Holiday Pastimes*, 180–2.

Yet representing the new Lord President guiding 'An old, and haughty Nation proud in Arms'—referring to Wales under the 'charge' of its President and evoking more generally the ancient British nation—is not, it turns out, the primary focus of Milton's experimental masque and its remaking of nationhood.

Rather, his work signals that other national issues, treated in his own terms, will continue to inform this aristocratic entertainment, as Milton's masque moves quickly into the family ritual that also defines this work:[26] depicting the Egerton children, those 'fair offspring nurs't in Princely lore', who in 'their tender age might suffer perill' (34, 40) and attempt to negotiate a labyrinthine world full of alluring and menacing temptations. Unlike *Coelum Britannicum*, Milton's Ludlow *Maske* dramatizes a perilous world of arduous Spenserian trial and struggle (the Egerton children wandering in a Wood of Error), as the young aristocrats symbolize a nation and its future leaders who embody its potential for, rather than fulfilment of, robust godly reform and virtue as, in the words of *Areopagitica*, the nation waxes 'young again, entering the glorious waies of . . . prosperous virtue destin'd to become great and honourable in these latter ages' (*CPW* 2:557). In the Ludlow *Maske*, moreover, we have the glamorized power of 'Chast austerity' and 'Saintly chastity' (450, 453) embodied in Lady Alice, rather than in Henrietta Maria, who denounces with her powerful 'sacred vehemence'[27] and the 'freedom of [her] minde' the court's 'lewdly-pamper'd Luxury', culture of 'vast excess' (795, 663, 770, 771), and conspicuous consumption—most recently displayed in *Coelum* (in which her own brothers danced)—as she lectures not only the Cavalier Comus but also the nation's nobility. Meanwhile, the charming, if not especially effective, exertions of the two youthful Egerton brothers (one aged 9, the other 11), sometimes treated with delicate irony,[28] dramatize chivalric ideals of chaste manliness and militant heroism, as well as their limitations, as the boys draw their swords in their attempt to 'Boldly assault the necromancers hall' (649) and free their endangered sister. Chastity and chivalry, embodied in the Egerton children and their trials, receive distinctive Miltonic treatment that diverges from the kind of Caroline extravaganza deifying the 'virtuous court' of Charles and Henrietta Maria, making that court a British model of chastity and decorum for the heavens themselves, as well as representing it as a model of revitalized chivalric values of British courage and assertiveness.[29]

Moreover, unlike other masques, where the triumph over the subversive forces of evil is usually more pronounced and decisive, in the Ludlow *Maske* Comus

---

[26] For a valuable discussion of *A Maske* as primarily a private work and family affair, see Stephen Orgel, 'The Case for Comus'. My critical emphasis differs: *A Maske* is a family affair with significant national implications.

[27] Such vehemence, including Comus's acknowledgement of the power of the Lady's speech, is even more pronounced in the 1637 printing of *A Maske* with lines 779–806 added there.

[28] The delicate irony with which Milton treats the ideals of the two boys is discussed well in Cedric Brown, *John Milton's Aristocratic Entertainments*, ch. 4.

[29] Cust, *Charles I: A Political Life*, 29; Malcolm Smuts, *Culture and Power*, 8–17.

escapes with his potent wand and remains a threat, despite the chivalric exertions of the Egerton boys. Milton's unease about a nation constantly vulnerable to new and protean kinds of ensnaring enticements comes into sharper focus if we consider that, fifteen years after the Ludlow *Maske*'s performance, Milton would recall quite precisely the language of *A Maske* to voice his acute disappointment in *Eikonoklastes* that so many English men and women had been transformed into a 'credulous and hapless herd, begott'n to servility, and inchanted with . . . popular institutes of Tyranny' by allowing themselves to succumb to 'glozing words and illusions' and become 'inchanted with the *Circæan* cup of servitude' (*Eikonoklastes, CPW* 3:601, 582, 488). Milton employs the language of *A Maske* to pour scorn on those compatriots, an 'Image-doting rabble' (*CPW* 3:601) who have been besotted by Charles Stuart's seductive apologia for his life and reign: the immensely popular book *Eikon Basilike*, published in no less than thirty-five English editions within 1649, not to mention versions printed in Ireland and on the Continent to serve the interests of royalist exiles. Having escaped in 1634, the sorcerer Comus had appeared in another guise in 1649, deluding many of Milton's English contemporaries (in the words of the Attendant Spirit) with 'som other new device' (941) and, once again, 'By sly enticement gives his banefull cup' with 'pleasing poison' (525–6). Indeed, at the very end of *Eikonoklastes* Milton writes of *Eikon Basilike* employing 'a new device of the Kings Picture at his praiers' that enhances the 'Sorcery' (*CPW* 3:601) of the king's book: the famous frontispiece depicting a Christlike Charles kneeling in a chapel. It is not only the language of sorcery that Milton recalls from *A Maske* but also the language of 'a new device' (that is, a trick or cunning contrivance: *OED* 6) to effect servitude and debasement in the English people and threaten the freedom of their minds. The difference in *Eikonoklastes* is that Milton is scathing about Charles's literary and aesthetic sensibility, whereas the accomplished sorcerer of the Ludlow *Maske*, however sinister, displays fulsome poetic language as he tempts Lady Alice with his Circean cup of sensual pleasure (666–755).

In the Ludlow *Maske*, Milton's anxieties about the threat of national and courtly servility are likewise expressed in the language of potent enchantment and brutish transformation or 'foul disfigurement' (74) unperceived by those who undergo it. These anxieties are evident in Milton's representation of the sly, seductive Cavalier poet, Comus, 'the foul inchanter' (645) and potent son of Circe (his arts excel hers), who *'appears with his rabble'* and antimasque *'rout of Monsters headed like sundry sorts of wilde Beasts, but otherwise like Men and Women . . . they com in making a riotous and unruly noise'* (pp. 89, 67) and filling 'the Air with barbarous dissonance' (550). Comus is an elegant, cunning, and sly enchanter, yet the disfigurement he causes in men and women already has in 1634 larger and more ominous national implications. Political and religious servility, brought about by cunning 'modern' politicians or prelates, Milton warned in *Of Reformation* (May 1641), tended 'to break a nationall spirit, and courage by count'nancing upon riot, luxury, and ignorance, till having thus disfigur'd and made men beneath men' (*CPW* 1:571–2). Milton's warning about a nation and its future aristocratic leaders threatened by servility and debasement induced by cunning artifice is dramatized as well in his depiction of Comus's 'mighty Art' (63), which combines seductive, subtle, and serpentine language with powerful spectacle and illusion: his 'dazzling Spells', his 'power to cheat the eye with blear illusion, / And give it false presentments', and his 'well-plac't words of glozing courtesie / Baited with reasons not unplausible'—the Miltonic double negative conveys his skilful equivocation—which 'Wind [him] into the easie-hearted man, / And hugg him [i.e. caress or court him] into snares' (154–6, 161–3).[30] Comus thus employs a combination of rhetorical and theatrical artifice (for example as a harmless but false rustic) to entice the 'fair off-spring' (34), Lady Alice, of that 'noble Peer' of England honoured on this masque occasion. Indeed, Milton conveys the Protestant national implications posed by the alluring but menacing Comus and his 'hellish charms' (613) by associating him, in his maturity, with the Catholic, papist foreign lands of France and Spain: as the Attendant Spirit observes, before settling in 'this ominous Wood' (61) near Ludlow, where he now practises his powerful arts, he had roved 'the *Celtick*, and *Iberian* fields' (60). Comus posed a danger to the aristocratic English Protestant nation and its future leaders in 1634; appearing in another guise in 1649, he would pose an even graver danger to the vulnerable people of the new English republic.

Milton's Sabrina and the Poetics of Nationhood

Only the power of Sabrina can match Comus's 'mighty Art' and Circean magic; she appears at the end of *A Maske* as a figure with major national and poetic significance. The immortal nymph and 'Goddess' (842) of the Severn, rather than a figure of royal magic, rises up from the river on her chariot and emerges as the agent of national renewal as she breaks Comus's powerful and numbing Circean spell, comes to the aid of ensnared chastity, and frees the distressed Lady. Sabrina is associated especially with the power of poetry—that is, 'the power of som adjuring [or exorcizing] verse' (858)—and with song and ritual. She thereby expresses Milton's sense of poetry as a potent force of individual and national recuperation and as a means of remaking national ideals. Furthermore, Sabrina remains guiltless and 'a Virgin pure' (826) after having been victimized; yet, unlike Orpheus in *Lycidas* (and by analogy, the potentially vulnerable poet), she is not violently dismembered but instead maintains her 'maid'n gentlenes' (843), her wholeness and integrity. She is also a local deity, enabling Milton to highlight the

---

[30] See *OED* s.v. 'hug' 1.c: 'to caress or court, in order to get favour or patronage'.

occasion and locale of his aristocratic entertainment. And yet she, a potent female figure rather than a Stuart *pater patriae* ('the politique father of his people', as James I described a godlike king and his wondrous powers),[31] is aligned with legendary British history and with the image of a godly nation as an 'imagined community', a literary-historical construct 'conceived in language'[32]—that is, by means of Milton's visionary poetry. The Attendant Spirit presents this revived and healing divinity as the 'daughter of *Locrine* / Sprung of old *Anchises* line' (922–3), evoking the legendary Trojan kings descended from Brute, traditional founder of Britain, and Anchises, father of Aeneas. She is simultaneously associated with a poetic vision of a flourishing, prosperous, and godly land—an image of national possibility—as the Attendant Spirit evokes, again through Milton's verse, a pastoral and biblical landscape adorned with beryl and gold, 'With many a tower and terrass round', and 'With Groves of myrrhe, and cinnamon' (935, 937).[33] In this way, Milton links legendary British history and the English–Welsh locale associated with Sabrina with national regeneration and religious reformation. The process of national renewal may ultimately be realized not by the power of a godlike Stuart monarch but instead by the arduous trials of the nation's youthful nobility and, no less, by the aesthetic power of its myth-making visionary poet who creates the representation of Sabrina and who has made the masque his literary medium in order to address the nation.

The association of Sabrina with the Severn (*Sabrina* in Latin), which flows near Ludlow and forms an ancient natural boundary between Wales and England, may prompt us, however, to ask additional questions about the national focus and significance of Milton's experimental Ludlow *Maske*. Does the regional setting—on the borderland of Wales and England, thereby linking Wales with England—enable Milton to modify the masque's nationalism and even perhaps give the work an anti-nationalist dimension? Does it give the political entertainment a more 'archipelagic' and consequently Welsh perspective?[34] The landscape of Wales is evoked in the Ludlow masque, its 'snowy hills' (927) appearing in the verses associated with Sabrina's mythic British identity deriving from 'old *Anchises* line'. Certainly, the regional dimension of the Ludlow *Maske* complicates the political dimension of Milton's work, enabling Milton to shift focus away from Charles's court in London and the spectacular dramatic representations, like *Coelum Britannicum*, performed at the city's great Banqueting House. The perspective on Wales and Welsh Marches in Milton's *Maske* also reminds us that

---

[31] James I, *Workes*, 529.

[32] Benedict Anderson, *Imagined Communities: Reflections of the Origins and Spread of Nationalism*, 145.

[33] Brown notes the biblical overtones of this passage: *John Milton's Aristocratic Entertainments*, 127. For cinnamon and myrrh, see e.g. Song of Solomon 4:14; Revelation 18:13.

[34] See e.g. John Kerrigan, *Archipelagic English: Literature, History, and Politics, 1603–1707*, and *British Identities and English Renaissance Literature*, ed. David J. Baker and Willy Maley.

there remains a tension between historicist criticism that is 'archipelagic' in focus and criticism that is focused on the construction of nationhood.

Indeed, ever since J. G. A. Pocock published a seminal article in 1975 arguing for historical work that was more 'archipelagic' and Atlantic in focus, there has been greater concern with encouraging historicist work that is less national in perspective and more 'pluralist and multicultural'.[35] Pocock's aim, understandably, was to challenge an unexamined Anglocentrism. Nonetheless, criticism of early modern British identities that is 'archipelagic' in focus exists in tension with criticism that attempts to stress and illuminate English nationalist concerns, and one of the challenges of ongoing work in these areas may be to negotiate this tension. An 'archipelagic' criticism might help to illuminate further the ways Milton's Ludlow *Maske* explores imaginatively the borderland between England and Wales. But we also need to be wary of an 'archipelagic' criticism that would refocus our attention away from the larger national dimensions of Milton's Ludlow *Maske*, diffusing its significance and the distinctive ways Milton envisions the remaking of national identity.

Consequently, I would argue that the regional dimensions of *A Maske*—partly embodied in the local deity of the Severn—do not undermine, but rather complement, the larger national implications of the political entertainment as Milton refashions them in new ways. The sense of reformed nationhood remains pronounced in the Ludlow *Maske*. The Welsh Marches, in any case, may have been considered, from a London perspective, wild and uncivilized borderlands, but they were nevertheless under English power and judicial authority. Since the Union of Wales and England in the reign of Henry VIII, English laws and county administration had been extended to Wales as a manifestation of English hegemony and its 'civilizing' process—at least until the abolition of the Council in the Marches of Wales in 1689.[36] Milton never questions this political and administrative situation—of Wales under English eyes—in the Ludlow *Maske*. Rather, the regional dimension of the Ludlow *Maske*, I suggest, enables Milton to separate his vision of England's *potential* exceptionalism from a sense of national exceptionalism that radiates from King Charles and his dazzling court depicted in *Coelum Britannicum*. It enables Milton to revise Stuart national ideology to create his own vision of nationhood formed by the arduous trials of its future aristocratic leaders and defined, in the end, by the intervention of a goddess, Sabrina, who is associated with national renewal and the power of visionary poetry rather than with any agent of royal power.

---

[35] J. G. A. Pocock, 'British History: A Plea for a New Subject'. See also *British Identities and English Renaissance Literature*, 1–3.

[36] The Union of England and Wales was legally accomplished by Acts of Parliament in 1536 and 1543; a statute in 1543 established the Council in the Marches of Wales.

Conclusion: on National Representation and National Exceptionalism

There are several points I would like to stress by way of concluding this discussion of *A Maske* and Milton's making of English nationhood in the 1630s. First of all, we need to rethink discussions of Milton's evolving nationalism to take account of the Ludlow *Maske* and the ways this early yet major work represents Milton as an author already engaged in the reformation and construction of his nation and, in this case, its nobility. The large issues of national identity and virtue that would obsess and challenge Milton during the upheavals of the Civil Wars and Interregnum are present in *A Maske*, even if the intense volatility characteristic of Milton's deeply conflicted relation to the English nation—sometimes providing a godly ideal, sometimes giving in to the temptation to backslide to a benighted royalist past—would develop more acutely in later writings and in different political and religious contexts. Moreover, vocational poetic issues, personal ideals, and the potential for national renewal all intersect in Milton's early work: these are all, as it were, on view in the Ludlow *Maske* and configured, I have been suggesting, in a highly distinctive way. Just as the political divine-right theory underlying early modern masques and extravagantly dramatized in *Coelum Britannicum* is notably displaced (Milton's Ludlow *Maske*, after all, nowhere mentions a Jove-like Charles I), so Milton takes the notion of refashioned English nationhood, central to the myth-making of the most extravagant Caroline masque, and invests it with fresh symbolic significance and potential. The concept of a refashioned English nationhood remains an ideal not yet realized in 'this dim spot, / Which men call Earth' (5–6) and itself must undergo strenuous testing, like the aristocratic Egerton children undergoing their '*hard assays*' in a perilous world. Just as the experimental Ludlow *Maske* reforms in more radical ways the politics of Stuart masques, as Barbara Lewalski, Leah Marcus, and David Norbrook have demonstrated,[37] so too the Ludlow *Maske* revises the masque as a courtly form of national self-representation. And it does so in unique ways that look forward to the arduous—though more anguished—trials and forgings of godly English nationhood that would characterize Milton's writings during the political and religious crises of the revolutionary decades and their aftermath. What it also shows is Milton already engaging, during Charles I's Personal Rule of the 1630s, in a contest for national representation and a debate about how the nation's leaders and their progeny prove their virtue as he rewrites the language and symbols of national construction in the Caroline masque.

---

[37] Marcus, *The Politics of Mirth*, ch. 6; David Norbrook, *Poetry and Politics in the English Renaissance*, 233–52; Barbara Lewalski, 'Milton's *Comus* and the Politics of Masquing'. See also Maryann Cale McGuire, *Milton's Puritan Masque*, esp. ch. 1.

Moreover, there is a final point I would stress about situating the Ludlow *Maske* in relation to the complex evolution of Milton's nationalism as he constantly challenges England to live up to her identity as a chosen nation. Milton's writings provide multiple opportunities and perspectives for us, as modern readers, to reflect on the nature of nationalism and its representations in the early modern period, as well as invite us to think more broadly and critically about the issue of national exceptionalism, a political and religious issue that today remains especially central to American national identity. To be sure, Milton provides his own perspectives on the meaning of national exceptionalism—promoting it at points, redefining it, using it to lament and castigate the shortcomings of a nation that has failed to live up to its reformist and revolutionary ideals. Milton's sense of national exceptionalism, shaped by the changing political and religious tensions and crises of seventeenth-century England, may not always be ours, though in other ways those of us who live in a country, such as the US, often obsessed by a sense of national exceptionalism have inherited his legacy and vision of a 'Nation chos'n before any other', 'a noble and puissant Nation', like the strong man Samson after sleep, 'rousing herself...and shaking her invincible locks' (*CPW* 2:552, 558). In February 2002 Margaret Thatcher, writing an opinion piece for *The New York Times*, quoted these famous words from *Areopagitica* and added: 'Milton's words perfectly describe America [the superpower] today' in the post-9/11 world, 'a power', she observed, 'that enjoys a level of superiority over its...rivals unmatched by any other nation in modern times'.[38] What she neglected to notice, as she co-opted Milton to support her own Conservative world view, is that Milton constantly reminds us that the idea of national exceptionalism can never simply be taken for granted—that Milton often struggles mightily with the very idea itself, and that, at the very least, he suggests that it must always be subjected to the most strenuous testing. Indeed, that is already one of the political messages of Milton's Ludlow *Maske* and its imaginative attempt to remake English nationhood.

---

[38] Margaret Thatcher, 'Advice to a Superpower'.

8

Inscribing Textuality

Milton, Davenant, Authorship, and the Performance of Print

Rachel Willie

Milton never completed a play intended for performance, and his involvement in masque culture seems limited to the Welsh Marches.[1] As David Loewenstein's analysis of the relationship between Milton's *A Maske* and national identity has demonstrated (Chapter 7), Milton did, however, engage with drama and with larger conversations about politics, language, and the stage throughout his career. Milton's engagement with the dramatic genre contributes significantly to his construction of his authorial identity. Later in this volume, Neil Forsyth also notes that 'Milton's imagination worked in dramatic terms' (p. 184). Indeed, sketches and fragments of dramas based mainly on biblical stories exist in the Trinity Manuscript and Milton defended drama in his commonplace book. The topic of Milton and drama goes through critical cycles. Jonas Barish's *The Antitheatrical Prejudice* (1981) has invited assertions that Milton's writing exudes a disdain for the stage, a poise that would be in keeping with his Puritan leanings.[2] Stanley Fish's influential work has led many to be of the opinion that the theatricality of Satan in *Paradise Lost* demonstrates Milton's dismissal of the stage as a fallen and corrupting force.[3] Others have proposed that Milton's tenacious use of blank verse and the reception of it as being old-fashioned and

---

[1] In addition to *A Maske at Ludlow Castle*, Milton also wrote *Arcades* (1634), a pastoral entertainment comprising song, dialogue, and masque-like elements in honour of Alice Spencer Egerton, dowager Countess of Derby. Towards the end of his life, Milton also published *Samson Agonistes* (1671), a closet drama not intended for performance. In his commonplace book, Milton asks, 'What in all philosophy is more important or more exalted than a tragedy rightly produced?' (*The Complete Prose Works of John Milton*, ed. Don M. Wolfe et al. (*CPW*) I:490–1). On Milton's commonplace book, see William Poole, 'The Genres of Milton's Commonplace Book'. On the Trinity Manuscript, see William R. Parker, 'The Trinity Manuscript and Milton's Plans for Tragedy'. See also Timothy J. Burbery, *Milton the Dramatist*, 33, 96.

[2] See, for example, Jonas A. Barish, *The Antitheatrical Prejudice*; T. H. Howard-Hill, 'Milton and "The Rounded Theatre's Pomp"', 95–121.

[3] Stanley Fish, *Surprised by Sin: The Reader in Paradise Lost*. For a sample of the large body of work that explores the theatrical inflections in Milton's epic, see Elizabeth Bradburn, 'Theatrical Wonder, Amazement, and the Construction of Spiritual Agency in *Paradise Lost*'; John G. Demaray, *Milton's Theatrical Epic: The Invention and Design of 'Paradise Lost'*; James Holly Hanford, 'The Dramatic Element in *Paradise Lost*'; Michael Lieb, 'Milton's "Dramatick Constitutions": The Celestial Dialogue in

Rachel Willie, *Inscribing Textuality: Milton, Davenant, Authorship, and the Performance of Print* In: *Making Milton: Print, Authorship, Afterlives*. Edited by: Emma Depledge, John S. Garrison, and Marissa Nicosia, Oxford University Press (2021).
© Rachel Willie. DOI: 10.1093/oso/9780198821892.003.0008

archaic is representative of the way in which Milton presents himself as being against the aesthetics of rhymed heroic couplets, and its associations with the politics present on the royalist Restoration stage and within the marketplace of print.[4] The antitheatricalism present in *Eikonoklastes* can thus be interpreted as strategically adopted to frame *Eikon Basilike* as a theatrical text; by so doing, the theatricality of the king's book can be attacked.[5] Other critics have highlighted the metaphorical quality of textual spectatorship and how drama connects to the *theatrum mundi* trope to show how Milton is not against *all* drama but instead uses drama as a form of moral representation.[6] Moving beyond a focus on Milton as dramatist, Brendan Prawdzik examines the problem that dramatic form presents for Milton in his attempt to reconcile the chaste, public poet with the stage: these insights highlight Milton's theatrical poetics and how it connects to embodiment, selfhood, and language.[7]

Milton certainly had a sustained interest in dramatic form, though whether this interest is for poetic or performative reasons is open to speculation. Deborah Milton stated that her father was 'most delighted with [reading] Homer, whom he could almost entirely repeat; and next, with Ovid's *Metamorphosis* and Euripides'.[8] Milton's love of reading classical authors provides some insight into his own reception and interpretation of drama: his heavily annotated copy of the plays of Euripides, which he purchased in 1634, survives.[9] It is annotated in four different hands, though Milton's scribal interjections seem to be limited to the period between his purchasing the two-volume edition and his total blindness in 1652, and most of his annotations were made before 1638.[10] As Maurice Kelley and Samuel D. Atkins contend, Milton not only engages with the text as an editor and translator by correcting the Latin translation appended to the Greek text, but also reads the text as a scholar and a poet.[11]

Milton's marginalia demonstrate his scholarly and poetic engagement with dramatic form: in his annotations of lines 754–71 in *Supplices*, he speculates that they are probably incorrectly given to the Chorus and the Messenger.[12] For

---

Paradise Lost, Book III'; Mary Nyquist, 'Reading the Fall: Discourse and Drama in *Paradise Lost*'; Paul Stevens, *Imagination and the Presence of Shakespeare in 'Paradise Lost'*.

[4] Elizabeth Sauer, *Paper Contestations and Textual Communities in England, 1640–1675*.
[5] Ibid., 57–76.
[6] Vanita Neelakanta, 'Theatrum Mundi and Milton's Theater of the Blind in *Samson Agonistes*'. Dennis Kezar juxtaposes the antitheatricalism within *Eikonoklastes* with the inescapability of drama to examine *Samson Agonistes* from the context of *ars moriendi* literature. See Kezar, 'Samson's Death by Theater and Milton's Art of Dying'.
[7] Brendan Prawdzik, '"Look on Me": Theater, Gender and Poetic Identity Formation in Milton's *Maske*'.
[8] John K. Hale, 'Milton's Euripides Marginalia: Their Significance for Milton Studies', 33.
[9] It is housed at the Bodleian Library: Don. d. 27 and 28.
[10] Maurice Kelley and Samuel D. Atkins, 'Milton's Annotations of Euripides', 684.
[11] Ibid., *passim*.
[12] Hale, 'Milton's Euripides Marginalia', 28–9. Hale notes that Christopher Collard agrees with Milton in his 1975 edition of the play.

John K. Hale, this engagement with dramatic form demonstrates not so much Milton's interest in staging as his concern with dramatic value, his metrical knowledge, and his sense of the 'staged moment'. Drama thus rematerializes upon the page, but this does not necessarily mean the words are a purely textual form. Hale suggests that Milton's annotations show how he read with his ears as well as his eyes as he restored the Greek scansion.[13] But reading itself sits at the threshold of hearing and seeing due to text being read aloud.[14] What this demonstrates is that Milton had a keen sense of the dramatic tradition—perhaps especially in relation to the legacies and reception of classical drama—and this comes through in his poetic works.[15]

In asserting Milton's theatricalism, critics wish to view Milton's poetry and prose as staged events. Conversely, those who seek to assert Milton's antitheatricalism tend to discreetly shy away from evidence that Milton might have inherited from his father a trusteeship of the Blackfriars Playhouse;[16] was involved in theatrics while at Cambridge;[17] wrote a poem expressing admiration for Shakespeare that was published in the 1632 second folio;[18] and collaborated with Henry Lawes in 1634 to produce *A Masque Presented at Ludlow Castle*, the focus of the previous chapter.[19] Instead, the antitheatricals often focus on Milton's final published closet drama, *Samson Agonistes* (1671), where Samson destroys the Philistine theatre. They suggest that this is indicative of blind Milton's desire to destroy the profane royalist Restoration stage. Other antitheatricals focus on comments in Milton's prose works that appear to be against the stage, and on how the theatrical elements of *Paradise Lost* could be aligning performed drama with the fallen angels. However, we are told that, with Milton's blessing, Dryden adapted *Paradise Lost* into a Restoration opera complete with heroic couplets.[20]

---

[13] Ibid., 28.

[14] For a detailed exploration of reading aloud in the early modern period, see Jennifer Richards, *Voices and Books in the English Renaissance: A New History of Reading*. See also Richards and Richard Wistreich, 'Voice, Breath and the Physiology of Reading'.

[15] Scholars have long identified 'theatrical residues' in Milton's poetry and prose, and the complex and sometimes contradictory ways in which he responded to drama, perhaps especially Shakespeare. See, for example, Paul Stevens, *Imagination and the Presence of Shakespeare in 'Paradise Lost'*; Nicholas McDowell, 'Milton's Regicide Tracts and the Uses of Shakespeare'.

[16] Gordon Campbell and Thomas N. Corns, *John Milton: Life, Work, and Thought*, 11–12.

[17] John K. Hale, 'Milton Plays the Fool: The Christ's College Salting, 1628'; Ann Baynes Coiro, 'Anonymous Milton, or, *A Maske* Masked'.

[18] 'An Epitaph on the admirable Dramaticke Poet, W. Shakespeare', *Mr VVilliam Shakespeares comedies, histories, and tragedies Published according to the true originall copies* (London, 1632), A5r. For discussion of Milton's engagement with Shakespeare, see Stephen B. Dobranski's chapter in this volume.

[19] Ian Spink notes that Lawes's posthumous reputation is predicated upon his collaboration with Milton, demonstrating that, while Milton's engagement with performance may be limited, it has lasting and far-reaching implications. See Spink, *Henry Lawes: Cavalier Songwriter*, 55–7.

[20] Diana Treviño Benet, 'The Genius of Every Age: Milton and Dryden'; Nicholas von Maltzahn, 'The First Reception of *Paradise Lost*'. See also Emma Depledge's chapter in this volume, where she notes that, although not performed, the opera was a very successful print commodity.

These apparent paradoxes in Milton's approach to stage plays mean that the debates regarding his view of drama are likely to be ongoing. In what follows, I aim to add another dimension to these discussions, which I hope will suggest that, far from being inconsistent, Milton's view of performance remains remarkably stable. In fact, one might go as far as to suggest that, like his engagement with the Pauline tradition and his use of Latin, Milton's engagement with language, the dramatic genre, and dramatic debates ought to be seen as one of the key ways in which he self-fashioned as an author.

In order to make this case, I will focus on two seemingly unrelated episodes in the performance of seventeenth-century drama, namely Thomas Heywood's publication of *An Apology for Actors* in 1612 and Davenant's publication of his preface to *Gondibert* (1650). I do not wish to suggest that Milton was directly influenced by Heywood's or Davenant's writing, but I would argue that their observations regarding words and performance show that Milton's views on drama are part of wider conversations about dramatic language, authorship, publication, authority, collaboration, and reception. As we will see, Heywood's *Apology* provides insights into performance culture that are vital for understanding why Milton might have struggled to write for the stage, and Davenant's observations regarding language provide important context for Milton's own views on literary legacy.

Apologizing for Actors, Attacking the Archaic

Heywood's *Apology for Actors* is centrally concerned with refuting antitheatrical tracts. Through allusion to antiquity, Heywood emphasizes the longevity and nobility of the profession of acting. By referencing Philip Sidney, he also emphasizes the ability of the theatre to teach and delight its spectators. However, the third and final treatise in the *Apology* ends with a plea to his fellow playwrights:

> Now to speake of some abuse lately crept into the quality as an inueighling against the State, the Court, the Law, the Citty, and their gouernments, with the particularizing of private mens humors (yet aliue) Noble-men, & others. I know it distates many; neither do I any way approue it, nor dare I by many means excuse it. The liberty which some arrogate to themselues, committing their bitternesse, and liberall inuectiues against all estates, to the mouthes of Children, supposing their iuniority to be a pruiledge for any rayling, be it neuer so violent, I could aduise all such, to curbe and limit this presumed liberty within the bands of discretion and gouernment. But wise and iuditial Censurers,

before whom such complaints shall at any time hereafter come, will (I hope) impute these abuses to any transgression in us, who have ever been carefull and provident to shun the like[21]

Absolving himself of involvement in iniquitous performances, Heywood is directly addressing Samuel Daniel, John Marston, Ben Jonson, George Chapman, John Day, and other playwrights for the boy acting companies. In the first decade of the seventeenth century, the two boy acting companies gained notoriety for the biting satire and politically risqué content of their plays.

Paul's boys were a little more cautious about attacking authority figures than the company based at the Blackfriars theatre, and this might be due to the paradoxical support which the Blackfriars had from authority figures. From 1604 until 1606, Anna of Denmark was the patron of the Children of the Queen's Revels, though before the company folded in 1608 they had lost their royal patron. In sponsoring the acting company, Anna's poet Samuel Daniel was appointed the boys' governor and given responsibility for licensing their plays. This does not appear to have been a productive career move: the same year, Daniel was called before the Privy Council after the allegory of his tragedy *Philotas* was interpreted as a narrative about the relationship between Elizabeth and Essex. A year later, in 1605, Marston went into hiding, and Jonson and Chapman (in fear of having their ears and noses cut) voluntarily imprisoned themselves and wrote obsequiously apologetic letters after anti-Scottish satire in *Eastward Ho!* offended the king. A year after that, the boys were reprimanded and some were jailed after Day's *The Isle of Gulls* annoyed the French ambassador and was also interpreted as being a personal attack on the king. Eventually, Anna appears to have lost interest in what the French ambassador had noted was her enjoyment of the railing performed at her husband's expense, and an exasperated James declared that the boys 'would never play more but should first beg their bread'.[22]

In the context of the theatrical climate of the 1600s and the liberties taken by the Children of the Queen's Revels, Heywood's concerns about the damage to the profession caused by using boys as mouthpieces for sedition have pertinence. Knowing the distaste that is generated by this 'presumed liberty', Heywood pleads with his fellow professionals to revise their text. In order to avoid inspiring the wrath and indignation of those in authority and the inevitable punishments that will be inflicted upon all who operate in the playhouse, Heywood requests that playwrights self-censor. By addressing 'all such' people who have been involved in the production of these dramas, Heywood's appeal is addressed not only to the

---

[21] Thomas Heywood, *An apology for actors containing three briefe treatises. 1 Their antiquity. 2 Their ancient dignity. 3 The true vse of their quality* (London, 1612), G3v.

[22] For a brief summary, see Martin Butler, 'Literature and the Theater to 1660', 571–5. For a detailed account of the repertory and theatre history of the company, see Lucy Munro, *Children of the Queen's Revels: A Jacobean Theatre Repertory.*

playwrights but also to the boy actors. Through acting the part, the boy actor could mediate the sedition present in the play text. This suggests that the performed text is not stable, that it can be altered by the actor speaking the words. The stage thus becomes a space where the reception and circulation of dramatic text is provisional and open to modification and change.

Sixty years later, London had experienced civil war, regicide, Commonwealth, and the restoration of the monarchy. Between 1642 and 1660, the playhouses were officially closed by three Acts of Parliament, though there is evidence to suggest that drama continued to be performed with and without the blessing of the state.[23] Through the many cultural and political shifts of the seventeenth century, the connection between actor, play text, and spoken word remained constant. As we will see, it is this malleability of the spoken word, shown in Heywood's reaction to the staging of plays, that is relevant when considering Milton's response to drama, but Davenant's views on language, as articulated in his preface to *Gondibert*, are also important for understanding how text circulates upon the stage and on the page.

Davenant may have been poet laureate, but some questioned whether he was deserving of his laurels:

> After so many sad mishaps
> Of Drinking, Ruining, and of Clappe
> I pitty most thy last misshappe.
>
> That having past the soldiers paines
> The Statesmans Axe, the Seamans gaines
> With Gondibert to butcher thy braines[24]

Thus began 'to Sr William Davenant', a poem penned by John Donne the Younger that circulated in manuscript in February 1652. Donne makes pretence of both congratulating and pitying Davenant. Having run the gauntlet of drunkenness, debauchery, and sexually transmitted diseases, it is suggested that Davenant continues to commit indecent acts. Private corruption is coupled with public heroics and the succinct biography goes on to refer to Davenant's prowess on the battlefield. After being knighted in 1643 for his services to the royalist cause, it seems inevitable that—following the execution of Charles I in January 1649 and the establishment of the Commonwealth—Davenant would become an enemy of the state. This notoriety would be consolidated in 1650, when Davenant was captured by the Commonwealth, imprisoned, and sentenced to death. However,

---

[23] Leslie Hotson, *The Commonwealth and Restoration Stage*; Janet Clare, *Drama of the English Republic: 1649–1660*; Susan Wiseman, *Drama and Politics in the English Civil War*; Rachel Willie, *Staging the Revolution: Drama, Reinvention and History, 1647–72*.
[24] John Donne the Younger, 'To Sr William Davenant', February 1651 [1652]. BL Thomason 669. f.15 (82) fol. 1.

within six years Davenant was not only pardoned but also producing 'reformed' dramas that celebrate Protectorate foreign policy. Davenant succeeded in negotiating regime change, but Donne's poem suggests a more sinister state of affairs. Regardless of Davenant's invidious status as an enemy of the state, Donne feels that he ought to be imprisoned for his crimes against poetry.[25]

John Donne the Younger was not the only person to comment upon Davenant's literary aspirations, and this is partly due to Davenant's interventions in the playhouse. As early as the 1630s, professional playwrights such as Philip Massinger were embroiled in a textual war with Davenant and his fellow courtier-playwrights.[26] At the outbreak of civil war in 1642, this literary controversy may have been suspended, but it would continue in the Restoration and be conjoined with memory of the civil war period. When the playhouses were officially reopened at the restoration of the monarchy in 1660, Thomas Killigrew and Davenant were granted patents that made them each a manager of one of the two acting companies that were licensed to perform drama, and Davenant was also permitted to mount productions in the 1650s.[27] Henry Herbert, who had been reinstated as Master of the Revels, noted this with perplexity. For Herbert, Davenant ranked amongst the most notorious of the turncoats and yet the restored monarchy chose to reward Davenant for his disloyalty.[28] The very act of granting the patent to Davenant would mean that he would hold considerable sway over the restored theatrical scene.

Davenant's ability to negotiate civil war, Commonwealth, and Restoration with his cranium still attached to his neck may have caused disquiet in some quarters, but it also meant that, for some, Davenant could be ridiculed. John Donne the Younger's comments regarding Davenant's lack of literary talent chime with many of the observations made by the London wits and within royalist circles; perhaps most notably, a literary community comprising John Denham and other Cavaliers satirically critiqued in print and in manuscript Davenant's lack of conformity to literary conventions.[29] Conversely, others—perhaps most famously Davenant's friend and occasional collaborator, John Dryden—praised Davenant for his ingenuity and blamed the circumstances of suspended theatre for Davenant penning 'unformed' Protectorate theatricals.[30] In this wider context where text is received, critiqued, and compared to past textual utterances, far from butchering

---

[25] Mary Edmond, *Rare Sir William Davenant: Poet Laureate, Playwright, Civil War General, Restoration Theatre Man*.

[26] Peter Beal, 'Massinger at Bay: Unpublished Verses in a War of the Theatres'.

[27] Willie, *Staging the Revolution*, 89–132.

[28] N. W. Bawcutt, ed., *The Control and Censorship of Caroline Drama: The Records of Sir Henry Herbert, Master of the Revels, 1623–73*, 223; Willie, *Staging the Revolution*, 119.

[29] Marcus Nevitt, 'The Insults of Defeat: Royalist Responses to William Davenant's *Gondibert* (1651)'; Timothy Raylor, *Cavaliers, Clubs, and Literary Culture: Sir John Mennes, James Smith, and the Order of the Fancy*, 197–9.

[30] Willie, *Staging the Revolution*, 134.

his brains with the tedium that is *Gondibert*, Davenant presses for a style of verse stripped of the follies to which celebrated poets of the past had succumbed. In a prefatory verse to *The Preface*, Abraham Cowley applauds Davenant's plainer style:

> Methinks Heroick Poesie, till now
>   Like some fantastic Fairy land did show;
>   Gods, Devils, Nymphs, Witches, & Giants race,
>   And all by man, in mans best work had place.
>   Thou like some worthy knight, with sacred Arms
>   Dost drive the Monsters thence, and end the Charms:[31]

Simultaneously adopting the rhetoric of knight errantry while condemning its negative connections as fantastical, Cowley celebrates Davenant for rescuing heroic poetry from the clutches of fairyland. Unlike his predecessors, Davenant focuses his narrative upon the known world and the actions of humanity. There is an implicit critique of earlier authors such as the Elizabethan writer Edmund Spenser, whose unfinished epic romance *The Faerie Queene* (books 1–3, 1590; books 4–6, 1596) was presented to the reading public as having the purpose of fashioning a gentleman into virtuous behaviour through the example set by various quests through fairyland.[32] The rich allegory of *The Faerie Queene* offers numerous references to contemporary concerns but, for Cowley, the recourse to the non-human renders these types of narrative flawed.

Both Cowley and Davenant wrote epics in the mid-seventeenth century that stripped the epic form of archaic language. As Lucy Munro has deftly demonstrated, archaism—both in terms of language and in terms of form—was integral to the epic, even if archaisms were unpopular by the time Cowley and Davenant were penning their epics. Munro's thesis also sheds light on how Milton uses archaism: Dryden assumed that Milton simply imitated Spenser in his recourse to the archaic, but, in *Paradise Lost*, archaic words cluster around Satan and Hell. For Munro, this precise use of words demonstrates how Milton deconstructs classical epic and reconstructs it as Christian epic.[33] Both Milton and Davenant are concerned with the 'fit' use of language, but they address how words are used differently. Milton, as Hannah Crawforth eruditely notes, uses the etymological roots of words to attempt to construct a national language of liberty, but the idealist use of language in his earlier work gives way to scepticism as the

---

[31] Abraham Cowley, 'To Sir William Davenant, upon his two first Books of Gondibert, finished before his voyage to America', A3r.
[32] See 'A Letter of the Authors Expounding His Whole Intention in the Course of this Work', appended to the 1590 edition *The Faerie Queene* (ed. Thomas P. Roche, 15).
[33] Lucy Munro, *Archaic Style in English Literature, 1590–1674*, 226–32.

republican agenda wanes.[34] Conversely, Davenant directly engages with how language in the present more broadly connects with language in the past: in *The Preface*, he praises and derides in equal measure. Starting with Homer, Davenant assesses the relative merits of deceased poets and completes his inventory with Spenser. While Spenser may be applauded for his ingenuity, he is also to be criticized for his vulgar use of language:

> Language (which is the onely Creature of Man's Creation) hath, like a Plant, seasons of flourishing, and decay; like Plants, is remov'd from one Soil to another, and by being so transplanted, doth gather vigour and increase. But as it is false Husbandry to graft old Branches upon young Stocks: so we may wonder that our Language...should receive from his [i.e. Spenser's] hand new Grafts of old wither'd Words.[35]

Spenser may have constructed a pastoral romance, but Davenant suggests that he knows little of horticulture. Rather than purifying language, in looking to the past and using archaic forms of English Spenser corrupts an evolving language, which prevents language from progressing. As Munro argues, Davenant presents archaism as a highly self-aware process that 'does not breach merely stylistic decorum, but also temporal decorum'.[36] For Davenant, the reception of text and the legacies of authorship rest in being part of an evolutionary process whereby language organically modifies, adapts, and changes over time.

As I have already noted, Milton was a keen reader of classical authors and, like Davenant, his writing thus becomes situated within a literary tradition that stretches back to antiquity. Later in this chapter, I will address how Milton asserts a sense of authorship through recourse to the old, but before returning to Milton it is worth noting Davenant's paradoxical engagement with past linguistic utterances. In the preface, we see not only the rationale for adapting old play texts but also a criticism of engaging with previous writing. As Michael Dobson, Paulina Kewes, and others have noted, the folios of Jonson, Shakespeare, and Beaumont and Fletcher, published in 1616, 1623, and 1647 respectively, established these writers as literary grandees.[37] Natural Shakespeare, artful Jonson, and the witty double act of Beaumont and Fletcher all produced texts that were worthy of being printed in folio, and the paratexts to each volume asserted the linguistic and literary achievements of each writer. The Restoration stage would continue to pay homage to past playwrights by reviving some pre-civil war play texts and altering

[34] Hannah Crawforth, *Etymology and the Invention of English in Early Modern Literature*, 147–84.
[35] William Davenant, 'The author's preface to his much honoured friend, Mr Hobbes', A9v.
[36] Munro, *Archaic Style*, 27.
[37] Michael Dobson, *The Making of the National Poet: Shakespeare, Adaptation and Authorship, 1660–1769*; Paulina Kewes, *Authorship and Appropriation: Writing for the Stage in England, 1660–1710*.

others.[38] However, for Davenant, old language needs to be handled with care. Lacking the purity of late seventeenth-century English, older play texts have to be modified to make them fit for a more refined age: whereas Heywood implores writers to take care in how they craft drama to maintain the decorum of the stage, Davenant presents language (and through it also drama) as in need of constant alteration and refinement. Through some cutting, rewriting, and grafting of new scenes onto the old play, the old language can be made relevant for a contemporary audience.

Such observations resonate with thoughts regarding the recovery of words and the relationship between heroic language and language as a living form that had currency in the Restoration; but they also emphasize the disconnection between heroic poetry and new ways in which words are used.[39] This disconnection is not reconciled through altering old texts: Davenant may reject archaic form, but the processes of adaptation could be conceived as recourse to the old. While the old play text has been modified, it still comprises 'old wither'd words'. There is a tension between the assessment of the evolution of language and how performing drama carries this language through to the Restoration stage. Another tension in Davenant's rejection of old words lies in the generic conventions that he employs. Unconventionally, the author's preface was first published separately from the poem and later enlarged and printed with the unfinished epic. In this respect, it not only serves the purpose of introducing the poem but also advertises the poem to its reading public—even if Denham and his coterie severely criticized Davenant for publishing a preface without the poem.

The perception that Davenant's poetics demonstrated a lack of understanding of generic conventions exposed him to ridicule. As Niall Allsopp has shown, the marginalia in one copy of Davenant's text show how readers actively engaged with each other's scribal annotations and with literary conventions to lampoon Davenant's literary pretensions.[40] Davenant may have attempted to utilize the paper stage to enact drama in textual form, but contemporaries questioned Davenant's grasp of poetics. Yet in these critiques, politics and poetics conjoin. Although Davenant gestured towards the poem as being his valediction to life as he stoically awaited his execution, early readers (somewhat cynically) understood that the poem was not a swansong. Instead, it could be interpreted as forming part

[38] The earliest Shakespeare adaptations did not reference Shakespeare as a source for the altered text. Through being attentive to the book trade and how Shakespeare circulated on the page and the stage, Emma Depledge has uncovered the rich afterlife of the Shakespeare text in the second half of the seventeenth century. See Depledge, *Shakespeare's Rise to Cultural Prominence: Print, Politics and Alteration, 1642–1700*.

[39] Milton's nephew and amanuensis, Edward Phillips, presents early modern lexicography as preserving language from 'the barbarisms and ruinous deformities of the time', suggesting that there is a disconnect between heroic language and spoken language that may be mediated through dictionaries (Crawforth, *Etymology and the Invention of English*, 171–5).

[40] Niall Allsopp, '"Lett none our Lombard Author blame for's righteous paine": An Annotated Copy of Sir William Davenant's *Gondibert*'.

of Davenant's lobbying of Parliament to pardon him. Later, Davenant composed a tract and a letter to Thurloe which advocated utilizing the stage for moral representations.[41] Protectorate poetics is thus infused with political didacticism and questions regarding ethics, yet *The Preface to Gondibert* heralds Protectorate poetics by drawing attention to aesthetics.

The poem, we are told, defies the generic conventions of heroic poetry and instead looks to the stage for its structure and form:

> I cannot discern by any help from reading or learned men...that any Nation hath in represention of great actions...digested Story into so pleasant and instructive a method as the English by their *Drama*: and by that regular species (though narratively and not in Dialogue) I have drawn the body of an Heroick Poem: In which I did not onely observe the Symmetry (positioning five Books to five *Acts* and *Canto's* to *Scenes*...) but all the *Shadowings, happy strokes, secret graces*, and even the *drapery*...I have (I hope) exactly followed.[42]

Davenant asserts that, in penning his heroic poem, he is drawing from both the beauty and the mechanics of drama. The stage rematerializes upon the page. Stripped of dialogue, drama still maintains its form. In appropriating English drama for poetic ends, Davenant suggests that he is purifying heroic poetry of the flaws that previous poets added to the form. As Timothy Raylor has demonstrated, in *The Preface to Gondibert* Davenant proposes a new literary aesthetic; this aesthetic is founded less upon improbabilities, poetic metaphor, and figurative language and more upon philosophical and scientific learning.[43] The virtually impenetrable poem that inspired John Donne the Younger's derision is based upon these tenets. However, this seems to be at odds with much of Davenant's dramatic output, both pre- and post-Restoration, where Neoplatonic love and honour seem to be the driving force.[44] This apparent contradiction emphasizes the difficulties in reconciling the need to draw from tradition and past textual events as a way of asserting the precedence and longevity of a type of writing, while at the same time suggesting that a new and radical form of writing is being developed. Generic conventions are being endorsed as they are being challenged because Davenant struggles to identify what the next development in the English language may be. The rejection of Spenser's archaism and the arguments for a

---

[41] C. H. Firth, 'Sir William Davenant and the Revival of Drama During the Protectorate'; James R. Jacob and Timothy Raylor, 'Opera and Obedience: Thomas Hobbes and "A Proposition for Advancement of Morality" by Sir William Davenant'.

[42] Davenant, 'The author's preface', B10r.

[43] Timothy Raylor, 'Hobbes, Davenant, and Disciplinary Tensions in *The Preface to Gondibert*', 59–72.

[44] For a study that examines Henrietta Maria's influence on court drama and how this connected to politics and aesthetics that in turn influenced Davenant's work, see Karen Britland, *Drama at the Courts of Queen Henrietta Maria*.

mode of writing that conforms to the unities of drama only emphasize the strong connection with the literary inheritance that Davenant seeks to reject. *Gondibert* thus signals a shift in literary culture on the page and upon the stage, but it is a transmission that is self-deconstructing and intensely concerned and indebted to the past that it is anxious to abjure.

Antitheatricalism, Authorship, and Reception

In different ways, Davenant's text and Heywood's *Apology* demonstrate the liminal space of the stage and emphasize the extent to which drama is a collaborative act between not only playwright and acting company but also the printed play text and audiences. Milton implicitly acknowledged this when he prepared *A Maske Presented at Ludlow Castle* for publication in 1637.[45] Rather than providing the text as it was performed in 1634, Milton revised it and in so doing asserted the primacy of his authorship. In 'Of that sort of dramatic poem, which is called tragedy', which prefaces *Samson Agonistes*, Milton makes the case for considering the poem as a tragedy:

> Tragedy, as it was anciently composed, hath been ever held the gravest, moralest, and most profitable of all other poems... The Apostle Paul himself thought it not unworthy to insert a verse of Euripides into the text of Holy Scripture, I Cor. xv.33, and Paræus commenting on the *Revelation*, divides the whole book as a tragedy, into acts distinguished each by a chorus of heavenly harpings and song between. Heretofore men in highest dignity have laboured not a little to be thought able to compose a tragedy... This is mentioned to vindicate tragedy from the small esteem, or rather infamy, which in the account of many it undergoes at this day with other common interludes; happening through the Poets error of intermixing comic stuff with tragic sadness and gravity; or introducing trivial and vulgar persons, which by all judicious hath been counted absurd; and brought in without discretion, corruptly to gratify the people... In the modelling therefore of this Poem, with good reason, the Ancients and Italians are rather followed, as of much more authority and fame... Division into act and scene referring chiefly to the Stage (to which this work never was intended) is here omitted.[46]

I have quoted the preface to *Samson Agonistes* at length because Milton's observations here are telling. Unlike Davenant, who conceived his heroic poem in five books to mirror the five acts of a play, Milton has stripped back the performance

---

[45] Cedric C. Brown, *John Milton's Aristocratic Entertainments*, 132–52.
[46] John Milton, 'Samson Agonistes', in *Milton: The Complete Shorter Poems*, ed. John Carey, 355–7.

elements of drama to focus upon the poetic. For Elizabeth Sauer, this presents a reconfiguration of theatrical culture, one which rejects the 'common interludes' of Restoration drama and the restored royalist stage. In so doing, Milton pre-empts the unpopularity of his poem and establishes a dramatic culture that is in opposition to the royalist stage and the marketplace of print.[47]

This interpretation of the poem thus imagines an authored reception history for the poem, echoing the 'fit audience . . . though few' (*Paradise Lost*, 7.31) Milton imagined reading his epic. Yet, in invoking classical tragedy as a poetic form to be read, Milton is positioning himself within a framework that presents him as the inheritor and redeemer of literary form. His annotations to Euripides—perhaps especially, his editorial interventions to correct error in the translation—also feed into this relationship between past and future textual utterances. Milton is concerned with the legacies of authorship and how the text is received through freeing the author's word from the interruptions and disruptions of the stage; by writing performance out of dramatic form, the uninhibited dramatic poetry can be transmitted to the judicious reader.

What has often been perceived as his antitheatrical response to the publication of *Eikon Basilike* also highlights the need for authorial integrity. When Milton famously attacked the frontispiece to *Eikon Basilike* as being 'drawn out to the full measure of a Masking Scene, and sett there to catch fools and silly gazers' (*CPW* III.342), it was not just visual representation and the dramatic that came under fire. Milton goes on to attack the disjunction between words and text. Assuming the reading public would be awed by a Latin inscription that many of them would not be able to translate, Milton undertakes the role of interpreter and condemns the opacity of the text:

> And how much their intent, who publish'd these overlate Apologies and Meditations of the dead King, drives to the same end of stirring up the people to bring him that honour, that affection, and by consequence, that revenge to his dead Corps, which hee himself living could never gain to his Person, it appears both by the conceited portraiture before his Book . . . and by those Latin words after the end *Vota debunt quæ Bella negarunt*; intimating, That what hee could not compass by Warr, he should atchieve by his Meditations. For in words which admit of various sense, the libertie is ours to choose that interpretation which may best minde us of what our restless enemies endeavor, and what wee are timely to prevent. And heer may be well observ'd the loose and negligent curiosity of those who took upon them to adorn the setting out of this Book: for though the Picture sett in Front would Martyr him and Saint him to befool the people, yet the Latin Motto in the end, which they understand not, leaves

---

[47] See Sauer's epilogue in *Paper Contestations*.

him, as it were a politic contriver to bring about the interest by faire and plausible words, which the force or Armes deny'd him.   (*CPW* III.341–2)

Milton registers the instability of words and how this instability can render text open to the interpretation of the reader, which makes the clarity of language all the more important as a way to impart meaning. The use of visual images ought to aid interpretation. However, instead of harnessing word to meaning, the 'conceited portraiture' renders the relationship between text and image fragmented: fools and silly gazers are caught in a performance designed to elicit sympathy because they fail to interpret the woodcut as an image that is full of conceit. Yet 'conceited' itself is a word that has varying meanings, which include 'ingenious' and having a favourable opinion of an object.[48] There is a tension between word, image, and interpretation, which is amplified by Milton's anxiety to recast the text into theatrical form.

Thomas Anderson intriguingly observes that Milton needs *Eikon Basilike* to be a theatrical text and this need is less concerned with the morality of staging plays and more focused upon the tension between Charles's word and deed. By mapping drama onto the king's book, Milton can destabilize sovereignty. In accepting Charles as the author of *Eikon Basilike*, Milton places the king's book within a dramatic literary tradition and thereby exposes the ways in which Charles appropriated the rhetoric of Shakespeare and plagiarized Sidney.[49]

However, Milton's discussion of the frontispiece complicates this reading. By comparing the frontispiece to a masque scene, Milton acknowledges the connection between sovereign authority and the specific way in which this was embodied in the Stuart court masque. It is not so much performance that comes under attack as the visual representation of sovereign power. Furthermore, Milton's analysis of the frontispiece brings into focus the apparent disparity between the image and the Latin text. Censuring idle authors who do not make their meaning clear, Milton is as much concerned with authorship as he is with theatrics. Milton is condemning not only the opacity of language but also the way in which *Eikon Basilike* has become a collaborative venture between word, image, and borrowings from other writers. Through grafting Shakespeare and Sidney's language and words onto a text that is presented as the word of the king, the meaning of the text becomes muddled. This eschews authorial integrity and blurs the sincerity of what is being conveyed. Non-authorial interventions and stealing from other writers lead to the corruption of the text.

This is a thread to which Milton returned: in *Colasterion* (1645), Milton attacks the writer of *An Answer to the Doctrine and Discipline of Divorce* (1644), arguing

---

[48] 'Conceited, adj. and n.'. *Oxford English Dictionary* Online. http://www.oed.com/view/Entry/38076?redirectedFrom=conceited (accessed 18 August 2017).

[49] Thomas Anderson, *Performing Early Modern Trauma from Shakespeare to Milton*, 169–87.

that 'his very first page notoriously bewraies him an illiterat, and arrogant presumer in that which hee understands not; bearing us in hand as if hee knew both Greek and Ebrew, and not able to spell it; which had hee bin, it had bin either writt'n as it ought, or scor'd upon the Printer' (*CPW* II.724–5). The anonymous author has exposed either their lack of learning or laziness in permitting an imperfect copy to be published. Given Milton's concern with the accuracy of print and the integrity of the author's word, Steven Zwicker's observation that our reading of *Eikonoklastes* is complicated by the way in which Milton asserts that he is a 'reluctant author' may seem ironic.[50] However, this emphasizes Milton's concern with textual integrity as he takes pains to let his reader know how irksome he has found the task. This apparent sincerity makes the ambiguity regarding his antitheatrical poise all the more remarkable.

Perhaps Milton's engagement with the stage is complex precisely because of his lack of engagement with drama as a performative form. As Heywood demonstrates, performed drama was (and is) a collaborative act, and Milton's response to *Eikon Basilike* shows a mistrust of collaborative ventures. In attacking *Eikon Basilike*, Milton draws attention to the way in which the king's book ventriloquizes drama; *Eikon Basilike* becomes an elaborate plagiarism and therefore lacks authenticity. This textual disagreement, when married with Heywood's plea to the boy actors and their playwrights, brings into focus the way in which an actor may mediate the author's word. Whereas the book is the repository for a writer's lively intellect and a means of presenting authorial integrity (as long as the author's word has not been mediated by non-attributed interpolations by other writers), the spoken word is more malleable. Providing freedom of speech is uninhibited, the mechanics of print production allow for tighter authorial control, even if the processes of printing mark an intervention in the reception of text between reader and author. The stage is a more unpredictable platform. Actors may act as mouthpieces for the author, but they can also alter the author's text through the act of performance.

It is not so much that Milton has antitheatrical or theatrical leanings; rather, he is sceptical of collaborative acts—despite his reliance upon his amanuensis and the processes of print production being collaborative. Through inscribing textuality, Milton can assert the importance of the written word as a way of conveying truth, and his deep understanding of etymology underscores his careful use of words. Using an actor as a spokesperson can only inhibit freedom of speech and the integrity of the author's word. What this emphasizes is an anxiety with regard to the flexibility of language, an anxiety that is neatly summarized by Plato:

---

[50] Steven N. Zwicker, *Lines of Authority: Politics and English Literary Culture, 1649–1689*, 46.

Every word, once it is written, is bandied about, alike among those who understand and those who have no interest in it, and it knows not to whom to speak or
not to speak; when ill-treated or unjustly reviled it always needs its father to help
it; for it has no power to protect or help itself.[51]

Rhetoric relates not only to the author's use of words but also to a listener's or
reader's cognition and anxieties with regard to how an author can reconcile ideas
and language in the material world. The author thus becomes the defender of the
word; as the parent from whom the word has sprung, the author protects it and
injects meaning into it. Yet reception is not linear, with an author imparting words
to a reader/spectator; instead, reception connects to wider networks of meaning.
Davenant and Milton are both considering authorship as part of broader discussions about dramatic language, authorship, and the collaborative nature of the
stage and the page. The author's reception of ideas thus informs their writings as
much as their writings are received and handed down to reader or spectator. Both
Milton and Davenant are concerned with authorial legacy and how to protect
words from being bandied about, but this anxiety of authorship manifests itself
differently. For Davenant, authorship is located in using language that encapsulates the idiom of the age and the malleable interplay between stage and page; for
Milton, authorship is located in the precise and uninhibited use of language.[52]

[51] Plato, *Phaedrus*, 565, 275e.
[52] I would like to thank Douglas Clark, Emma Depledge, Marissa Nicosia, and John Garrison for
comments upon earlier drafts of this essay, and Tom Charlton and Daniel Starza Smith for helpful
conversations.

9

'Londini sum natus'

the Latin Voice of Milton's Life Account
in *Defensio Secunda*

John K. Hale

This chapter explores Milton's construction of an authorial persona by paying
close attention to his use of Latin in the *Defensio Secunda*, a 1654 political tract he
produced to defend both his own reputation and Oliver Cromwell's regime. Milton's
reputation had been called into question by royalist tracts such as *Regii Sanguinis
Clamor* ('The Cry of the Royal Blood') by Pierre du Moulin (1652). The original
words of *Defensio Secunda*, which was a sequel to Milton's *Defensio pro Populo
Anglicano* (1651), rarely receive close reading. One thing that perhaps keeps the
words unread is the deflection of scholarly interest from them onto their content,
which has become so central to biographers that the Latin words' expressive power
and self-revelation take second place.[1] David Masson, for example, said he had
already used 'every atom' of its information, and 'quoted it piece by piece' in his *The
Life of John Milton*.[2] And yet, to give a simple example, early in the autobiographical
section of *Defensio Secunda*, Milton declares, *'Londini sum natus'*. Translators tend
to use the natural English word order, 'I was born in London'. But the original gave
more weight than this to the place of birth, reversing the words of the verb, 'In
London was I born'. Besides sensing more balance and weight in this word order, we
can also note Milton's pride in his birthplace. This pride features in other Latin self-
lives, from Ovid's Sulmo in *Tristia* IV. x to Hobbes's Malmesbury in his verse *Vita*:
Latinist or humanist, they generally like to place themselves, by origin, within the
republic of Rome and the republic of letters. Consequently, this part of *Making
Milton,* one that dwells on Milton's authorial persona and reputation, provides an
ideal opportunity to do the celebrated narrative more justice.

The present life account was the second of three *Defences*. After English
publications which attacked the trial and execution of Charles I, the first Latin
one—commissioned by the royalists in exile—came from the eminent Continental

---

[1] For those seeking an introduction to Milton's Latin writing and to the context of Latin readership
in the early modern period, see *The Oxford Handbook of Neo-Latin*, edited by Sarah Knight and
Stefan Tilg.
[2] IV, 593.

John K. Hale, 'Londini sum natus': *the Latin Voice of Milton's Life Account in* Defensio Secunda In: *Making Milton: Print,
Authorship, Afterlives.* Edited by: Emma Depledge, John S. Garrison, and Marissa Nicosia, Oxford University Press (2021).
© John K. Hale. DOI: 10.1093/oso/9780198821892.003.0009

classical scholar Claudius Salmasius: *Defensio Regia* (May 1649). Milton replied in *Defensio pro Populo Anglicano* (February 1651). He was answered (and personally attacked) in *Regii Sanguinis Clamor* (August 1652); this was by Pierre du Moulin, but Milton thought it was by Alexander Morus. His *Defensio Secunda* (May 1654) replied to *Clamor*, attacking Morus. Morus himself replied, and Milton replied to that reply. Indeed, Salmasius had replied too, but died in 1653 well before the publication of that reply in 1658. Milton said his own last word on the whole thing when he revised *Pro Populo* in 1658, with stylistic titivations, as well as adding a final resonant retrospect.

In this chapter I examine how Milton's Latin voice in *Defensio Secunda* defends his reputation, so as to present a distinctive persona, doing so for the needs of immediate context (to refute the attacks on his character in *Clamor*) and to record his life to date, with its formation and motivation. That Latin voice, besides using the normal resources of Latin, makes revealing choices within its wide repertoire. Not that his Latin differs totally from the Latin of his milieu; but repetitions, intensity, and inventiveness distinguish him from them. Again, the features and figures we shall trace do not occur rigidly in the sequence of this analysis, nor in isolation from one another. Nonetheless, it is in this sequence that close reading identifies them, as one then another attracts attention and makes the main impact. And as to their combination, the impact will be greater still: this *a fortiori* is briefly sketched in a final fast-forward to Milton's impassioned peroration.

Contexts

The Latin of this mid-century milieu is classical, and oratorical. Humanists proved themselves to each other by striking Ciceronian, principled, and preferably Roman attitudes, naturally matched with Ciceronian periodic Latin. It was in such terms that Milton achieved the shock effect of an unknown's attack on the big-name Salmasius in *Prima Defensio*, David against Goliath—commissioned by the Senatus Populusque Anglicanus (SPQA), no less.[3] One of the terms of debate was correctness in the Latin, so that opponents twit each other for false quantities or lapses of idiom. Such things become hard to fathom in translation, where good and bad Ciceronian sound much the same in English prose. However, since Leo Miller's pioneering work with the divergences of Milton's 'good'—that is, more classical Latin and the clunky practicality of diplomatic Latin (resembling the shapeless English of insurance policies)—greater attention must be paid to the

---

[3] 'The Senate and People of England', modelled on that formidable badge of Roman authority, *Senatus Populusque Romanus*, '*SPQR*'.

actual words and their stylistic norms.[4] Reliance on translations can only be a drawback: the Latin style matters.

Miller did further good service in explaining that what is most tedious to our minds in the *First Defence* (and its sequels)—the arguing down of every last detail in the preceding propaganda and obloquy—was necessitated by the attacks as made by Salmasius. What is more, Miller's comparison of Salmasius's text with the advice offered by his close friend Claudius Sarravius demonstrates his willed servility towards his royalist instructors.[5] Miller's work adds to evidence from the letters of other Continental humanists which show them following the Latin quarrel between Salmasius and Milton.[6] The Continental readership of Latin was widespread and vocal.

The Life Account in *Defensio Secunda*

What, then, does a closer engagement with its Latin contribute to our understanding of Milton's life account in the *Second Defence*? Could we even see it with fresh eyes, and indeed ears? For, as shown by the opening example of *Londini sum natus*, English translation needs more words, in a different sequence, forfeiting balance and rhythm. 'In London was I born' does secure the gist, and by artificial word order keeps the Latin emphasis. But even so the succinctness is lost, the proclamatory self-identification. Milton's Latin self-life seeks *gravitas*, where the Latin word again means more, and in shorter compass than English accommodates: weight *and* seriousness. This befits Milton's sense of himself, as well as the need to set self-defence within the greater defence of the Commonwealth. Whether or not that Roman dignity and decorum can be off-putting when it becomes self-importance (for the Romans too took themselves very seriously), the effect in English can only be wordier, looser, and weaker. Milton is wearing his Roman robes, justifying in a Roman way himself and his life.

Other Life Accounts

Before examining the passage within the *Second Defence* (*Londini sum natus...*, 81),[7] let us review his other life accounts, since by their differences they may suggest the

---

[4] Leo Miller, *John Milton's Writings in the Anglo-Dutch Negotiations 1651–54*. He recovered many compositions of Milton's during his work for the Office of Foreign Tongues, because the more classical diction and idiom in his drafting distinguished them from the surrounding workaday idiom of officialdom.

[5] Leo Miller, 'In Defence of Milton's Pro populo anglicano Defensio'.

[6] See, for example, Gordon Campbell and Thomas N. Corns, *John Milton. Life, Work, and Thought*, 238.

[7] Reference is to the pages of the first edition, which gives the copy-text for the edition I am currently compiling for the new *Complete Works* from Oxford University Press, and also for its English

stance and purpose of this one. In his *Apology,* Milton makes much of his reading, his poems, and hope of becoming a 'true poem', whereas in the *Second Defence* he speaks only generally of his studies, and not at all of his poems. In *Areopagitica* Milton tells of visiting 'the famous Galileo grown old, a prisoner to the Inquisition for thinking of astronomy otherwise than . . . the licencers thought'—an anecdote most apt to his theme in that oration. In the *Defence,* however, this makes us notice Galileo's absence, part of a dearth of intellectual adventurers or outsiders. If anything, its life account dwells on orthodoxy and solidarity.

In the first *Defence,* now in Latin, and composed as a spokesman, Milton gives no life account, being for Europeans an unknown David confronting Goliath/Salmasius, who must make his way without reputation, by his own voice. But the *Second* dwells more on *ethos,* characterization, probity, beginning with Milton's own. What the *First Defence* does share with the *Second* is a surprising, prophetic-patriotic finale, adjuring the English people to choose aright, namely as Milton advises them to. The peroration of the *Second* continues and extends it, instructing England more than defending it. And since the 1658 addendum to the *First* speaks proudly of Milton himself, in his acts, his thoughts are further turning away from European hearers to English ones. In the third *Defence,* of *Himself,* while Milton uses attack as his main form of defence, he writes some further explanations of his own travels, as snatches of rebuttal. All in all, the tactics and purpose of the life accounts keep varying. That in the *Second Defence,* though using some of the same life materials, stands alone in purpose, scope, and shaped Latinity. Milton's use of the Latin medium is unique in its form of witness to Milton's persona and reputation: for the first and only time he is testifying to his own character, for the sake of an official role or duty, exploiting the lexis of the Latin of *officium.*

Purposeful Sentence Length

Before commencing the life account itself, he declares the text's purpose in a lengthy sentence, 131 words of Latin, 185 in our English. It is all about reputation. We can learn something from the varying lengths of Milton's sentences, over and above the obvious contemporary use of periodic ones. As their punctuation is lighter than ours, we can see an entire act of thought within a long sentence, where modern practice might use paragraphing instead (and English translations tend to divide periods into more manageable sentences). The long periods make us join

translation. This pagination differs slightly from that of Yale, which is using a different copy-text: Oxford's [81]–[95] = Yale's [80]–[94]. Other editions or translations consulted are Columbia; Yale; and my selection of passages in my *BLN* volume, *John Milton. Selected Latin Writings.* I give brief citations from the Oxford *Defences* volume, which gives the page numbers of the first edition of *Defensio Secunda* (whose title is shortened henceforth to *2 Def,* and similarly *1 Def* and *PSD* for the other *Defences*).

up the whole sense, by reading to the end before absorbing the whole; for example, to grasp a whole causality or (as in the present case) motivation. Indeed, causality and motivation tend to take turns, the former shaping the latter, once Milton's account of the great public events begins to explain his own life choices.

In the introductory sentence of 131 words, however, he sets out to define his motives for the whole life account. It addresses a threefold audience. Discussions of audience or readership imply Europe, since the work is in Latin, but Milton makes us think of how his life looks to the particular notables whom he later characterizes in turn—not even only Cromwell. And then to the people whom he is defending officially, as a duty (*officium*). All are worthies: his own worthiness must be known too.

Consider this passage:

> First, [81] in order that so many good and learned men, who throughout the neighbouring nations now read our works, and do not think ill of me, may not be dissatisfied with me because of this fellow's insults, but may thus convince themselves that I am not such as ever to have disgraced honourable speech with dishonourable habits, or free statements with slavish actions; and that our life has, with God's good help, always been far removed from all depravity and iniquity: next, in order that those distinguished and praiseworthy men whom I take as subjects for praising may know that I consider nothing more shameful than if I proceeded to my praises of them while blameworthy and vicious myself; in order that, finally, the English people – whom, whether as my destiny or my duty, their own virtue has impelled me to defend – may know that if I have always led a shame-free and honourable life, my defence will bring them – whether honour or renown, I do not know – [but] certainly never shame and disgrace. Who, therefore, and whence I am, I shall now state.[8]

First, [81f] he does not want European readers to believe the aspersions cast by Morus, but to know he is of good character. Next, he does not want the English worthies whom he praises to recoil from eulogies by someone vicious, unworthily. And thirdly, he wants the English people to know their defender is a person of honourable, not shameful, life. Presumably, the third readership, coming last, is the worthiest. Their defence is his 'fate or his duty'—*sive fatum sive officium*. He

---

[8] Primum [81] ut tot viros bonos atque doctos, qui per omnes vicinas gentes nostra iam legunt, deque me haud malè sentiunt, ne propter huius maledicant mei poeniteat; verùm ita sibi persuadeant non eum esse me, qui honestam orationem inhonestis moribus, aut liberè dicta, serviliter factis unquam dedecorârim; vitamque nostro Deo bene iuvante, ab omni turpitudine ac flagitio remotam longè smper fuisse; deinde ut quos laudandos mihi sumo viros ullustres ac laude dignos, hi sciant nihil me pudendum magus existimare, quam si ad eorum laudes vituperandus ipse ac nequam accederem; sciat denique populus Anglicanus, quem ut defenderem, meum sive fatum sive officium, sua virtus impulit, si vitam pudenter atque honestè semper egi, meam defensionem, nescio an honori aut ornamento, certè pudori aut dedecori nunquam sibi fore: qui igitur, et unde sim, nunc dicam.

returns to address them, the key component of his work's title, in its final pages (162–73). The copy-text makes a single long, new paragraph beginning with the ringing admonition—Nam et vos, ô cives, 'For you also, O fellow-citizens'—to be assessed in a moment here. But first, we may also wonder if Europe is not in some sense the ultimate as well as explicitly here the first audience, for reputation within the republic of letters; and wonder too what the Commonwealth leaders thought of this life account. Did Fairfax, the odd man out among the leadership worthies, read any of the *Defences*? Did he need help with their Latin? And did all the readers read the Latin sentences silently, or had they someone to read them aloud? The approach through sentence length prompts such new questions: even if they cannot be answered, we can at least register some impact from the shortness of the short ones.

Like the first sentence of the life story itself, short by contrast with its precursor. It joins birthplace and parentage. The main clause comes first, in which three words in hyperbaton make *Londini* stand out. Three ablative phrases follow, of two, then three, then eight words; for ancestry, father, and mother respectively. The impression made is of artful bluntness (the hyperbaton), of simplicity expanding (3, 2, 3, 8 = 16).

Over- and Understatement

The first sentence works also by ascending superlatives: *viro integerrimo, matre probatissima*, who is then again *potissimum nota*—'a man of the utmost integrity, my mother of the highest esteem and especially well known'. These superlatives for characterizing persons, to select and maximize their salient qualities, tend to become routine later on. As when a speech of thanks drags on! When a speaker names a whole succession of names, utterly splendid persons, doing a great job, superlatives have diminishing returns. In starting off the roll call, however, Milton makes his mother's works of mercy (*eleemosynis*) stand out; not by some third superlative adjective, but instead by the resounding adverb with simple adjective, *potissimùm notâ*, 'especially well known'. The change of the superlative idiom secures a glow of emphasis, to make a gracious tribute, simple and short. Worthy parents predispose us to expect worth of the son. No siblings are mentioned, though he had two; no one is given a name. The effect of *potissimum nota*, last word in the phrase and the sentence, is a 'need I say more?', or 'Enough said'. That is how I would read it aloud. The comparative bluntness of the sentence reads aloud finely, as an understated proclamation of ancestry.

In the next sentence, we register length and hypotaxis (124 words). It binds together all stages of his formal education till he 'left' Cambridge, *reliqui*. That is the last word in several senses. He left for home 'of his own volition': that scotches the slander that he left on the run (*profugus*), headed for the brothels of Italy. He 'left' for further studies at home in the country. Most telling of all, in grammar he 'left' the fellows of his college 'missing him' (*mei etiam desiderium*). The sentence explains in passing the beginning of his eye troubles as owed to late-night study (not divine retribution for supporting regicide). It comes at some cost to details of this prolonged studying, we should note—just what he does emphasize in his *Apology* account: he has his eye on something different in weaving this account. I call it tact, the tact of calm sobriety, so far rather featureless and normal or orthodox, but at any rate blameless.

Tact explains one striking omission, the awkward fact that he fell out with his first tutor, Chappell, who had him rusticated. The opponents had missed this, or garbled it. Milton is silent about it here, even while *Poems 1645* did glance at it (in *Elegia Prima*). Instead, the fellows pay him no mediocre attention (*haud medio-criter cultus*), and will even 'miss' him when he has left. No superlatives here: instead, though, the understatement of litotes. True, nowadays we hear negativity in the double denials of persons caught out in sharp practice ('I did nothing *wrong*', meaning nothing actually illegal, merely greedy, cruel, self-serving, harm-ful to others, and so on). Such nuance was not heard by Milton, who keeps the old figurative power of understatement, as in 'no mean city'. Understatement is joined to a figure, zeugma, of leaving—*reliqui*, final word of this sentence and this narrative phase—'leaving' not only place and people but also their emotion, their sense of loss. Plain style has its own ways of emphasizing.

Understatement is felt locally in a further way, the words of selected emotion, Milton's: *avide, studui*, etiam ... *reliqui* ('avidly', 'I studied', 'I even left'). Then he wonderfully collocates two very precise reasons for book buying. By Maths and Music *oblectabar*, 'I was delighted', or even 'beguiled'.[9] He goes back to London to buy books in these subjects for the sake of *addiscendi: ad-* prefixed hints at love of 'extra' learning, 'further' to his humane Letters.[10] The keynotes are: tact, judicious choice, all-round accomplishment; all in all, the *good* use of time and opportunity.

Emotion is as yet infrequent and understated. It begins to increase in the next sentence. Twenty-three words get him from five years of study in retreat via his mother's death to his desire for travel: *Italiam potissimum* ['Italy in particular', that adverb again, which not merely varies the routine superlatives but outweighs them] *videndi* cupidus, exorato *patre* ... ['eager to see, after securing my father's permission', where the prefix *ex-* means beseeching or gaining by ...]. The next sentence, as the travelling commences, returns to the sound of superlatives and relies on corroboration by superlatives, not of self-praise but, rather, of corrobor-ation by his consorting with very worthy hosts. Their worth vouches for his.

---

[9] OLD s.v., senses 1 and 2 respectively.

[10] Milton's love and practice of music was lifelong. Did he pursue maths so far, as it is a subject where you know at once when you have hit your ceiling? The two disciplines followed Arts in the university curriculum.

Superlatives return, and he drops names plentifully: Wootton, representative of King James; Scudamore, Earl of Sligo, representing King Charles; the great Grotius, Ambassador to France of the Queen of Sweden—taken together, the names exude more than a whiff of rank. The big names name excellences and notables, who put themselves about to be of service to Milton (and they begin to be European ones as well). For, it is implied, they know him to be worthy of it.

Camaraderie

As he reaches Italy in general, but in particular Florence and its Academies of the young like-minded, Milton changes his mode of naming. He does not name Galileo by name, despite meeting him. Instead, further to deride the opprobrium of smears about Italy, he speaks of equality in friendship.[11] He changes to the second person. The apostrophe is in the affectionate singular, *Tui*, even though he is naming several people: each one is a *Tu*. Gaddi, Dati, Frescobaldo, Coltellini, Buonmatthei, Chimentelli, Francini, and many others. All are *Tu*, and 'time will never erase their memory – ever pleasant and delightful!'

This way of naming names strikes a new note in the narration. No friends have been named from school, university, or afterwards, not even Milton's closest friend, Charles Diodati. Now in Florence, Milton names a whole lively new group of equals. He does place Gaddi first, he being 'centre and chief of an academy kept up by himself',[12] the Svogliati (the 'disgusted', a jokey blokeish name of these friendly gatherings). Dati, second, was actually a closer friend: named first, and alone with Francini, in the *Epitaphium Damonis*, and recipient of Milton's impetuous frank Letter 10, homesick for Florence. Of the other friends, two stand out. Buonmatthei was a senior member of another society, the Apatisti: when Milton wrote to him (*Ep. Fam.* VIII], it was more deferentially, urging him to make his Italian dictionary more helpful to foreigners. By contrast Malatesti, poet of the risqué *Tina* cycle, is mentioned in the Dati letter but omitted from the present life account. So, Milton is editing, to present himself in selective company, not retelling the whole story.

Something similar happens in Rome, on both visits: he meets the scholarly German Holstenius, yet makes no mention of poets whom he met, like Salsillus, nor of his host, Cardinal Barberini. For Naples, he makes the most of Mansus, who gives the focus for his account of Milton's religious profession while in Italy. Mansus is a nobleman and Viceroy of Naples, poet and patron of poets. Also an

---

[11] See further Estelle Haan, *From Academia to Amicitia: Milton's Latin Writings and the Italian Academies*; also John K. Hale, ed. *John Milton: Select Latin Writings*, 97–155.
[12] Masson, *The Life of John Milton*, I. 723. Masson's account of the Florence visit remains entertaining. A fuller account is found in Haan, *From Academia to Amicitia*.

older, respected personage. His name ticks several boxes for Milton's profile, only to make a quite new point in a moment.

Milton so selects and arranges the names of these friends as to secure a clear impression—of being among equal and kindred spirits. He still does *not* mention poetry, though this was what opened doors for him in Florence.[13] Scholarship is held over till Rome and Holstenius. Even in Naples, where he keeps company with the older, graver Mansus, he does not mention the poetry on either side: only that the *insignis poeta* ('famous poet') Tasso had written to his friend Mansus in MS, a work on friendship. Milton is building the picture of sobriety in companionship, vouching for his own reputation by bigger and older ones; in a word, playing safe. As well he might do when in danger, both in defence of himself now and when in Italy too.

And yet not so! Mentioning Mansus brings the crucial, dangerous, relevant topic forward: Mansus could not do more for him in Naples 'because I was unwilling to be more guarded in speaking of religion'—*quod nolebam in religione esse tectior*. Though the verb is negative, and so partly is the colouration of its adjective *tectior*, this at once changes. Having shown himself to be of virtue and blameless so far, his account changes from reputation to initiative, and conviction. From sounding inclusive and without opinions, Milton emerges with a strong one, jarring among so much camaraderie. *Turpe enim existimabam*, 'I thought it shameful' to be travelling for pleasure while my countrymen were fighting it out for freedom, *de libertate dimicarent*. The full-blooded vigour of the second verb does not obscure that of Milton's verb for his own action, *existimabam*, 'I judged it', too casually Englished as 'I thought'. I return to this, after wider consideration of verbs in Latin, and verbs of cognition and decision in this passage. They begin to require notice here.

Verbs of Cognition and Volition

In Latin, the verb as such has greater force than in English. Its verbs are concrete. Routinely, they come last for impact. They conclude syntax and sense together. Or else, departing from that norm, they can be placed strategically. The Latinate nouns in *-ation* which festoon English academic prose, though they derive from Latin verbs, are more static and have less force, concerned with state more than with efficacy: in Latin they keep their sense of verb as action, agency. *Abstractio*, for example, would mean the action of pulling away, not the abstract idea of

---

[13] His poems 'met with acceptance above what was lookt for'—presumably another modest understatement, because some 'were received with written encomiums', such as the fulsome praises of the commendatory verses in *Poems 1645* (in the autobiographical portion of *Reason of Church-Government*).

abstraction. The verb *abstrahere* would retain the metaphor of 'pull away': *abstractare*, formed from the supine 'to abstract', does not exist in classical Latin. If it had existed, it would keep the older, frequentative function of such formations, to 'go on and on pulling away', like stripping off old wallpaper. And as for Milton, his way with verbs follows this exemplar, even in his verse and his English too: the delayed verb '*Sing*, heavenly Muse...' is only an extreme and climactic instance.

In the particular Latin which this chapter considers, Milton naturally shows the same muscularity and leverage throughout. We noted how *reliqui*, hardly the most semantically potent among verbs, had great force by understatement placed last, just as 'returned' has the last word in *Paradise Regained*. We can trust Milton to know what he is doing with his verbs throughout. Consequently, when we wait to hear the verbs of his Continental travels *without* feeling the earth move, we know it is only a matter of time before they do shake it. That time comes when he reaches Naples, meets Manso, and, for the first time in this narrative, faces the fact he is a Protestant in the heartland of the Church of Rome. Here, thanks to the verbs, he seems to grow up.

Those verbs I call verbs of cognition, if that term gathers up thought, choice, hope, apprehension in both senses, and judgement, with an eventual sense that in this account of his fate he 'can [do] no other' than these acts of the mind. Along with cognition goes volition, as in the Naples sequence: *nolebam... existimabam.* Then, decision: *nolebam, existimabam—statueram* ('I was unwilling, I was judging, I had decided'.) The verbs, and their placing and how they sit among the many other parts of his measured periodic sentences, demonstrate how he came to act a part on the kingdom's great stage; that is to say, gradually, reluctantly, inescapably, just as Cincinnatus or Isaiah came only slowly to their personal moments of fate. I hope to justify these portentous phrases now, by selecting evidence from the sheer weighty eloquence of Milton's Latin hereabouts.

Back, then, to *existimabam*. *Existimo* is a verb favoured for gravitas by Roman historians, especially Sallust, whom Milton greatly admired.[14] It keeps, but extends to considered opinion, the sense of *-aestimare*, to weigh, measure, estimate; to weigh up, after reflecting. Milton 'kept on' weighing it up too: he uses the continuous imperfect—'I was regularly judging my own behaviour abroad once the bad news reached me'. He must act. He does: he abandons further travel, to return homewards. And more cognition follows: he must decide how to conduct himself as he goes back through Rome, where Jesuits may ambush him for his previous (though unmentioned) free-speaking. For *Sic enim mecum statueram*: 'For I had [already] decided thus with myself, not indeed to initiate conversations on religion, but if I was asked about my faith, to conceal nothing, whatever I might

---

[14] These points are made more fully in my essay 'Milton on the Style Best for Historiography'.

then suffer' [86]. The decision's content has been well recognized, the verb of cognition less so. It is bolder and clearer than the first hint of attitude in *nolebam*. The pluperfect tense insists on the decision being earlier (just as the Jesuits must have been alerted on the outward journey). The grammatical modality is indicative, not subjunctive: not of thought being thought, but of its outcome in action. The verb phrase comes first in its sentence, as the declarative *sic mecum statueram*. Nothing like this has preceded within the narrative. This is not just reputation, let alone in the negative form of blamelessness. It is initiative, conviction, speech as action, albeit remaining speech about his religion when asked: *de religione quidem iis in locis sermones ultro non inferre; interrogatus de fide, quicquid esse passurus, nihil dissimulare* ('not to initiate conversations about religion in those parts, but when asked about my beliefs to conceal nothing, regardless of consequences' [86]).

I see no reason to mistrust what Milton declares here. He became imprudently outspoken later, in 1649 and 1659. The same attitude is plain in *Lycidas* (1637), published then and again in 1645. What we are following in the present summary is the reticence owed to prudence and to hospitality. And the self-picture is developing, into the account of public events which makes him go public with his views, from opportunity and urgency. Then, after further prolonged reticence about the King's trial, he goes public for solid reasons, on *principle*; when (as he argues it) he can do no other. Rhetoric and self-presentation do play some part in this account. What might be less recognized is, once again, the part played by verbs of cognition: these combine to express conviction, considered acts of a weighty boldness. He *wields* these verbs, to explain his integrity, for precision, sincerity, and principle.

Next, accordingly, I ignore all other aspects of style, to make plainer this case about verbs, as seen now in the writings by which Milton put his head decisively, irrevocably above the parapet.

Cognition and Volition in Defending the Polemical Writings

The life narrative continues into a series of realizations and disclosures. Just as in Italy he 'was unwilling, judged, and decided', so when the pride of the bishops 'detumesced' (*detumuit*, 88i)—those powers including censorship—Milton was 'aroused' (*experrectus*). He was aroused to think out the basic liberties and to publish his ideas, because *consuluissem ecquando ullius usus essem futurus si nunc patriae...deessem* ('I had asked of myself how I would ever be of any use [89] if I were now to fail my country'). 'I decided', *statui* (that verb of deciding again) to switch my whole strength from 'some other things I was planning',[15] to writing on

---

[15] Such as a tragedy or epic.

liberties like church reform. It was Now or Never. The long sentences concatenate the circumstances and motives before explaining his interior debate with precision. The latter process (*meque consuluissem*) has moved past the negatives of condition and restraint (speaking of faith only when *interrogatus*). He takes a direct initiative, in fact a whole series of them,[16] from 1641 to 1645.

Then, after another lull, the wars return, the Commonwealth abandons negotiation with the King, and puts him on trial instead. Milton returns to publication. Yet what he stresses in the narrative is his delaying, a deliberative slowness. *Neque de jure regio quicquam a me scriptum est, donec Rex hostis à Senatu judicatus, belloque victus, causam captivus apud Judices diceret, capitisque damnatus est* ('Nor did I write anything about the right of kings, until the King – judged an enemy by the Senate, and defeated in war – would plead his cause as a prisoner before the Judges, and [until] he was [actually] condemned to death' [92]). And moreover, when the Presbyterians changed sides and made trouble, not even then did I write about Charles, but showed (*ostendi*) what must be said against tyrants, as a species. The syntax keeps on and on, retarding and withholding the moment when, finally, and last in the sentence of 136 words, *prope concionabundus incessi* ('almost orator-fashion I attacked'). The ample sound of concionabundus helps us register that he writes like (*prope*) a Roman, haranguing in 'public' for the public good.

The effect is of circumstantial precision, of principle not personal animus, of painstaking sincerity. The effect is gained by features of the Latin which may be muted in translation, for instance if the single 136-word sentence becomes several in English: ease of comprehension forfeits the precise, personal, ratiocinative effect, whether during the writing of *Tenure* or here in the retrospect. Why, for example, does Milton not say, 'I wrote nothing about the right of kings', but instead use the strange passive locution 'nothing had been written by me about' it (*neque de jure regio quicquam a me scriptum est*)? And note the careful differentiation of *donec... diceret* (subjunctive, he is waiting with purpose) from [*donec*] *capitis damnatus est* ([until] sentence of execution was actually passed on Charles). These hesitations are explained by the next words, *Tum vero tandem*, 'Then indeed at last' among the conflicting and tumultuous responses of the factions, and because of these, Milton *thinks* (*ratus*, 93) to rebut their falsehoods. And 'not even then' (*ne tum quidem*) did I write or urge (*scripsi aut suasi*) 'in order to settle' (*ad statuendum*) anything about Charles, but only in general against tyrants. Principle is again upheld. *Scripsi* brings out the written status of *Tenure*, but *suasi* brings out its advocacy, and looks ahead to *concionabundus* ('orator-fashion'). Writing is action, persuasion of the public. Does *neque quicquam a me scriptum* mute the idea of agency, or highlight it? Does *nihil* insist that not only

---

[16] Aimed by a further series of noteworthy verbs of thought, volition, and decision: *conscripsi, ratus, didiceram, dicturum, respondi*, garnered from 89 alone.

did he not write *Tenure* (yet) but nothing other or smaller either? Or is he cheating, saying nothing 'was written' though he must have thought it? These interpretations can all be maintained, though not equally. Latinists should be heard when the reasons are being ranked, for this is a central, vital declaration. To me, then, this self-expression combines principle, timing, and public spirit, Milton's sense of *officium*.[17]

None of this could cut any ice with those who opposed the regicide, and for some of them his expounding a principle or ideology of punishing tyrants would only make matters worse—it being more, not less, abominable to assent to it with mind, not emotion, for that would render it more likely to happen again, and again. Milton goes on and on affirming his good conscience: *bonam conscientiam, bonam apud bonos existimationem*. Principle and integrity are proclaimed: that is more provocative, but he is defending himself *apud bonos*, to men of good conscience, such as himself, including himself. Yet again, verbs of cognition carry or sum up his burden—*ratus, ostendi, incessi*, and words of thought like *conscientiam* or *existimationem*. They are what the *boni* have and judge by.

So, the man of faith acts in good faith. His cognitive verbs guide the syntax, subordinating the pieces of the lengthy train of thought into a concatenation which (dragging us along) may persuade us of its conclusions. And while this is the case with hypotactic styles generally, Milton in defence of his own actions offers an overplus. That may be why he returns to the wider principle in his singular finale, the appeal which (within a defence of the English people) he voices *to* them.

A Calculated Indecorum or the Compulsion of Sincerity?

Milton's reputation must be worthy of England's. His self-account may increase his reputation. It speaks gradually more about himself, in the voice and persona of a published thinker. Thereby, having defended himself more than worthily, Milton thinks to qualify himself to advise England how best to defend itself. This last move, surprising and illogical in a work addressed on *behalf* of England, *to* Europe, extends the impassioned close of his *First Defence*, as if to say to England, 'I have done my part: now you do yours'. After the self-characterization with its narrative of public events, interwoven with his own part in them, Milton characterizes the Commonwealth's leaders, culminating in Cromwell. Thereupon, the peroration tells them what to do next. A bold, confident move, exemplifying his individualistic conception of who the 'English people' *are*. They are those who are worthy of his defence, which worth they must show by

---

[17] Cf. the epigraph to *Areopagitica*, taken from the Greek of Euripides's *Supplices*, and set into English verse by Milton himself.

doing as he advises. Circularity, egocentricity, and eccentricity come to dominate the developing picture of upright self-worth.

This chapter has shown how reputation is upheld by the Latin of the persona, one which creates personality, to the point where it usurps centre stage. Comparison with Milton's other life accounts shows us this, too, as do certain silences in this one. Far from dusting off or updating his curriculum vitae, as academic wretches must do today, Milton makes it all new, enforcing attention to his thoughts and choices preceding action.

Persona and Voice in the Final Appeal

Thus, as part of this self-life excursus, Milton accounts for his actions by recalling how, why, and when he chose to go public. Throughout, public action was compelled by events and conscience, overcoming reluctance for the sake of a greater good. The delaying effect of his thought-preceding action is matched by the syntactical effect of hypotaxis up to the verbs of cognition and choice. Its hyperrational impression need not invalidate Milton's good faith for several further reasons. (1) It has the sanction of Milton's ancient exemplars, Romans or prophets. (2) It chimes with other life decisions, from the letter to a friend in the Trinity MS and the sonnet 'How Soon Hath Time', to his decision to share *De Doctrina* in its Epistle. It is a responsible Protestant freedom, to speak his mind, do his best, account for the faith that is in him. (3) In the same spirit, Milton ends his *Second Defence* by even more blatantly exhorting the 'people' to act wisely in the continuing crisis, that is, to do what he advises. (4) The work is becoming more oratorical, a stance and genre which small details of the Latin reveal: mention of *oratio* and *contio*, personal pronouns, and (5) the whole peroration, modelled on that of *Prima Defensio*, moves into a more specific advocacy than there. (6) This astonishing, late self-assurance continues the growing confidence with which the life narrative depicts Milton. The difference which a reader experiences at the close is that the voice moves from a rationalizing *ethos* to an outright patriotic *pathos*. It now harangues the people. They, not readers in Europe, are *vos. Scitote . . . scitote*; he repeats, 'I would have you know', in the Latin, 'You are to know that . . .'. It has an urgent impulsion to it, repeated in the cognitive imperative. It would speak aloud well.

Or does this overstate my case? Woodcock's *New Latin Syntax* says: 'this second or so-called "future" imperative in –*to*, –*tote*, expresses an order that is not to be obeyed immediately . . . Accordingly this form is regularly found in the texts of laws, and in general precepts or proverbs . . . A few verbs are regularly used in this form in all circumstances, e.g. *scito, memento . . .*' (126 n. 1, p. 96).[18] This

---

[18] E. C. Woodcock, *A New Latin Syntax*.

strengthens more than it moderates my point. And it is better, one might say, to over- than to under-interpret the tonality of Milton's original Latin. Better to show by as many routes as possible how Milton indulges (to no avail) in vociferous fervour. Also, the concurrence of his verbs of cognition, reiterated, as this strange appeal nears its climax. His voice is rising in passion and register, as (poignantly) he harangues only those of his fellow countrymen who are literate and have Latin, instead of the Europeans to whom he is supposed to be defending the whole of England.

Who could possibly doubt his sincerity when it must express itself out of turn, dangerously, even straining a hitherto well-kept decorum? He was the same public trumpet in 1659. *Defensio Secunda* in its life account shows how he became this, in a steepening parabola. On reflection, the slight jolt felt when Milton addresses England as 'you' resembles the appreciation we all feel when Cicero harangues Catilina or Rome: we listen in, and let the Latin play over and around us. Overridingly, it must indeed be the Latin, not a stumblingly literal or merely approximative English.

10

Milton among the Iconoclasts

Antoinina Bevan Zlatar

> Thus to herself she pleasingly began.
>   O sovereign, virtuous, precious of all trees
> In Paradise, of operation blest
> To sapience, hitherto obscured, infamed,
> And thy fair fruit let hang, as to no end
> Created; but henceforth my early care,
> Not without song, each morning, and due praise,
> Shall tend thee, and the fertile burden ease
> Of thy full branches offered free to all;
> Till, dieted by thee I grow mature
> In knowledge, as the gods who all things know;
> . . .
>   So saying, from the tree her step she turned;
> But first low reverence done, as to the power
> That dwelt within, whose presence had infused
> Into the plant sciential sap, derived
> From nectar, drink of gods.[1]

Eve's first act after eating the forbidden fruit is to offer a hymn of praise to an apple tree, promising to do so every morning thereafter, and then to bow down to it 'as to the power / That dwelt within' (9.835–6). It is, of course, Satan in the serpent who has taught Eve to fetishize the forbidden fruit, persuading her that it is forbidden because it is mind-expanding or 'intellectual food' (9.768), and that in eating it she may ascend the chain of being even to godhead. God, whom Adam and Eve had so memorably praised as 'universal Lord' (5.205) in their morning orison, becomes in Satan's account a god in a pantheon of gods. The danger of robbing the one true God of honour by worshipping false gods—idolatry—and the association of false gods—idols—with devils is introduced early and explicitly in the poem in the lengthy catalogue of the gods of the land of Canaan, Egypt, and Greece that concludes Book I. Thereafter it will be an insidious, pervasive danger,

---

[1] John Milton, *Paradise Lost*, in *John Milton: The Complete Poems*, ed. John Leonard, 9.794–838. All subsequent references to this work in this chapter will be cited within the text.

Antoinina Bevan Zlatar, *Milton among the Iconoclasts* In: *Making Milton: Print, Authorship, Afterlives*. Edited by: Emma Depledge, John S. Garrison, and Marissa Nicosia, Oxford University Press (2021). © Antoinina Bevan Zlatar. DOI: 10.1093/oso/9780198821892.003.0010

one to which Adam ultimately succumbs in putting his love of Eve before his love of God. Raphael, disconcerted by the fervour of Adam's love for his spouse, had firmly recommended 'and love, but first of all / Him whom to love is to obey' (8.633–4); after the Fall, the Son's immediate response to Adam's confession is, 'Was she thy God, that her thou didst obey / Before his voice' (10.145–6). Indeed, the idolatrous connotations of Adam's love of Eve are subtly and poignantly intimated in the lines following the passage with which we began:

> Adam the while
> Waiting desirous her return, had wove
> Of choicest flowers a garland to adorn
> Her tresses, and her rural labours crown
> As reapers oft are wont their harvest queen.
>
> (9.838–42)

In *De corona*, Tertullian had dissuaded Christians from wearing garlands because of their association with pagan idolatrous worship; Heinrich Bullinger would cite Tertullian's treatise in *De Origine Erroris* (1539), and the English *Homily against Peril of Idolatry* would echo Bullinger.[2] Within fifty lines, this garland will fall from Adam's slack hand 'and all the faded roses shed' (9.893), the first sign of mortality in the poem and a prolepsis of Adam's Fall.

Milton's preoccupation with the dangers of idolatry is not confined to *Paradise Lost*. It is one of the key ways in which he constructed his authorial identity. Achsah Guibbory has observed that Milton's oeuvre is driven by an 'obsession with idolatry',[3] while Barbara Lewalski deemed idolatry to be 'a central concern for Milton from his first major poem, the "Nativity Ode," through many prose tracts written during the Civil War and Protectorate, to his profound engagement with that issue in his greatest poems'.[4] This should not surprise us. As Margaret Aston, pre-eminent historian of English Protestant image debates and iconoclasm, suggested thirty years ago, in the early modern period idolatry 'became deeply engraved on the English conscience. The Reformation made it the deadliest of sins... which no believer could be unaware of. It was impressed upon every individual as part of the faith he or she grew up in'.[5] Protestants would accord Exodus 20:4–6 the status of a separate commandment, promulgating it through a plethora of newly printed catechisms and inscribing it on church walls.[6]

---

[2] Bullinger, *De Origine Erroris* (1539), cap. 29, fol. 142a, quoted in Griffiths, ed., *Book of Homilies*, 180–1.

[3] *Guibbory, Ceremony and Community*, 147.   [4] Lewalski, 'Milton and Idolatry', 213.

[5] Aston, *England's Iconoclasts*, 342.

[6] See *England's Iconoclasts*, 343–79; Ian Green, *The Christian's ABC*, and Tara Hamling, *Decorating the Godly Household*, 43–4.

But does such a preoccupation necessarily make Milton an 'iconoclast'—a breaker of images? Milton did not literally wield a hammer or a crowbar to smash images in English churches, but there is ample evidence of his engagement with the idea of religious iconoclasm in his prose and poetry. The most explicit and sustained example is *Eikonoklastes*, the treatise in which he systematically breaks the potentially idolatrous image and text of the King's book, the *Eikon Basilike*, aligning himself in the preface with those Greek emperors surnamed 'Iconoclastes' who sanctioned the breaking of religious images in Byzantium, and towards the end with Zorobabel of 1 Esdras 3–4 who freed the people of God from the Captivity of Babylon.[7] *Samson Agonistes*, meanwhile, whose protagonist pulls down the temple and theatre of Dagon, one of the gods in the catalogue of idols in *Paradise Lost*, suggests that Milton continued to debate the uses of violent destruction of idols for reformist ends until the very end of his life.[8]

Propelled by historicism and the 'religious turn' in early modern studies generally, in the course of the last thirty-five years Milton criticism has focused our attention on Milton's reception of the Reformation, and on image debates and iconoclasm in particular. E. B. Gilman's *Iconoclasm and Poetry in the English Reformation* (1986) was pioneering in this regard, arguing that the Reformation suspicion of pictorial representations of the divine changed the formerly companionable relationship between *pictura* and *poesis* into one of embattled rivalry, with the consequence that the poetry of Spenser, Donne, and Milton enacted 'a continuous interplay, and the occasional major collision, between strongly iconic and strongly iconoclastic impulses'.[9] Subsequently, monographs by David Loewenstein, Lana Cable, Linda Gregerson, and Achsah Guibbory have discussed Miltonic iconoclasm from different theoretical perspectives.[10] In the wake of 9/11, John Carey's *Times Literary Supplement* article equating Samson's destruction of the temple of Dagon with the act of a suicide bomber provoked a vehement defence of *Samson Agonistes* from Feisal Mohamed.[11] In *Under the Hammer: Iconoclasm in the Anglo-American Tradition* (2010), James Simpson argues that Milton is an iconoclast on a par with the arch image-breaker William Dowsing. Following the parliamentary ordinance of 1643, Dowsing had broken and removed fixed altars, altar rails, chancel steps, crucifixes, crosses, images of any of the three persons of the Trinity, the Virgin Mary, and saints from East Anglian

---

[7] John Milton, *Eikonoklastes*, *The Complete Works of John Milton*, Vol. VI, 282; 414–15.

[8] *Samson Agonistes*, *The Complete Works of John Milton*, Vol. II. For the 'Sea Monster' Dagon, see *Paradise Lost* I.457–66.

[9] *Iconoclasm and Poetry*, 3.

[10] See Loewenstein, '"Casting down Imaginations": Iconoclasm as History', 51–73; Cable, *Carnal Rhetoric*; Gregerson, *The Reformation of the Subject*; and Guiborry, *Ceremony and Community*.

[11] Carey, 'A work in praise of terrorism?'; and Mohamed, 'Confronting Religious Violence'. For a broader discussion of how contemporary writers connect Milton's work to political radicalism, see Nigel Smith's chapter in this volume.

churches, and then carefully recorded his acts in a journal.[12] Daniel Shore begs to differ in 'Why Milton is Not an Iconoclast': 'Far from destroying idols, Milton seeks to capture and preserve them under judgement, investing them with poetic care even as he hollows them out from the inside, thereby refashioning them as the instruments of their own disenchantment'.[13]

The most persuasive accounts of Milton's iconoclasm emphasize its complexity, ambivalence, and the ways in which it is creative in its destruction, fashioning new images as it destroys the old.[14] Yet some pernicious assumptions have emerged from this line of inquiry—the notion that a Protestant sensibility to the dangers of idolatry and an engagement in image-breaking, variously defined, involves a fundamental distrust of the workings of the imagination or a repudiation of all material images, an assumption that as a Puritan Milton 'detested images'.[15] Such premises have provoked varied responses. In *Milton among the Puritans*, Catherine Gimelli Martin finds no evidence for a Puritan suspicion of visual representations of the divine in Milton's poetic oeuvre.[16] In *Milton's Visual Imagination*, Stephen B. Dobranski bypasses the issue, instead shining a light on Milton's exuberant visuality in *Paradise Lost*, and aligning it with the theory of Quintilian and Longinus.[17]

Rather than focusing on Milton's engagement with, and disempowerment of, false gods, this chapter will explore the other end of the idolatrous spectrum, namely the false worship of the true God through misrepresentation or *false imaging*. The false imaging of the three persons of the godhead had been a central concern in the debate on the dangers of using visual images in devotion both on the Continent and in England's long Reformation. It was discussed in the *Homily against Peril of Idolatry* (1563), a key text in the English image debates, and was an issue that came to the fore again in the 1620s and the 1630s as fixed altars adorned with crucifixes and candles returned to churches and biblical scenes, often with a clear Christological focus, reappeared on their walls and in glass windows.[18] Milton, who would attack the ceremonialism of those very bishops at the forefront

---

[12] Simpson, *Under the Hammer*, 86–95. See *The Journal of William Dowsing*, ed. Trevor Cooper.

[13] Shore, 'Why Milton is not an Iconoclast', 23.

[14] For Gilman, Milton the poet is neither iconoclast nor idolater but puts the eye 'to trials no less severe than those faced by Adam, Christ, and Samson' (*Iconoclasm and Poetry*, 151). For David Loewenstein, Milton does not simply destroy the image of Charles I fashioned in the *Eikon Basilike* but, aware of the power of images, instead forges a new image in the *Eikonoklastes*; 'his literary iconoclasm emerges as both a destructive and a creative response to the drama of history in his age' (*Milton and the Drama of History*, 72).

[15] James Simpson finds it 'paradoxical' that Milton the Puritan iconoclast should have commissioned a portrait of himself, *Under the Hammer*, 95–6. In *Glory, Laud and Honour*, Graham Parry summarily declares that Milton 'detested images', 13.

[16] Gimelli Martin, *Milton among the Puritans*, 169–73, especially 169–70.

[17] Dobranski, *Milton's Visual Imagination*, 1–35, especially 8–17.

[18] Seminal discussions of the refurbishment remain Peter Lake, 'The Laudian style: order, uniformity and the pursuit of the beauty of holiness in the 1630s', 115–37, and Fincham and Tyacke, *Altars Restored*.

of the re-embellishment of the churches in his antiprelatical tracts, would have known that giving a material form to any of the three persons of the godhead was an incendiary issue. Yet, in *Paradise Lost* Milton's narrator dares to take the reader to heaven and audaciously to represent in word pictures God the Father, the Son, and the Spirit. Other Protestant poets such as Joseph Fletcher, Lucy Hutchinson, and Abraham Cowley would be far less intrepid, either absenting God from their narratives or else resorting to heavy allegory.[19]

Why was imaging the godhead so problematic? If Catholics, following Gregory the Great, John of Damascus, and Thomas Aquinas, allowed religious images as visual analogues to the written Word with significant didactic potential, Protestants argued that images, while not intrinsically heinous, were dangerous in that they tempted the fallen mind to worship a man-made artefact—a puny bit of created matter—instead of the one true invisible, immeasurable, incomprehensible Creator who was beyond representation. This had the soundest biblical foundations, principally Isaiah 40, Psalms 115 and 135, and Romans 1:23. It will come as no surprise that the most absolute formulation against falsely representing God is found in John Calvin's *Institutes*: 'only those things are to be sculptured or painted which the eyes are capable of seeing: let not God's majesty, which is far above the perception of the eyes, be debased through unseemly representations'.[20] God had revealed himself in the Scriptures, in the sacraments of baptism and the Eucharist, and in his created universe; man's images of God were therefore 'lies', 'fictions', 'imagination', and were to be removed from churches and the home and destroyed.

Yet, the Calvinist repudiation of religious images, what Patrick Collinson termed 'iconophobia' in his brilliant if flawed 1985 Stenton Lecture, was but the most extreme end of a rich spectrum of Protestant attitudes to images in England, a spectrum of opinions that would translate into an array of practices.[21] Cultural historians such as Tessa Watt, Tara Hamling, Anthony Wells-Cole, and Alexandra Walsham have shown that a far more elastic understanding of images prevailed across the long Reformation, one inflected by subject matter, medium, place, and function.[22] It mattered what was depicted, how, where, and for what purpose. A statue of the Trinity was an idolatrous abomination for many, but a two-dimensional picture of Christ in a secular setting or even on a church wall or in a glass window was acceptable to more than just the so-called Laudians. This needs to be emphasized as a way of moving beyond the binary that posits an

[19] Samuel Fallon, 'Milton's Strange God: Theology and Narrative Form in *Paradise Lost*', 41 n. 6; Fallon observes that the Catholic Vida and Tasso had no such aversion to representing God in their epic poems.

[20] Calvin, John, *Institutes of the Christian Religion*, Vol. I, 112.

[21] Patrick Collinson, 'From Iconoclasm to Iconophobia', 22–5.

[22] See Hamling, *Decorating the Godly Household*; Walsham, *The Reformation of the Landscape* and 'Angels and Idols'; Watt, *Cheap Print and Popular Piety*; and Wells-Cole, *Art and Decoration in Elizabethan and Jacobean England*.

iconophobic Puritanism versus an iconophilic Laudianism, a binary that reinforces the assumption that as a Puritan Milton must have 'detested images'.

In order to better understand Milton's attitude to images, it is important to
consider the spectrum of attitudes prevalent in Milton's England. As I intend to
demonstrate, the transcript of the 1633 Star Chamber trial of the window-breaker
Henry Sherfield provides the requisite contextual evidence. Sherfield stood
accused of sneaking into his parish church of St Edmund's in Salisbury in the
dead of night in 1630 and breaking 'an antient and fair' [sic] stained-glass window
depicting God the Father at the Creation.[23] The Sherfield case was one of the more
notorious of the Star Chamber trials, and would be brought against William Laud
at his own trial. Milton was now in Hammersmith, but his brother Christopher
was at the Inner Temple, where the goings-on in Star Chamber were hot gossip.[24]
Like William Prynne, who would suffer so horribly at the hands of this court,
Sherfield was a common lawyer of puritan leanings.[25] In his sixties, he was a
bencher of Lincoln's Inn, a former MP for Southampton, JP for Wiltshire and,
since 1623, Recorder of Salisbury.[26] He had been one of the first to oppose
Buckingham and Montague in 1625, and the historiography of this trial has
tended to focus on its political implications, seeing it as a showcase for episcopa-
lian and ultimately royal control over common lawyers of a puritan disposition.
Indeed, all his judges concur that Sherfield's 'crime' or 'error' was to undertake
reformation without his bishop's authority. He was sentenced to a fine of £500,
committed to the Fleet, and ordered to make public acknowledgement to John
Davenant, Bishop of Salisbury. He died a year later a broken man.[27]

Of Sherfield's twenty judges, only Archbishop Richard Neile and Bishop
William Laud were ecclesiastics, the rest being privy councillors, Chief Justices,
and members of the House of Lords. They were speaking on record in public
persona and their political allegiances were often patent, especially in their
recommended punishments. Nevertheless, each of these men voiced their opinion
on the uses and abuses of having pictures of the three persons of the godhead in
the church, often at great length, which suggests that imaging God was not an
issue confined to men of the cloth but instead of general public concern in 1633.
Moreover, the labels 'Puritan' and 'Laudian' do not do justice to the spectrum of
opinions in evidence. By reading Milton's representation of God the Father, Son,

---

[23] All citations from the trial are from Howell, 'Proceedings in the Star-Chamber against Henry
Sherfield', 519–62; 519.

[24] Campbell and Corns, John Milton, 68.

[25] For Prynne's Star Chamber punishments, see Campbell and Corns, John Milton, 94–5.

[26] Paul Slack has usefully positioned Sherfield within various force fields—familial, local, and
national. See Slack, 'Sherfield, Henry (bap. 1572, d. 1634), lawyer and iconoclast'; Slack, 'The Public
Conscience of Henry Sherfield', 151–71; and Slack, 'Religious Protest and Urban Authority: the Case of
Henry Sherfield, Iconoclast, 1633', 295–302.

[27] See Aston, Broken Idols, 663–77.

and Spirit in *Paradise Lost* in the context of this trial, I hope to make the case for a more iconophile poet.

The Sherfield Trial as Context for *Paradise Lost*

According to Sherfield the pictured window had to be carefully dismantled because

> [it] was not a true Representation of the Creation; for that it contained divers forms of little old men in blue and red coats, and naked in the heads, feet and hands, for the picture of God the Father; and in one place he is set forth with a pair of compasses in his hands, laying them upon the Sun and the Moon ... and the woman naked in some part, as much as from the knees upwards, rising out of the man ... whereas this Defendant conceiveth this to be false, for there is but one God, and this representeth seven Gods ... nor did the Lord God so create woman as rising out of man, but he took a rib of the man ... in all which the workman was mistaken: in regard of which falsifications ... [this was] an abuse of the true and lively Word of God.   (523)

Sherfield is denouncing the craftsman for false imaging. By representing God with multiple fleshly bodies subject to the ravages of time, the window-maker had traduced the invisible, eternal Creator, rendering his wondrous acts of creation ludicrous and indecorous. But it was also a matter of conscience: believing the window to be the cause of idolatrous worship and likely to be so again, he had been impelled to take parts of the window down. Indeed, Vicar Thatcher, a witness for the defence, testifies that he had seen one Emma Browne bowing to the picture because 'My Lord God (was) ... In the Window';[28] another witness testifies that a stranger and reader of Bellarmine had doffed his hat to it.

But William Noy, the Attorney General, dismisses Sherfield's plea.[29] Yes, Elizabethan and Jacobean injunctions do stipulate that 'all relics of idolatry and superstition should be taken away; but every memorial, or story of a saint and prophet, is not a relic of idolatry and superstition'.[30] Noy is making the by then old distinction between images and idols: not every image is an idol. Some images were illustrations of biblical narratives or memorials of exemplary lives; these were permissible. This line of argument was wholly reformed: Zwingli had said as much in Zurich in the 1520s, and the *Homily against Peril of Idolatry* (1563) would echo

---

[28] Howell, 'Proceedings in the Star-Chamber against Henry Sherfield', 531–2.
[29] James S. Hart Jr, 'Noy, [Noye], William (1577–1634)', suggests that Charles I moved Noy to bring the case to Star Chamber. Noy's antipathy to puritans would be evident again in his prosecution of Prynne.
[30] Howell, 'Proceedings in the Star-Chamber against Henry Sherfield', 538.

him.[31] The window in St Edmund's church conveyed a story in pictures; it functioned as a memorial of God's feats at the Creation and a spur to pious gratitude and not as an object of idolatrous worship. Francis Cottington, Chancellor of the Exchequer, follows Noy, stating that to claim that this window is idolatrous 'is as light as to affirm, that Idolatry may be committed to any thing, which for ornament the painter hath made'.[32] Again this echoes Zwingli, who had judged picture windows to be ornamental rather than 'scandalous' and had allowed them to remain in churches in the city and canton of Zurich.[33] For Cottington, devoted servant to the crown, Sherfield's act was 'the act of a madman'; it aligned him with 'Puritans and Brownists' and deserved to be punished by loss of office as Recorder and a fine of £1000.[34]

Sir Robert Heath and Sir Thomas Richardson, Inner Temple and Lincoln's Inn lawyers, beg to differ, however.[35] No, the picture in question *is* offensive, and if the bishop had been told of it, he would have reformed it, says Heath.[36] Richardson points out that the *Homily against Peril of Idolatry* recommends the removal of images with idolatrous potential.[37] Secretary John Coke reiterates Richardson's point and adds that 'our Church doth not allow ... the image of God the Father to be in the church' (546). Heath recommends a token fine of 500 marks, as does Richardson; Coke suggests no fine or loss of office but that Sherfield should acknowledge his fault to the bishop.

It is true that representations of God the Father had been problematic in England from the Lollards onwards.[38] The *Homily* saw images of God the Father as a double transgression—a falsification of his incorruptible nature and a lack of faith in the viewer 'thinking not God to be present except they might see some sign or image of him'.[39] For William Perkins, even thinking in such terms was idolatrous. The right way to think of God was not to conceive of any form but instead to consider 'his properties and proper effects. So soone as the minde frames unto it selfe any forme of God (as when he is popishly conceived to be like

[31] Zwingli, *Eine kurze christliche Einleitung*, p. 658, and *Homily*, 192. For a discussion of the hierarchy of peril encoded in the *Homily* and its debt to Zwingli, see Bevan Zlatar 'Flowers Wrought in Carpets: Looking afresh at the *Homily against the Peril of Idolatrie*'.
[32] Howell, 'Proceedings in the Star-Chamber against Henry Sherfield', 540.
[33] Zwingli, *Eine Antwort, Valentin Compar gegeben*, 96.
[34] Howell, 'Proceedings in the Star-Chamber against Henry Sherfield', 540; Fiona Pogson, 'Cottington, Francis, first Baron Cottington (1579?–1652)'.
[35] Paul E. Kopperman, 'Heath, Sir Robert (1575–1649), *judge*'; Brian Quintrell, 'Richardson, Sir Thomas (*bap.* 1569, *d.* 1635), *judge*'; and Michael B. Young, 'Coke, Sir John (1563–1644) *politician*'.
[36] 'Proceedings in the Star-Chamber', p. 542. Historians debate whether Bishop John Davenant was the prime instigator of the prosecution or whether Devenant's moderate Calvinism made him sympathetic to Sherfield. See Vivienne Larminie, 'Davenant, John (*bap.* 1572, *d.* 1641), bishop of Salisbury', and Aston, *Broken Idols*, p. 665 n. 165.
[37] 'Proceedings in the Star-Chamber', 544.
[38] Aston, *Broken Idols*, 544–69, discusses attitudes towards depictions of God the Father in relation to the Trinity.
[39] *Homily against Peril of Idolatry*, in *Book of Homilies* (1601), ed. John Griffiths, 215.

an old man sitting in heaven in a throne with a sceptre in his hand) an idol is set up in the minde'.[40] One wonders how John Milton would have responded to Henry Sherfield. Like all the judges at the trial, Milton would have condemned the idolatrous worship of images, but he would not have seconded Sherfield's critique of the glazier for having traduced the Almighty into a series of puny little old men. Judging by his narrator-poet's rigorously biblical representation of God the Father in *Paradise Lost* discussed below, and by the idiosyncratic understanding of the theory of biblical accommodation outlined in *De Doctrina Christiana*, Milton might have replied that:

> Our safest course is to encompass God with our mind as he shows himself and describes himself in sacred literature. For although it be granted that God is always either described or outlined not as he really is but as we can grasp him, yet it will be no less our duty to imagine him in our mind exactly as he – in adapting himself to our grasp – wants to be imagined.   (*De Doctrina Christiana* I.2, 29).

In the divinely inspired books of the Bible, the Creator God has 'back parts', he feels 'regret', he 'rests' after his labours. More conventional interpretations of accommodation explained such anthropomorphism as God's condescension or 'baby talk' used for the benefit of his human audience. Yet, Milton concludes by asking 'if God assigns himself a thoroughly human body and aspect, why should we be afraid to assign him what he assigned himself, so long as we believe that what is imperfect and feeble in us is most perfect and beautiful wherever assigned to God?' (*De Doctrina Christiana* I.2, 31). Milton's point is not that God has a human body and emotions, nor that these are metaphors for a reality beyond language, but rather that we should allow the veracity of these images in that they are the images God has used to represent himself in his Scriptures for our benefit. Neil Graves has made the persuasive case that in Milton's idiosyncratic theory the biblical image of God is not a metaphor for a differentiated reality but instead a synecdoche which partakes to a certain degree in the true appearance of God; that God reveals part of himself in his writings, that these parts are true but not the whole truth.[41]

What of pictures of the New Testament and of Christ? Sir Thomas Richardson tells the court that as Judge of the Western Assizes he has seen 'in some churches in my circuit, some stories of the New Testament, some in windows, some in needle-work and woven-work; God forbid these should be taken away'.[42] Christocentric imagery had been a key feature of the refurbishment of the churches in the late 1620s and 1630s. We need only think of the painted-glass

---

[40] Perkins, *A Warning against the Idolatrie*, 107–8.
[41] See Graves, 'Milton and the Theory of Accommodation'.
[42] 'Proceedings in the Star-Chamber', 544.

windows by the van Linge brothers in Oxford and Cambridge college chapels.[43] Bishop Laud had much to say on the matter: 'I do not think it lawful to make the Picture of God the Father: but it is lawful to make the Picture of Christ, and Christ is called the express Image of the Father. I do not mean to say that the Picture of Christ, as God the Son, may be made; for the Deity cannot be pourtrayed or pictured, though the Humanity may'.[44] This was a contravention of the *Homily* which, taking a harder line than Zwingli, outlawed images of Christ: 'For Christ is God and man: seeing therefore that of the Godhead, which is the most excellent part, no image can be made, it is falsely called the image of Christ...Images of Christ be not only defects, but also lies'.[45] Laud's insistence that 'Christ is called the express Image of the Father' is Pauline, however. It is this that gives Archbishop Neile his cue: 'No man ever took upon him to paint the essence of the Deity. The question is whether it be lawful to express God the Father by any representation? I think it not unlawful in itself. The eternity of Alpha and Omega doth appear in Christ, and Christ is the Image of his Father'.[46] Neile is here evoking Revelation 1:7–8 as well as Hebrews 1:3 and Colossians 1:15—all of which do seem to sanction a visible representation of the godhead.[47] What might Milton have said to this? Putting politics to one side, he presumably would have acknowledged the force of Laud's and Neile's appeal to the Paul of Hebrews 1:3 and Colossians 1:15. As we shall see, it is these Pauline texts that are fundamental to the narrator-poet's description of the Son in Book III of *Paradise Lost*.[48]

For Laud and Neile, Sherfield's trial serves as an exemplary platform to articulate their fear of iconoclasm and the virtues of images. Laud is nevertheless quick to disallow the adoration of images and condemns the Council of Nicaea, the key Catholic authority, as 'gross'.[49] Instead, he subtly aligns himself with Luther, invoking Luther or Lutherans positively three times in the course of his judgement.[50] And once again we see Archbishop Neile going one step further than Laud, this time in valorizing the use of the crucifix in devotion. Looking at the crucifix, says Neile, serves as a powerful reminder of our sins and of God's love in sacrificing his son. I suggest that this valorization of a controversial object takes its inspiration from Lancelot Andrewes's remarkable Good Friday sermon of 1597, a

---

[43] See Peter Yorke, 'Iconoclasm, ecclesiology and 'the beauty of holiness', 138–207; and Graham Parry, *Glory, Laud and Honour*, 59–86.

[44] 'Proceedings in the Star-Chamber', 550.

[45] *Homily against Peril of Idolatry* in *Book of Homilies* (1601), 217. Compare with Zwingli, *Eine Antwort, Valentin Compar gegeben*, 119.

[46] 'Proceedings in the Star-Chamber', 557.

[47] See Anthony Milton, 'Laud, William (1573–1645), *archbishop of Canterbury*', and Andrew Foster, 'Neile, Richard (1562–1640), *archbishop of York*'.

[48] In addition to the discussion that follows, see Noam Reiser's chapter on Milton's 'Pauline temper' in this volume.

[49] 'Proceedings in the Star-Chamber', 550.

[50] See 'Proceedings in the Star-Chamber', 549, 550, 551. For Luther and the visual arts, see Joseph Leo Koerner, *The Reformation of the Image*.

sermon that had appeared in the omnibus edition of Andrewes's sermons, first published under Laud's supervision in 1629 and reissued shortly before the trial in 1632. Peter McCullough has argued that the theology behind Andrewes's Passion sermons is that of Martin Chemnitz, a second-generation Lutheran.[51]

Another point of controversy concerned depictions of the Holy Spirit. In the course of the refurbishment of the churches begun in James's reign, baptismal fonts had reappeared at the west end of churches, sometimes decorated with a two-dimensional or even a three-dimensional dove. This had been the case at Durham Cathedral and had famously incited the ire of Peter Smart.[52] Edward Sackville, Earl of Dorset, is the only one to raise this issue at Sherfield's trial: he thinks the third person of the Trinity can be pictured because 'the Holy Ghost appeared in the similitude of a dove', a reference to the dove of Matthew 3:16.[53] Calvin would have disagreed, however, arguing ingeniously in the *Institutes* that because the dove at Christ's baptism had vanished at once, 'who does not see that by one moment's symbol the faithful were admonished to believe the spirit to be invisible in order that, content with his power and grace, they might seek no outward representation for themselves?' (102). Where might we situate Milton in this spectrum of attitudes? Judging by the narrator-poet's decision to give his heavenly muse a 'dovelike' form at the opening of *Paradise Lost*, Milton would seem to have more in common with Edward Sackville than with Calvin.

By the late 1630s, the more radical voices against images were making themselves heard. Edmund Gurnay, a minister in Norfolk and fellow of Corpus Christi, Cambridge, published *Towards a Vindication of the Second Commandment* (Cambridge, 1639), a response to the images that had reappeared in Cambridge in the 1630s as college chapels were refurbished in accordance with the 'beauty of holiness'. Gurnay condemned religious images as well as pictures of princes, animals, and parents, a repudiation of secular images that would extend to funeral monuments in his later polemic, *An Appendix unto the Homily against Images* (1641). Indeed, 1641 saw a surge in iconoclastic publications following the collapse of press censorship. In *A Treatise against Images and Pictures in Churches*, George Salteren argued vehemently against the Arminian claim that iconoclastic measures were no longer necessary. Given the wicked heart of man, idolatry could not be avoided without the destruction of all images in churches, whether graven, molten, carved, or painted. In *The Sinfulness and Unlawfulness of making or having the Picture of Christ's Humanity*, John Vicars denounced

---

[51] Peter McCullough documents the Laudian appropriation of Andrewes's ninety-six sermons in 'Making Dead Men Speak: Laudianism, Print, and the Works of Lancelot Andrewes, 1626–1642', 401–24. For Andrewes's Lutheran theology of the Passion, see McCullough, 'Lancelot Andrewes's Transforming Passions', 573–88.

[52] Aston, *Broken Idols*, 595–604; for Durham's new font and Smart's reaction, see 600–1.

[53] 'Proceedings in the Star-Chamber', 554. For a study that demonstrates how difficult it can be to determine religious affiliation in this period, see David L Smith, 'Catholic, Anglican or Puritan? Edward Sackville, Fourth Earl of Dorset, and the ambiguities of Religion in Early Stuart England', 105–24.

pictures of Christ, the Holy Ghost as a dove, as well as angels in both religious and secular settings. By 1644 William Dowsing, with the endorsement of Parliament, would be wielding his hammer in East Anglia:

> At Clare, Jan. 6. We brake down a 1000 pictures superstitious; and brake down 200, 3 of God the Father, and 3 of Christ, and the Holy Lamb, and 3 of the Holy Ghost like a dove with wings....[54]

Anatomizing the Sherfield trial has revealed a rich spectrum of attitudes towards pictorial representations of God the Father, Son, and Holy Spirit in churches, ranging from a Calvinist repudiation of all images, through a Zwinglian tolerance for images as visual analogues to the biblical narrative, to a Lutheran acceptance of them. By the 1640s some at the more radical end of this spectrum were keen to extend the list of prohibited images to include representations of angels, secular portraits, and effigies, even pictures of animals; by 1644 Dowsing was translating iconophobia into iconoclastic action.

Paradise Lost and Iconophilia

Milton may have begun writing *Paradise Lost* as early as the 1640s when these debates over images were being hammered out.[55] As we saw at the outset, *Paradise Lost* is acutely aware of the perils of idolatry and yet dares to represent in word pictures God the Father, the Son, and the Spirit.

> And chiefly thou O Spirit, that dost prefer
> Before all temples the upright heart and pure,
> Instruct me, for thou knowst; thou from the first
> Wast present, and with mighty wings outspread
> Dovelike satst brooding on the vast Abyss
> And madst it pregnant: what in me is dark
> Illumine, what is low raise and support;
> That to the height of this great Argument
> I may assert eternal providence,
> And justify the ways of God to men.
>
> (1.17–26)

[54] *The Journal of William Dowsing*, 214. The iconoclastic tracts and Dowsing's campaign are surveyed in Julie Spraggon, *Puritan Iconoclasm during the English Civil War*, 32–60 and 120–8 respectively.
[55] Campbell and Corns, *John Milton*, 192–3.

In true epic mode, the poet calls on his Muse for inspiration. Given that this is biblical epic, it seems fitting that the poet should invoke the aid of the Spirit. Which Spirit? Why, the Spirit of God of Genesis 1:2: 'And the earth was without form, and void; and darkness *was* upon the face of the deep. And the Spirit of God moved upon the face of the waters' (King James Bible). Yet, in the light of Calvin's prohibition of visual representations of the invisible Spirit, Peter Smart's strictures, and Dowsing's iconoclasm against all pictures of the Holy Ghost 'like a dove with wings', the poet's choice to give the disembodied Spirit of Genesis 1:2 a 'dovelike' form catches our attention. The Spirit here would seem to be an amalgam of that of Genesis 1:2 and the spirit 'like a dove' that appeared at the baptism of Christ in the Gospels. In *De Doctrina Christiana*, in the course of a discussion which argues that the Holy Spirit 'is plainly lesser than both the father and the son, as being obedient and subservient in everything' (257), Milton explicates the dove of Matthew 3 as 'a symbol and minister of divine power . . . a certain representation of the father's utmost love and affection towards the son, communicated by the holy spirit in the very gentle [mansuetissima] image of a dove' (251). In *Paradise Lost* the 'dovelike' of 1.21 is polysemic. It draws attention to the poem's salvific narrative and God's use of symbols to communicate with mankind. But in invoking a Spirit that is represented as a dovelike creature of cosmic proportions with 'mighty wings outspread' and a body vast enough to sit on the 'vast Abyss', a body that broods and impregnates simultaneously, Milton is also, I would like to suggest, announcing his monist project in the poem.[56] In his pioneering book *Milton among the Philosophers*, Stephen Fallon outlined Milton's theory of matter or animist materialism thus:

> Instead of being trapped in an ontologically alien body, the soul is one with the body. Spirit and matter become for Milton two modes of the same substance: spirit is rarefied matter, and matter is dense spirit. All things, from insensate objects through souls, are manifestations of this one substance.[57]

Where spirit and matter are two modes of the same substance rather than two ontologically separate entities, representing the Holy Spirit as 'dovelike', especially where there is biblical precedent for doing so, is wholly acceptable. The Holy Spirit appears again in implicitly bird-like form in Raphael's account of Creation in Book VII: 'His brooding wings the spirit of God outspread' (235). As at 1.23,

---

[56] Alistair Fowler glosses 'brooding . . . / And madst it pregnant' as a 'Mixed metaphor implying the Hermetic doctrine that God is both masculine and feminine, and indicating a vitalistic tradition'. See *Paradise Lost*, 60. For the different valences of the dove in Milton's oeuvre as a whole, see Karen Edwards's 'Milton's Reformed Animals: An Early Modern Bestiary'.

[57] Fallon, 80–1. For responses to Fallon, see Phillip J. Donnelly's '"Matter" versus Body: The Character of Milton's Monism'; and N. K. Sugimura's *'Matter of Glorious Trial'*.

'brooding' renders 'Spiritus Dei *incubabat*' (my emphasis), the Latin translation of Genesis 1:2 favoured by St Basil and others.[58]

At the beginning of Book III, the poet seeks inspiration once more, and well he might for this is the book in which he will show us God the Father and the Son, and allow us to eavesdrop on their dialogue. The assistance invoked is now the light of divine illumination—'Hail, holy light' (Book 3.1)—which the physically blind poet, deprived of the light of the sun, craves.

> So much the rather thou celestial light
> Shine inward, and the mind through all her powers
> Irradiate, there plant eyes, all mist from thence
> Purge and disperse, that I may see and tell
> Of things invisible to mortal sight.
>
> (3.51–5)

With Calvin's, the English Homilist's, and the increasingly vociferous Puritan strictures against giving a visible form to the invisible God in mind, the poet's request that the Light allow him to see and tell 'Of things invisible to mortal sight' seems audacious. But the wish is seemingly granted in the very next line:

> Now had the almighty Father from above,
> From the pure empyrean where he sits,
> High throned above all height, bent down his eye,
> His own works and their works at once to view.
>
> (3. 56–9)

Here is God the Father sitting on a throne 'above all height' and looking calmly down at Creation. Is not this the heresy of anthropomorphism? Is not this a crass literalization of a metaphor, a word picture akin to the stained-glass image of God the Creator as an old man with a pair of compasses in his hand, the false imaging of godhead which Sherfield had been impelled to remove? The poet and the author of *De Doctrina Christiana* would retort that no, this was rigorously biblical, carefully conforming to Psalm 102:19: 'For he hath looked down from the height of his sanctuary; from heaven did the Lord behold the earth' (King James Bible). If God has chosen to represent himself looking down on the earth from on high in his writings, then, according to Milton's idiosyncratic theory of accommodation outlined above, this is the image the poet should use and honour as true, true in part if not the whole truth. Besides, in using a curiously anthropomorphic metaphor to denote the act of divine looking—he 'bent down his eye'—the poet draws attention to the metaphoricity of language, acknowledging that all attempts

---

[58] Alistair Fowler, ed., *Milton, Paradise Lost*, 60 and 403.

to know God are necessarily dependent on the images intrinsic to human language. We note, too, the poet's wise decision not to let his gaze linger on God the Father. Instead, he moves swiftly on to the objects of the divine gaze—his Creation. Like Isaiah and Paul, the poet knows that God is best seen in his works. And best of all his works is the Son:

> Beyond compare the Son of God was seen
> Most glorious, in him all his Father shone
> Substantially expressed, and in his face
> Divine compassion visibly appeared,
> Love without end, and without measure grace
>
> (3.138–42).

The biblicism here is perhaps even more pronounced, with each line, each clause declaring its firm anchoring in Paul: 'Who being the brightness of his glory, and the express image of his person... when he had by himself purged our sins, sat down on the right hand of the Majesty on high' (Hebrews 1:3, KJB); 'Who is the image of the invisible God, the firstborn of every creature' (Colossians 1:15, KJB).[59] We remember that Laud had used Hebrews 1:3 to substantiate his acceptance of images of Christ in churches at the Sherfield trial. What strikes us here is the idea of the Son's visibility relative to the Father's invisibility, an idea that is given its fullest expression in the narration of the angels' hymn:

> Thee Father first they sung omnipotent,
> Immutable, immortal, infinite,
> Eternal king; thee author of all being,
> Fountain of light, thyself invisible
> Amidst the glorious brightness where thou sitt'st
> Throned inaccessible, but when thou shad'st
> The full blaze of thy beams, and through a cloud
> Drawn round about thee like a radiant shrine,
> Dark with excessive bright thy skirts appear,
> Yet dazzle heaven, that brightest seraphim
> Approach not, but with both wings veil their eyes.
> Thee next they sang of all creation first,

---

[59] The nature of the Pauline 'image' has been much debated. For a succinct account that distinguishes between Plato, Plotinus, Philo, and Paul see Alain Besançon, *The Forbidden Image*, 25–86, especially 81–6. For a reading that foregrounds Paul's visual piety by dissociating it from a Platonizing denigration of the material world, see Jane Heath, *Paul's Visual Piety*, 13–61, 65–142. Milton's antitrinitarianism continues to be a subject of debate. The extent of his heterodoxy with regard to the Son is surveyed in John Leonard, *Faithful Labourers*, 477–525, and Hillier, *Milton's Messiah*, 9–36. For a subordinationist reading, see MacCallum, *Milton and the Sons of God*, 71–9.

> Begotten Son, divine similitude,
> In whose conspicuous countenance, without cloud
> Made visible, the almighty Father shines,
> Whom else no creature can behold.
>
> (3.372–87)

The emphasis on looking and veiling of eyes prompts us to ask the forbidden question: what does the Father look like? According to the angels, the Father is the 'Fountain of light', invisible amidst the brightness in which he dwells, paradoxically discernible through cloud, yet still too bright for the brightest seraphim to see. This is the negative theology of *deus absconditus*.[60] More positively, God the Father is rendered visible in the 'divine similitude' (384), in the Son in whose 'conspicuous countenance' (385) he shines. The Son, we are told, renders visible the invisible Father, 'Whom else no creature can behold' (387).

The hymn suggests that it is precisely visibility that marks a difference between Father and Son. Once again this finds support in *De Doctrina Christiana*. Explicating scriptural proof texts that refer to the Son as 'only-begotten', Milton adds '– not, however, one with the Father in essence, since he was *visible*, given and sent by the Father, and issued from him' (135, my emphasis). If the Father is too bright to see, what does the Son look like? The Son is the radiant reflection of the Father's brightness 'substantially expressed' (140). He is the perfect likeness of the Father, 'Beyond compare . . . Most glorious' (138–9). There is a sense in which the exact nature of the divine similitude cannot be expressed because he cannot be compared to something below him on the ontological scale. And yet, in offering to become man and die for the sins of mankind, the Son becomes part of the material, visible world. It is through the Incarnation that the Son renders visible the invisible Father and sanctifies the material world. After all, the angels were privy to the Son's earlier conversation with the Father in which he had offered to atone for the Fall by becoming man and dying, and where the Father had foretold the Son's wondrous birth, death and rising, and ultimate exaltation. God the Father had specified:

> Therefore thy humiliation shall exalt
> With thee thy manhood also to this throne;
> Here shalt thou sit *incarnate*, here shalt reign
> Both God and man, Son both of God and man,
> Anointed universal king.
>
> (3.313–17, my emphasis)

In the first of his three *Treatises on Images*, the Byzantine theologian John of Damascus had defended the use of religious images in worship by appealing to the

---

[60] Cf. *Paradise Lost*, 5. 598–9. See Michael Lieb, *Poetics of the Holy*, 205–7.

Figure 10.1 York Minster, 'God the Creator holding a compass', *c.*1420. © Crown copyright. Historic England Archive.

Incarnation: 'I am emboldened to depict the invisible God, not as invisible, but as he became visible for our sake, by participation in flesh and blood.'[61] For Damascus, the fact that the Son of God had appeared not as an angel but instead as a human being had sanctified the material world. This sanctification of the material world had in turn sanctioned the making and use of images in worship.

---

[61]   *Three Treatises on the Divine Images*, trans. Andrew Louth, 22.

By reading Milton's word pictures of God the Father, Son, and Spirit in the early books of *Paradise Lost* in the context of the rich spectrum of attitudes to imaging the divine evidenced by the Sherfield trial, I hope to have drawn attention to Milton's insistent visualization of the invisible. What should we then make of Milton, and of Milton's construction of an authorial persona in *Paradise Lost*? I propose that the poet in *Paradise Lost* should be placed not at the iconoclastic, puritan end of the spectrum in the company of Sherfield or Dowsing. Indeed, the Milton that emerges from this study is instead at the more iconophile end, perfectly content to have Raphael ventriloquize Proverbs 8:27 and say of the Son at Creation, 'and in his hand / He took the golden compasses' (7.224–5) (see Figure 10.1).

11

Do I Amuse You?

Milton's Muse and the Dangers of Erotic Inspiration

Kyle Pivetti

I begin with a pun, one that challenges the prophetic persona in which Milton so often presented himself. The blind 'seer', granted divine knowledge and compelled to recite its insights, begins *Paradise Lost* (1667) by proclaiming, 'Sing Heav'nly Muse'.[1] Traditionally, the classical figure of the muse serves as a conduit to revelation, offering insight to the chosen singer. But when Eve hears Satan's temptation at the climactic moment of *Paradise Lost,* another type of muse instead suggests itself. Satan finishes speaking, and Eve finds herself staring at the fruit with something less than divine insight on her mind. Here, Milton makes a curious word choice: 'Pausing a while, thus to herself she *mused*' (9.744, emphasis mine). A long internal monologue follows in which she debates the merits of Satan's argument, wondering about the precise definitions of 'good' and 'death', but the conclusion is foregone. Her musing leads to self-deception, tragedy, and—not to overstate things—the corruption of all humankind.

What does Eve's act of musing have to do with Milton's invocation of the muse? If the beginning of *Paradise Lost* implies that spiritual truth descends from the 'Heav'nly Muse', then why does the poem associate Eve's experience of the muse with temptation and failure? What does it mean for the poet-narrator, let alone Milton, to associate his work with satanic persuasion? According to the *Oxford English Dictionary*, the etymological links between the 'muses' as divine figures and the verb 'to muse' used here by Milton are thin, but in a poem on listening to (sometimes formerly) angelic beings, the questions nonetheless invite analysis.[2] The apparent contrast suggests a great deal about Milton's conception of himself as a poet, one torn between a religious dedication to truth and an evocative—if not dangerous—propensity to temptation, deception, and eroticism.

The wordplay inherent to 'Heav'nly Muse', that is, can tell us what is at stake in the dedication to poetry, and what Milton gives up to become the author of

---

[1] John Milton, *Paradise Lost*, in *John Milton: The Complete Poems*, ed. John Leonard, 119–406, 1.6. All subsequent references to this work in this chapter will be cited within the text.

[2] See, 'muse, v.', *Oxford English Dictionary Online*, http://www.oed.com, accessed July 2018.

Kyle Pivetti, *Do I Amuse You? Milton's Muse and the Dangers of Erotic Inspiration* In: *Making Milton: Print, Authorship, Afterlives*. Edited by: Emma Depledge, John S. Garrison, and Marissa Nicosia, Oxford University Press (2021). © Kyle Pivetti. DOI: 10.1093/oso/9780198821892.003.0011

Paradise Lost. He claims his authorial reputation by attempting to deny the eroticism implicit in the relationship to the muse and at moments of poetic inspiration. What we get, finally, is a vexed association that at once identifies writing as sexualized—indeed homoerotic—activity and as a divine pursuit of truth. To purify his youthful voice to become the recipient of the 'Heav'nly Muse', the author will render the eroticism and temptation of his past satanic, and so cast his own poetic ambitions as potentially dangerous a*muse*ments.

Discussion of Milton's muse have often centred on her precise identity, especially as the figure appears in the four invocations of *Paradise Lost*. In the classical tradition, Zeus and Mnemosyne gave birth to the nine sisters, each dedicated to separate branches of learning. Milton adopts this tradition at the opening of Book VII, when he specifically names one of these sisters: 'Descend from Heav'n Urania' (7.1). Urania, the muse of astronomy, seems well suited to a poem reaching from Hell to Earth to Heaven. Milton, however, goes on to complicate the matter: 'The meaning, not the name I call: for thou / Nor of the Muses nine, nor on the top / Of old Olympus dwell'st, but Heav'nly born' (7.5–7). The classical invocation associates Milton's work with that of Hesiod, Homer, and Virgil, but no sooner does he do that than he differentiates his Christian epic from its generic roots. It is such oscillation that leads to continuing dispute among scholars. William Bridges Hunter and Stevie Davies, for instance, read the muse as three separate figures in *Paradise Lost*, each corresponding to a different figure in the Holy Trinity.[3] John Shawcross similarly treats the muse as 'the spirit of God...regardless of which specific person of the Trinity is intended'.[4] One can see that the conversation centres on Milton's dedication to both classical poetry and Christian theology. He depends on the figure of the muse as a metaphor for truth and insight, yet that muse puts him at odds with the very subjects of *Paradise Lost*, namely Christian teleology.

In that tension, Milton enters a longer literary history of Christian appropriation. Philip E. Phillips sums up what is at issue for the inheritors of Hesiod or Virgil:

> With the advent of Christianity and the decline of paganism, the concept of the muses came under increasing attack, and their rejection became a topos in itself in Christian poetry from the fourth to the seventeenth centuries, when many religious poets preferred to invoke the Holy Spirit, Christ, or God. Perhaps the most famous example of rejection of the muses comes in Boethius's *De Consolatione Philosophiae*, in which Lady Philosophy banishes the muses of poetry for clouding reason, inciting passion, and acclimating her student to his ills.[5]

---

[3] William Bridges Hunter, Jr, and Stevie Davies, 'Milton's Urania: "The Meaning, Not the Name I call"'.

[4] John T. Shawcross, *With Mortal Voice: The Creation of Paradise Lost*, 14.

[5] Philip E. Phillips, 'muses', in *The Milton Encyclopedia*, 250.

The daughter of memory thus transforms into a crux of adaptation and authorial self-fashioning. To become the epic poet, Milton will invoke the muse, but the muse also symbolizes questionable sources, the sort of passionate inspiration that may serve Satan better than the angels. Critics have suggested a number of ways in which Milton is made, in which his authorship is shaped by his use of the muse. In Phillips's reading, Milton strives to reduce the contradictions across his career, moving from the pagan characteristics to the Christian icon of *Paradise Lost*. Resolution comes through balance; the muse retains her classical origins yet discovers new purpose in speaking to the Christian poet of 'upright heart and pure' (1.18).[6] In this version of Milton's career, he learns to refine himself and his sources, never abandoning outright the muse's classical associations with passion, yet turning those passions to the spiritually 'upright'. It is a narrative that Barbara Lewalski echoes in her reading of the muse. She draws upon an allusion from 'On the Morning of Christ's Nativity' (1629) to make the comparison to Isaiah, who must lay a coal on his lips before accepting holy words. Milton thus 'emphasizes through Isaiah the element of needed preparatory cleansing' and the need to 'live chastely and frugally'.[7] Milton will assume control of his poetry, eventually wrestling agency from the muses, but to do so he must prepare himself. He must be recreated, remade, instructed, and purified. In the case of both Phillips and Lewalski, the epic poet is fashioned anew, mastering the potentially fraught inspiration of the muse.

Yet not all readers treat the Milton of *Paradise Lost* as the self-possessed poet who has resolved the tensions between classical and Christian influences. Stephen M. Fallon, for instance, shows that Milton's invocations move 'from prophetic confidence ... toward anxiety and awareness of the possibility of error and alienation', far from the balanced poet who masters the trope.[8] Instead, conflict endures, just as it does in the view of Stanley Fish, who witnesses a Milton facing the threat of powerlessness before the muse's authority. 'Promise and threat are thus indissoluble,' he writes, 'intertwined with one another, and are experienced as such by all creatures, poets not excepted.'[9] The muse figures a crisis of just what a poet does in the act of writing, and what is required of the author to indeed become the author. Milton, I will argue, actively resists the very conventions that he employs, proposing in the process a vexed understanding of convention and autonomy. Sexuality, I will go on to argue, resides at the centre of these anxious deliberations.[10] When we attend to the erotic and passionate associations with the

---

[6] For the extended version of this argument, see Philip E. Phillips, *John Milton's Epic Invocations*.
[7] Barbara Lewalski, 'Milton: The Muses, the Prophets, the Spirit, and Prophetic Poetry', 63.
[8] Stephen M. Fallon, *Milton's Peculiar Grace*, 211.
[9] Stanley Fish, 'With Mortal Voice: Milton Defends against the Muse', 513.
[10] Shawcross writes, 'We cannot help but being struck by the sexual overtones of the metaphor of inspiration' (*With Mortal Voice*, 20). For Shawcross, these erotic elements reinforce the relationship to God. I will suggest an inherent tension to the eroticism drawing Milton's narrator to satanic 'musing'.

muse, we will discover that lust forever lingers in the relationship to the muse, despite what may be Milton's best attempts to live 'chastely and frugally', to attain the 'upright heart and pure'. The muses remain a dangerous presence in Milton's later works; they threaten a return to what may seem frivolous amusements, satanic indulgences, and erotic abundance.

When Eve muses over the serpent's words, she therefore troubles the distinctions between truth and lies, between inspiration and temptation. In fact, when she succumbs to Satan, Milton turns to the language of irrational hunger and eroticism, that which seems far removed from the influence of the divine muses. The full passage reads,

> Meanwhile the hour of noon drew on, and waked
> An eager appetite, raised by the smell
> So savory of that fruit, which with desire,
> Inclinable now grown to touch or taste,
> Solicited her longing eye; yet first
> Pausing a while, thus to herself she mused.
>
> (9.739–44)

At the moment of her new 'inspiration', the very appearance of the fruit changes, transformed by her 'desire' into something she can already taste and touch. This is the condition of her musing, staring at the fruit with desire—and sensual desire at that. It is no coincidence that after Adam eats, he stares at Eve with similarly eager intentions: 'Carnal desire inflaming; he on Eve / Began to cast lascivious Eyes' (9.1013–14). His sexual desire matches Eve's hunger, and the ways in which they turn their eyes to the objects of attention tell us something about what happens when she muses. Eve works hard to justify her newly aroused hunger; she describes the serpent as 'author unsuspect, / Friendly to man, far from deceit or guile' (9.771–2). He is a trustworthy source in her eyes, corrupt and desirous as those eyes may be. The serpent seems to be an authority that would not dare to deceive her. Her mistakes point to the divine sisters dictating Milton's own composition, making him author in his own right. The muses too promise truth to their subjects, but not without the eroticism that follows from the sensual pleasures of musing. If divine poetry requires a cleansing, it also requires the contradictory indulgence of lust.

These vexed relationships emerge with more force when we look across Milton's career, from his earliest commentaries on poetic inspiration. 'Sonnet I', composed in 1629, offers a fairly conventional comparison between the songs of the nightingale and the cuckoo. The contrast, rather than denying the erotic potential of poetic inspiration, reinforces the responses surrounding Eve's fall. The sonnet begins with an invocation of the nightingale, figured here as a spokesperson for love, who must sing before the cuckoo interrupts:

> O nightingale, that on yon bloomy spray
> Warblest at eve, when all the woods are still,
> Thou with fresh hope the lover's heart dost fill,
> While the jolly Hours lead on propitious *May*
> Thy liquid notes that close the eye of day,
> First heard before the shallow cuckoo's bill,
> Portend success in love; O, if Jove's will
> Have linked amorous power to thy soft lay,
> Now timely sing, ere the rude bird of hate
> Foretell my hopeless doom in some grove nigh[.][11]

The nightingale's song inspires in its own way, filling the 'Lover's heart' with 'fresh hope' as night begins to fall, and it sings before the cuckoo can intervene with its own disturbing song. The nightingale offers abundant possibility, promising a future of sensuality and emotion. When Milton suggests that 'Jove's will' has 'linked that amorous power to thy soft lay', he ascribes to the nightingale Olympian connotations and, unlike the Christianized inspirations of Milton's later work, the bird cultivates classical and erotic connotations alike. In fact, the nightingale's song merges explicitly with the muses in the closing lines, with far less devastating consequence than we see in Eve's moment of musing. 'Sonnet I' concludes with a pledge: 'Whether the Muse, or Love call thee his mate, / Both of them I serve, and of their train am I.'[12] The muse delivers amorous potential, just as the nightingale does. And the young Milton dedicates himself to all, seemingly satisfied with the ambiguity in just what the muse will deliver.

The same conceit of the nightingale appears with decidedly opposite connotations in the fifth book of *Paradise Lost*, when Eve recounts her worrying dream—one secretly inspired by Satan—to Adam. She quotes Satan's words: 'Now is the pleasant time...where silence yields to the night-warbling bird, that now awake / Tunes sweetest his love-labored song' (5.39–41). The nightingale still 'warbles' in *Paradise Lost*, and its subject remains sexual attraction, of the sort that will morph into Eve's desirous glimpses of the fruit. Satan is playing the muse, speaking to Eve with what is described as 'inspiring venom' (4.804). He too inspires, and he too sings of the 'night-warbling Bird'; his amorous song, though, corrupts those who hear it. In 'Sonnet I', the speaker commits himself equally to love and the muse, collapsing one into the other. By the time of *Paradise Lost*, that relationship has transformed, and Satan assumes the properties of the 'night-warbling Bird' who fills the lover's heart. And if we remember the conclusion of 'Sonnet I', we recognize that Satan has taken on the role of muse, with dangerous implications.

---

[11] John Milton, 'Sonnet I: O Nightingale!', in *John Milton: The Complete Poems*, ed. John Leonard, 30, ll. 1–10.
[12] Ibid., ll. 13–14.

The contradictions arise in an especially forceful mode in the poem Milton writes to his father defending a career in poetry. 'Ad Patrem' dates to 1638, nearly a decade after the composition of 'Sonnet I'.[13] It begins with an invocation: Milton asks that the muse allow him to speak to his father. He writes,

> Nunc mea Pierios cupiam per pectora fontes
> Irriguas torquere vias, totumque per ora
> Volvere laxatum gemino de vertice rivum;

(Now I wish that the Pierian fountains would send their waters flooding through my breast and make my lips the channel for the whole stream that pours from the twin peaks.)[14]

The reference to Pierian fountains, a site on Mount Pierus and a haunt of the muses, establishes Milton's subject. Milton pleads for a flooding that will permeate mouth and breast, references that bring to mind Eve's desiring visions of the fruit. The purpose here, though, is refinement: 'Ut, tenues oblita sonos, audacibus alis / Surgat in officium venerandi Musa parentis' ('so that my Muse—her trivial songs forgotten—might rise on bold wings to do honor to my revered father') (4–5). The muse partakes in the celebration of Milton's father; indeed, she legitimizes the entire plea for respect. Of particular note, though, is that she abandons the 'tenues... sonos' ('trivial songs') in doing so.

Milton's central aim in the poem is to demonstrate his father's place in leading the son to a life of literary pursuits. He writes, 'Tu tamen ut simules teneras odisse Camenas, / Non odisse reor' ('You may pretend to hate the delicate Muses, but I do not believe in your hatred') (67–8). The rejection of the muses follows certain academic traditions, especially in the Christian contexts that read the muses as unimportant, distracting, and seductive. Milton, however, challenges that account and insists that his father fostered the love of language, of music, and of learning that leads to a career in poetry. Milton thus turns what could be a conventional rejection into a celebration, and, once again, the language of eroticism accompanies the divine knowledge given to the poet:

> Dimotaque venit spectanda scientia nube,
> Nudaque conspicuous inclinat ad oscula vultus,
> Ni fugisse velim, ni sit libasse molestum.

(From the opening cloud science appears and, naked, she bends her face to my kisses, unless I should wish to run away or unless I should find her enjoyment irksome.) (90–2)

---

[13] I follow the chronology given by Gordon Teskey in The Poetry of John Milton, 559–68.

[14] Ad Patrem, in John Milton: Complete Poems and Major Prose, ed. Merritt Y. Hughes, ll. 1–3. Throughout, I employ the translations of Hughes. All subsequent references to this work will be cited within the text.

'*Scientia*', translated here as science, refers as well to the knowledge available to the poet, knowledge with potentially dangerous traits. The figure is '*Nuda*' ('naked') and leans into the speaker's '*oscula*', his kiss or mouth. He does maintain a possibility for escaping her 'enjoyment', the '*libasse*' that also translates as 'taste', a secondary meaning implied by the verb '*libo, libare*'.[15] The act of kissing anticipates the act of eating of the fruit, both of which can entrap or enervate those who come under their influence. The poet could run away, but everything in the verse lets us know that is not going to happen. The young writer remains dedicated to love and muse alike, just as he did in 'Sonnet I'.

By the end of '*Ad Patrem*', Milton implores his early works to survive, hoping that their perseverance would also protect the father's legacy. Even so, the sexual undertones remain. He concludes,

> *Et vos, O nostri, iuvenilia carmina, lusus,*
> *Si modo perpetuous sperare audebitis annos,*
> *Et domini superesse rogo, lucemque tueri,*
> *Nec spisso rapient oblivia nigra sub Orco,*
> *Forsitan has laudes, decantatumque parentis*
> *Nomen, ad exemplum, sero servabitis aevo[.]*

(And you, my juvenile verses and amusements, if only you dare hope for immortality and a life and a glimpse of the light beyond your master's funeral pyre and if dark oblivion does not sweep you down into the throngs of Hades, perhaps you will preserve this eulogy and the name of the father whom my song honours as an example to remote ages.) (115–20)

Milton gives his promise in terms of memory, begging that '*oblivia negra*' ('dark oblivion') does not take over the songs of his youth. Even these—amusements for a young writer—do honour to the name of the father. He calls these early works '*lusus*', translated here as 'amusements', but that term comes with its own particularly evocative etymology. The editors of the *OED* write that the sense of 'sport' as fun and pleasurable entertainment develops from the 'classical Latin *lūsus*'.[16] Its definition encompasses not just 'playing' but also 'amorous play'. In fact, the word blends into the classical Latin '*lūdus*', a term 'often used to denote a recreation chiefly of young men involving physical exercise and military training'.[17] When Milton refers to his youthful '*lusus*', he invokes such associations— that of 'amorous play' between writers or recreation between young men. He begs his early songs to survive into perpetuity; so too will their 'amorous' associations. The muse, whether intentionally or not, has made sure.

[15] '*libo*', in D. P. Simpson, *Cassell's Latin Dictionary*, is defined as 'to taste'.
[16] 'sport, *n.*', in *The Oxford English Dictionary*, http://www.oed.com, accessed July 2017.
[17] Ibid.

The erotic connotations of '*lusus*' are embedded in the models from which Milton derives his inspiration. Among his early Latin poetry, Milton wrote a number of elegies, a genre with a rich literary history, although one seemingly separated from the grand epics he would later write. These poems instead delighted in the sexual, the witty, and the personal. On the classical writers of the Latin love elegy, Georg Luck writes, 'Obviously they were not concerned with great religious and national issues. Sometimes they make a half-hearted attempt to defend their "naughtiness," *nequitia*. They always seem to remember that the love-elegy is a "playful" kind of poetry (*lusus*).'[18] Milton's amusement encompasses his own elegies, and that suggests the 'naughtiness' in these early works, the sexual elements that the muses may try to purify by the time of *Paradise Lost*. Among the authors invoking '*lusus*' is, of course, Ovid, but another poet of the classical period offers more insight into Milton's own amusing ventures into writing.[19]

Catullus is remembered for his epigrammatic poetry on intimate and daily life, and critics turn often to Poem 50 to illuminate his attitudes towards both the act of writing and homosocial relationships of the late Roman period. Catullus addresses the epigram to Gaius Licinius Calvus, a poet friend with whom Catullus spent an evening immersed in the pleasures of wine and poetry. Of particular note is a term foregrounded in the first two lines:

> *Hesterno, Licini, die otiosi*
> *multum lusimus in meis tabellis,*
> *ut conuenerat esse delicatos.*
> *scribens uersiculos uterque nostrum*
> *ludebat numero modo hoc modo illoc,*
> *reddens mutua per iocum atque uinum.*
> (At leisure, Licinius, yesterday
> We'd much fun with my writing-tablets
> As we'd agreed to be frivolous.
> Each of us writing light verses
> Played now with this metre, now that,
> Capping each other's jokes and toasts.)[20]

Catullus depicts a frivolous scene in which these poets work on nothing of much importance. They had much fun ('*multum lusimus*') fiddling with the 'writing-tablets', and had even played ('*ludebat*') with one another's meters. Milton's '*lusus*' derives from the very same verb. These activities do not amount to important or upstanding behaviours; this is leisure ('*otiosi*'), differentiated from the '*negotium*'

---

[18] Georg Luck, 'Introduction to the Latin Love Elegy', in *Latin Erotic Elegy: An Anthology and Reader*, 308.

[19] Luck writes, 'Ovid knew that he would be remembered by posterity as the "playful author of love-poems," *tenerorum lusor amorum*' ('Introduction to the Latin Love Elegy', 308).

[20] Catullus, 'V', in *The Poems of Catullus*, ed. and trans. Guy Lee, 48–51, ll. 1–6.

or Roman business. Yet Catullus still leaves the exchange physically affected: *'atque illinc abii tuo lepore / incensus, Licini, facetiisque'* ('Yes, and I left there fired by / Your charm, Licinius, and wit').[21] The speaker is so insatiable that food cannot satisfy, and he spends the night tossing and turning until he can meet his poet friend again (*'ut nec me miserum cibus iuuaret / nec somnus tegeret quiete ocellos'*).[22] This agitation comes from the playful act of poetry—an act that arouses the body as much as the intellect. 'The word *ludere*', Elizabeth Marie Young notes, 'might alone connote something vaguely naughty, if not altogether indecent, for it could also be used to refer to sexual play.'[23] Their exchange of verse blurs into the acts of sex, a shift that illuminates Milton's dedication to his own poetry. In Milton's exchanges with his close friend and fellow poet Charles Diodati, the muses provoke and prod each other, with the same associations of food, sex, and diverting play.

Milton in fact uses the language of '*lusus*' in a poem that critics have often read in terms of sexuality and writing: *Epitaphium Damonis*. Milton composed the lines at least a year after hearing that Diodati had died, and what follows renders his grief in an extended series of complaints and allusions. Speaking of himself in the persona of Thyrsis, Milton imagines what the nymphs would say to this devastated shepherd:

> *'Quid te, Thyrsi, futurum est?*
> *Quad tibi vis?' aiunt: 'non haec solet esse iuventae*
> *Nubila frons, oculique truces, vultusque severi;*
> *Illa choros, lususque leves, et semper amorem*
> *Iure petit'*[.]

('What is to become of you Thyrsis? What do you wish? The brow of youth is not usually clouded, nor its eyes severe nor its aspect stern. Youth's lawful pursuits are dances and frivolous sports and love always.')[24]

Thyrsis's youthful friendship was filled with '*lusus*', the same 'frivolous sports' or amorous amusements that described Milton's first attempts at literature. With the death of the partner comes the end of youth, and all of its erotic delights. That Milton assigns the same word in both cases speaks to the homoerotic potential in the relationship with Diodati, and what it means that his verse partner has died. If Catullus turned in his bed thinking of the enjoyment he shared with another poet, Thyrsis here laments the passing of the moment, the realization that no verse exchange can follow.

---

[21] Ibid., ll. 7–8.   [22] Ibid., ll. 9–10.

[23] Elizabeth Marie Young, *Translation as Muse: Poetic Translation in Catullus's Rome*, 121. Paul Allen Miller, in *Subjective Verses: Latin Love Elegy and the Emergence of the Real*, goes even further in his analysis of the implications of Poem 50: 'It has long been recognized that Catullus in this poem mixes the vocabulary of sexual attraction with that of literary admiration to create an image of ideal homosocial, homoerotic bonding between two poets' (71).

[24] John Milton, *Epitaphium Damonis*, in *John Milton: Complete Poems and Major Prose*, ed. Merritt Y. Hughes, 132–9, ll. 82–6. See also Blaine Greteman's and Stephen B. Dobranski's discussion of *Epitaphium Damonis* in their respective chapters in this volume.

Scholars have often looked to *Epitaphium Damonis* to illuminate the connec-tions between Diodati and Milton, connections that include affectionate letters and multiple poems delivered throughout their relationship. Although Cedric Brown may minimize the sexual elements in these exchanges, others, such as John Rumrich, discover complicated and at times contradictory experiences of eroticism.[25] Stephen Guy-Bray encapsulates the intertwined strains within the poem: '*Epitaphium Damonis* is a poem that talks about sex at least as often as it talks about poetry; indeed the two aspects of the poem cannot be separated.'[26] Guy-Bray goes on to suggest that physical sex almost certainly was part of exchanges, but this is not to say that *Epitaphium Damonis* escapes without contradiction, uneasiness, or shame.[27] The affection for Diodati forces attention from the serious business of writing, from epics to the sexually charged '*lusus*'.

Those vexations reappear with the muses in *Elegia Sexta*, an epistolary poem from Milton to Diodati composed in early 1630. Diodati had apologized to Milton for the poor quality of verses that accompanied an earlier message, and, notably, this problem is presented in terms of the muses. In the preface, we read that '*inter lautitias quibus erat ab amicis exceptus, haud satis felicem operam Musis dare se posse affirmabat*' ('in the magnificence of his reception by his friends, [Diodati] was not able to cultivate the Muses very prosperously').[28] Because friendly celebration distracted him, Diodati apparently lost the serious effort required for literary merit and apologized. Milton disagrees—uncharacteristically so for a bookish scholar of ancient languages and scripture. He envisions muses who enjoy community, indulgence, and bodily pleasure:

> *Quid quereris refugam vino dapibusque poesin?*
> *Carmen amat Bacchum, Carmina Bacchus amat.*
> . . .
> *Saepius Aoniis clamavit collibus Euoe*
> *Mista Thyoneo turba novena choro.*

(But why do you complain that poetry is a fugitive from wine and feasting? Song loves Bacchus and Bacchus loves songs. . . . On the Aonian hills the chorus of the Nine has often mingled with the rout of Thyoneus and raised the cry, *Euoe*.)[29]

Diodati need not worry about serious study to write fine verses; Bacchus will help him just as well by turning poetry into a pleasure akin to drinking and eating, as if it were not so much an intellectual activity as a physical one. Joining Bacchus

---

[25] See Cedric C. Brown, 'John Milton and Charles Diodati: Reading the Textual Exchanges of Friends'; and John P. Rumrich, 'The Erotic Milton'.
[26] Stephen Guy-Bray, *Homoerotic Space*, 118.
[27] See Guy-Bray, *Homoerotic Space*, 119. Bruce Boehrer, in 'Animal Love in Milton: The Case of *Epitaphium Damonis*', also finds uneasiness in the poem. It is Milton's passion for Diodati that informs his defence of heteronormative marriage.
[28] John Milton, 'Elegia Sexta', in *John Milton: Complete Poems and Major Prose*, ed. Merritt Y. Hughes, 50–3, p. 50.
[29] Ibid., ll. 13–18.

are the muses. This 'chorus of nine' merge together as a group and unleash their songs. The relationship is not imagined as one divine figure whispering to the solitary and purified male poet; instead, the muses link with the Bacchae—the 'rout of Tyoneus' referring to those dedicated to Bacchus's mother—and together shout the triumphant cry, 'Euoe'. It is an ecstatic image, a delirious vision of literature as a group activity pursuing not so much truth as pleasure. In turn, Diodati morphs into one of the Bacchae, partaking in the feminine throng. Milton goes on to imagine Diodati penetrated by the muse of comedy: '*perque... digitumque sonantem / Irruet in totos lapsa Thalia sinus*' ('and through... music-making fingers Thalia will glide into full possession of your breast').[30] In the next line, she is joined by Erato, muse of erotic poetry.[31] The muses take delight in their productions, just as the poet is encouraged to indulge his own delight for the sake of writing. The joys of the body are the joys of literature, and Milton begs Diodati not to feel shame.

Milton frames his own writing as part of the same celebration, with sexual implications. He asks Diodati, '*At tua quid nostrum prolectat Musa camenam, / Nec sinit optatas posse sequi tenebras?*' ('But why does your Muse provoke mine, instead of permitting her to seek the obscurity she craves?')[32] Diodati had originally proclaimed that the muses fled the festivities of friendship; in this case, the muses partake with Diodati and actually draw in Milton's own muse. Literary pursuits become yet more communal, with temptation playing an active role.[33] Milton's choice of verb '*prolectat*' signals the sexual elements at work. Hughes translates the phrase as 'provoke', but the Latin verb '*prolectare*' means 'to coax forth' as well as 'to lure, entice', as in the *Oxford Latin Dictionary*. The *OED*'s entry for the English derivation 'prolectation' includes 'Enticement, attraction'.[34] Diodati's muse, delighting in wine and eroticism, cannot help but entice Milton's. She tempts the gods of poetry, just as Eve is tempted to hear the nightingale's songs or to wonder on the taste of the fruit. Poetic inspiration, at least in this moment, is attraction and enticement. It enables Milton to partake in a bacchanal of literary composition.

In *Elegia Sexta*, Milton does briefly envision the life of an epic poet. Those who wish to write on matters of great import must '*parce... vivat*' ('live sparingly').[35] This writer cannot drink wine nor join into the choral shouts of the Bacchae; he

---

[30] Ibid., ll. 47–8.   [31] Ibid., l. 51.   [32] Ibid., ll. 3–4.

[33] On the group identities associated with Diodati and Milton's relationships, see John Garrison, 'Plurality and *Amicitia* in Milton's *Epitaphium Damonis*'. As in the culminating image of *Epitaphium Damonis*, plurality dominates *Elegia Sexta*, despite the elegy being written from one male to another. Indeed, in his discussion of *Epitaphium Damonis* in the present volume, Greteman finds that the poem 'was not merely the product of private grief [but also a poem that] carefully affirms, reconstitutes, and expands the social, poetic, and political networks that Milton established during his schooling in England and his travels abroad during the 1630s'.

[34] 'prolectation, *n.*', in *The Oxford English Dictionary*, http://www.oed.com, accessed July 2017.

[35] *Elegia Sexta*, ll. 59–60.

must abstain and live with moral uprightness, drinking only the '*Sobriaque e puro pocula fonte*' ('sober draughts from the pure spring').[36] The mocking image offers a glimpse of Milton's future as the prophetic author of *Paradise Lost*. The joyous pleasures of Diodati's muses disappear with the friend's death. Enticement, attraction, and appetite are the affects of Eve, the victim of satanic seduction. By the time of *Paradise Lost*, the eroticism of the muse seems at once enablement and inhibition. The writing necessitates the sexuality of inspiration, and the attendant shame of succumbing to temptations.

Milton also envisions a bacchanal in *Paradise Lost*, and in the middle of an invocation. He opens Book VII by calling upon Urania to illuminate him with spectacular knowledge of the heavens, and he asks the muse for protection:

> But drive far off the barbarous dissonance
> Of Bacchus and his revellers, the race
> Of that wild Rout that tore the Thracian bard
> In Rhodope, where woods and rocks had ears
> To rapture, till the savage clamor drowned
> Both harp and voice[.]
>
> (7.32–7)

Lewalski reads these Bacchae as the 'revelers of Charles II's court', images of failed intellect and debased identity.[37] The community has turned. No longer do the joys of wine and abundance spur the acts of literature; now, Milton separates his own literary activity from that of the Bacchae, and one can imagine Diodati watching the epic poet leaving the celebration. Wine and '*lusus*', it seems, no longer help. Bacchus leads a destructive group to the murder of Orpheus, the 'Thracian bard', and replaces music with 'savage clamor'. In the letter to Diodati—at least temporarily—the clamor did not have to be this way. It was an enticing exchange, shameless and productive, a 'wild Rout' that did not seek justification from Christian tutelage. It grasped amusement in concert with literary production. By the time of the epic, the muse seeks the refined speaker, yet the promise of the throng persists, offering a version of literary production never fully eliminated in Milton's self-fashioning.

At the climax of *Paradise Lost*, Eve muses to her own corruption. Milton, one might say, does the same. He lets Diodati's muse entice his own, to images of wine and lines of verse traded happily and easily. If lust follows, if the '*lusus*' detracts from the serious business, then it is a welcome distraction in the early career. To become the epic writer, Milton tries to do away with the frivolity and to drink only from the purest of springs. We can imagine, though, him hearing the nightingale sing or the muses join with Bacchus. In fact, we saw in *Ad Patrem* that he

---

[36] Ibid., l. 62.   [37] Lewalski, 'Milton: The Muses', 72.

wondered whether his youthful verses would survive 'dark oblivion', whether they would last even as he turned to more serious subjects. An analysis of the muses indicates just that; amorous love and amusement lingers in Eve's dream, a poetic possibility that is satanic, tragic, yet irresistible all the same. Such analysis also offers important insight into Milton's authorial identity; Milton's invocations do not appear balanced nor the work of the 'purified poet'. They are the conflicted writer committed to his serious business, yet wondering whether musing could be something else, with someone else. Just do not mention it to Urania.

PART III

MILTON'S AFTERLIVES

12

Making Milton's Bogey

or, Anne Finch Reads John Milton

Lara Dodds

This chapter takes the volume's focus away from the ways in which Milton constructed his authorial identity, be it in his writings or else through negotiations with the book trade, into his posthumous history. I intend to explore Milton's reception by asking whether he was a bogey for women writers. Or, to put the question more generally, whether women writers responded to Milton's poetry, particularly *Paradise Lost*, in distinctly gendered ways. Did Milton's poetry help to shape the tradition of women's writing during the decades following his death? The chapter examines these questions through a case study of the poetry of Anne Finch (1661–1720), a poet whose varied responses to Milton include stylistic imitation, direct allusions, and reworkings of Milton's own adaptation of the myth of the Fall. Finch's poetry provides the occasion for an examination of Milton's afterlife and also for the examination of how gendered categories such as Milton's bogey, and even the idea of women's writing itself, have shaped literary history.

Finch's poetry has previously served as evidence for competing and even contradictory arguments about Milton's influence on women's writing. On the one hand, Finch demonstrates an awareness of and resistance to the limitations Milton placed on women. For instance, we can detect Milton's Adam's exquisite condescension to Eve—'for nothing lovelier can be found / In woman, than to study household good, / And good works in her husband to promote' (9.232–4)—in Finch's 'The Introduction', an impassioned complaint against those who view a woman who writes as an 'intruder on the rights of men':

> To write or read or think, or to enquire
> Wou'd cloud our beauty, and exhaust our time
> And interrupt the Conquests of our prime;
> Whilst the dull mannage, [*sic*] of a servile house
> Is held by some, our outmost art, and use.[1]

---

[1] For ease of reference I cite Finch's early manuscript poetry from Reynolds, ed., *The Poems of Anne Countess of Winchilsea*, 5.

Lara Dodds, *Making Milton's Bogey: or, Anne Finch Reads John Milton* In: *Making Milton: Print, Authorship, Afterlives.* Edited by: Emma Depledge, John S. Garrison, and Marissa Nicosia, Oxford University Press (2021). © Lara Dodds. DOI: 10.1093/oso/9780198821892.003.0012

Here, as Sandra M. Gilbert and Susan Gubar argue in their groundbreaking feminist literary history *The Madwoman in the Attic* (1979), Milton's bogey is the obstacle that patriarchal authority poses to the development of women's writing, and Finch is one of the many women who 'recorded anxieties about [Milton's] paradigmatic patriarchal poetry'.[2] On the other hand, Finch also responded to Milton as a poet of married love, so that we can also find Milton in Finch's description of an Edenic retreat where she can find

> A *Partner* suited to my Mind,
> Solitary, pleas'd and kind;
> Who, partially, may something see
> Preferr'd to all the World in me[.][3]

As Joseph Wittreich argued in *Feminist Milton* (1987), in some cases *Paradise Lost* offered women readers and writers resources for the negotiation of patriarchal tradition. Finch, Wittreich suggests, was able to cast her 'own hopes in Miltonic dreams', discovering in Milton's Eve possibilities for female desire that, perhaps, Milton could not recognize.[4]

Previous scholars have thus identified Finch as both a victim of and a victor over Milton's bogey. In this chapter I suggest that Finch's varied and even contradictory responses to Milton's poetry make her works particularly useful for a re-examination of the relationship between Milton—both as a source of poetic inspiration and as a synecdoche of literary tradition—and women's negotiations of authorial identity and literary history. During the period in which Milton's poetic reputation was forming, Finch wrote frequently and perceptively about the problem that would become Milton's bogey. In her poetic reworkings of *Paradise Lost* and in a remarkable collection of metapoetic fables such as 'The Circuit of Appollo', 'The Critic and the Writer of Fables', and 'The Miser and the Poet', Finch constructs a sophisticated understanding of literary history that allows for multiple versions of Milton and his bogey. In her printed poetic collection *Miscellany Poems* (1713) Finch engages with Milton quite extensively and in ways that demonstrate the value of the bogey as a critical framework for thinking about her work and, more importantly, for the gendered analysis of literary history. In two earlier manuscript collections, however, Milton does not loom so large, and Finch engages more fully with women's literary tradition and influence. Her references to Milton, both explicit and oblique, illustrate a

---

[2] Gilbert and Gubar, *The Madwoman in the Attic*, 188.
[3] Finch, *Miscellany poems, on several occasions*. Further references in this chapter will be to this edition, cited parenthetically. *The Cambridge Edition of the Works of Anne Finch, Countess of Winchilsea*, edited by Jennifer Keith and Claudia Thomas Kairoff, was not available at the time of writing this chapter but will provide the foundation for future scholarship on Finch.
[4] Wittreich, *Feminist Milton*, 54.

conflicted legacy for women's literary history; neither bogey nor proto-feminist, Finch's Miltons are shaped by the varied contexts—public and private, manuscript and print—in which women made themselves into poets.

Making the Bogey

Milton's bogey began life in the peroration of Virginia Woolf's *A Room of One's Own* (1929):

> For my belief is that if we live another century or so – I am talking of the common life which is the real life and not the little separate lives which we live as individuals – and have five hundred a year each of us and rooms of our own; if we have the habit of freedom and the courage to write exactly what we think; if we escape a little from the common sitting-room and see human beings not always in their relation to each other but in relation to reality; and the sky too, and the trees or whatever it may be in themselves; if we look past Milton's bogey, for no human being should shut out the view; if we face the fact, for it is a fact, that there is no arm to cling to but that we go alone and that our relation is to the world of reality and not only to the world of men and women, then the opportunity will come and the dead poet who was Shakespeare's sister will put on the body she has so often laid down. Drawing her life from the lives of the unknown who were her forerunners, as her brother did before her, she will be born.[5]

Bringing together the ideological and economic strands of her argument, Woolf imagines a time—still impossibly far in the future from her perspective—when financial independence would allow women to define themselves in relation to reality rather than through the patriarchal constructs that have so often confined them. Appearing in both the opening and the closing pages of *A Room of One's Own*, Milton frames Woolf's discussion of the relation of women to literary tradition in multiple ways. In the essay's opening pages, Milton appears as the author of *Lycidas,* a poem preserved in a library in 'Oxbridge'(4).[6] Woolf's narrator hopes to consult the manuscript, to discover which 'word it could have been that Milton had altered', to engage, in other words, with the young Milton in the process of becoming a poet. But she cannot do so: 'ladies are only admitted to the library if accompanied by a Fellow of the College or furnished with a letter of introduction' (7–8). She is turned away by the first of many male figures who,

---

[5] Woolf, *A Room of One's Own*, 117–18.
[6] See Stephen B. Dobranski's chapter in Part I of this volume for more on how Milton sent copies of his work to the Bodleian Library, Oxford, beseeching 'the librarian to preserve his publications' (p. 29).

throughout *A Room of One's Own*, deflect women from their desires and ambitions: the beadle, Dr Johnson, Professor Trevelyan, the writer of letters to *The Times*, a metonymic chain that culminates on the final page of the book in Milton, now transformed into the father of a bogey that shuts out the view. *A Room of One's Own* anatomizes the making of Milton's bogey in order to kill it off; Milton's bogey must die in order for the female poet to live.

For Gilbert and Gubar in *A Madwoman in the Attic*, Milton's bogey thus became a useful heuristic for describing the development of women's literary history. Gilbert and Gubar observe that Woolf's creation has multiple potential meanings. 'Enigmatic' and 'ambiguous', Milton's bogey may be Milton himself, 'the real patriarchal specter'; Adam, 'who is Milton's (and God's) favored creature'; or Milton's 'inferior and Satanically inspired Eve, who has also intimidated women and blocked their view of possibilities both real and literary'.[7] The bogey transforms Milton into a polyvalent figure that conjoins two of the challenges faced by women writers: a literary tradition that has historically excluded women and a powerful religious myth that is used to authorize women's subordination. The bogey is useful as a theoretical concept because of this multiplicity; like Shakespeare's sister, the other great myth of *A Room of One's Own*, the bogey persists because it efficiently describes the mixture of social, cultural, and personal factors that frame the literary activities of historical women like Anne Finch as 'Women's Writing', a category in literary history that identifies women's writing with and through gender.

It is for these reasons that I believe the bogey remains useful even in light of research that has complicated Gilbert and Gubar's original argument. In *Feminist Milton*, Joseph Wittreich suggests that the bogey properly belongs to the eighteenth- and nineteenth-century editors and critics who presented misogynist and patriarchal interpretations in their editions and commentaries. Editors such as Thomas Newton, who 'everywhere insists upon "Milton's orthodoxy"', created the conditions for Woolf's invention of the bogey. Against this conservative, and male, authority, Wittreich arrays a 'radical female readership that searched his writings for arguments against female oppression'.[8] The most useful contribution of *Feminist Milton* is its identification of numerous previously unknown or little-known female readers of Milton whose responses to Milton's poetry, especially *Paradise Lost*, reveal a broad range of political and spiritual positions. A full account of women's contributions to the making of Milton awaits further scholarly investigation of texts such as Jane Adams's fascinating paraphrase of *Paradise Lost* in her *Miscellany Poems* (1734), Elizabeth Bradburn's *The Story of Paradise Lost for Children* (1828), Sarah Siddons's *An Abridgement of 'Paradise Lost'* (1822), or Lucy Hutton's *Six Sermonicles, or Discourses on the Punishment of*

---

[7] Gilbert and Gubar, *The Madwoman in the Attic*, 188.   [8] Wittreich, *Feminist Milton*, 17, 30.

Eve (1787). Shannon Miller's study of Milton and seventeenth-century women writers begins this work by seeking alternatives to the agonistic relationships that underlie most narratives of literary history. Miller shows how *Paradise Lost* is partially made from 'debates over gendered culpability, the portrait of Eve, and the narrative of the Fall' in early seventeenth-century texts by women, just as later writers such as Hutchinson, Astell, and Finch remade Milton in their own adaptations of the Fall narrative.[9]

Milton and Anne Finch's *Miscellany Poems* (1713)

Of the four surviving collections of Finch's poetry, Milton's influence is most prominent in her printed collection *Miscellany Poems, on Several Occasions* (1713). Revealing a poet of 'astonishing range and versatility',[10] *Miscellany Poems* is the work of a mature poet fully engaged in contemporary literary culture. In addition to fables, Finch's primary genre at this stage in her career, the volume includes many of the popular poetic forms of the period: songs, translations, pastoral dialogues, odes, hymns, epistles, and a blank-verse tragedy. Like many eighteenth-century poets, Finch's greatest debts to Milton may be to the companion poems: her popular ode 'The Spleen' responds directly to Milton's *Il Penseroso*, and the tetrameter couplet is a favourite metre throughout the *Miscellany Poems*.[11] In this chapter, however, I focus on Finch's responses to *Paradise Lost*, which extend from the stylistic burlesque of 'Fanscomb Barn' to varied meditations on the characters of Adam and Eve. Engaging with Milton's poetics and his influential adaptation of the myth of the Fall, Finch's poetry contributes to a long tradition of Genesis commentary and critique.

The one reference to Milton by name in *Miscellany Poems* is also Finch's one foray, outside of drama, into blank verse. Finch's 'Fanscomb Barn: in Imitation of Milton', describes Strolepedon and Budgeta, a pair of beggars who retreat to Fanscomb Barn for much needed food and rest. Inspired by the beauty of the landscape, and by the liquor he has been drinking, Strolepedon describes his humble environment in a heroic mode:

> My Wife (acknowledg'd such thro' maunding Tribes
> As long as mutual Love, the only Law,
> Of Hedge or Barn, can bind our easy Faiths)
> Be thou observant of thy Husband's Voice,
> Sole Auditor of Flights and Figures bold;

---

[9] Miller, *Engendering the Fall*, 4.
[10] Backscheider, *Eighteenth-Century Women Poets and their Poetry*, 39.
[11] Miller, 'Yet Once More', 232.

Know, that the Valley which we hence descry
Richly adorn'd, is *Fanscomb-Bottom* call'd:
But whether from these Walls it takes the Name,
Or they from that, let Antiquaries tell,
And Men, well-read in Stories obsolete,
Whilst such Denomination either claims,
As speaks Affinity contiguous –
Thence let thy scatter'd Sigh, and oft-grieved Smell
Engulf the Sweets, and Colours free dispos'd
To Flowers promiscuous, and redundant Plants
And (if the drouzy Vapour will admit,
Which from the Bowl soon triumphs o'er thy Lidds,
And Thee the weaker Vessel still denotes)
With Looks erect observe the verdant Slope
Of graceful Hills, fertile in Bush and Brake,
Whose Height attain'd, th'expatiated Downs
Shall wider Scenes display of rural Glee;
Where banner'd Lords, and fair escutcheon'd Knights,
With gentle Squires, and the Staff-griping Clown,
Pursue the trembling Prey impetuous;
Which yet escaping, when the Night returns,
And downy Beds enfold their careless Limbs,
More wakeful *Trundle* (Knapsack-bearing Cur)
Follows the Scent untrac'd by nobler Hounds,
And brings to us the Fruit of all their Toil.

(*Miscellany Poems*, 61–3)

I cite this long passage because it demonstrates just how carefully Finch has studied the poetics of *Paradise Lost*. Here, Milton signifies as style, and Finch has mastered it, skilfully employing Miltonic technique such as enjambment, extended sentences with multiple subordinate clauses, and syntactical features such as doublets and grammatical inversion. Finch's reasons for imitating Milton in 'Fanscomb Barn', which appears only in *Miscellany Poems*, likely included participation in the contemporary literary fashion for Miltonic blank verse inspired by John Philips's *The Splendid Shilling* (1701) as well as a desire to display her technical virtuosity. As Dustin Griffin writes of *The Splendid Shilling*, the importance of Philips's burlesque lies not in its detraction of Milton but rather in showing 'how Milton might be turned to creative use'.[12] Finch's creative use of Milton's poetics is visible not only in the direct imitation of 'Fanscomb Barn' but

---

[12] Griffin, 'The Bard of Cyder-Land'.

also in a poem such as 'A Nocturnal Reverie'. Praised by Wordsworth as providing one of the few 'new image[s] of external nature' between 'the publication of the Paradise Lost and the Seasons',[13] this 'technical tour de force', a fifty-line poem made up of a single sentence with the main verb delayed to line 47, effectively adopts a Miltonic syntax to new circumstances.[14]

In 'Fanscomb Barn', Finch's appropriation of Miltonic blank verse expands the possibilities of the mock-heroic. Like Philips, Finch uses Miltonic blank verse to emphasize the distance between readerly expectations of the heroic and the poem's humble subject matter. The action of this poem is nothing if not slight: Strolepedon and Budgeta find refuge in Fanscomb Barn, and indulge in food and drink until Strolepedon's extravagant praise of their surroundings lulls Budgeta to sleep in the straw, 'unvex'd with Cares' (*Miscellany Poems*, 65). But though there is humour in the poem, its treatment of Strolepedon and Budgeta is generous and empathetic. Finch's use of heroic verse to describe these humble characters imbues them with dignity and also allows for commentary on the political uses of Adam and Eve as a myth of origins. Strolepedon and Budgeta are able to reproduce a Miltonic state of nature in which 'wedded love' offers the 'sole propriety / In Paradise of all things common else' (4.750, 751–2) only because they are excluded from the social norms that link marriage and property. Budgeta is Strolepedon's wife by the law of 'mutual love': 'the only Law, / Of Hedge or Barn, [that] can bind our easy Faiths'. By locating the Miltonic ideal of mutual love outside of society— in a marriage that cannot be recognized as a marriage—Finch simultaneously acknowledges the possibility for women's fulfilment in marriage and also the loss it represents. Finch's treatment of these questions is light-hearted and humorous—Budgeta is inferior, the 'Weaker Vessel', because she cannot drink as much alcohol as her husband—but the poem nonetheless engages with debates about women's place in the development of the social contract.[15]

In 'The Petition for an Absolute Retreat', Finch likewise adapts a Miltonic vision of prelapsarian Eden to contemporary political circumstances. Addressed to Catherine Cavendish Tufton, Countess of Thanet, 'The Petition for an Absolute Retreat' addresses 'indulgent Fate' with a detailed blueprint for 'A sweet, but absolute Retreat', where the speaker's 'unshaken Liberty' is protected from the 'Intruders' of the outside World (*Miscellany Poems*, 33–4). Drawing upon a long tradition of royalist poetry, Finch proposes retirement as a solution to political defeat. Associating the pleasures of retirement with prelapsarian Eden, Finch imagines a retreat where needs are fulfilled free of the curse of Genesis 3:17–19 ('Courteous Fate! Afford me there / A *Table* spread without my

[13] 'Essay Supplementary to the Preface of Lyrical Ballads' cited from Barash, 'The Political Origins of Anne Finch's Poetry'.
[14] Wright, *Producing Women's Poetry*, 180. See also Miller, 'Staying Out Late'.
[15] Pateman, *The Sexual Contract*.

Care' (*Miscellany Poems*, 35)), and where the bounty of Nature underwrites a state of nature that is not threatened by prohibition and Fall. The speaker describes a landscape graced with 'All' the fruits 'that did in *Eden* grow, / All, but the *Forbidden Tree*, / Wou'd be coveted by me' (35). This simultaneous avowal and disavowal of desire places Finch's speaker in a complicated relationship to the myth of the Fall and to Milton's version of that myth. When Milton's serpent brings Eve to the Tree of Knowledge of Good and Evil, she also abjures desire. 'Fruitless to me', she explains, 'though fruit be here to excess' (9.648), but of course the serpent's temptation ends with a fulfilled desire that becomes the basis of her subjection (Genesis 3:16). Finch reclaims Eve's desire—her speaker 'covet[s]' 'All'—by pre-emptively excluding the possibility of temptation and transgression. Finch's poem suspends its speaker between the awakening of Eve's desire—'what hinders then / To reach, and feed at once both body and mind?' (9.778–9)—and the epic voice's report, 'she plucked, she ate' (9.781). Finch uses Miltonic imagery to imagine political retreat as a prelapsarian space in which desire does not lead to disobedience and disaster but, rather, allows for the creation of space that resembles Eden because it is separated from the temptations of the larger social world.

Like 'Fanscomb Barn', 'The Petition for an Absolute Retreat' offers a reconsideration of Milton's representation of the relationship between Adam and Eve. In *Paradise Lost*, of course, Milton adapts the Genesis account of the creation of Eve in order to demonstrate Adam's fitness and to confirm his social status. Thus, Milton's Adam recognizes man's 'single imperfection' and identifies 'Collateral love, and dearest amity' as the condition of his own happiness (8.423, 426), a judgement that God confirms and rewards. God knew 'ere thou spak'st' that 'it [was] not good for man to be alone' (8.444, 445), and because Adam 'pleased' (8.437) God by 'Expressing well the spirit within thee free' (8.440), God will 'please' (8.449) Adam by fulfilling his desire for 'Thy likeness, thy fit help, thy other self, / Thy wish exactly to thy heart's desire' (8.450–1). Eve's creation and eventual union with Adam represents both a fulfilment of Adam's desire and an affirmation of his self-knowledge.

In 'The Petition for an Absolute Retreat', by contrast, it is the female speaker who engages in a process by which the identification of a partner contributes to development of her sense of self. She asks Fate to give her 'A Partner suited to my Mind' because 'Heaven has shown / It was not Good to be alone' (*Miscellany Poems*, 39). Like Milton, Finch appropriates Genesis 2:18 ('And the Lord God said, It is not good for man to be alone, I will make him an helpmeet for him') for her own purposes. Finch recasts the verse into gender-neutral terms in order to privilege the speaker's desires for a husband just as Milton retains and intensifies the gender specificity of the source in order to, as Mary Nyquist argues, ensure 'that the doctrine of marriage is both produced and understood by the person for whom it is ordained'.[16] Finch's speaker describes a partner who will value her companionship above the demands of the outside world:

> Who, partially, may something see
> Preferr'd to all the World in me;
> Slighting, by my humble Side,
> Fame and Splendor, Wealth and Pride.
>
> *(Miscellany Poems*, 39–40)

In this passage, Finch engages with Adam's praise of Eve in Book VIII of *Paradise Lost*. Adam admits to Raphael that he finds Eve 'so absolute' that he believes her to be 'wisest, virtuousest, discreetest, best' (8.547, 550), and the reaction of Raphael (and generations of Miltonists) has been to deny this desire, to correct Adam's error and to remind us of Eve's inferiority: 'For what admir'st thou, what transports thee so, / An outside?' (8.567–8). As we have seen, Wittreich cites this poem as evidence that Finch draws upon Milton to describe a husband suited to her mind, but I would suggest that, as with the poem's speaker's simultaneous avowal and disavowal of her desire for the Forbidden Fruit, this poem suggests a more complex circuit of desire. The speaker seeks a partner who will not have to disavow his 'partiality', who will not have to insist upon her inferiority. This possibility is not allowed by the Adam and Eve story or by *Paradise Lost*, as suggested by the fact that 'The Petition for an Absolute Retreat' is not addressed to the speaker's husband but instead to Arminda, the friend and feminine principle whose love draws Ardelia from 'Dark Oblivion' and warms 'anew her drooping Heart' (*Miscellany Poems*, 42). Finch turns to the tradition of female friendship poetry, exemplified by Katherine Philips, the poetic forebear whom Finch addresses more directly in the manuscript volumes discussed below, in order to describe an ideal companionship that, for the female speaker, coexists and perhaps even competes with the model of marital happiness drawn from *Paradise Lost*.

Finch's confident engagement with Milton's poetics and her creative adaptation of his characters put into question the narrative of the bogey as a hindrance to women's writing, but it does not mean that we can give it up entirely. Finch's 'Adam Pos'd' suggests that the bogey persists as a function of literary history. What would happen if 'our First Father, at his toilsome Plough, / Thorns in his Path, and Labour on his Brow', were to meet a modern woman of fashion?

> Cou'd he a vain Fantastick Nymph have seen,
> In all her Airs, in all her antick Graces,
> Her various Fashions, and more various Faces;

[16] Nyquist, 'The genesis of gendered subjectivity in the divorce tracts and in *Paradise Lost*', 117.

How had it pos'd that Skill, which late assign'd
Just Appellations to Each several Kind!
A right Idea of the Sight to frame;
T'have guest from what New Element she came;
T'have hit the wav'ring Form, or giv'n this Thing a Name.

(123)

Drawing upon a long tradition of anti-feminist satire, this poem suggests that the foolish and vain variety of women's fashions would overpower the discernment that allowed Adam, in the State of Innocence, to name the world. The Adam in this poem is recently fallen and, as we know from *Paradise Lost* Book X, the recently fallen Adam was indeed able to name this creature: 'Thou serpent', 'Crooked by nature, bent, as now appears', 'This novelty on earth, this fair defect / Of nature' (10.867, 885, 891–2). By giving Adam this quick facility with gendered insults, Milton shows misogyny to be one of the first consequences of the Fall, and Finch's poem, even as it acknowledges the harm in men's attempts to assign a 'Name' to women, suggests its stubborn persistence.

Conclusion: Alternative Miltons and Women's Literary History

In a prose introduction to *Miscellany Poems and Two Plays by Ardelia*, a manuscript collection of her poetry, Finch offers an origin story for her vocation as a poet, though, on the surface, this story has little to do with Milton.[17] Recalling 'some of the first lines I ever writt', Finch describes an invocation to Apollo and the god's 'wise and limited answer':

I grant thee no pretence to Bays,
     Nor in bold print do thou appear;
Nor shalt thou reatch Orinda's prayse,
     Tho' all thy aim be fixt on Her.[18]

In these lines Katherine Philips, the 'Matchless Orinda', is presented as a figure for emulation. Though Apollo warns Finch that she will never achieve her ambition to match Orinda in poetic achievement or in praise, Philips is, like the epigraph from Spenser's *Shepheardes Calender* on the manuscript title page, part of what Gillian Wright describes as this manuscript's 'attempt to write Finch into the high canon

---

[17] For a full discussion of Finch's manuscript and print poetry collections see Wright, *Producing Women's Poetry*, 146–91.
[18] Reynolds, *The Poems of Anne Countess of Winchilsea*, 7.

of English poetry'.[19] Philips appears throughout the paratextual materials of this volume to establish Finch's reputation and skill as a poet: later in the prose introduction Finch defends her selection of genres in the context of Philips's choices; in a commendatory poem by Mrs Randolph, Finch is an heir of Orinda's 'Poetique Monarchy'; and when Finch describes herself as 'harden'ed in an error' by persisting in the exposure of her 'uncorrect Rhimes',[20] she likely recalls Philips's apology for her 'incorrigible inclination to that folly of riming' in *Poems* (1667).[21] The paratextual materials of *Miscellany Poems and Two Plays by Ardelia*—the elaborate apology and defence of her writing in 'The Preface', the poetic 'Introduction' defending women's ability to write, and the commendatory poems that comment on the author's sex—echo printed poetry collections by women of the second half of the seventeenth century.[22] Finch acknowledges and responds to a tradition of women's writing that offers her, on the one hand, resources for negotiating the challenges of writing as a woman and, on the other, a model for literary achievement.

Two decades later, in the printed collection *Miscellany Poems* (1713), Orinda, and the apparatus that connects Finch to a previous generation of women writers, are gone.[23] Instead, the volume opens with a poem that describes a reading practice that turns all women's writing into a singular category. In 'Mercury and the Elephant: A Prefatory Fable', Mercury cannot be bothered with the petty differences of mere mortals, a moral that Finch applies to the publication of her poetry. For friends and critics, gender—'then she has Writ'—may be all there is to say about her poetry (*Miscellany Poems*, 3). In this brief conclusion I suggest that the disappearance of Philips when Finch's poetry moved from manuscript to print is of a piece with the making of Milton's bogey. Virginia Woolf wrote that 'we think back through our mothers if we are women', and when she could not find them—Orinda is missing from *A Room of One's Own* as well—she invented Shakespeare's sister and Milton's bogey to fill the gap. Two of Finch's many poems about poetry, 'The Circuit of Appollo', which appeared only in the manuscript *Miscellany Poems and Two Plays by Ardelia*, and 'The Critick and the Writer

---

[19] Ibid., 165. The lines quoted are from the June eclogue: 'I never list presume to Parnass hill, / But piping low, in shade of lowly grove, / I play to please my self, albeit ill.' This disavowal of ability as a means of asserting ambition is a conventional gesture on the title pages of seventeenth-century poetry collections and is analogous to the citation from Virgil's *Eclogue* 7 on the title page of Milton's *Poems of Mr John Milton* (1645).

[20] Reynolds, *The Poems of Anne Countess of Winchilsea*, 7.

[21] The poem by Mrs Randolph is not included in Reynolds's edition but can be found on fol. 3 of Folger MS N.b.3. Katherine Philips, *Poems* (1667), A2v.

[22] Examples include Philips's *Poems* (1667), Cavendish's *Poems and Fancies* (1653), and Bradstreet's *The Tenth Muse* (1650).

[23] Philips's influence can be seen in a retirement poem such as 'The Petition for Absolute Retreat', but explicitly marked references to Philips are absent. I have restricted my discussion to Finch's differing treatment of literary history in her manuscript and print volumes. For a more comprehensive account of the differences between the volumes, including discussion of Finch's Jacobite politics, see Barash, 'The Political Origins of Anne Finch's Poetry', 327–51.

of Fables', which appeared only in the printed *Miscellany Poems*, in their commentaries on what it means for a female poet to seek tradition, suggest the tradeoffs that Finch made as she sought different audiences for her poetry.

In the 'Circuit of Appollo', Finch writes herself into a tradition and community of women. In 'The Circuit', Apollo laments the death of Aphra Behn (d.1689) because he does not expect to find her 'superior in fancy, in language, or witt', but when he searches Kent he finds four female poets, including Ardelia (Finch's pseudonym), who can compete for the laurel.[24] As Susannah Mintz argues, 'The Circuit of Appollo' is distinctive in its radical suggestion 'that women are capable of multiple and multiply impressive forms of creative production'.[25] Like most sessions poems, however, the conclusion of the poem is satirical. Apollo examines the relative claims of the four candidates, but, recalling Paris's adventure with the golden apple, a choice that led to the 'ruine of Troy' since 'in Witt, or in Beauty, itt never was heard, / One female cou'd yield t'have another preferr'd', he divides the laurel among all the competitors. Drawing upon the conventions of anti-feminist satire, Apollo acts to diffuse women's envy: who would 'be so imprudent, so dull, or so blind, / To loose three parts in four, from amongst womankind?' Apollo's unwillingness to make a judgement reduces the women writers to their gender. Finch writes women's literary history into its own forgetting.

'The Critic and the Writer of Fables' suggests what may be gained and lost by this forgetting. Cast as a series of exchanges between a poet and her critic, this poem describes a poet's search for her place in literary tradition. The speaker, in an allusion to Finch's well-regarded (and Miltonic) poem 'The Spleen', is 'Weary' of the '*Pindarick* way' (*Miscellany Poems*, 162), so she turns to the writing of fables, which promise

> To fill my Page, and rid my Thoughts of Care,
> As they to Birds and Beasts new Gifts impart,
> And Teach, as Poets shou'd, whilst they Divert.
>
> (*Miscellany Poems*, 163)

With their pragmatic outlook on human folly, fables offer an antidote to the fickle power of spleen, but the Critic rejects fables because they are insufficiently ambitious: no poet can 'purchase Fame by childish tales' (*Miscellany Poems*, 163). The remainder of the poem follows this pattern: the Critic interrupts and the Poet-speaker responds to critique by trying on an alternate poetic identity. If fables are unsatisfactory, she will try epic; when epic is rejected, pastoral. Finally, the Critic suggests that satire is the only form suited to the age and insists that, to

---

[24] Apollo acknowledges Behn's scandalous reputation but emphasizes her poetic excellence, a rare stance. See Medoff, 'The daughters of Behn and the problem of reputation'.

[25] Mintz, 'Anne Finch's "Fair Play"', 80.

'move' her readers, the Poet must 'shew us private, or the publick Faults' (*Miscellany Poems*, 165).

Milton is not mentioned by name in Finch's 'The Critick and the Writer of Fables', but his status as the pre-eminent author of English epic haunts this poem about the making of literary tradition. When the critic denies the validity of Finch's chosen form—fables are the one generic constant in *Miscellany Poems*— the speaker responds by temporarily inhabiting different poetic identities, each of which suggests alternate versions of the literary tradition to which she aspires.[26] The Poet-speaker's first choice is epic, though, of course, Finch never attempted the form:

> The Walls of *Troy* shall be our loftier Stage,
> Our mighty Theme the fierce *Achilles* Rage.
> The Strength of *Hector,* and *Ulysses* Arts
> Shall boast such Language, to adorn their Parts,
> As neither *Hobbes,* or *Chapman* cou'd bestow,
> Or did from *Congreve,* or from *Dryden* flow.
>
> (*Miscellany Poems*, 163–4)

The Critic dismisses the Poet-speaker's epic ambitions as outdated, sending her, in a reversal of the Virgilian progression imitated by Milton and other male poets, to pastoral and satire. But first the Poet-speaker eagerly inhabits the identity of epic poet, briefly substituting her own ambition for Milton's: if his poem ascends 'above the Aonian mount', her imagined epic will 'boast such Language' as Dryden, Chapman, and Hobbes, Homer's mere translators, never achieved. But the Critic does turn the Poet away from epic, and from pastoral, while the speaker herself rejects satire, the dominant poetic form of her contemporaries. Finch concludes the poem with a motto that transforms this poem against fables back into a fable and the Poet-speaker's rejection of satire into a subtly satirical comment on the limits of critical tradition: '*Happy the Men, whom we divert with Ease, / Whom Opera's and Panegyricks please*' (*Miscellany Poems*, 166).

The bogey has been trapped in the debate about Milton's misogyny, the dynamic of critique and defence that structures much critical discussion of Milton and, especially, of Milton and gender. Finch's poetry suggests, by contrast, that the bogey remains useful because it enables an analysis of the gendering of literary history. In *A Room of One's Own*, Woolf described Finch's poetry as 'harassed and distracted with hates and grievances', and she laments that Finch

[26] Lewis, *The English Fable*, 129–55.

did not have the freedom to write a pure poetry.[27] There is, of course, a strong irony in Woolf's identification of anger as a source of literary failure in her own righteously angry work. Finch's multiple and contradictory representations of her relationship to literary history allow these negative emotions to do their work, showing us how the bogey is made.[28]

[27] Woolf, *A Room of One's Own*, 62.   [28] Ngai, *Ugly Feelings*.

13

Mexican Miltons

Angelica Duran

John Milton as cultural artefact has been constructed primarily through Milton's texts themselves and by readers centred geographically in England and Anglo-America.[1] This is to be expected, given linguistic and commercial circuits. 'Milton' necessarily changed as he radiated out in time and space. We think readily of the impact of French and German literary authors, critics, politicians, and translators starting in the seventeenth century. Hispano-American contributors, conversely, have been dilatory and muted, but are no less incisive, as recent, if sparse, critical work has demonstrated.[2] Key instances of the reception and construction of Milton in colonial (1521–1810) and postcolonial Mexico provide a sense of the roots of the Hispano-American tradition in relation to Western European texts in the hemisphere. My argument is that early Mexican Miltons reflect and participate in Hispano-America's colonial and postcolonial structures and restructurings of its literary culture.[3] Further, these Mexican Miltons are dynamic constructs with extensions that lead back to Milton's native England, outward to eighteenth- and nineteenth-century England, France, Rome, and Spain, and forward to twentieth- and twenty-first-century Latin American literary culture. Equally importantly, these Mexican Miltons can lead us to new and renewed understandings of Milton's works.

Milton's Circulation in Colonial Mexico

The earliest traces of Milton's presence in Mexico reflect the typical colonial method of cultural and material importation and dissemination. On the one

---

[1] See the previous chapter, 'Making Milton's Bogey: Or, Anne Finch Reads John Milton', for a similar dynamic.

[2] For German and French influence in Milton studies, see Curtis Whitaker's 'Domesticating and Foreignizing the Sublime: *Paradise Lost* in German', 115–37; and Christophe Tournu's '"The French Connection" among French Translations of Milton and within Du Bocage's *Paradise terrestre*', 139–63. For Latin American engagements with Milton, see Miriam Mansur's 'Machado de Assis and Milton: Possible Dialogues', 167–82; Angelica Duran's 'Three of Borges's Miltons', 183–200; and Mario Murgia's 'Milton in Revolutionary Hispanoamerica', 203–22 and Murgia's 'Either in Prose or Rhyme: Translating Milton (in)to Latin America', 279–92.

[3] See the extensive collection of thoughtful studies, *Literary Cultures of Latin America: A Comparative History*, Vols. 1–3, ed. Mario J. Valdés and Djelal Kadir.

Angelica Duran, *Mexican Miltons* In: *Making Milton: Print, Authorship, Afterlives.* Edited by: Emma Depledge, John S. Garrison, and Marissa Nicosia, Oxford University Press (2021). © Angelica Duran.
DOI: 10.1093/oso/9780198821892.003.0013

hand, this is to be expected. Starting in 1519, European books came through Veracruz, Mexico, the site of Hernán Cortés's colonizing efforts on behalf of the Spanish Crown and the only authorized port city in Spanish America for decades. On the other hand, Milton's works should not have circulated in colonial Mexico from perhaps 1707 onwards, although more likely after 1734, and certainly in the last decades of the eighteenth century.

Why this variable time frame for the proscription of Milton's works in Mexico, and by extension Spanish America? The short answer is the Inquisition, but that answer is unhelpfully vague. In popular culture and even some critical literature, the Roman Catholic Inquisition and Spanish Catholic Inquisition are often conflated, even though they are two separate—though related—entities.[4] For the focus of this study, the most important difference between the two is their autonomous sets of the *Index librorum prohibitorum*, the infamous series of indexes of proscribed works and authors. Attending to Milton's differing entries on the two sets of indexes provides us with insights into cultural power relations between the colonizing and colonized institutions operating in colonial Mexico, as well as between the two Inquisitions.

The prefatory material in the Spanish Catholic Inquisition's indexes are mostly in the Spanish vernacular common to the majority of users: local clergy, booksellers, merchants, and readers. The lists themselves, however, are primarily in Latin, which is the language in which Milton's name appears, for the first time, in the Spanish Catholic Inquisition's 1707 index: '* IOANNES MILTHONIVS, Anglus, Hæ- | retic. *Pro Populo Anglicano Defenſio, con-* | *tra Claudij Salmasij Defenſionem Regiam.* | Londini'.[5] The entry appears in the Class I section of the index. As the (Latin) headnote in the lists states, this section is reserved for 'authors of damned memory, whose published and forthcoming Works are prohibited: but individual works [by those authors] are permitted which have been expurgated or else because they seem harmless'.[6] Users who did not read Latin would not have direct access to the definition. Further, users who did read Latin were faced with some ambiguity. After all, the judgement of 'harmless' is subjective. To obviate confusion, the 1707 Spanish Catholic index includes asterisks next to the names of Class I authors whose entire body of work is proscribed. Those familiar with the index would know that the designation of 'IOANNES MILTHONIVS' as an asterisked and named 'Hæ- | retic' indicated that all works

---

[4] For a detailed discussion of the differences of the two Inquisitions, see ch. 1 of Duran, *Milton among Spaniards.*

[5] Diego Sarmiento y Valladeres and Vidal Marín. *Novissimus librorum prohibitorvm et expvrgandorvm,* 1.660.

[6] Sarmiento y Valladeres and Marín, *Novissimus,* 1.1. All English translations of non-English originals are mine, with originals provided in the notes with their orthographic characteristics maintained. For help with this translation from the Latin, I thank John K. Hale. Latin original: 'Prima classis avctorum damnatæ memoriæ, quorum Opera edita, & edenda sunt prohibita: nisi expurgata, aut, quod videantur innoxia, nominatum permittantur'.

bearing his name as author were prohibited. Still, the use of Latin would leave room for error for those who could not correctly link the Latin name to the English name that appeared on book covers and title pages, *John Milton*.

Two external factors in colonial Mexico also mitigated the Spanish Catholic Inquisition's proscription of all of Milton's works: the presence of the Roman Catholic Inquisition's indexes and the changing nature of the Spanish American branch of the Spanish Catholic Inquisition. Shifting Spanish, native, and Roman Catholic mandates, laws, and practices in Spanish America resulted in both the Spanish Catholic Inquisition's and the Roman Catholic Inquisition's indexes circulating in Mexico.[7] Milton does not appear in the Class I 'M' sections in the 1704 and 1734 Roman Catholic indexes issued directly before and after the 1707 Spanish Catholic index.[8] Rather, his name appears as a primary entry in the Roman Catholic Index for the first time in 1758: 'Miltonus, Joannes. Literæ Pseudo-Senatus Anglicani, | Cromwellii, reliquorumque perduellium nomine, ac | jussu conscriptæ | *Decr. 12. Decemb.* 1700. | – Il Paradiso perduto. Poema Inglese, tradotto in no- | stra lingua de Paolo Rolli. *Decr. 21. Jan.* 1732'.[9] The first work is a collection of state papers, posthumously published, that circulated internationally under Milton's name.[10] The second work, Paolo Rolli's Italian translation of Milton's *Paradise Lost*, had appeared in the Class III 'P' section, based on its title, in a 1734 appendix to the 1704 Roman Catholic Index.[11] Class III entries are anonymous and corporate works either requiring expurgation or entirely prohibited; and published translations provided opportunities for the introduction of heretical material by translators, editors, and printers. Neither the appended Class III entry of 1734 nor the Class I entry of 1758 make a claim on the state of Milton's soul.

Monelisa Lina Pérez-Marchand notes that 'the American Inquisition, dependent on the Spanish one and with a similar organization to it, had freedom of action in its dominions, but it was not autonomous from the Spanish one, as it was from the Roman one'.[12] Nonetheless, both regulatory tools circulated in

---

[7] I accessed both sets of indexes in libraries in Mexico City, Puebla, Oaxaca, and Veracruz. Lack of acquisition records for holdings in these libraries renders it impossible to confirm their presence during colonial times, although a number of the volumes possess strong indicators, such as institutional stamps.

[8] Milton's name would have appeared in *Index librorum prohibitorum Innoc. XI. P. M.*, 195, and *Index librorum prohibitorum usque ad diem 4. Junii Anni MDCCXLIV. Regnante Benedicto XIV. P. O. M*, 274 or 291.

[9] *Index librorum prohibitorum Sanctissimi domini nostri Benedicti XIV Pontificis Maximi iussu recognitus, atque editus*, 195.

[10] Gordon Campbell and Thomas N. Corns, *John Milton: Life, Work, and Thought*, 382–3.

[11] *Index librorum prohibitorum Innoc. XI. P. M.*, 2nd appendix, 506. For the Italian translation in the 1734 appendix, see Edward Kenrick, '*Paradise Lost* and the Index of Prohibited Books'.

[12] Monelisa Lina Pérez-Marchand, *Dos etapas ideológicas del siglo XVIII en México: a través de los papeles de la Inquisición*, 49. Spanish original: 'La Inquisición americana, dependiente de la española y con una organización similar a la de aquélla, tenía libertad de acción en sus dominios, pero no era autónoma de la española, como ésta con respecto a la romana.'

colonial Spanish America, resulting in an uneven and destabilizing experience for the educated reading elite and others in its book trade. Mario Murgia calls attention to a case that indicates Mexican authorities adhering to the 1707 Spanish Catholic index in its strictest sense; Charles 'Loret, a young French surgeon residing in the Mexican city of Jalapa in 1768' was 'accused of having Milton's *Paradise Lost*, and tried and punished with abjuration and banishment to Spain'.[13] It is unlikely that Loret possessed the Italian *Il Paradiso perduto*, listed in the Roman Catholic appendix at the time. It is more likely that he possessed an English version or one of the three French translations or imitations of *Paradise Lost* available at the time, all of which were proscribed on the 1707 Spanish Catholic index. Conversely, Canon Antonio Carbonel recommended censoring a French '*Le Paradi Perdu*, de Milton' which had reached him in Guatemala. The canon's censure, based on 'various propositions that appear to favor Materialism and Calvinism', is redundant with the complete proscription of Milton's works in the 1707 Spanish Catholic index, thus indicating a lack of understanding of or capitulation to the meaning of the asterisk in that index or the use of the Roman Catholic index.[14] Also, the poised tone of the letter to his fellow cleric in Mexico evinces the unguarded discussion of Milton's works in the second half of the eighteenth century.

The Guatemalan–Mexican exchange is indicative of the second major factor in the circulation and reception of Milton in Mexico: the changing nature of the Spanish American branch of the Spanish Catholic Inquisition, specifically its increased religious self-determination and cultural autonomy from Spain and Rome. Martin Austin Nesvig traces 'the establishment . . . of local, noncentralized inquisitional authorities beginning in the 1520s', through a growing institution-alization with 'a central tribunal' for Spanish America in Mexico in 1571, then the decline of 'the activity of censorship and the Inquisition' after its 'nadir' in the 1630s.[15] The 'Holy Mexican Office' oversaw a network that extended from the city and 'Archbishopric of Mexico' to all the realms and provinces of New Spain, with the dioceses of 'Tlaxcala, Michoacán, Guatemala, Guadalaxara, Chiapas, Yucatán, Oaxaca, Vera Paz, Honduras, Nicaragua, Nueva Vizcaya, Islas Philipinas sus distritos y jurisdicciones'.[16] These Spanish American branches of the Spanish Inquisition communicated with each other with greater speed and many more shared assumptions than with the Ibero-Spanish source. This combined with the circulation of two at times conflicting sets of Western European-based indexes to increase the notion and practices of independence among Spanish American inquisitorial members and readers. Further, Nesvig notes that, through the

---

[13] Murgia, 'Revolutionary', 204.

[14] Pérez-Marchand, 111. Spanish original: 'varias proposiciones qe. al paracer favorecen al Materialismo y al Calvinismo'.

[15] Martin Austin Nesvig, *Ideology and Inquisition: The World of the Censors in Early Mexico*, 10.

[16] Pérez-Marchand, 49. Spanish original: 'El Santo Oficio Mexicano'; 'arzobispado de México'.

mid-seventeenth century, 'overall there was no vigorous prosecution of the sole act of possessing prohibited books. Indeed, there were only eight trials in over a century for the specific crime of possessing prohibited books'; yet 'the mere threat of excommunication for possessing a book banned by the Inquisition was enough: Books were relinquished, though grudgingly and people came forth to deposit them with their local comisario'.[17] Pérez-Marchand draws attention to a change in reader reception by the second half of the eighteenth century, with book merchants, clerics, government officials, military, shipmen, doctors, and cooks finding themselves 'in a dramatic spiritual tension, taken between curiosity for the new, sympathy with modern ideas, and the weight of a religious tradition that put brakes on those tendencies'.[18] Her study of Mexico's National Archive of the Inquisition indicates that French works were increasingly the source of those fresh, modern ideas and moved readers to overcome misgivings. Manuel Brioso y Candiani notes independent Mexican reader reception reflected in private library holdings as well: inquisitorial 'prohibitions did not reach individuals in Mexico's high society and . . . were more theoretical than practiced. The elevated classes took little note of the Holy Office and at times almost openly derided it. In their libraries were to be found the works of the major French and English philosophers, the same with the large number of political writings, even those that incited a revolutionary spirit at the end of the eighteenth century.'[19]

The marked Francophilia in Spanish America in the decades surrounding Mexico's independence in 1821 would have buoyed Miltonic reception in Mexico, through France's Miltonophilia. The holdings of two notable Mexican libraries, the Biblioteca Palafoxiana in Puebla and the State Library of Oaxaca, reflect the active, welcome importation of select sets of Western European literature replacing a primarily passive, Spanish cultural colonization during Mexico's transition to national independence.[20] It is worth mentioning that these libraries also possess copies of the indexes of both the Spanish and Roman Catholic Inquisitions.

---

[17] Nesvig, 231.

[18] Pérez-Marchand, 127–36, 146. Spanish original: 'en una tensión espiritual dramática, cogido entre la curiosidad por lo nuevo, la simpatía hacia las ideas modernas, y el peso de la tradición religiosa que le imponía frenos a esas tendencias'.

[19] Manuel Brioso y Candiani. *Ensayo de una historia científica acerca de Oaxaca*, 56. Spanish original: 'no alcanzaba a las personas de la alta sociedad mexicana y . . . las prohibiciones lo eran más en la teoría que en la práctica. Las clases elevadas se cuidaban poco del Santo Oficio y aun lo despreciaban casi abiertamente. En sus bibliotecas se hallaban las obras de los gran filósofos franceses e ingleses, los mismo que gran número de escritos políticos, aun los que el genio revolucionario esparcía a fines del siglo XVIII.'

[20] For a brief history of Oaxacan libraries, see Carmen Vázquez Mantecón, *Historia de las bibliotecas en Oaxaca*. For the colonial Hispano-American book trade, see Irving A. Leonard's stalwart *Books of the Brave, Being an Account of Men in the Spanish Conquest and Settlement of the Sixteenth-century New World*.

The Biblioteca Palafoxiana is the Americas' first major public library, 'founded in 1646 through the donation of 5,000 books from the private collection of its namesake Juan Palafox y Mendoza, bishop of Puebla from 1640 to 1655 and viceroy of New Spain' and reaching its estimated holdings in 2003 of 41,000 volumes acquired primarily 'after the governmental Reform of President Benito Juarez (1854–76)' and 'through the relocation, in 1773, of the libraries of five Jesuit colleges, upon the ouster of the Jesuits'.[21] Pre-independence works include the famous French imitation of Milton's *Areopagitica* (1644), *Sur la liberté de la presse: imité de l'anglois, de Milton* (1789) by Mirabeau, and two French translations of *Paradise Lost* (1667), from the complete works of Jacques Delille (1805) and of Louis Racine (1808). The next three works date from after Miguel Hidalgo y Costilla's Grito de Dolores, 16 September 1810, which spurred the Mexican Revolution, and come from various Western European countries: the Spanish verse translation of *Paradise Lost* by the Ibero-Spanish politician Benito Ramón de Hermida (Madrid, 1814), the English *The Poetical Works of John Milton* (Leipzig, 1827), and Chateaubriand's French translation of *Paradise Lost* (Paris, 1841).[22]

The francophone presence of Milton holdings is repeated in the State Library of Oaxaca, a hotbed of Mexico's liberal movement in the nineteenth century. The library's special collection of the Institute of Arts and Sciences (established in 1826), among the first public schools in Mexico, includes French originals and Spanish translations of French works that circulated Milton's works and figure, such as Spanish translations of Chateaubriand's *Essay on English Literature* from 1857 and *The Genius of Christianity* from 1863. The library's special collection of Benito Juárez, the much-loved Oaxacan-born president, includes French originals that laud Milton as a revolutionary thinker, such as P. J. Proudhon's *Système des contradictions économiques ou philosophie de la misère* (Paris, 1850) and Edgar Quinet's *Oeuvres Complètes* (Paris, 1857). It is worth mentioning that the book Juárez was reading in the days preceding his death was the French *Cours d'histoire des législations comparées* (1838) by Jean Louis Eugène Lerminier.[23] Further, Milton also appears in the State Library's general collection, for example as a minor character in its two French editions of Victor Hugo's play *Cromwell* (Paris, 1840; Paris, 1881) and in the Spanish translations of the French originals *Los cuatro Estuardos* (Madrid, 1854) and *Historia de la república de Cromwell* (Madrid, 1858). These last two works accurately indicate the overlap of Ibero-Spanish and Mexican Francophilia.

---

[21] Angelica Duran, 'Milton in Puebla, Mexico'; Jacques Lafaye, *Albores de la imprenta: el libro en España y Portugal y sus posesiones de ultramar (siglos XV-XVI)*, insert between pp. 96 and 97. Spanish original: 'mediante la traslación, en 1773, de las bibliotecas de cinco colegios de jesuitas, a raíz de la compañía de Jesús'.

[22] Duran, 'Milton in Puebla'.

[23] The book is on permanent display at the Homage Precinct of Benito Juárez in the National Library of Mexico.

Milton's Translation in Postcolonial Mexico

Milton circulated minimally in colonial Mexico as an English author whose works in Latin and Italian translation in particular were targeted by the Spanish and Roman Catholic Inquisitions. Then, Mexican libraries reflect Milton's increased presence in light of his French vogue in the years surrounding Mexico's independence. Among the active contributions to the construction of Milton that start emerging in Mexico is the first hispanophone translation of *Paradise Lost* published in Latin America. The paratexts of this postcolonial work articulate clearly the sociopolitical elements at the forefront in the circulation of Milton in independent Mexico, and the translation itself displays with equal clarity the religious elements. Perforce, *El Paraíso perdido* (1858), translated by the Mexican poet Francisco Granados Maldonado and published by the oft-lauded Mexico City printing house of Ignacio Cumplido, ultimately relies on Western European colonial systems for the Spanish language into which it was translated, the English work itself, and the multinational European printing press introduced to Mexico City in the sixteenth century. What is new and engaging in this work is its eschewal of a primarily subordinate status within the hierarchical cultural system. Instead, it advertises and enacts an active creation of a national Mexican literature situated within a transatlantic literary network and Christian religious structure.[24]

In the prefatory paratexts of *El Paraíso perdido*, Granados exhibits and recommends to 'my beloved compatriots' unmediated cultural relations with Western Europe (he does not mention the US or other Latin American countries).[25] The title page of *El Paraíso perdido* announces the work to be a primary translation, 'Translated from the English', rather than a secondary translation from one of the three Ibero-Spanish translations or fifteen French translations and imitations published by 1858.[26] In the prefatory 'Dedicatory', Granados laments that 'among us, very few have dedicated themselves to the study of foreign literature', that 'some of our young compatriots' know 'more of the French than of their own language', and that they possess little knowledge of 'German, English, and Italian literature'.[27] Further, the prefatory 'To the Readers' situates his Mexican

---

[24] For a contrastive and marked use of the humility topoi in a colonial Mexican translation of another epic, see Publio Virgilio Maron, *Traduccion de las obras de el príncipe de los poetas latinos Publio Virgilio Maron a metro castellano.*

[25] John Milton, *El Paraíso perdido*, ed. and trans. Francisco Granados Maldonado, XX. Spanish original: 'mis benévolos compatriotas'.

[26] Milton, *El Paraíso perdido*, trans. Granados Maldonado, title page. For a list of French translations and imitations, see Tournu's '"The French Connection" among French Translations of Milton and within du Bocage's *Paradis terrestre*', 160–2, and, for a list of Ibero-Spanish translations, see Angelica Duran's '*Paradise Lost* in Spanish Translation and as World Literature', 276–7. Spanish original: 'Traducido del Inglés'.

[27] Milton, *El Paraíso perdido*, trans. Granados Maldonado, I–II. Spanish original: 'Dedicatorio'; 'entre nosotros son muy pocos los que se han dedicado al estudio de las literaturas estrangeras'; 'algunos de nuestros jóvenes compatriotas'; 'mas de la francesa que la de su lengua'; 'literatura alemana, inglesa, é italiana'.

translation among a primarily English and French republic of letters that includes John Dryden, Joseph Addison, and chief figures in the French reception and translation of Milton's works, 'Chateaubriand', 'Dupré, Saint-Maure, Racini', and 'Mommeron'.[28] The paratext also gives rise to a claim to be made for Granados's own limited exposure to Ibero-Spanish literary culture. Granados states, 'Among us, I do not remember anyone having occupied himself with a work of this type' and presents himself 'as the first who claims to have passed Milton's beauties into the Spanish language', suggesting his ignorance of the three Ibero-Spanish translations available by 1858.[29]

Granados's claim for the primacy of his translation coordinates with the national claims he stakes on the Spanish language and the development of his personal 'effective post-colonial voice', to use Bill Ashcroft and Helen Tiffan's salient term.[30] Granados's postcolonial Mexican voice positions itself in direct conversation with the English and French literary canons that enjoyed the greatest international status at the time, in contrast to the Spanish literary canon that Mexican anthologies often depict as bygone, at its most powerful during its *Siglo de Oro*, or Golden Age, from the early sixteenth through mid-seventeenth centuries. In the prefatory paratexts, Granados claims the Spanish language, unobtrusively and thus powerfully, as 'their [fellow Mexicans'] own language' ('su lengua')—and later 'our language' ('nuestra lengua')—and ties language to nation-building and literary art, as do Dante's *De vulgari eloquentia*, Milton's prefatory 'The Verse' added to the 1674 edition of *Paradise Lost*, and the paratexts of myriad translations.[31] Murgia notes Granados's 'cultural and nationalistic – if also somewhat romanticised – purposes', in his preface to the translation: 'the yearning I have that the desire to know the works of the genius be awakened among us, so that, without neglecting our tongue, we may seek to enrich our [Mexican] literature'.[32] Granados avers that 'it cannot be denied either that such a national literature, with the awareness of foreign ones, can acquire new expressions and, without altering anything of the language, enrich itself and make itself wise; and a wise literature is one of the greatest advantages that a country can have'.[33]

---

[28] Milton, *El Paraíso perdido*, trans. Granados Maldonado, IV, V. For a thorough discussion of how Addison's writings contributed to Milton's afterlife in print, see the essay by Thomas Corns in this volume. Spanish original: 'A los lectores'.

[29] Milton, *El Paraíso perdido*, trans. Granados Maldonado, IV. Spanish original: 'Entre nosotros, no recuerdo que alguno se haya ocupado de un trabajo de esta naturaleza'; 'como el primero que pretenda haber hecho pasar à la lengua española las bellezas de Milton'.

[30] Bill Ashcroft and Helen Tiffan. *The Empire Strikes Back*, 7.

[31] For a sampling of these paratexts, see Lawrence Venuti, ed., *The Translation Studies Reader*.

[32] Murgia, 'Revolutionary', 206.

[33] Milton, *El Paraíso perdido*, trans. Granados Maldonado, II. Other nineteenth-century Mexicans, such as José Vasconcelos, sought to promote the development of Mexican literature in indigenous languages. For the choice of native and self-authorized languages among the 'Themes of Resistance Culture', see Edward Said's *Culture and Imperialism*, 209–20. Spanish original: 'no puede negarse

The paratexts of *El Paraíso perdido* also reflect a Christianity inflected at times with Catholicism, in line with the plurality of Catholicisms evinced by the inquisitorial indexes and their reception. In 'To the Readers', Granados praises Milton's choice of religious topic as the 'most worthy..., elevated and sublime'. In his three-page 'Hymn of Thanksgiving, from the Translator to God' nestled between the 344-page translation and 107-page 'Notas de Addison', Granados extols his access to a glorious vision of Christianity initiated by Milton and abetted by God: 'From the immortal Milton, harmonies / Awakened my agitated spirit / And I was able – oh, God! – then with your help / To interpret the Glory of the angels.'[34] Granados's translation itself reinforces this Christian vision in myriad instances, such as in the use of 'Holy / sainted muse!' ('¡Musa santa!'), for the personal pronoun 'Thou' referring to 'Urania' (*PL* 7.9, 7.1).[35] Granados's heavy hand here contrasts with Milton's refined balancing of classical and Judaeo-Christian traditions in his use of terms with inclusive connotations such as 'Heav'nly Muse' (*PL* 1.6), which Granados translates accurately as 'Musa celestial' early on in the epic.[36]

Granados's ecumenism also involves realigning Milton's more radical representations of the Son. In the preface, Granados specifies 'the Messiah, the Son of God, who is God himself', in contradistinction to Milton's erasure of the coexistence of God the Father and Son.[37] He is also more emphatic in depicting Jewish figures as 'shadowy types to truth' (*PL* 12.303) in the archangel Michael's descriptions of 'Sainted Moses' and Joshua, 'Precursor of *the* Jesus so long awaited by the people. / From *the* Jesus who will open to humans / The desired port to the holy homeland'.[38] Milton's typology is firm but light-handed in calling attention to the Hebrew-named 'Joshua whom the Gentiles Jesus call' (*PL* 12.310), the Greek equivalent, compared to Granados's. In Granados's translation, 'Jesus' refers only to the Messiah and is preceded by the article 'el', as emphasized in my English translation. In nineteenth-century Spanish, the article is used as an honorific, as is

tampoco que esa literatura nacional, con el conocimiento de las estrañas, puede adquirir nuevos giros y sin alterar en nada el idioma, enriquecerse y hacerse sábia; y una literatura sábia es una de las mayores ventajas que puede tener un pais.'

[34] Milton, *El Paraíso perdido*, trans. Granados Maldonado, V, 345, 346. Spanish original: 'mas digno... elevado y sublime'; 'Himno de gracias, del traductor a Dios'; 'De Milton inmortal las armonias / Despertaron mi espíritu abatido, / Y pude ¡oh Dios! entónces con tu ayuda, / Interpretar la Gloria de los ángeles'.
[35] Milton, *El Paraíso perdido*, trans. Granados Maldonado, 191. All English quotations of Milton's poetry are from John Milton, *The Complete Poems*, ed. John Leonard, and are cited parenthetically in the text.
[36] Milton, *El Paraíso perdido*, trans. Granados Maldonado, 1.
[37] Milton, *El Paraíso perdido*, trans. Granados Maldonado, VII. Spanish original: 'el Mesías, el Hijo de Dios, que es Dios mismo'.
[38] Milton, *El Paraíso perdido*, trans. Granados Maldonado, 335. Spanish original: 'Moises el Santo'; 'Precursor del Jesus que ansían las gentes. / Del Jesus que abrirá á los humanos / El puerto ansiado de la patria santa'.

still the case in English and Spanish with *the* Messiah. Granados's translation is slightly shorter than Milton's original; thus Granados's expansion from sixteen to twenty-one lines of Milton's famously brief mention of the First Coming of Jesus shortly after this passage (*PL* 12.356–71) indicates yet another instance of what Granados describes in the opening paratexts as 'licenses' taken 'to render the nature of the English language, and the character of ours'.[39]

Granados's translational licences sometimes spill into Catholicizing. After translating Milton's scene (*PL* 12.413–20) of Christ's 'cruel death' on the 'shameful cross' with fidelity, Granados has Adam reinforce the Christian doctrine of a 'sublime Redeemer' conceived 'by the pure workings / Of the Holy Spirit' and has Michael sanction future displays of the adoration of the cross, anathema to Milton the author of *Paradise Lost* and *Eikonoklastes* (*Iconoclast*): 'People by the thousands convinced / Will adore the cross, and before the altars / Of Christianity.'[40] Granados's regular practice of omitting, reducing, and replacing classical allusions also serves to prioritize Catholic elements, as at the start of Book 11. Milton likens Adam and Eve's prayer of repentance for their sin of eating of the Tree of Knowledge to 'th' ancient pair / In fables old, less ancient yet than these, / Deucalion and chaste Pyrrha', which 'then clad / With incense, where the golden altar fumed, / By their great Intercessor, came in sight / Before the Father's throne: them the glad Son / Presenting, thus to intercede began' (*PL* 11.10–12, 17–21). Granados replaces the allusion to the story from Ovid's *Metamorphoses* with a heavy-handed reference to the pope:

> their prayer rises, traversing
> The camps of light, to the august throne,
> At the temple in which the supreme pontiff,
> The happy mediator, God's son,
> Above the gold altar amid the perfume,
> From the eternal incense of the archangels,
> Receives it and takes it to the foot
> Of the Increating being, and says to him as follows...[41]

Granados imitates Milton's practice of coinage with 'Increating being' ('Increador') and imitates equally his religious independence, albeit in another

---

[39] Milton, *El Paraíso perdido*, trans. Granados Maldonado, 338, XX. Spanish original: 'licencias'; 'facilitar la índole de la lengua iglesa, y el carácter de la nuestra'.

[40] Milton, *El Paraíso perdido*, trans. Granados Maldonado, 337, 338, 340. Spanish original: 'muerte cruel'; 'afrentosa. cruz'; 'el Redentor sublime'; 'por obra pura / Del Espíritu Santo'; 'Los pueblos á millares convencidos / Adorarán la cruz, y ante las aras / Del cristianismo'.

[41] Milton, *El Paraíso perdido*, trans. Granados Maldonado, 299. Spanish original: 'sube su oracion atravesando / Los campos de la luz, al sólio augusto, / Al templo en que el pontífice supremo, / El mediador feliz, de Dios el hijo, / Sobre el altar de oro entre el perfume, / Del incienso eternal de los arcángeles, / La recibe y la lleva ante las plantas / Del Increador ser, y así le dice'.

direction. Granados's alignment of the Son with the pope rather than St Peter is radical even within Catholicism.

Despite Granados's stated hopes and active engagement with the epic and despite the prestige of the Cumplido press, the translation never gained even moderate circulation in Mexico, as is the case with all but two of the twenty-three hispanophone translations published between 1812 and 2005.[42] Its circulation, however, has been substantial in another sense: Harvard possesses a copy, a 1929 bequeathal from a memorial fund of the Harvard professor and US Hispanist Henry Wadsworth Longfellow (1807–82), and the University of Texas at Austin has in its circulating library the copy that once belonged to the Zacatecan Genaro García (1867–1925), whose many accomplishments include being Director of Mexico's National Museum of History, Archaeology, and Ethnology. These holdings indicate that, during at least its first century of circulation, Granados's translation gained the appreciation of key leaders in the formation of the canon in the Americas and, especially with Longfellow, internationally.

Hispanophone Miltons in Milton Studies

When his works and fame arrived in Hispano-America, Milton resonated anew yet once more, in low yet powerful tones. In eighteenth-century Mexico, Milton was not a fixed figure of heresy given the inclusion of his name or his works' titles in indexes inherited from Spain and Rome but, rather, a figure worth careful examination given the varied assessments of the status of his soul or his works. Mexican special collections evince another major Western European force in shaping the predispositions of Mexican readers' reception of Milton: French Miltonophilia. Then, in the second half of the nineteenth century, Granados's hispanophone translation of *Paradise Lost* emerges, blithely yet firmly engaging with these cultural and religious elements and reflecting a postcolonial hybridity that moves us to look anew at specific sets of word choices, allusions, and character representations in Milton's original.

These early Mexican Miltons are key instances in a genealogy that extends vibrantly into twentieth- and twenty-first-century Mexico. From Puebla, a centre of Mexican theatrical activity, we find the play *Paradise Lost: Drama in 4 Acts Arranged by Ambrosio Nieto, Upon the Inspiration of the Immortal Milton* (c.1900). We also find a 1967 hispanophone edition of Milton's epic that exemplifies another kind of postcolonial hybridity. The anonymous prose text is a revision of the Ibero-Spanish translation of 1812 by Juan Escóiquiz and its

---

[42] The two are Escóiquiz's 1812 translation, which seems to have endured in the hispanophone world in large part because of its precedence, and Dionisio Sanjuán's 1868 translation, which circulates widely in Mexico today due to the backing of the major press Porrúa.

illustrations are comprised of twenty-four images in the vibrantly coloured *cromo* genre popular in Mexico by a little-known Mexican artist, Miguel Fernández de Lara, interposed among thirty-six of the fifty illustrations by France's Gustave Doré, first published in an English *Paradise Lost* of (*c.* 1866) and then used in translations into, for example, Arabic, Bulgarian, Chinese, Dutch, Finnish, German, Japanese, and Portuguese, as well as other Spanish translations through the twenty-first century. But, as we have already seen, *Paradise Lost* is not the only Milton work to attract Mexican readers. The hispanophone modernist pastoral elegy 'París: Bactra: Skíros' (1981) by the globetrotting Mexican 1990 Nobel Prize in Literature laureate Octavio Paz, uses the headnote to Milton's *Lycidas*, in its original English, as its epigraph and refers directly to it early on in the poem.

The genealogical branches also extend south of Mexico's borders, as might be expected given the Latin American network that the Spanish Catholic Inquisition inadvertently established early on. Two hispanophone translations of *Paradise Lost* by Colombians followed Granados's hendecasyllabic blank-verse translation: one in prose by Aníbal Galindo in 1868, another in ottava rima by Enrique Álvarez Bonilla in 1896. Argentine Jorge Luis Borges (1899–1986) remained in lifelong conversation with Milton; his first reading of Milton's poetry in English took place at the age of 15, when he and his family were in Paris. And we find Cuba's Fidel Castro (1926–2016), in his October 1983 speech 'History Will Absolve Me', citing Milton's *Tenure of Kings and Magistrates*, the first two separate hispanophone translations of which were published in Spain in 2009 and in Mexico in 2011.[43]

Milton's seventeenth-century works have 'walked the town a while', and, as has recently begun to be explored, the pueblos (towns) too.[44] The circulation and reception of Milton in Hispano-America can tell us much about a whole set of reading practices, interpretations, and heretofore undetected elements of Milton's works, and about their international, multilingual readers. Their obscurity already tells us much about not only hispanophone but also non-hispanophone reading practices. It confirms Barbara Fuchs's claim that the dearth of critical attention to 'Spanish influences' in and Spanish responses to English literary works 'continue to limit the field' of early modern literary studies, which she attributes in part to a carry-over of the Black Legend of Spain's colonial enterprises.[45] She joins Walter Mignolo in striving to create 'a truly cosmopolitan world' within critical studies that would advance aesthetic sensibilities.[46] Our attention to major canonical Western writers like Milton can impel and strengthen the sort of golden age of shared interpretive power that Jonathan Culler articulated just over a decade ago, one marked by a sophisticated 'understanding of discourse' driven 'largely by postcolonial theory', and one, according to Homi Bhabha, requiring vigilance, so

---

[43] My thanks to Stephen Fallon for alerting me to this reference.   [44] 'A book was writ', l. 3.
[45] Barbara Fuchs, 'Imperium Studies: Theorizing Early Modern Expansion', 84.
[46] Walter Mignolo, *The Darker Side of Western Modernity: Global Futures, Decolonial Options*, 23.

as to carve out a third space that 'enables other positions to emerge. This third space displaces the histories that constitute it and, in its place, sets up new structures of authority and political initiatives.'[47]

My aim in this discussion of a small set of the traces of the early modern English author and political figure John Milton to be found in Mexico has been to disclose a Milton that has been a contentious but ultimately 'enabling resource' for Mexican readers, publishers, translators, and writers wrestling to redefine their literary practices and by extension cultural and aesthetic power.[48] The few texts explored in this discussion are representative of the rich reception and manifold manipulations of Milton's works in Hispano-America that warrant further exploration—and, frankly, enjoyment—within and outside of Mexico's borders.[49]

[47] Jonathan Culler, 'Comparative Literature, at Last', 244; Jonathan Rutherford, 'The Third Space. Interview with Homi Bhabha', 211.

[48] Seamus Heaney, *Preoccupations: Selected Prose, 1968–1978*, 180.

[49] I wish to thank Mario Murgia and Nair Anaya Ferreira, who provided me with a forum in which to share an early version of this paper at the National Autonomous University of Mexico in May 2017, and Marissa Nicosia for her suggestions on draft versions.

14

Milton's Erotic Dramas

Neil Forsyth

In recent years, performances of Milton's works, even the non-dramatic ones, have made audiences aware of how much Milton's imagination works in theatrical terms, and also, for this audience member at least, the erotic aspects of what the poems express. At a recent conference for Medieval and Early Modern scholars in Zurich, Switzerland (on 9 September 2016), for example, I was as captivated as everyone else by a performance, in the confined space of the Zunfthaus zur Saffran restaurant, of Book IX of *Paradise Lost*. It was preceded—a happy choice—by a play in Middle English from the York Mystery Cycle also telling the Fall of Adam and Eve. Watching the two together I was made aware, yet again, of the intensity with which Milton dramatizes the quarrel and the Fall sequence. The only false note, I felt, was that the actor playing the serpent/Satan embraced Eve in a rather erotic way. Not that this is inappropriate for the way Milton represents the reasons for Eve's attraction to Satan, but I felt the physical embrace was simply too obvious, too explicit, for the understated eroticism of the scene in Milton's poem. Otherwise, the production was a brilliant reminder of how theatrical the scene is, and how it echoes, or anticipates, the other major dramas among Milton's works. Both the earlier *A Maske Presented at Ludlow Castle* and the (probably) later *Samson Agonistes* dramatize in their different ways erotic attractions, and there are even parallels in the prose.[1] Seeing the scene from *Paradise Lost* in relation to the medieval play made it obvious how Milton's imagination worked in dramatic terms, and indeed reminded me that Milton had originally set out to write a tragedy of the story.[2] He even introduces Book IX by announcing that he must now change these notes to tragic—not simply a statement of mood, but also a statement of genre.

The erotic dimension of *A Maske* also became obvious in a performance, this time by the Royal Shakespeare Company, at the indoor theatre named after Sam

---

[1] Elsewhere in this volume, David Loewenstein discusses Milton's *A Maske Presented at Ludlow Castle* and national identity, and Rachel Willie considers his *Samson Agonistes* in the context of lively debates about English theatre.

[2] Ann Coiro thoroughly reviews the relation of Milton's epic to dramatic forms in 'Drama in the Epic Style'.

Neil Forsyth, *Milton's Erotic Dramas* In: *Making Milton: Print, Authorship, Afterlives*. Edited by: Emma Depledge, John S. Garrison, and Marissa Nicosia, Oxford University Press (2021). © Neil Forsyth. DOI: 10.1093/oso/9780198821892.003.0014

Wanamaker, which I saw on 10 November 2016.[3] The director of this intensely enjoyable production was Lucy Bailey, who has long been involved with musical theatre, but who first made her name at the Globe in her gruesome and powerful production of *Titus Andronicus*. It was Emma Rice, in her first season as Artistic Director, who had invited Bailey to return to the Globe, but Bailey herself who wanted to do Milton. Shortly before this performance Rice had announced she would step down after the 2018 season. Her many critics argued she was violating the spirit and purpose of Shakespeare's Globe by introducing microphones and state-of-the-art lighting. The Wanamaker is admittedly a different kind of space, but nonetheless, as a *Telegraph* reviewer put it, 'if Emma Rice's critics are perturbed by what she's doing to Shakespeare they should see what she has done to John Milton' (2 November 2016).

The candle-lit setting of the Wanamaker was especially apt for Milton's masque, most of which takes place in 'a wild wood' at night. *A Maske Presented at Ludlow Castle* soon became known as *Comus* after the central character, a sorcerer who lives in these woods attended by his variously attired 'monstrous rout' and described as a son of Bacchus and Circe. The theatre itself was decorated with variously grotesque heads or masks, perhaps making a complex pun with the genre of the piece, but certainly adding allure to the partly sinister, partly comic, monsters who cavorted on stage (see Figure 14.1). Milton's original title is *A Maske Presented at Ludlow Castle*, which gives simply the location on the Welsh border where on Michaelmas night, 29 September 1634, John Egerton, Earl of Bridgewater, was being officially and ceremonially installed as President of the Council of Wales and Lord Lieutenant of Wales and the Marches. In this production, however, the title became *Comus, a Masque in Favour of Chastity*, highlighting what is perhaps hardest for a modern sensibility to accept about the masque—the colourless and rather passive figure of the Lady as she wards off the challenges of sensuality. In trying to undo that interpretation of the masque, the production came close to the one advocated by Melissa Sanchez in a challenging essay. She writes: '*Comus* makes visible an alternative way of being in the world, one that follows from reflection on what it means to embrace the dark and disturbing aspects of sexuality and one that the Spirit and the Lady cannot fully defeat or resist.'[4]

This production added to Milton's original a clever frame story designed to introduce the idea of a masque to a contemporary London audience. Written by the well-known writer of comedy Patrick Barlow, it pretended to be the final dress rehearsal, just minutes before the audience arrives for the performance itself, and it turned on the sudden refusal of the Lady Alice Egerton (Emma Curtis), the

---

[3] I reviewed the production in *European Stages* Vol. 9 (https://europeanstages.org/category/volume-9/); see also Forsyth, 'Comus Performed at the Wanamaker Theatre in London'.
[4] Sanchez, 'What Hath Night to Do with Sleep?'.

Figure 14.1 'Lustful creatures with dirty faces': *Comus* at the Sam Wanamaker Playhouse. Photograph: Sheila Burnett. Susannah Clapp, 'Comus review – Milton meets the National Theatre of Brent', *The Observer*, 6 November 2016. By permission of Shakespeare's Globe Theatre.

obstinate 15-year old daughter of the house, to perform her role as Milton's Lady. In Barlow's play she gives no reason, nor does she seem to understand herself, but she is clearly a girl used to having her own way, and also a rebellious teenager. Her younger brothers, who are due to perform with her, try to persuade her, as does the hapless Henry Lawes, the musician and director of the masque and also the Attendant Spirit. A hilarious Philip Cumbus, doubling as Lawes and Spirit and Thyrsis,[5] gets a great deal of unexpected humour from Milton's text as well as from Barlow's, or his own, wry asides. The boys also tease Lady Alice by suggesting that she has a crush on the stable boy, who (it soon transpires) is to play Comus himself. The suspense is drawn out briefly until her father, in whose honour the masque is being produced, steps in—at first appealing to her better nature, and then simply ordering her to perform: 'You will do as you are told. Is that clear?' A pause before she says quietly, 'Yes', and the masque itself can begin.

In this production, having made his point, Egerton (Andrew Bridgmont) took his seat along the lower gallery and prepared rather pompously to watch the show,

---

[5] Coiro ('Drama in the Epic Style') suggests that Comus and Spirit might be doubled, as the two 'masked musical genius[es] of the woods': the theatrical logic would be 'hard for a director to resist' (84). In this production, however, that would have destroyed the sharp opposition of the two— bumbling middle age versus seductive youth.

as the cast performed a harmless little dance. But soon there came a loud and spectacular crash, Egerton's chair tipped him forward, and he fell down into the pit below the stage. Much dry ice floated up along with an eerie, greenish light. Dreadful, scary things could now happen. Danny Lee Wynter played the pagan Comus lusciously, savouring Milton's verse but also revolving his pelvis in time to the poetic rhythms.[6] He led his 'rout of monsters' in dance ('What hath night to do with sleep?'), and ordered them to 'beat the ground, / In a light fantastic round'; then, when he heard the Lady singing, he declared that 'Such sober certainty of waking bliss / I never heard till now' (122, 143–4, 263–4).[7]

Having been separated from her brothers during the night as they were all making their way through those sinister woods to Ludlow, she was singing in hopes they could hear her. Comus, however, disguised as a villager, persuades her to come with him to look for them and takes her offstage for safety to his 'low / But loyal cottage' (319–20). The boys meanwhile engage in a longish dialogue about chastity, fearful of what might befall their absent sister. In this production their rather flat, undramatic speeches were enlivened by the monstrous inhabitants of the wood, who molested the boys even though they could not see them. The audience laughed as one boy told the other to 'be not over-exquisite' (359), but listened also as he explained that 'he that hides a dark soul, and foul thoughts / Benighted walks under the midday sun; / Himself is his own dungeon' (383–5). After the jokey beginning, there was an uneasy quiet in the theatre as the Elder Brother (Rob Callender) delivered his speech about the hidden strength of chastity and virginity. Doing their best to avoid their mysterious assailants, the boys finally managed to escape. They were helped in all this by the Attendant Spirit, who has been presiding over the action since he descended, comically, from the heavens after the crash. Taking the form of the family's shepherd, Thyrsis, he offered them as protection the magic herb haemony, and told them how to find their sister. Later he insisted, again comically, that they use the 'root' (629).

Then Comus and the Lady reappeared for the great central confrontation, in which the Lady is made to sit in a magical chair brought on stage by the monster chorus and 'Smeared with gums of glutinous heat' (917). She is stuck there and must hear and then reply to Comus's blandishments and threats. Comus holds a necromancer's wand, pointing it at the space that has opened between her legs as her dress is pulled above her knees. He also offers a drink from his magic cup. But the Lady refuses: 'Fool do not boast, / Thou canst not touch the freedom of my mind / With all thy charms' (662–4). He denounces 'the lean and sallow

[6] Susannah Clapp, the theatre critic of *The Observer*, reviewed the performance in these terms in 'Comus review'.
[7] Milton, *A Masque of the same Author Presented at Ludlow Castle, 1634 Before the Earl of Bridgewater Then President of Wales ['Comus']*, in Orgel and Goldberg, eds., *The Major Works*, 44–71, stage direction on p. 47. Further quotations from *A Maske* in this chapter come from this edition and are cited parenthetically in the text.

Abstinence' and praises the Lady's looks: 'Beauty is Nature's brag' (709, 745). Comus's speech is clearly influenced by the rhythm and sparkle of Shakespeare, and the young actor (Danny Lee Wynter) put on his best imitation of what we may expect to hear from Globe training.

The language is magnificently anti-puritan and thrilling. If we do not make the best use we can of the natural world God has given us,

> we should serve him as a grudging master,
> As a penurious niggard of his wealth,
> And live like Nature's bastards, not her sons,
> Who would be quite surcharged with her own weight,
> And strangled with her waste fertility;
> The earth cumbered, and the winged air darked with plumes[.]
>
> (725–30)

The images and rhythms are Shakespearean, but the theme has reached beyond and behind Shakespeare, behind to the world of fairy lore that he exploited in *A Midsummer Night's Dream*, with its added layer of classical myth, and beyond to the conflicts that were beginning to define the new, capitalist world. God has given a wealth of which to be 'a penurious niggard' is a major crime.

The Lady, who is one of the few characters in Milton to resist temptation, replies with increasing heat in an argument that becomes a defence of a puritan socialism, a covert sermon about conspicuous expenditure in big houses like the one where the masque is supposedly being performed. Nature has enough for everyone if not exploited by the rich:

> If every just man that now pines with want
> Had but a moderate and beseeming share
> Of that which lewdly-pampered luxury
> Now heaps upon some few with vast excess,
> Nature's full blessings would be well-dispensed
> In unsuperfluous even proportion[.]
>
> (768–73)

The younger brothers soon rush in to rescue her and Comus escapes. But the Lady has need of a higher power to be rescued from her frozen posture. Sabrina, who embodies the nearby River Severn, and so celebrates the border country over which Bridgewater now presides, has to intervene. In this production she was played by a black actress (Natasha Magigi). There is music to accompany her, but she also represents the power of poetry to 'unlock / The clasping charm, and thaw the numbing spell' (851–2).

Though the world of the masque seems ethereal or other-worldly, its vocabulary and rhythms frequently evoking Shakespeare's fairies, in fact there was much in the immediate context that had deeply serious implications.[8] The Bridgewater children, Alice in particular, had recently complained of demonic possession and had been treated with protective amulets and St John's wort. In a sense the masque replays her cure. The Earl himself in his capacity as a judge had recently given an extremely fair-minded ruling in the long-drawn-out case of rape of a 14-year-old girl, Margery Evans, by a powerful local official. This may have been in the minds of those present on this big occasion, more especially as Michaelmas was a holiday associated with public administration and justice. In church the lessons for the day, from Ecclesiasticus 38 to 44, are about greatness ('Let us now praise famous men'), about sitting on the judges' seat and the wisdom of ancient prophecies. The gospel for the day, from Matthew 18, denounces the man who offends against children: 'it were better for him that a millstone were hanged about his neck, and that he were drowned in the depth of the sea.'

There was another related and even more important reason why the subject of the masque was extremely risky and needed to be handled with great delicacy. Patrick Barlow's frame play made this explicit. The elder brother told his younger sibling the story of a family scandal, and the Earl commented sarcastically how glad he was that the boy brought this up. An extraordinary sexual scandal had in fact recently afflicted the family of the Dowager Countess's eldest daughter Anne (sister of Frances, Bridgewater's wife, the boys' aunt). Her husband, the infamous Earl of Castlehaven, had had his servants frequently rape both his wife and his stepdaughter, who was married to his own son. He was also accused of sodomy. He had been executed in May 1631. One reason for the choice of subject for the masque may thus have been to insist on the chastity, and so marriageability, of the Lady. Milton had to be careful not to insult his Ludlow hosts, and especially not the young virgin playing the Lady. In particular, he needed to avoid having the references to rape and chastity seem ironic. Bridgewater, an upright judge, and now Lord President of Wales, was no Castlehaven.

The intensity of her commitment to chastity makes the Lady of *A Maske* unnervingly like the 'Lady of Christ's'—as Milton had been called as a student at Cambridge. But it also implies an equally strong need to struggle with its opposite. The Elder Brother evokes that contrary state of the soul in a speech with a remarkable profusion of liquid *l* sounds:

> when lust
> By unchaste looks, loose gestures, and foul talk,
> But most by lewd and lavish act of sin,

---

[8] For more on this context and the related scandal, see Forsyth, *John Milton: A Biography*, 43–4.

> Lets in defilement to the inward parts,
> The soul grows clotted by contagion,
> Embodies, and imbrutes, till she quite lose
> The divine property of her first being.
>
> (463–9)

To which the Second Brother replies with a line that usually raises a laugh in the theatre, as it did this time: 'How charming is divine philosophy' (476).

When the text of the masque was published, in late autumn 1637, Milton added, or reinstated, a long and passionate speech for the Lady in praise of 'the sun-clad power of chastity' (782) and 'the sage / And serious doctrine of virginity' (786–7), as well as Comus's response: 'She fables not, I feel and I do fear / Her words set off by some superior power' (800–1). In this production, his words were shifted forward and became one of Comus's earliest responses to the Lady. The masque's concluding lines, spoken by the Attendant Spirit, sum up the moral lesson:

> Mortals that would follow me,
> Love Virtue, she alone is free,
> She can teach ye how to climb
> Higher than the sphery chime;
> Or if Virtue feeble were,
> Heaven itself would stoop to her.
>
> (1018–23)

Virtue, that is, can teach you to climb above the music of the spheres to heaven. The last two lines Milton wrote in Count Camillo Cerdogni's guestbook when he was visiting relatives of Charles Diodati in Geneva, on 10 June 1639. The association of freedom and virtue became a dominant theme in Milton's writings.

The production concluded with a serious return to Barlow's frame drama: the Earl asked his children what they learned from performing in this masque. The two young, still foppish, brothers responded briefly that they had learned to pay attention and to obey their father. But the Lady, to their joint consternation, defied him, and insisted she had learned what her mother had always told her—to go her own way and be her own woman. That, finally, is the larger doctrine of chastity conveyed by the masque—that it will be tested certainly, but we must rise above the lesser and more worldly doctrines, predatory enchanters, being peddled around us. It had an obvious appeal to Lucy Bailey. She wrote in the programme notes that chastity here means something like integrity. The Lady's argument for control over her life and for freedom of the mind is as relevant as ever for women. Milton's masque indeed has a special status among his works because of its attention to, and sympathy for, women. Though the masque is a genre usually performed at court, this one is written for a faraway place, Ludlow, on the Welsh Marches, and even celebrates its estrangement from the dominant trend of Caroline politics and the treatment of women in its courtly culture.[9]

Read in the light of what he had already achieved in *A Maske*, so warmly revived by that sensual Globe production, Milton's odd choice to retell the myth of Adam and Eve as a love story is perhaps easier to understand. As the Zurich production made us see, the drama of *Paradise Lost* Book IX is all about love and jealousy. Indeed, love, explicitly sexual love, is all over the poem: in the invocation to Book I, in the role of Satan with Eve, in the sexualized creation, in the fact that angels too make love—'union of pure with pure / Desiring' (8.627),[10] as Raphael explains with a blush, and in the psychology that leads to the redemption in Book X.

The roll call of devils includes the first sexual beings in the poem, as the names Baalim and Ashtaroth are general terms for male and female spirits.

> For Spirits when they please
> Can either Sex assume, or both; so soft
> And uncompounded is their essence pure,
> Not tied or manacled with joint or limb,
> Nor founded on the brittle strength of bones,
> Like cumbrous flesh; but in what shape they choose
> Dilated or condensed, bright or obscure,
> Can execute their airy purposes,
> And works of love or enmity fulfil.
>
> (1.423–31)

Indeed, the original heterosexuality in Milton's world is not the relationship of Adam and Eve but, rather, the union of Satan and his offspring, Sin. In the strange dialogue between them in Book II, Sin tells Satan that, when he first plotted against God, she 'shining heavenly fair, a goddess armed / Out of thy head I sprung' (2.757–8). While the angels at first found her repellent, she eventually became attractive, especially to Satan himself:

> full oft
> Thyself in me thy perfect image viewing
> Becam'st enamoured, and such joy thou took'st
> With me in secret, that my womb conceived
> A growing burden.
>
> (2.763–7)

---

[9] Marcus, 'John Milton's *Comus*'.

[10] Milton, *Paradise Lost*, in Orgel and Goldberg, eds., *The Major Works*, 355–618. Quotations will be cited parenthetically in the text.

The result of this conception is the birth of Death, and so we see that the original pattern of heterosexuality and of family life is both incestuous and disastrous. What is more, this is a heterosexuality based on similarity and not on difference— something that is also true of Adam and Eve themselves, since the story of Eve's origin as Adam narrates it in Book VIII bears a close resemblance to the story of the origin of Sin and Death.

The story gets worse before it gets better: once Death is born, he rapes his mother and begets 'yelling monsters' (2.795), which 'when they list into the womb / That bred them...return' (2.798–9). Such, it seems, are the miseries of family life. It is characteristic of the poem that we hear first about the perverted aspect of sexuality.[11]

Sin continues with the account of the birth of her son, conceived in incest:

> He my inbred enemy
> Forth issued, brandishing his fatal dart
> Made to Destroy[.]
>
> (2.785–7)

Just as Satan and Sin establish a grim precedent for heterosexuality, so the first familial relationship in the poem establishes an equally gloomy precedent for family life, and one that foreshadows Abel's murder, which is shown to Adam near the end of the poem. Similarly, Death's 'fatal dart'—at once the spear with which Death as a warrior does his work and the phallus with which he will repeatedly rape his mother—links the penis not primarily to sexual enjoyment but instead to reproduction. In this first ever example of sexual activity, both male and female genitals are condemned even when they are used for what was traditionally felt to be their proper purpose. Milton undermines any straightforward sense of human sexuality even before we meet the humans themselves.

Both Adam and Eve tell of their emotions at the moment of the Fall, and both ascribe their actions to love. But with a difference. Adam announces immediately that he will eat the fruit in order to stay with Eve: the speech is moving and recalls what he tells Raphael in Book VIII about his reaction to Eve's birth and to her overpowering beauty. Now 'with thee / Certain my resolution is to die' (9.906–7). Adam is then said by the rather severe narrator to be 'fondly overcome with female charm' (9.999). Satan seems to have understood this, since he conspicuously leaves the whole plot to work itself out once he has convinced Eve to eat: he seems to know Eve will give the fruit to Adam, and that he will be bound to eat:

> He after Eve seduced, unminded slunk
> Into the wood fast by, and changing shape

---

[11] Some of these comments are borrowed from Guy-Bray, 'Fellowships of Joy'.

> To observe the sequel, saw his guileful act
> By Eve, though all unweeting, seconded
> Upon her husband, saw their shame that sought
> Vain covertures[.]
>
> (10.332–7)

Slunk must be one of the ugliest and yet most expressive words in the English language, almost onomatopoeic.

Eve's announced motive for giving Adam the fruit is not so different from his, though rather more complicated. She wants that Adam not be lost to her and acquire another wife (9.817–33), and says so in a powerful speech of self-questioning. She recognizes she has been made somehow inferior, as indeed the narrator apparently told us when we first saw them: 'not equal, as their sex not equal seemed' (4.296). She imagines she now has 'the odds of knowledge in my power' and so may, by keeping Adam ignorant, 'add what wants / In female sex, the more to draw his love' (9.820, 821–2). That very knowledge, she thinks, '[may] render me more equal, and perhaps, / A thing not undesirable, sometime / Superior; for inferior who is free?' (9.823–5). The speech is one of the reasons for the common accusation of Milton's misogyny. Eve is 'fallen' at the moment she makes the speech that reveals her selfish (but still sympathetic) motivation, whereas when Adam says the same thing ('how can I live without thee, how forego / Thy sweet converse and love so dearly joined / To live again in these wild woods forlorn?', 9.908–10), he is still unfallen: the distinction, however, of fallen and unfallen is making less and less of a difference now. He too rejects the idea of another Eve. In C. S. Lewis's severe view (1942: 21–3), the act was murder (of all posterity), and Milton himself seems to concur in his theological treatise.

So, 'love' is the main motive for the Fall, as it is for the redemption, indeed for the Creation itself. It extends, within Book IX, from Adam's agonizingly simple recognition that he cannot force Eve to stay with him ('Go; for thy stay, not free, absents thee more', 9.372) all the way to Eve's response to Adam's decision: 'O glorious trial of exceeding love' (9.961). In between come the extraordinary moments, one when Satan himself is smitten, affected by Eve to become 'stupidly good' (9.465), the other being nature's sympathetic reaction to the Fall when from Adam's 'slack hand the garland wreathed for Eve / Down dropped, and all the faded roses shed' (9.892–3). The subsequent reaction to the 'new wine' is explicitly, even blatantly, sexual. The 'false fruit ... / Carnal desire inflaming, he on Eve / Began to cast lascivious eyes, she him / As wantonly repaid; in lust they burn' (9.1011–15), and soon 'high winds' from within torment them 'both in subjection now / To sensual appetite' (9.1122, 1128–9).

'Earth felt the wound' and now again 'Earth trembled from her entrails', but neither Adam nor Eve pay any attention (9.782, 1000). The quasi-divine human couple become no longer masters of themselves. They are on a high, and repeat the intoxicated lovemaking of Hera and Zeus (also Helen and Paris) in Homer's *Iliad*.[12] But when they calm down, after sleep, the result is characteristically Miltonic:

> up they rose
> As from unrest, and each the other viewing,
> Soon found their eyes how opened, and their minds
> How darkened; innocence, that as a veil
> Had shadowed them from knowing ill, was gone,
> Just confidence, and native righteousness
> And honour from about them, naked left
> To guilty shame he covered, but his robe
> Uncovered more, so rose the Danite strong
> Herculean Samson from the harlot-lap
> Of Philistean Dalilah, and waked
> Shorn of his strength, they destitute and bare
> Of all their virtue: silent, and in face
> Confounded long they sat, as stricken mute[.]
>
> (9.1051–64)

This recovered power of sight, which Eve had been willing to die for, now tells them only that they are naked, and ashamed.

The parallel between Adam and Samson was traditional, since both are uxorious and are betrayed by a woman. Milton was perhaps already writing, or maybe had already written, his own drama on the subject, *Samson Agonistes*. In this *Paradise Lost* reference Dalilah has a 'harlot-lap', which does not necessarily mean, as some assume, that she is not Samson's wife. Here though, the curious text reads as if both Adam and Eve are likened to Samson ('*they* destitute'). In the absence of punctuation between 'shame' and 'he' in line 1058, we cannot strictly tell whether it is honour (as it might be nowadays) or shame that draws the robe over nakedness, or whether it is Adam who covers himself. In either case the Fall is first felt emotionally, psychologically, in the complex and uncertain syntax around this idea of shame/honour/nudity. No longer are they 'in native honour clad' (4.289), which had been so powerful a substitute for clothes when they were innocent. A further oddity here is the robe: where did it come from, since they are both still naked, as in line 1074 where the result of knowledge, says Adam, is that it 'leaves us naked thus, of honour void'. Fowler's notes explain helpfully that the robe refers to the covering of guilty shame, since mankind has no clothing till 10.216. 'Shame is personified (as at 1097); with his *robe* (a vestige of Adam's "robe

---

[12]   See Forsyth, 'Homer in Milton', 67–71.

of righteousness") he *covered* them, but no longer adequately. The absent object mimes the absent covering.'[13] The paradox of a robe which uncovers is only one further sign of the potentially misleading images generated by 'the force of that fallacious fruit' (9.1045), a phrase which in its playful alliteration reproduces the 'amorous play' with which in the previous line Adam and Eve are now 'wearied'. The weariness itself is reproduced in the images of the next lines, as the 'exhilarating vapour bland' is now 'exhaled, and grosser sleep / Bred of unkindly fumes, with conscious dreams / Encumbered, now had left them' (9.1047, 1049–51). They then awaken, or rather, in a brilliant and mildly alliterative phrase, 'up they rose / As from unrest' (9.1046–52). Decidedly, Milton tries to make us feel as well us understand the unpleasant effects of the first sex after the Fall.

The 'veil / Had shadowed them from knowing ill' (9.1054–5) is akin to the veil which concealed a beloved face from Milton even in dream, as the famous sonnet tells, and indeed that sonnet is worth remembering here for the similarity of vocabulary and the parallel sense of loss. She

> Came vested all in white, pure as her mind:
> Her face was veiled, yet to my fancied sight,
> Love, sweetness, goodness, in her person shined
> So clear, as in no face with more delight.
> But O as to embrace her I inclined,
> I waked, she fled, and day brought back my night.
>
> (9–14)

What is lost in both cases is purity and innocence, and in both cases two kinds of vision are contrasted. In the sonnet, though, Milton wakes to his own darkness again, but in *Paradise Lost* this is only one movement of the symphony. What Adam and Eve together now know they have lost can eventually be recovered: 'thus these two / Emparadised in one another's arms / The happier Eden' (4.505–7), as Satan views them in his envy, will eventually be picked up by the discovery of a paradise within, happier far. But that is not yet, and the couple now have to suffer all the agonies of mistrust and hatred and denunciation. In this poem, love is the best thing about being alive, and also the worst. And, indeed, the paradox is deeper than that: Adam's best impulse, his rapid decision to stay with Eve in spite of what he knows to be the consequences, leads to the tragic event of the poem, the Fall itself. Indeed, it is itself that tragic event. Conversely, at his worst, emotionally most hateful ('Out of my sight, thou serpent', 10.867), Adam discovers or remembers what can redeem them, 'calling to mind with heed / Part of our sentence, that thy seed shall bruise / The serpent's head' (10.1030–2).

---

[13] Fowler, *Milton: Paradise Lost*, 531.

In sum, the narration of the Fall comprises several set pieces, each of which has sexual implications: the separation, in which love is shown to be the basic motivating emotion (Eve's love, but for whom?—herself perhaps, or the serpent, as in many parallel versions and myths; Adam's love for Eve); the temptation by Satan at the tree with 'many a wanton wreath' (9.517, 503–30), in which he 'glozed', recalling Comus's 'glozing courtesy / Baited with reasons not unplausible' (161–2); Eve's offering the fruit to Adam 'with liberal hand' and his acceptance, though 'not deceived' (9.995, 996); their mutual feeling of enhanced power and especially of lust; the aftermath in which they awaken to their new fallen state and to contemplate the difference.

Adam praises adventurous Eve's bold deed at the beginning of the speech (9.921) in which he comes to his decision to eat. Genesis 3:3 imposed a ban on touching the fruit, and Milton reiterates it, saying that 'Adam or his race' are 'charged not to touch the interdicted tree' (7.45–6). Now Adam adds to the praise, saying she 'hath dared / Had it been only coveting to eye / That sacred fruit, sacred to abstinence, / Much more to taste it under ban to touch' (9.922–5), lines which seem to establish a hierarchy of interdictions, from seeing to touching to tasting. The odd repetition of 'sacred' suggests to John Leonard that Adam is making an idol of the fruit,[14] and it is true that his mind is beginning to turn as he invents the notion that even to look at the fruit was part of Eve's boldness. Indeed, he is already using the language of the Decalogue by speaking of 'coveting' anything at all.

In the dialogue with Dalila in *Samson Agonistes*, Milton's final version of erotic experience, the sense of touch marks the climax of the exchange. Although the play is in fact a closet drama, there was a brilliant semi-staged reading at St Giles' Church, Cripplegate, where Milton is buried, during the Ninth International Milton Symposium on 10 July 2008. This inspired Hiroko Sano, as the organizer of the Tenth International Milton Symposium in Tokyo in 2012 to commission a Noh-style adaptation. She writes that 'the conversation between Samson and Dalila inspired Mutsuo Takahashi to depict their love-hate relationship in his *Shinsaku-noh Samuson* [New Noh Samson]'. She quotes part of the dialogue with her own translation, which was 'displayed on the back of the seats for the benefit of the English-speaking audience at the National Noh Theatre'.[15] This version of the exchange put much stress on the 'love' dimension: part of it reads as follows.

Chorus: Let us live happily together,
          Forevermore, my beloved.

She persuades him, taking his hand.

Samson: If you had truly loved me,
          Why did you have my hair shaven?

---

[14] Leonard, ed., *John Milton: The Complete Poems*, 836.
[15] Sano, 'Translating Milton's Poetry into Japanese'.

Dalila: So that you may not go elsewhere.

Samson: Why did you have my eyes put out?

Dalila: So that you may not look at other women.

Samson: Why did you receive silver as a reward?

Dalila: So that I may maintain our life together.

Samson: I still have a doubt about you.
                  Yet I am going to the court for the feast.

Dalila: You told me to take your hand and lead you. How delighted and
                  pleased I am!

Milton's original is quite different, and this rather sentimental Noh version makes
us more closely aware of what Milton is doing: there is certainly no taking of
hands. Already when she had first come on the scene and the Chorus identified
her, Samson exclaimed, 'My wife, my traitress, let her not come near me' (725). At
the climax of the dialogue she says, 'Let me approach at least, and touch thy hand',
to which Samson, alert to the danger, replies, 'Not for thy life, lest fierce remem-
brance wake / My sudden rage to tear thee joint by joint. / At distance I forgive
thee, go with that' (951–4). Prior to that moment, Dalila appeals at length to the
marriage bond, and even uses it to justify her betrayal of Samson. Fearing that
Samson might leave her, as he had the woman of Timna, she sought, she claims,
'How to endear, and hold thee to me firmest' (796). Knowing 'that liberty /
Would draw thee forth to perilous enterprises', she fears like Hotspur's Kate to sit at home
'full of cares and fears / Wailing thy absence in my widowed bed; / Here I should
still enjoy thee day and night / Mine and love's prisoner, not the Philistines'
(803–8). No need when Samson is beside her to fear 'partners in my love. / These
reasons in love's law have passed for good, / Though fond and reasonless to some
perhaps; / And love hath oft, well meaning, wrought much woe' (810–14). Samson
gives no credence to any of this (except obviously the last clause), and so Dalila
leaves the scene in the hope that she will be famed for saving 'Her country from a
fierce destroyer' (985). The Chorus makes the definitive comment on this: 'She's
gone, a manifest serpent by her sting / Discovered in the end' (997–8). This is not
the only Miltonic variant on the risks of the erotic world, as we have seen, but it is
certainly a frightening one. It may indeed help us see that Milton imagines all of
the threats to human sexuality as in some way serpentine, or at least monstrous.

15

Milton and Radicalism

Nigel Smith

When we talk about a recurrent and distinctive theme in the study of Milton's reception, the matter of his radicalism, or his alleged radicalism, stands out. Perhaps it is second only to the supreme issue in his reception: the appreciation and interpretation of *Paradise Lost*. A radical is someone who advocates a drastic transformation of society, perhaps with a set of views notably in advance of that society's general practices and values. The word was not used in this way until the early nineteenth century, but it is regularly applied to the early modern world in this sense. The concern with form as opposed to history in early modern studies in the last two decades might have obscured this issue in some quarters, but recent investigations of temporality in Milton see a return of concern with context and of the aesthetic coding in his poetry of the revolutionary transformations of his times, a process in which he took part as a controversial writer and as a civil servant for a revolutionary government, and emerging sharply in the early 1640s after a conformable youth.[1] In this chapter I do not interpret Milton's poetry and prose as would be my usual practice and preference: instead I discuss the ways in which he has been regarded as a radical and why that issue remains a valuable aspect of his legacy.

Milton's prose writings of the 1640s imaginatively and enthusiastically engage with the spirit of reform that existed in the Long Parliament, in the Assembly of Divines, and in many parts of the country, but especially London and East Anglia. It may not have been particularly daring to argue against episcopacy, but it was incendiary to argue for divorce, and certainly to place oneself with the less conservative wing of the Parliamentarians to argue against prepublication censorship. Milton appeared to be with the 'Independent' party when he justified regicide on the grounds of the right to resist a tyrant, and he then defended first the English republic (1649–53) and second the Protectorate (1653–9) in Latin to a European audience. This would make him a mouthpiece for two kingless regimes, the establishment of each connected with some kind of military coup, but Milton's private views have been seen to contain surreptitious criticism of aspects of these

---

[1] Rachel Trubowitz, 'Introduction' to 'Milton and the Politics of Periodization', 292; David Quint, 'Milton, Waller, and the Fate of Eden'; Marissa Greenberg, 'Milton Much Revolving'; Nicholas McDowell, *Poet of Revolution*.

Nigel Smith, *Milton and Radicalism* In: *Making Milton: Print, Authorship, Afterlives.* Edited by: Emma Depledge, John S. Garrison, and Marissa Nicosia, Oxford University Press (2021). © Nigel Smith.
DOI: 10.1093/oso/9780198821892.003.0015

MILTON AND RADICALISM   199

regimes, and he later spoke in defence of Puritan desiderata that were never satisfied by the Commonwealth regimes, such as the abolition of tithes and the complete separation of Church and state.

It is very hard to find a general account of Milton from the earliest biographies onwards that was not invested in a historical understanding of his activities, sometimes approvingly, but often not. Since he very publicly defended the execution of King Charles I, he was for many a terrible rebel, and a social demon in his argument for divorce. Milton's status as either Whig or republican hero or Tory demon was located within the division of political views that descended in time from the English Revolution itself. William Winstanley's condemnation quoted in this collection's first chapter is a good example of Restoration royalist opinion, and Milton's stock in the opposing camp would be greatly assisted in the publishing enterprises of John Toland, all of which appeared in the wake of the Glorious Revolution of 1688–9. This well-explored material provided the picture of a republican poet that could be developed and amplified in the age of the American and French Revolutions, when like-minded English franchise reformers, republicans, and other kinds of radical would find in Milton's writings, poetry and prose, a spokesperson for a spirit of revolutionary transformation that was indeed quintessentially English. This was one of the understandings central to the interest in Milton of the English Romantic poets, not least the younger Wordsworth.[2]

The view inherited from the historical and literary scholarship of the nineteenth century that followed was that he was a kind of political proto-Whig, a religious Puritan, a devotee of toleration yet philosophically a largely backward-looking pre-Cartesian who accepted the Ptolemaic view of the universe.[3] This view continued to evolve in a social democratic direction with the American scholarship of the earlier and mid-twentieth century, even as Milton's poetic reputation was taking a tumble across the Atlantic at the hands of the literary modernists. Milton was seen through communist spectacles during the controversial era of the McCarthyite persecutions, when, at the same time and by contrast, elitist Straussians also claimed Milton for a conservative vision.[4] All of these views were concerned to redeem a Milton with partisan political and religious views, an actor in the public sphere as opposed to someone who was primarily poet of the nation, a view constructed after his death and achieved mostly through editions of his poetry, especially *Paradise Lost*.

[2] See Philip Connell, 'Wordsworth's "Sonnets Dedicated to Liberty" and the British Revolutionary Past'.
[3] David Masson, *The Life of John Milton: Narrated in Connection with the Political, Ecclesiastical, and Literary History of his Time*.
[4] See Sharon Achinstein, 'Red Milton: Abraham Polonsky and You Are There (January 30, 1955)'; Nigel Smith, *Is Milton better than Shakespeare?*, 13–14.

The 'radical' Milton of scholarly inquiry in the second half of the twentieth century, signalled most strongly in the writings of Christopher Hill, accepted that the poet was decidedly a republican, and hence to the 'left' of being a proto-Whig (given the choice, the poet would not have countenanced the return of a monarchy; his mature position was that a republic is *always* better than a monarchy), and he was not a Puritan but instead a *radical* Puritan. His ideas on divorce, on the mortality of the soul, on the continuity of spirit and matter, soul and body (monism), on free will, on the nature of the godhead, all make him distinctively of an extreme, even minority, position, way beyond the boundaries of what we can define as an English Commonwealth 'Puritan consensus', even though Milton remained for eleven years an important civil servant of the 'Puritan state', and even though few deny that he covertly voiced his doubts about the rise of singular Cromwellian authority—the governments of first the republic (January 1649–December 1653), then the Cromwellian Protectorate (December 1654–April 1659), and finally the briefly restored republic (April 1659–April 1660). Hill wanted Milton in or near the company of the extreme and largely non-elite Puritan sects who were the focus of his most famous work: 'open to the left and closed to the right'.[5] We should remember that Milton was twice interrogated by the highest authority in the state for his publications: by Parliament in 1643 for the *Doctrine and Discipline of Divorce* and by the Council of State in 1652 for sanctioning the publication of the Socinian (that is, anti-trinitarian) *Racovian Catechism*.

To return to a point made at the beginning of this chapter, 'radical' meaning someone who wants a fundamental and drastic transformation of society was not used until 1819, so when we use that word we risk looking back at the seventeenth century through a nineteenth-century franchise reform and working-class movement lens.[6] Nonetheless, and bearing this in mind, Milton was still a shockingly bold intellectual and saw a consonance between his own proposals and the turbulent events of his time. In this sense we talk of him as a political and religious radical, and we think of his writings in prose and poetry as both painstaking reflections of these issues and agents in intended projects of consciousness transformation among his readers.

Much of the 'historicist' work on Milton of the later twentieth century was really concerned with unpacking the meaning of Milton's prose works in their historical context, once they had been given a fully prepared and annotated

---

[5] Christopher Hill, *Milton and the English Revolution*, 470; and *The Experience of Defeat: Milton and Some Contemporaries*. The degree of originality and persuasiveness in Hill's approach, and his influence on other Miltonists, is assessed with discrimination in Thomas N. Corns, 'Christopher Hill on Milton, Bunyan and Winstanley'.

[6] See Glenn Burgess and Matthew Festenstein, eds., *English Radicalism, 1550–1850*; Laurent Curelly and Nigel Smith, eds., *Radical Voices, Radical Ways*.

modern edition, first with the Columbia Milton, then with the Yale Prose.[7] From the mid-twentieth century onwards this enterprise was concerned to rectify a view of Milton as a relatively orthodox figure that prevailed among many experts on the poetry: that Milton was theologically orthodox, and that the poetry represented a more transhistorical, universal set of values for the human race than the prose. This was the view of C. S. Lewis, who was defending Milton as a Christian poet against the devastating attack on his *poetic* reputation by T. S. Eliot and F. R. Leavis earlier in the twentieth century.[8] Slowly but surely between the 1960s and the first decade of the twenty-first century the 'radical' and 'heretical' Milton gained ground, and was widely accepted in the international world of Milton scholarship, where prose and poetry were reconciled in a series of studies and editions. The attempt to argue that Milton was not the author of *De Doctrina Christiana* (*DDC*), and that therefore Milton was at least not such an extreme theological radical, is a decidedly minority view.[9] Few now take it seriously, but it is not an extinct view. Recent work confirms the view that Milton's heresies were seen in his poetry in the earlier eighteenth century, nearly a century before *DDC* was known, even as he himself importantly, remarkably even, returned the word 'heresy' to its earlier meaning of 'choice', as opposed to that which we decide is the forbidden thought.[10]

Hill was able to identify and bring out the significance of the times when Milton and his works were visible among the English Revolution radicals. The alleged brandishing of the first divorce tract by a Baptist preacher, 'Mrs. Attaway', at a conventicle meeting is a famous example.[11] She was said to have used the *Doctrine and Discipline of Divorce* (1643) to think through her predicament of being married to a man who was not of her church; she would re-partner with another Baptist preacher, William Jenney. Further work showed how these configurations found their way into the poetry.[12] We now have full accounts of how Milton might be read as a republican and radical religious or radical Puritan poet, and understood by his contemporaries as such. After the work of Hill and Barbara K. Lewalski, this is where Milton studies has come to stand, in serving an author

---

[7] Frank Allen Patterson, ed., *The Works of John Milton*; Don M. Wolfe, ed.,*Complete Prose Works of John Milton*.

[8] C. S. Lewis, *A Preface to Paradise Lost*.

[9] William B. Hunter, Jr, C. A. Patrides, and J. H. Adamson, eds., *Bright Essence: studies in Milton's Theology*; Gordon Campbell et al., *Milton and the Manuscript of De Doctrina Christiana*.

[10] John Leonard, *Faithful Labourers: A Reception History of Paradise Lost, 1667–1970*, I, 481; David Loewenstein, *Treacherous Faith: The Specter of Heresy in Early Modern English Literature and Culture*.

[11] Thomas Edwards, *Gangraena*, 3 pts (1646), II.9; Hill, *Milton and the English Revolution*, 131–2, 135, 160, 222, 274, 308, 312, 318. See now Jason A. Kerr, 'Elizabeth Attaway, London preacher and Theologian, 1645–1646,' *The Seventeenth Century*, DOI: 10.1080/0268117X.2020.1825230.

[12] David Norbrook, *Poetry and Politics in the English Renaissance*, ch. 10; and, *Writing the English Republic: Poetry, Rhetoric, and Politics, 1627–1660*, ch. 10; Loewenstein, *Milton and the Drama of History: Historical Vision, Iconoclasm, and the Literary Imagination*; and, *Representing Revolution in Milton and his Contemporaries: Religion, Politics, and Polemics in Radical Puritanism*; Blair Worden, *Literature and Politics in Cromwellian England: John Milton, Andrew Marvell, Marchamont Nedham*.

of a new kind because he put extraordinary learning in the service of radical politics and the revolutionary power of politics.[13] One must add the work of Laura Knoppers on how aware and engaged the blind Milton was in the anti-Commonwealth culture of the Restoration and how he resisted this in his great poetry, some of it published by men like John Starkey with subversive reputations.[14] Those who are skilled with archive searching have found evidence of Milton as a much reviled and feared presence among defenders of the monarchy and the Church of England.[15] At stake here is Milton's deep knowledge not merely of ancient philosophy but also of an entire tradition of legal learning that derives from the Roman understanding of slavery.[16] This work precedes Mary Nyquist's broad-based contextual meditation on Milton and the long history of slavery discourse.[17] The degree to which Milton may be seen as an extraordinarily engaged explorer of the first man and woman, of paradisal marriage, an interest of religious radicals and libertines, is superbly explored by James Grantham Turner, and as an observer of the 'new science' by Joanna Picciotto.[18] William Poole's consideration of the different ideas of the Fall of man as they relate to Milton's treatment in *Paradise Lost* might be said to broaden and deepen heterodoxy as a category of Hill's political and religious radicalism, although Hill himself never saw this material as outside of the criteria of a widespread, seventeenth-century, intellectual revolution.[19] It is now a standard technique to compare proper radical religious theology, such as the use of a section of the Bible or a theological concept

---

[13] Barbara K. Lewalski, *The Life of John Milton: A Critical Biography*; see also John T. Shawcross, *The Development of Milton's Thought: Law, Government, and Religion*, 49–50.

[14] Laura Lunger Knoppers, *Historicizing Milton: Spectacle, Power, and Poetry in Restoration England*; these findings inform Knoppers's important edition of Milton's 1671 poems: *The Complete Works of John Milton. Vol. 2*. Jonathan Goldberg, 'What dost thou in this world?', discusses interpretive complexity in *Paradise Regained* against what he regards as a reductive obsession to find the republican component in Milton's writings and activities. But *Paradise Regained* in all of its complexity has long been read in the context of Milton's republican politics and his radical Puritan affiliations. As Ryan Netzley puts it, 'the essay misrepresents material print culture studies... "an account bent on the singularity of the moment and its definitive meaning" [Goldberg] ... is not what historicism means' ('Milton Now: Alternative Approaches and Contexts', 193).

[15] See, e.g., Nicholas von Maltzahn, 'Laureate, Republican, Calvinist: An Early Response to Milton and *Paradise Lost*'.

[16] Quentin Skinner, 'John Milton and the Politics of Slavery'; Martin Dzelzainis, '"In These Western Parts of the Empire": Milton and Roman Law'; Dzelzainis, 'Conquest and Slavery in Milton's History of Britain'; Dzelzainis, '"In Power of Others, Never in My Own": The Meaning of Slavery in *Samson Agonistes*'; Alison Chapman, *The Legal Epic: Paradise Lost and the Early Modern Law*.

[17] Mary Nyquist, *Arbitrary Rule: Slavery, Tyranny, and the Power of Life and Death*.

[18] James Grantham Turner, *One Flesh: Paradisal Marriage and Sexual Relations in the Age of Milton*; Joanna Picciotto, *Labors of Innocence in Early Modern England*; see also Kristen Poole, *Radical Religion from Shakespeare to Milton: Figures of Nonconformity in Early Modern England*, ch. 6.

[19] William Poole, *Milton and the Idea of the Fall*; see, e.g., Christopher Hill, *The Century of Revolution, 1603–1714*.

like the incarnation, alongside Milton's works for degrees of similarity and difference.[20]

These views resonated with, and fed or were fed by, the rise of a European or Western New Left, a reorientation of left-wing politics after the repudiation of Soviet and Warsaw Pact communism in the wake of the Hungarian Risings in 1956, culminating in the 'student revolution' of May 1968, of which the most famous, but by no means only, locale was Paris. One strand of scholarship seeking an alternative path to Hill was nonetheless dedicated to finding a more historically accurate understanding of early modern republicanism, with its debts to ancient Greek and Roman political thought, as opposed to the Protestant biblicism, frequently in an apocalyptic or millenarian mode, that powered the Puritans. But in all of this work it is not a matter of whether Milton was a radical or not, but in what ways he was one, and how much more knowledge can be added to the picture. In this way too, a reasonably broad consensus for teaching the political aspects of Milton's great poetry, especially *Paradise Lost*, in university, college, and high-school classrooms has been shown to have been widely practised, and to be possible, in the light of the English Revolution debates and the history of the events of that time.[21]

What is left to be said? If we are to believe those working on the latest collected works of Milton, under the general editorship of Gordon Campbell and Thomas N. Corns, quite a lot. The results thus far have been very encouraging, ranging from the welcome construction of new texts and translations, fascinating and revealing early commentary on the reception of Miltonic texts, and important new discoveries about textual history, such as the recovery of the lost English translation of Milton's first Latin Defence of the English People (*Defensio pro Populo Anglicano*). The translation was by Thomas Margetts, and appears to be the text commissioned by the Council of State, but it was not issued in print, for reasons that are yet to emerge. The text was located in the library of Victoria University in Wellington, New Zealand, by Joad Raymond, the volume editor, and belongs to the collection assembled by G. H. Turnbull.[22] William Poole's forthcoming edition of Milton's *Commonplace Book* represents a very considerable reassessment of the grounding of his heterodox views in enormous learning, while Sharon Achinstein places Milton's divorce arguments in the longer history of the law of marriage while exposing the complicated matter of Milton's attempts to revise his divorce

---

[20] See, e.g., Brian Adams Hampton, *Fleshly Tabernacles: Milton and the Incarnational Poetics of Revolutionary England*; Paul Cefalu, *The Johannine Renaissance in Early Modern English Literature and Theology*, chs. 3–4; Ryan Hackenbracht, *National Reckonings: The Last Judgment and Literature in Milton's England*.

[21] See, e.g., David Loewenstein, 'Radical Politics in *Paradise Lost*'.

[22] Joad Raymond, 'Thomas Margetts: A New Milton Manuscript, and a New Defender of the People of England'.

writings while they were in press.[23] Other contributions to this edition of the complete works are mentioned later in this chapter.

How do those approaching Milton for the first time now react to the mention of a 'radical Milton'? Does the idea of Milton the radical sound tired, a mantra from former times, more to be associated with their grandparents? They might, almost two decades into the twenty-first century, well question 'radical' since it is now usually used to describe 'radical Islamic terrorists' or 'radical white supremacists': those dedicated to violence in the name of Islam or against it wherever they are on the globe, but associated in Western Europe, North America, and Australasia with bombing, gun and knife attacks on unarmed civilians. A larger collection of terrorist events stretching back in time comes to mind, involving violence and the deaths of innocent civilians in the name of various frustrated nationalities, racial bigotry, and other kinds of religious or ethnic anger. This is not a romantic picture with which to associate a venerated poet, even when we feel sympathy for people who are reacting to evident oppression. Indeed, such violence is usually directed against the tolerant values with which Milton is associated. When I went to university in October 1977, the student revolutions of 1968 were less than a decade old and the issues of those heady times still echoed around campuses. It was easy to see Milton as a hero of liberation, in line with how, for instance, the Romantic-era radical poet Percy Bysshe Shelley also saw Milton. Several studies at the time showed how Milton's radical afterlife had been taken as such by people later in history.[24] As if to underline a swing in perception, a recent collection of essays indexes 'revolution' (mostly in connection with Milton's reception in the French Revolution era), 'rebellion', 'antityrannicism', 'arbitrary power', 'liberty', 'republicanism', and 'slavery', but not 'radicalism'.[25] It is true that radicalism is not often indexed in earlier studies because it is a general term, and Milton scholars have referred to the specific terminology of the debates in which he engaged, reminding us once again that radicalism as a word with its current meaning does not belong to Milton's lifetime.

We are no longer at a point at which 'radical Milton' is either obvious or unproblematic: indeed, the label is uncomfortable. The matter is put into further relief by a high-quality study of a long-standing issue that underlines Milton's own apparent elitism when it comes to defining the 'people', that disapproval of the ignorant and untrustworthy vulgar, primarily for Milton those who do not know Latin.[26] The Romantic-era idea of Milton as poet-prophet on the side of the

---

[23] See John Milton, *Manuscript Writings*, ed. William Poole, *Complete Works*, vol. XI; Sharon Achinstein, 'Early Modern Marriage in a Secular Age: Beyond the Sexual Contract'; I am also grateful to have heard Prof. Achinstein's discussion of her forthcoming edition in 'John Milton in the Printing House (1644)', Workshop in the History of Material Texts, University of Pennsylvania, 1 April 2019.

[24] See Annabel Patterson, *Early Modern Liberalism*.

[25] Gray and Murphy, eds., *Milton Now: Alternative Approaches and Contexts*.

[26] Paul Hammond, *Milton and the People*.

English people slips further away, even as the same study produces heartening evidence that, despite his elitism, Milton enjoyed even in Restoration London at the point of his death a measure of popular affection. This is to be juxtaposed with the recent invocation of Milton's name as a patriot in a nationalistic, if not also jingoistic, journalism naming Milton as an obvious support for the Brexit cause in the 2016 EU referendum campaign, perhaps with a hint of nativist populism: I doubt that very much indeed. As David Marquand rightly replied, 'Milton saw himself as part of a Europe-wide Protestant movement'.[27]

An uncomfortable aspect of the charge of radicalism was brought home in the wake of the 9/11 attacks. On their first anniversary in September 2002, John Carey published a piece in *The Times Literary Supplement* in which he argued that we should question whether we ought to teach *Samson Agonistes* since its conclusion appeared to sanction irrational violence when Samson, apparently moved by an impulse of some kind, and of uncertain origin ('I begin to feel / Some rousing motions in me which dispose / To something extraordinary my thoughts' (ll. 1381–3)), caused the Philistine theatre to collapse, so killing the Philistine elite and himself.[28] The voices of outrage in the debate were predictable, but Carey had chosen his ground carefully. His real intention was to show up Stanley Fish for closing the door on literary interpretation after establishing that Samson finally demonstrates he is a man of faith: beyond that, after his prayer (l. 1637), ours is not to reason why. Not good enough, said Carey: we never really know Samson's final state of mind before he acted because Milton gives us a simile: 'And eyes fast fixed he stood, as one who prayed.' The debate was strong enough in the literary journals at the time for Feisal Mohamed to investigate the matter of a faith-bound politics, and to find resonances between the present and some of Milton's fellow travellers, such as Sir Henry Vane, who also articulated a relationship between faith and force. Mohamed was able to continue a blog, remains strongly audible in the public sphere, and brought his thoughts to a book-length statement in *Milton and the Post-Secular Present*.[29] He has been charged with underestimating the role played by reason in Milton's writing: Milton did not simply support strong political positions purely in the name of faith.[30] Mohamed objects to what he sees in both Carey and J. A. Wittreich's characterization of ambiguity in Milton as a humanistic 'dogmatism' with regard to the interpretation of that very vexing simile, 'as one who pray'd, / Or some great matter in his mind revolv'd' (ll. 1637–8). Carey and Wittreich believe that Milton leaves the matter of what

[27] Rich Lowry, 'Brexit and the Case for Modern Nationalism'; David Marquand, 'Britain's problem is not with Europe, but with England'. Rich Lowry is an American conservative journalist, editor of the *National Review; Politico Magazine* is an American publication.
[28] John Carey, 'A work in praise of terrorism?'
[29] Feisal Mohamed, *Milton and the Post-Secular Present: Ethics, Politics, Terrorism*. See also Mohamed, 'Milton, Sir Henry Vane, and the Brief but Significant Life of Godly Republicanism'.
[30] Ben Labreche, '*Areopagitica* and the limits of pluralism', 323–9.

it means open to the reader. I believe that position is true, yet with Mohamed I also think that these lines still uphold a 'faithful' reading, one that in context invokes the defeated but unbowed righteousness of the Commonwealth 'good old cause' and that invokes alarm and awe for all of us in just how this outcome was reached.[31] Mohamed also succeeds in making a coherent study of aspects of Milton's writing that urgently connect with our world, and that embrace 'radical' political activity in Milton's time and ours. Bravely and rightly, like John Carey and against the views of others, Mohamed makes us see that there are ways in which today's terrorism and the seventeenth-century understanding of biblical violence connect. The study is a demonstration of the role that intellectuals play in our current world, howsoever fraught, pressurized, or marginal. We might have hoped that these painful issues would not matter by 2019, but they do just as much as they did in September 2002.

It may also be the case that the Milton who unquestioningly believed in the force of Providence is too readily conceded: 'Wittreich's position, like Carey's, forecloses discussion of Milton's radicalism in an effort to present him as a poet sympathetic to the values of modern humanism.'[32] But Wittreich points to Milton's engagement with Greek tragedy: there are in the subject matter of *Samson Agonistes* inscrutable forces at work. We may not know them, but we *must* think about them. That is tragedy in the truest Greek sense. Milton himself does not say that Samson's death is not a suicide: that is what the Chorus says. We do not need to turn to Milton's free-will theology to see that his 'humanism', with all of its subtle understanding of the recuperation of lost literatures, is the way in which he and his contemporaries grappled with their sense of the operation of divine will in this world.[33] Others have discussed Milton's explicitly stated reservations with regard to the use of violence, not least in *Samson's* companion poem, *Paradise Regained*.[34] Neither is it difficult to imagine Milton's profound reflections on civilization being considered today in philosophically grounded discussions of the need for social justice in a world suffering from swelling income inequality and the 'violence' of world capitalism.[35]

Elsewhere we encounter degrees of denial. Some have questioned Milton's republicanism and the very idea of him as a radical. William Walker has been foremost.[36] His method relies upon very close textual readings that aim to show

[31] Mohamed, *Milton and the Post-Secular Present*, 114.

[32] Mohamed, *Milton and the Post-Secular Present*, 120.

[33] See Russ Leo, 'Milton's Aristotelian Experiments: Tragedy, *Lustratio*, and '"Secret refreshings" in Samson Agonistes (1671)'; Leo, *Tragedy as Philosophy in the Reformation World*, Conclusion.

[34] David Norbrook, 'Republican Occasions in *Paradise Regained* and *Samson Agonistes*'.

[35] See Andrew Anthony, 'Srećko Horvat: 'The current system is more violent than any revolution', *The Guardian*, 21 April 2019, https://www.theguardian.com/books/2019/apr/21/srecko-horvat-poems-from-the-future-interview (accessed 22 April 2019).

[36] William Walker, 'Milton's "Radicalism" in the Tyrannicide Tracts'. Walker's earlier articles culminate in his two monographs *Antiformalist, Unrevolutionary, Illiberal Milton: Political Prose, 1644–1660* and *Paradise Lost and Republican Tradition from Aristotle to Machiavelli*.

Milton is not saying what he is held to say. Hence his reading of the regicide writings and the Latin defences, in which he insists that Milton is not a 'radical' because he always maintained that the Parliament on whose behalf he writes has only ever sought to defend the ancient constitution against the depredations of Charles I, who has become a tyrant, and Archbishop Laud. So, the kingless republic, which had never before existed in England, established in the wake of the abolition of monarchy (never happened before in post-Norman Conquest English history), the House of Lords (ditto), and the episcopacy (ditto), was a reversion to a status quo ante, and Milton supported that. There is no discussion of resistance theory, the necessary conditions for resisting a tyrant and the means to do so, despite Milton's well-known use of them, and the closeness of his arguments to those of some of the more radical parts of the New Model Army. Much of this material is set down in Volume IV of the Clarendon Works by one of its editors, Nicholas McDowell, which Walker does not cite, published the year before his article appeared, but the material was easy to find before then. Recent work on the French Protestant resistance theory that Milton knew and cited has shown that it did in places embody antimonarchical views, and Milton's know-ledge of rabbinic commentary has been adduced as a further source of such views.[37] Walker is guilty of a very selective reading of the tracts, and one that very largely ignores the intellectual context in which they were written and the political context in which they circulated. If he is correct, Charles II might well have said in 1660, 'Oh I am so sorry about my Dad: he did let it go to his head, didn't he? And that bumptious bishop didn't help at all. Sorry for your trouble of having to put him on trial and then execute him. Tell you what, let's shake hands and carry on as normal, according to the rules of the ancient constitution.' To some degree, the Act of Oblivion sanctioned 'forgive and forget', but Charles hunted down those who had signed his father's death warrant in Britain, Europe, and colonial North America, trying and executing many of them: they were hanged, drawn, and quartered, their remains boiled, tarred, and impaled on spikes in public view.[38] Milton was lucky to be let off as lightly as he was. The legal reforms of the Commonwealth were erased from the statute book: to this day they are regarded as a legal nullity. Milton supported all of the innovation of the Commonwealth and the means by which a political revolution was achieved, and in some important respects argued that it had not gone far enough. The regicide and the revolution were regarded as an unjust outrage in the Europe of the time, even in the few states that were republics at the time. What the English

---

[37] See Freya Sierhuis, 'The Idol of the Heart: Liberty, Tyranny, and Idolatry in the Work of Fulke Greville'; Eric Nelson, *The Hebrew Republic: Jewish Sources and the Transformation of European Political Thought*, ch. 1.

[38] A brilliant essay by Blair Worden convincingly connects the treatment of the regicides to Milton's *Samson Agonistes*, especially the trial and execution of Sir Henry Vane in 1662: 'Milton, Samson Agonistes, and the Restoration'.

Parliamentarians had done was simply not sympathetically understood. This is also true of their political writings, Milton's included, that were publicly burned across the Continent. Yet there is good evidence to show that he personally thought the new government of the early 1650s was not acting fast enough: Milton was a godly revolutionary republican intellectual.[39] I can see that Walker would be upset by too much emphasis on 'classical' over godly republican (itself a reaction against an earlier predominance of interest in Puritanism), but this minority view is unpersuasive.

Yet at least Walker engages in a scholarship that attempts to reread primary materials, whereas James Simpson's anti-Reformation writing appears to accept stereotypical views of Milton and reverse their moral polarity. Since in his view the Reformation did not deliver religious freedom but instead established a mental tyranny (predestination) and violent barbarism (iconoclasm), Milton is a scion not of liberty but authoritarian mind control that is never wholly committed free-will theology, and a destructive commitment to image breaking, as in the conclusion of *Samson Agonistes*. Walker's position at least attempts originality from research; Simpson confirms old stereotypes in reverse fashion, and that is surely the less worthy gambit.[40]

Nonetheless, these debates remind us to think hard about Milton's uses of the Bible, the fundamental ground for the interpretation of his mature poetry, and the great territory of sophisticated imagistic and narrative invention within it. Moreover, as Warren Chernaik reminds us, English republicanism was a biblical as well as classical matter.[41] Milton's own latitude with biblical interpretation is instanced in Erin Murphy's rich discussion of the way in which the Holy Family in *Paradise Regained*, especially the relationship between the Son and Mary, offers a non-patriarchal, non-monarchist genealogy: a 'commitment to epistemological uncertainty and temporal deferral' that 'resists the promise of birth' in any conventional way; the 'brief epic' offers a wholly transformed view of the biblical account of genealogy and hence 'filiation'.[42]

Milton put great faith in the right of individuals to return to fundamental texts, above all the Bible, in order to figure out the 'truth'. We can agree on very simple common beliefs in a Christian commonwealth, and then there is a great deal of latitude to research and debate. This applies to Scripture and all texts from the deep past, especially if they precede the long period of corruption that manifested itself in the Roman Church through the Middle Ages. In political theory it means a

---

[39] See Stephen Fallon, 'Nascent Republican Theory in Milton's Regicide Prose'.

[40] James Simpson, *Permanent Revolution: The Reformation and the Illiberal Roots of Liberalism*, 101–2, 256. The latter reference reworks a section of the current author's work in order to assert Milton's arrogance: that he thought he was better than Shakespeare (Nigel Smith, *Is Milton Better than Shakespeare?*, 17).

[41] Warren Chernaik, *Milton and the Burden of Freedom*, ch. 4.

[42] Erin Murphy, 'Radical Relations: The Genealogical Imaginary and Queer Kinship in Milton's *Paradise Regained*'.

return not merely to biblical and Roman but also to Greek political thought, and here Rachel Foxley valuably reminds us of these Hellenic categories: with political liberty being invested in the male head of a household, and whose liberty might be threatened by the dangerous passions of the disordered and violent mob.[43] 'Radical' in the old sense of 'return to roots' is what Milton did.

How did this reflex sit with the politics of the English Revolution? One of the disabling problems with studying Milton in the context of revolutionary politics or radical religion is the apparent need to align him with this or that group or position. David Williams has recently argued that Milton, like his sometime fellow republican journalist Marchamont Nedham, was really sympathetic with the Levellers, or both were even Levellers.[44] Much evidence is drawn from alleged similarities between Milton's writings and texts published by Leveller writers before they were Levellers and before there was a Leveller movement. The analysis of late 1640s politics is distorted by the assumption that the Levellers were the only extant good cause, that they represented the true will of the people, and were fighting a pitched and ultimately unsuccessful battle with elite Parliamentarians and army commanders who were their plain opposites. Matters were much more complicated than that. At crucial points in 1649 the separatist churches that had been the bedrock of Leveller support swung instead firmly behind the authorities of the new republic as the 'Free State' took shape. Recent historiography pays more careful attention to the precise kinds of agency involved in the production of petitions and pamphlets, as campaigns were built out of fragile and temporary alliances, before they were opposed, frustrated, and fractured. We also need to be aware of which interest was funding the production and distribution of a pamphlet in order to understand the full intent of the publication.[45] This, as we will see, takes us back to the world of Christopher Hill's diverse but interacting radicals.

In *The Tenure of Kings and Magistrates* Milton uses the same biblical texts to support the removal of the tyrant that had occurred in a number of Army pamphlets. It is doubtful that many of the more prominent Levellers would have supported this: John Lilburne regarded Pride's Purge of the House of Commons, the Army's physical exclusion of the Presbyterian MPs that made possible the trial and execution of the king, as illegal. Milton feared new tyranny growing up in cabal-like government, and hence his publication in 1658 of Sir Walter Ralegh's *Cabinet Council*. More forthright republicans, like John Streater, Edward Sexby, and Miles Sindercombe, called for the assassination of the Lord

[43] Rachel Foxley, '"Due libertie and proportiond equalitie": Milton, democracy, and the republican traditio'.

[44] David Williams, *Milton's Leveller God*, ch. 1.

[45] See Jason Peacey, *Print and Public Politics in the English Revolution*; Peacey, *Politicians and Pamphleteers: Propaganda during the English Civil Wars and Interregnum*.

Protector.[46] Milton thought of the instruments of government as a means of channelling virtue, godly virtue seamlessly fused with political liberty as learned from the Bible and classical antiquity. Hence it is that the angels in *Paradise Lost* seem to appear as high-ranking state administrators.[47] He did not see an equation that linked property and political representation, as did James Harrington (surely merit would overcome property qualifications), and he rejected Hobbes's authoritarian justification of sovereignty. He nonetheless thought that true liberty would also result in greater prosperity.[48] These positions brought disputes in print with Sir Robert Filmer, the apologist for political patriarchy, and Harrington. It was Harrington whose republicanism would be more immediately and extensively understood in continental Europe, while Milton's poetry would find itself converted into the categories of a reborn idealistic philosophy.[49] Milton also inferred his dislike of colonial exploitation.[50]

Milton's 'radicalism' is nuanced and does not fit with some older stereotypical views of what a seventeenth-century radical was. There has been a fashion of denouncing Christopher Hill's search for a lower-class activism visible in army rank and file, and in beer-drinking at inns, that in fact turns out to be either of the middling sort or even elite, and quite sober.[51] But that critical view misses the point that Hill was often quite accurate with the importance of the kind of evidence that attracted him. The man who married Milton for the third time was Robert Gell,[52] former fellow of Milton's alma mater, Christ's College, Cambridge, an extreme opponent of predestination theory who also called for a new translation of the English Bible, and allegedly with a congregation of perfectionist sectaries in his living of St Mary Aldermary, London. He was the Cambridge Platonist Henry More's tutor and the go-between between More and the speculative philosopher Anne, Viscountess Conway, eventual convert to Quakerism. Gell represents the kind of latitude towards belief that was in many ways beyond the boundaries of public Commonwealth parameters, and he managed to survive in his living both during the Commonwealth and after the Restoration. David Como provides important new evidence of Gell's activities as

---

[46]   Nigel Smith, 'Milton and Popular Republicanism in the 1650s'; James Holstun, *Ehud's Dagger: Class Struggle in the English Revolution*, ch. 5.

[47]   See Julianne Werlin, 'Paper Angels: *Paradise Lost* and the European state system', *Milton Studies*, 61 (2019), 212–38.

[48]   See Lorenzo Sabbadini, 'Property, Liberty and Self-Ownership in the English Revolution', ch. 3.

[49]   Eco O. G. Haitsma Mulier, *The Myth of Venice and Dutch Republican Thought in the Seventeenth Century*; Arthur Weststeijn, *Commercial Republicanism in the Dutch Golden Age: The Political Thought of Johan & Pieter de la Court*; Gaby Mahlberg and Dirk Wiemann, eds., *European Contexts for English Republicanism*.

[50]   See, in particular, Eric B. Song, *Dominion Undeserved: Milton and The Perils of Creation*; David Armitage, 'John Milton: *Poet Against Empire*'; J. Martin Evans, *Milton's Imperial Epic: Paradise Lost and the Discourse of Colonialism*.

[51]   John Morrill, 'Which World Turned Upside Down?'

[52]   David Como, 'The Family of Love and the Making of English Revolutionary Religion'; see also Nigel Smith, 'Retranslating the Bible in the English Revolution'.

a religious radical, showing that he actively cultivated an artisan/petty merchant congregation in pre-Civil War London, some of whose members understood him to be preaching Familism and tried (unsuccessfully) by petition to win toleration for this group and others at the point of the Restoration. True 'radicals', those who would be agents of popular political movements, like the Levellers, we now know to have been sometimes learned, educated in universities or not, and to have views which do connect directly with Milton's and, with regard to mortalism and creation, may have influenced him.[53]

Milton addressed this context in his last prose pamphlet, *Of True Religion* (1673), urging a broad-based faith with a simple acceptance of a few biblical truths, and of the truth of the Scripture itself. His own antitrinitarianism had been offensive to the Commonwealth regime and would have continued so in the eyes of the reconstituted Church of England. This would have put Milton at odds with a man he knew well, the influential Independent divine, chaplain to Oliver Cromwell, and sometime Vice-Chancellor of Oxford University, John Owen, who attacked the Socinians in his *Vindiciae Evangelicae* (1655) with many literary examples.[54]

Owen saw the matter of limits to the toleration of religious beliefs as one involving literary attitude: how to fashion the right kind of poetry, a theme that takes us right to Milton's front door. This is not surprising given his interest at this point in overseeing undergraduate education, and also manifesting a very public concern with the writing of godly poetry and the proper way to do it. Owen would have been offended by Paul Best's (the first true English Socinian of whom we know) lost epic, which seems to have been Spenserian verse with the beast standing for the doctrine of the Trinity rather than Rome.[55] Owen's polemic is seeded with literary criticism. In his longer history of Arianism and Socinianism, poetry becomes the piece of evidence by which we judge the soundness of someone's doctrine. Too much worship of the Trinity leads to idolatry: he quotes at length from the Jesuit poet Clarus Bonarsius (aka Carolus Scribanius), *Amphitheatrum honoris* (1606), a Latin poem on the Virgin of Halle, and the poetic Mariolatry of Franciscus de Mendoza: two full pages in quarto of Latin verse.[56] Why does Owen go to these texts in particular? It is Owen's intention to show that, since Socinianism began in Italy, it retained crucial aspects of Roman Catholic idolatry (possibly amplified by the exile in Poland of Faustus and Lelio

---

[53] Nicholas McDowell, 'Ideas of Creation in the Writings of Richard Overton the Leveller and Paradise Lost'; for the broader situation, see McDowell, *The English Radical Imagination: Culture, Religion, and Revolution, 1630–1660.*

[54] For the broader context see Sarah Mortimer, *Reason and Religion in the English Revolution: The Challenge of Socinianism*; Paul C. H. Lim, *Mystery Unveiled: The Crisis of the Trinity in Early Modern England.*

[55] Nigel Smith, '"And if God was one of us:" Paul Best, John Biddle, and anti-Trinitarian heresy in Seventeenth-Century England', 165.

[56] John Owen, *Vindiciae Evangelicae* (1655), 57–9.

Sozzino), especially as it is known in verse. No one should be in any doubt, argues Owen, that the Socinians are still in a sense Catholics, are indeed still idolaters: 'when they had left the Papacy, and set up their opposition to the Blessed Trinity, in all their books they still made mention of those Idols and Pictures ... they knew how abhorrent it was to the very principles of reason it was, that God should be such, as by them represented; and therefore set themselves at liberty (or rather gave up themselves to the service of Sathan) to find out another God whom they might worship.'[57] Of the devil's party then; as bad as the papists, but worse in that their faith stressed reason (in the attack on the concept of the Trinity) and yet crucially violated it when it mattered. By separating Christ from God, they further institute idolatry by using the Catholic doctrine of 'divine adoration', the 'shield of the Papists doctrine'.[58]

Pagan poetry by contrast and in this context, says Owen, indubitably defines God in a Protestant way. Thus, Xenophon is quoted from Clement of Alexandria on the nature of God; Owen quotes the Greek distiches, presented here in English prose translation: 'He who shakes all things, and is Himself immoveable, is manifestly one great and powerful. But what He is in form, appears not. No more does the sun, who wishes to shine in all directions, deem it right to permit any one to look on himself. But if one gaze on him audaciously, he loses his eyesight.'[59] Yet in another work, *Animadversions on a treatise intituled Fiat lux, or, A guide in differences of religion, between papist and Protestant, Presbyterian and independent* (1662), written against the Roman Catholic John Vincent Canes's *Fiat Lux* of the same year, Owen attacks those who would use ancient literature as a proof of the existence of purgatory, listing Virgil, Cicero, and Lucretius as pagan authors who can be so mistakenly construed.[60] Perhaps the dark days of the early Restoration pushed Owen away from the degree of more liberal speculation he appeared to manifest when at the height of his influence during the Commonwealth. Scholarly interest today places us in a Lucretian moment, and the 1650s was also such a time, thanks, among others, to John Evelyn, Lucy Hutchinson, and John Milton.[61] The difference between Owen and Milton in one sense may be judged by the relative degree of tolerance of Lucretius. As Jerry Passannante shows us, the Cambridge Platonist Henry More was busy writing in Spenserian stanzas an anti-epicurean poetry designed to dispel the materialism of Lucretius. Because he read Lucretius carefully—as carefully, it would seem, as John Owen—More could not accept a partial accommodation of the ancient poet to a Providentialist framework. To this extent More's work was faithfully Lucretian

[57] Owen, *Vindiciae Evangelicae*, 56–7.   [58] Owen, *Vindiciae Evangelicae*, 57–58.
[59] Owen, *Vindiciae Evangelicae*, 71–2; Clement of Alexandria, *Stromata*, V.
[60] Owen, *Animadversions on a treatise intituled Fiat lux*, 405–6.
[61] See, e.g., Stephen Greenblatt, *The Swerve: How the World Became Modern*; David Norbrook, Stephen Harrison, and Philip Hardie, eds., *Lucretius and the Early Modern*.

and acknowledged, if with regret, the pervasive rise of materialist perspectives.[62] It is Lucretius who is probably the most significant force of reconciliation with Milton's verse in the mind of his erstwhile colleague and after 1660 political opposite, John Dryden, a client of the Duke of York, the future James II. Paul Hammond writes:

> Odd though it may have seemed for Lucretius and Milton to lie side by side on Dryden's table, both writers challenged him to see the animation of the natural world, to imagine chaos and creation, and to develop his own understanding of true happiness. In translating these writers, by drawing them into this improbable dialogue, Dryden was both essaying their respective imagined worlds and defining his own place.[63]

The presence of Lucretius and atomism on the one hand and Socinianism on the other in the poetry and prose of Milton bespeaks a fundamental difference from Owen, despite the links, personal, professional and doctrinal, between them. Owen's epic poet was Dante. Milton built atomism into his epic, not least, as is famously discussed, in Satan's journey from Hell across Chaos to the solar system and the Earth in Books II and III.

Yet when Milton licensed the Latin London edition of the Socinian *Racovian Catechism* in February 1652, Owen was infuriated. Milton wrote his sonnet to Cromwell in May 1652 on the occasion of a petition urging limited toleration and signed by fifteen Independent ministers, Owen among them. The sonnet praises Cromwell as guardian of liberty but almost certainly hints at the danger of further censorship and persecution of more extreme views than the Independents were prepared to tolerate. Christoph Arnold was a young German student visitor to England in 1651, and he claimed to have met some remarkable people. He describes a Milton who is a 'strenuous' defender of the republic who converses readily, with 'pure style' and terse writing. Of 'old English' Scripture and commentary he 'seemed altogether to entertain a too harsh if not an unjust opinion'. To Milton specialists the letter is well known, but often misunderstood. In a sentence that has, I believe, been utterly overlooked, Arnold notes *Areopagitica* and argues that while it is seemingly out of date ('written as long ago as 1644'), 'this very observant author foresaw the present liberty'.[64]

In the 1650s, not for the first time but in a way that signified the most profound challenge yet to the idea of the English confessional polity, the grounds of faith, not least as known to literate and educated people through poetry, were

[62] Gerard Passannante, *The Lucretian Renaissance: Philology and the Afterlife of Tradition*, 185–97.
[63] Paul Hammond, 'Dryden, Milton, and Lucretius'.
[64] Frans Blom, *Christoph and Andreas Arnold and England: The Travels and Book-Collections of Two Seventeenth-Century Nurembergers*, 75–80, 90.

profoundly undermined. God and Jesus in different ways were claimed to be knowable as if they were people, atomism would not be denied, and the state Bible could be refuted in countless instances of erroneous translation. The Elizabethan and Jacobean ideals of Protestant literary nationhood were considerably extended in Milton's prose writings and then unpeeled in the moment of *Paradise Lost*'s composition, in a fusion of various anti-Calvinist liberalisms, and where the literary was an instrument of that undermining and an affirmation of another way of being a believer—one without coercion. Milton's version, as is well known, had no room for Roman Catholics, and his republican constitution as expressed in 1660 proposed the permanent presence of proven virtuous men in a council of state, the only limitation being mortality: not democratic in our sense of the word, and unlike the systems of regular election proposed at the time, by the Levellers or republicans like Harrington and Streater. Facilitated by print, by the proximities of the early modern city, and by the social disruption of the mid-century, this knowledge had the ability to travel across the borders between the social strata within city congregations, and eventually across international borders.

Yet Milton's position is also consonant with the reading of 'weakness' proposed by Ross Lerner: 'this loving, wandering inability to know', that is to say another position of difference from those who would assert a faith-certain Milton, one we learn about from proems and incidental comments where the poet appears to be confessing his state of mind as he composes: a confession of self-awareness on the road on which he travels.[65] I am much less persuaded by calls for 'atheist' Milton proved by the same body of material, and would maintain that in the seventeenth century antitrinitarianism was more of a threat to an orthodox Calvinist than mere 'sensuous libertinism'.[66] Making Jesus more like a man was the result of much mid-century theological speculation, and that process continued into the following century.[67] It certainly helps to explain how we arrive at an 'ontology of the human' in Milton, a description of the human rooted in the unfallen experience of Adam and Eve: 'in the pluralist constitution of human personhood in the epic, we may derive a starting point for sociality, equality, indeed for a democratic potential of what may come in the realm of the political . . . the basis of a right to have rights', although it remains in my view very much to be seen how this understanding fits with the commercial transformation of seventeenth-century England.[68] Milton witnessed the transformation of England 'from a society in which a uniform state church, claiming allegiance of all but small groups of self-

---

[65] Ross Lerner, 'Weak Milton'. See also the investigation of Milton's notion of free speech, vulnerability, and pleasure in James Kuzner, *English Renaissance Republicans, Modern Selfhoods and the Virtue of Vulnerability*, ch. 5.

[66] Michael Bryson, *The Atheist Milton*.

[67] Donald John, 'They Became What They Beheld: Theodicy and Regeneration in Milton, Law and Blake'.

[68] Sharon Achinstein, 'Milton's Political Ontology of the Human'; Liam Haydon, '*Paradise Lost* and the Politics of the Corporation'; see also Mohamed, *Sovereignty*, ch. 3.

conscious separatists or recusants, splintered into the hopelessly fragmented world of civil-war sectarianism', and that endured despite Restoration persecution.[69] That was Robert Gell's world. Milton was in part the theorist and in all of his writings one of the most compelling observers of this process. Milton's writings fit resoundingly well with what we call early modern radicalism: they were definitive parts of its literature. Of this scene and its archive there is still very much to discover, and the topic remains vitally relevant to our own concerns today. That our notion of what is radical has been recently so exposed to reassessment only makes our interest in Milton and his works all the more keen and searching.

[69] Como, 'The Family of Love'.

16

Afterword

Making Milton Matter

Elizabeth Sauer

Milton's cultural capital is invested in books, both those that serve as mediums for his self-fashioning endeavours and those that participate in ongoing conversations about 'why Milton matters'. While already prosperous and profitable, the industry capitalizing on this question has experienced even more growth since the four-hundredth anniversary of the poet's birth. The products thereof materialized voluminously in library exhibits, conference presentations, and the broadest array of publications, which have successfully assessed 'why we studied Milton, [and] what exactly constituted his cultural value'.[1] By taking up the matter of Milton, print and book history, authorship, and afterlives, *Making Milton* advances the project of gauging the poet-polemicist's significance and the received tradition of his work, while presenting pioneering readings, especially of the material Milton.

This book on making Milton and making him matter navigates the author's text life, defined by his 'continu[ous] reading' practices.[2] Milton's Künstlerroman begins with a Humanistic education, the amassing of his own library, and corres-pondence with teachers and scholars, editors, and associates like Thomas Young, Charles Diodati, and Vatican librarian curator Lukas Holste. One of the most revealing episodes in the narrative of his book consultations and acquisitions is captured in a letter to Holste. The (material) manuscript evidence thereof remained undiscovered until the mid-twentieth century when Milton reappeared in the Vatican Library, over four centuries after his first visit. 'Courteously admitted [in]to the [Vatican] Library,' recalls the young Milton, 'I was permitted to browse through the invaluable collection of Books, and also the numerous Greek Authors in manuscript annotated by your nightly toil', a nocturnal labour

---

[1] Paul Stevens, 'Milton and the Marginalization of the Humanities,' 77. Contributions to the literature on Milton's value include Leonard's *The Value of John Milton* and Wittreich's *Why Milton Matters*, to which *Making Milton* adds the material Milton. Not considered in the present volume is Milton's monism and philosophy of matter.

[2] Milton, 'To Charles Diodati, 1637', in Orgel and Goldberg, eds., *John Milton: The Major Works*, 717–19, 718. Boswell identified hundreds of titles in reassembling Milton's library and history of book ownership (*Milton's Library*). However, only a few of Milton's extant books have been recovered. See William Poole, 'John Milton and Giovanni Boccaccio's *Vita di Dante*'.

Elizabeth Sauer, *Afterword: Making Milton Matter* In: *Making Milton: Print, Authorship, Afterlives*. Edited by: Emma Depledge, John S. Garrison, and Marissa Nicosia, Oxford University Press (2021). © Elizabeth Sauer.
DOI: 10.1093/oso/9780198821892.003.0016

that Milton and his muse would later imitate in their engendering of *Paradise Lost*. The annotation of the manuscripts, for which Milton credits Holste, animates those documents, "as if in readiness for action, like Vergil's—*souls shut deep within a green valley, and about to cross the threshold of the upper world*; they seemed to demand only the ready hands of the Printer and a delivery into the world'.[3] The process of annotating the writings and preparing them for dissemination compares with the 'progress the soul' described in Virgil's account of the unborn souls 'poised for action' and awaiting only the assistance or conduct of a midwife.[4] The printer assumes the midwife's position in Milton's description of the birth. Made in the image of their authors, and brought forth at the hands of the printer, the newly begotten writings bear and preserve the 'potency of life' of their progenitor's 'living intellect' and the imprimatur of their deliverer.[5]

The development of what would become the key work in the English literary canon was likewise a laborious corporeal act, but also a slow home birth, marked by setbacks. Jonathan Richardson reports that Milton 'frequently Compos'd lying in Bed in a Morning... [;] when he could not Sleep, but lay Awake whole Nights, he Try'd; not One Verse could he make; at other times flow'd *Easy his Unpremeditated Verse*, with a certain *Impetus* and *Æstro*, as Himself seem'd to Believe. Then, at what Hour soever, he rung for his Daughter to Secure what Came.'[6] Composition is an act of embodiment, as well as a visceral, verbal, collective, and material practice involving the poet and, in this case, one of his daughters. The resulting manuscript remains a work in progress, requiring assembly, correction, and emendation: 'I had the perusal of it [the poem] from the very beginning', explains Edward Phillips, to whose Milton biography Richardson was indebted; 'for some years, as I went from time to time, to Visit him, in a Parcel of Ten, Twenty, or Thirty Verses at a Time, which being Written by whatever hand came next, might possibly want Correction as to the Orthography and Pointing'.[7] On the basis of Phillips's testimony, Gordon Campbell and Thomas N. Corns have concluded that copies of *Paradise Lost* were already in circulation in the mid 1660s.[8]

Past and present biographers in fact participate in the ongoing industry of making Milton, the focus of the current volume. *Making Milton* is a major contribution more specifically to the burgeoning field of inquiry that brings

---

[3] *Aeneid* 6.679–80; 'To Lukas Holste in the Vatican at Rome', Wolfe, ed., *Complete Prose Works of John Milton*, 1:333.

[4] Reputedly a midwife, Phaenarete—'she who brings virtue to light'—might have inspired her son Socrates's comparison of philosophical inquiry with midwifery (Plato, *Theaetetus*, 149a).

[5] Milton, *Areopagitica*, in Orgel and Goldberg, eds., *The Major Works*, 236–73, 239–40.

[6] Jonathan Richardson, Jr and Sr, *Explanatory Notes and Remarks on Milton's 'Paradise Lost'... With the Life of the Author*, 291. Cf. *Paradise Lost* 9.23–4. On the legal and material conditions that led to the publication of *Paradise Lost*, see also William Poole, *Milton and the Making of* Paradise Lost, ch. 13.

[7] Phillips, *The Life of Mr John Milton*, 73.

[8] Campbell and Corns, *John Milton: Life, Works, and Thought*, 271, 327. Cf. Festa, 'Milton's Sensuous Poetics'.

Milton Studies into conversation with the scholarship on material culture, the history of the book, and the mechanisms of public dissemination. The volume is an especially timely intervention in the drama of Milton writing himself into sense, that is, the shaping of his persona and public reception so reliant on evolving print technologies. While the tripartite structure of the book invites distinctions among the terms and conditions of printing, authorship, and the generation of afterlives, the historical and material operations of 'making Milton' create a dynamic among all three practices and the collective achievements of the contributors.

That the making of Milton is the labour of the book trade, editors, stationers, and social networks in which his writings circulated and were reproduced is amply and adeptly explicated in Part I. The material Milton is fabricated by the sociopolitical conditions that fostered or (like censorship) derailed book production and trade. In the opening chapter, Stephen B. Dobranski, whose influential scholarship has made groundbreaking inroads into Milton's place in the publishing world, reconstructs Milton's early views on authorship and print as mechanisms for tangible embodiment and self-perpetuation. The following chapters concern Milton's status, legacy, and cultural and material environs, as well as his monetary worth in the marketplace. Dovetailing with Dobranski's essay is Blaine Greteman's study of *Epitaphium Damonis*—the first work Milton had printed (the anonymously published *Maske Presented at Ludlow Castle* notwithstanding)—from which radiate the social, poetic, and political networks Milton established. The expansive set of relations defining and promoting Milton's authorial identity and career included stationers involved in a commercial rivalry. The canonical folio edition of *Paradise Lost* emerged from this contest (Emma Depledge). And thanks to Thomas N. Corns's contribution, we learn of the re-evaluation of Milton in a narrative of *Paradise Lost*'s domestication and distribution as an octavo and a pocket edition. The early modern and eighteenth-century book trade made Milton matter for the people.

The first English author about whom reports, correspondence, and life records are in abundance, Milton inspired numerous lives of the poet and biographies throughout his life and legacy, even though he himself left no diary. These lives of the poet are based, as Edward Jones reminds us, on little corroborated evidence.[9] But the recovery of Milton through examinations of the large body of his literary writings has proven enormously fruitful.[10] Well over a

---

[9] Jones, 'Ere Half My Days', 3. No biographer has more zealously and seductively claimed Milton for the twenty-first century than David Hawkes. His cultural materialist reading fashions a Milton with *far-sighted* views on society, sexuality, economics, and politics that animate his life and literary career (Hawkes, *John Milton: A Hero of Our Time*).

[10] The most recent and significant biographies of Milton profitably emphasise the *making* of the poet: Nicholas McDowell's *Poet of Revolution: The Making of John Milton* (Princeton: Princeton University Press, 2020) and William Poole's *Milton and the Making of* Paradise Lost.

generation ago, Stephen Greenblatt spawned a new era of scholarly historicist inquiry in *Renaissance Self-Fashioning*, which probed structures of selfhood in key literary figures of the sixteenth century. Identities, Greenblatt illustrated, are ideological products of power relations within social laboratories.[11] The material world in *Renaissance Self-Fashioning* is demarcated by population increase, urban and industrial development, and economic advancements. In *Making Milton*, self-fashioning is more specifically a product of textual and material embodiment, thus raising alternative questions about, and encouraging new ways of, making Milton.

In Part II, 'Milton's Construction of an Authorial Identity', Milton's print persona emerges in various venues. These range from his participation in a republic of letters, by way of the *Defensio Secunda* (John K. Hale), to a refashioned nationalism, which, by virtue of *A Maske Presented at Ludlow Castle*, manifests new symbolic power (David Loewenstein). Stories of the book featuring Milton's relationship with his muse (Kyle Pivetti) and Milton's biblical hermeneutics and rereadings of Pauline texts (Noam Reisner) confirm that self-formation is a simultaneous act of conformity, intervention, and resistance—local, national, and international. Rachel Willie's reading of the shared concern of Milton and William Davenant with authorial legacy intersects with Dobranski's earlier chapter on Milton's struggles at self-memorialization in and through print, though Willie concentrates on authorial preservation in early modern theatre culture. Milton's visual imagination is central to Antoinina Bevan Zlatar's eye-opening investigation of the poet's visualization of the invisible in the context of reimaginings of divinity, and in terms of contemporary critical debates on Milton's iconoclasm.[12]

As the final part demonstrates, interpreters of Milton's reputation and adapters of his works reconfigure Milton. Readers, audiences, and critics write back, becoming performers in and directors of Milton's uneven and vibrant reception history. Showcased here is a rich array of critical rereadings of Milton's oeuvre, designed as 'projects of consciousness transformation' (Nigel Smith). Heading the critical agendas scrutinized in Part III is Milton and gender. Lara Dodds analyses Restoration poet Anne Finch's engagement and adaptation of *Paradise Lost*, which was for women writers both a source of inspiration and a monument to an enshrined literary tradition. A dramatically different approach to *Paradise Lost*, one focused on its eroticism, is advanced in Neil Forsyth's account of *A Maske Presented at Ludlow Castle*, as informed by the early modern stage's rematerialization of the page, authorial practice, and textual interpretation.

---

[11] Greenblatt, *Renaissance Self-Fashioning*, 256. On Milton and self-fashioning, see Stevens's 'Discontinuities in Milton's Early Public Self-Representation'.
[12] See Dobranski, *Milton's Visual Imagination*.

Making Milton disrupts not only the narratives of Milton's carefully plotted literary career and 'transcendent authorship' but also establishes new and blended methodologies for approaching these subjects. For example, John K. Hale demonstrates that Milton's self-life is Latinized, his reputation sustained by the Latin of his distinctive persona. Angelica Duran's examination of the early Mexican Miltons underwrites valuable novel understandings of the international, multilingual nature of Milton's circulation. In this case, the evidence exposes a material Milton who serves as an 'enabling resource' for Mexican readers and critics wrestling to realize or refine their own forms of literary critical engagement. Smith reviews Milton's and Milton's readers' critical agendas by detailing the ways Milton scholarship then and now consciously resonates with the times. In that regard, Milton and Miltonists are radical and/or rooted. Throughout, *Making Milton* cautions against bookbinding 'John Milton, Englishman'—in the vernacular—or cordoning off Milton's self-life and material life from the republic of letters and from international milieux. Milton's identity and territory are global and multilingual, and that is ultimately where this collection leads us in our pursuit to appreciate how, where, and why Milton matters.[13] Marking a material turn in Milton Studies, *Making Milton* serves, then, as a welcome enabling resource and rewarding contribution to the cultural capital of collective book production and reception.

[13] On the global Milton, see Duran, Issa, and Olson, eds., *Milton in Translation*; and Gordon Teskey's acceptance speech in Sauer, 'MSA Platinum Jubilee at the 2018 MLA'.

Works Cited

Achinstein, Sharon. *Milton and the Revolutionary Reader.* Princeton: Princeton University Press, 1994.

Achinstein, Sharon. 'Milton's Spectre in the Restoration: Marvell, Dryden, and Literary Enthusiasm'. *Huntington Library Quarterly* 59 (1997): 1–29.

Achinstein, Sharon. *Literature and Dissent in Milton's England.* Cambridge: Cambridge University Press, 2003.

Achinstein, Sharon. 'Red Milton: Abraham Polonsky and You Are There (January 30, 1955)'. In *Visionary Milton: Essays on Prophecy and Violence*, ed. Peter E. Medine, John T. Shawcross, and David V. Urban. Pittsburgh: Duquesne University Press, 2010: 50–61.

Achinstein, Sharon. 'Early Modern Marriage in a Secular Age: Beyond the Sexual Contract'. In *Milton in the Long Restoration*, ed. Blair Hoxby and Ann Coiro. Oxford: Oxford University Press, 2016: 365–78.

Achinstein, Sharon. 'Milton's Political Ontology of the Human'. *ELH* 84 (2017): 591–616.

A Choice Catalogue of the Library of John Parsons (London, 1682).

Allsopp, Niall. '"Lett none our Lombard Author blame for's righteous paine:" An Annotated Copy of Sir William Davenant's *Gondibert*'. *The Library* 16 (2015): 24–50.

An Abridgement for the late remonstrance of the army. London: printed for Laurence Blaikloche, 1648.

An Answer to a Book. Intituled, 'The Doctrine and Discipline of Divorce'. London: G.M., 1644.

Anderson, Benedict. *Imagined Communities: Reflections of the Origins and Spread of Nationalism.* London: Verso, 1991.

Anderson, David K. 'Internal Images: John Donne and the English Iconoclast Controversy'. *Renaissance and Reformation* 26.2 (2002): 23–42.

Anderson, Thomas. *Performing Early Modern Trauma from Shakespeare to Milton.* Aldershot: Ashgate, 2006.

Andrewes, Lancelot. 'A Sermon Preached at the Court, on the XXV of March, A.D. MDXCVII. Being Good-Friday'. In *Selected Sermons & Lectures*, ed. Peter McCullough. Oxford University Press, 2005: 122–37.

Anthony, Andrew. 'Srećko Horvat: The current system is more violent than any revolution', *The Guardian*, 21 April 2019: https://www.theguardian.com/books/2019/apr/21/srecko-horvat-poems-from-the-future-interview.

Arber, Edward, ed. *The Term Catalogues, 1668–1709 A.D.*, 3 vols. London: Privately printed, 1903–6.

Armitage, David. 'John Milton: *Poet Against Empire*'. In *Milton and Republicanism*, ed. David Armitage, Armand Himy, and Quentin Skinner. Cambridge: Cambridge University Press, 1995: 206–25.

Ashcroft, Bill, and Helen Tiffan. *The Empire Strikes Back: Theory and Practice in Post-Colonial Literatures.* 2nd edn. London: Routledge, 2003.

Aston, Margaret. *England's Iconoclasts: Laws against Images.* Oxford: Oxford University Press, 1988.

Aston, Margaret. *Broken Idols of the English Reformation*. Cambridge: Cambridge University Press, 2015.

Atkyns, Richard. *Original and Growth of Printing*. London, 1664.

Aubrey, John. 'John Milton'. In *Brief Lives*, ed. Richard Barber. Woodbridge: Boydell Press, 2004.

Backscheider, Paula R. *Eighteenth-Century Women Poets and their Poetry: Inventing Agency, Inventing Genre*. Baltimore: Johns Hopkins University Press, 2010.

Baker, David J., and Willy Maley, eds. *British Identities and English Renaissance Literature*, Cambridge: Cambridge University Press, 2002.

Barabási, Albert-László. *Network Science*. Cambridge: Cambridge University Press, 2016.

Barash, Carol. 'The Political Origins of Anne Finch's Poetry'. *Huntington Library Quarterly* 54.4 (1991): 327–51.

Barish, Jonas A. *The Antitheatrical Prejudice*. Berkeley: University of California Press, 1981.

Barkan, Leonard. *Transuming Passion: Ganymede and the Erotics of Humanism*. Palo Alto: Stanford University Press, 1991.

Barnard, John. 'Dryden, Tonson, and Subscriptions for the 1697 Virgil'. *PBSA* 57 (1963): 129–51.

Barnard, John. 'Large- and Small-Paper Copies of Dryden's *The Works of Virgil* (1697): Jacob Tonson's Investment and Profits and the Example of *Paradise Lost* (1688)'. *PBSA* 92 (1998): 259–71.

Barnard, John. 'London Publishing, 1640-1660: Crisis, Continuity, and Innovation'. *Book History* 4 (2001): 1–16.

Barnard, John. 'Etherege, Sir George (1636–1691/2), playwright and diplomat'. In *Oxford Dictionary of National Biography*. Oxford: Oxford University Press, 2004.

Baron, Sabrina A. 'Licensing Readers, Licensing Authorities in Seventeenth-Century England'. In *Books and Readers in Early Modern England,* ed. Jennifer Anderson and Elizabeth Sauer. Philadelphia: University of Pennsylvania Press, 1992: 217–42.

Bawcutt, N.W., ed. *The Control and Censorship of Caroline Drama: The Records of Sir Henry Herbert, Master of the Revels, 1623–73*. Oxford: Oxford University Press, 1996.

Beal, Peter. 'Massinger at Bay: Unpublished Verses in a War of the Theatres'. *The Yearbook of English Studies* 10 (1980): 190–203.

Beer, Anna. *Milton: Poet, Pamphleteer, and Patriot*. London: Bloomsbury, 2010.

Bennett, John S. *Reviving Liberty: Radical Christian Humanism in Milton's Great Epics*. Cambridge: Harvard University Press, 1989.

Besançon, Alain. *The Forbidden Image: An Intellectual History of Iconoclasm*. Chicago: University of Chicago Press, 2000.

Bevan Zlatar, Antoinina. 'Flowers Wrought in Carpets: Looking afresh at the *Homily against the Peril of Idolatrie*'. In *Crossing Traditions: Essays on Reformation and Intellectual History in Honour of Irena Backus*, ed. Maria-Cristina Pitassi. Boston: Brill, 2017: 386–404.

Blayney, Peter W. M. 'The Publication of Playbooks'. In *A New History of Early English Drama*, ed. John D. Cox and David Scott Kastan. New York: Columbia University Press, 1997: 405–10.

Blethen, H. T. 'Bishop John Williams's Recantation of his "Holy Table, Name and Thing", 1638'. *Journal of Theological Studies* 29 (1978): 157–60.

Blevins, Jacob. *Humanism and Classical Crisis: Anxiety, Intertexts, and the Miltonic Memory*. Columbus: Ohio State University Press, 2014.

Blom, Frans. *Christoph and Andreas Arnold and England: The Travels and Book-Collections of Two Seventeenth-Century Nurembergers*. Nuremberg: Stadtarchiv Nürnberg, 1982.

Boehrer, Bruce. 'Animal Love in Milton: The Case of *Epitaphium Damonis*'. *ELH* 70.3 (2003): 787–811.

Bond, Donald F., ed. *The Spectator*, 5 vols. Oxford: Clarendon Press, 1965.

Boswell, Jackson. *Milton's Library: A Catalogue of the Remains of John Milton's Library and an Annotated Reconstruction of Milton's Library and Ancillary Readings*. New York: Garland, 1975.

Bourne, Claire M. L. '*Vide Supplementum*: Early Modern Collation as Play-Reading in the First Folio'. In *Early Modern English Marginalia*, ed. Katherine Acheson. New York and Abingdon: Routledge, 2018: 195–233.

Bradburn, Elizabeth. 'Theatrical Wonder, Amazement, and the Construction of Spiritual Agency in *Paradise Lost*'. *Comparative Drama* 40 (2006): 77–98.

Braddick, Michael J. *The Oxford Handbook of the English Revolution*. Oxford: Oxford University Press, 2015.

Bradner, Leicester. 'Milton's *Epitaphium Damonis*'. *Times Literary Supplement* (18 August 1932): 531.

Brioso y Candiani, Manuel. *Ensayo de una historia científica acerca de Oaxaca*. Mexico: Tipografía Oaxaca en México, 1939.

Britland, Karen. *Drama at the Courts of Queen Henrietta Maria*. Cambridge: Cambridge University Press, 2006.

Brooks, Cleanth, and John Edward Hardy. *'Poems of Mr. John Milton': The 1645 Edition and Essays in Analysis*. New York: Harcourt, Brace, 1951.

Brooks, Douglas A. *Printing and Parenting in Early Modern England*. London: Routledge, 2005.

Brown, Cedric C. *John Milton's Aristocratic Entertainments*. Cambridge: Cambridge University Press, 1985.

Brown, Cedric C. 'John Milton and Charles Diodati: Reading the Textual Exchanges of Friends'. *Milton Quarterly* 45.2 (2011): 73–94.

Brown, Cedric C. 'Milton, the Attentive Mr Skinner, and the Acts and Discourses of Friendship.' In *A Concise Companion to the Study of Manuscripts, Printed Books, and the Production of Early Modern Texts: A Festschrift for Gordon Campbell*, ed. Edward Jones. Chichester: Wiley-Blackwell, 2015: 106–28.

Brown, Cedric C. *Friendship and its Discourses in the Seventeenth Century*. Oxford: Oxford University Press, 2016.

Brown, Eric C. *Milton on Film*. Pittsburgh: Duquesne University Press, 2015.

Bryson, Michael. *The Atheist Milton*. Farnham and Burlington: Ashgate, 2012.

Bullinger, Heinrich, *De origine erroris libri duo, Heinrychi Bullingeri, Ecclesiae Tigurinae ministri*. Zurich, 1568. Zentralbibliothek Zürich. Signatur: 5.38,4. http://dx.doi.org/10.3931/e-rara-18524.

Burbery, Timothy J. *Milton the Dramatist*. Pittsburgh: Duquesne University Press, 2007.

Burgess, Glenn, and Matthew Festenstein, eds. *English Radicalism, 1550–1850*. Cambridge: Cambridge University Press, 2007.

Burt, Stephen. '"To The Unknown God:" St. Paul and Athens in Milton's *Areopagitica*'. *Milton Quarterly* 32, no. 1 (1998): 23–31.

Butler, Martin. 'Literature and the Theater to 1660'. In *The Cambridge History of Early Modern Literature*, ed. David Loewenstein and Janel Mueller. Cambridge: Cambridge University Press, 2003: 565–602.

Cable, Lana. *Carnal Rhetoric: Milton's Iconoclasm and the Poetics of Desire*. Durham: Duke University Press, 1995.

Callon, Michel, John Law, and Arie Rip. 'How to Study the Force of Science'. In *Mapping the Dynamics of Science and Technology*, ed. Michel Callon, John Law, and Arie Rip. Houndmills: Macmillan, 1986: 3–15.

Calvin, John. *Institutio christianae religionis, in libros quatuor nunc primum digesta, certisque distincta capitibus, ad aptissimam methodum: aucta etiam tam magna accessione ut propemodum opus novum haberi possit.* Geneva: Robert I. Estienne, 1559.

Calvin, John. *Institutes of the Christian Religion*, Vol. I. Ed. John T. McNeill. Trans. Ford Lewis Battles. Louisville: Westminster John Knox Press, 2006.

Campbell, Gordon, and Thomas N. Corns. *John Milton: Life, Works, and Thought*. Oxford: Oxford University Press, 2008.

Campbell, Gordon, Thomas N. Corns, John K. Hale, and Fiona J. Tweedie. *Milton and the Manuscript of De Doctrina Christiana*. Oxford: Oxford University Press, 2007.

Carey, John, ed. *Milton: The Complete Shorter Poems*, 2nd edn. Harlow: Pearson Education, 1997.

Carey, John. 'A work in praise of terrorism?' *Times Literary Supplement*. September 6 (2002): 15–16.

Carter, Philip. 'Kit-Cat Club (*act.* 1696–1720)'. In *Oxford Dictionary of National Biography*. Oxford: Oxford University Press, 2005.

Catullus. 'V'. In *The Poems of Catullus*, ed. and trans. Guy Lee. Oxford: Oxford University Press, 1990: 48–51.

Cefalu, Paul. *The Johannine Renaissance in Early Modern English Literature and Theology*. Oxford: Oxford University Press, 2017.

Chapman, Alison. *The Legal Epic: Paradise Lost and the Early Modern Law*. Chicago: The University of Chicago Press, 2017.

Charles II. *Proclamation, for calling in and suppressing of two books written by John Milton*. London: John Bill, 1660.

Chartier, Roger. 'Texts, Printing, Reading'. In *The New Cultural History*, ed. Lynn Hunt. Los Angeles: University of California Press, 1989: 154–75.

Chernaik, Warren. 'Books as Memorials: The Politics of Consolation'. *Yearbook of English Studies* 21 (1991): 207–17.

Clapp, Susannah. 'Comus review – Milton meets the National Theatre of Brent'. *Observer*, 6 Nov. 2016.

Clare, Janet. *Drama of the English Republic: 1649–1660*. Manchester: Manchester University Press, 2002.

Clement of Alexandria. *Stromata*, V.

Coiro, Ann Baynes. 'Milton and Class Identity: The Publication of *Areopagitica* and the 1645 *Poems*'. *Journal of Medieval and Renaissance Studies* 22 (1992): 261–89.

Coiro, Ann Baynes. 'Anonymous Milton, or, *A Maske* Masked', *ELH* 71 (2004): 609–29.

Coiro, Ann Baynes. 'Drama in the Epic Style: Narrator, Muse and Audience in *Paradise Lost*'. *Milton Studies* 51 (2010): 63–100.

Collinson, Patrick. 'From Iconoclasm to Iconophobia: The Cultural Impact of the Second English Reformation'. The Stenton Lecture, 1985, 1–37. Reading: University of Reading, 1986.

Como, David. 'The Family of Love and the Making of English Revolutionary Religion: The Confession and "Conversions" of Giles Creech'. *JMEMS* 48 (2018): 553–98.

Connor, Francis X., 'Henry Herringman, Richard Bentley and Shakespeare's Fourth Folio (1685)'. In *Canonising Shakespeare: Stationers and the Book Trade, 1640–1740*, ed. Emma Depledge and Peter Kirwan. Cambridge: Cambridge University Press, 2017: 38–54.

Corns, Thomas N. 'Christopher Hill on Milton, Bunyan and Winstanley'. *Prose Studies* 36 (2014): 209–18.

Corns, Thomas N. 'Roman Catholicism, *De Doctrina Christiana*, and the Paradise of Fools'. In *Milton and Catholicism*, ed. Ronald Corthell and Thomas N. Corns. Notre Dame: University of Notre Dame Press, 2017: 83–100.

Cowley, Abraham. 'To Sir William Davenant, upon his two first Books of Gondibert, finished before his voyage to America'. In *A Discourse Upon Gondibert. An Heroick Poem Written by Sr. William Davenant. With an Answer to it by Mr Hobbs*. Paris: Chez Matthieu Guillemot, 1650.

Crawforth, Hannah. *Etymology and the Invention of English in Early Modern Literature*. Cambridge: Cambridge University Press, 2013.

Cruickshank, Frances. *Verse and Poetics in George Herbert and John Donne*. Surrey: Ashgate, 2010.

Culler, Jonathan. 'Comparative Literature, at Last'. In *World Literature in an Age of Globalization*, ed. Haun Saussy. Baltimore: Johns Hopkins University Press, 2006: 237–48.

Cust, Richard. *Charles I: A Political Life*. Harlow: Longman, 2005.

Darbishire, Helen, ed. *The Early Lives of Milton*. London: Constable, 1932.

Davenant, William. 'The author's preface to his much honoured friend, Mr Hobbes'. In *A Discourse Upon Gondibert. An Heroick Poem Written by Sr. William Davenant. With an Answer to it by Mr Hobbs*. Paris: Chez Matthieu Guillemot, 1650.

de Filippis, Michele. 'Milton and Manso: Cups or Books?'. *PMLA* 51 (1936): 745–56.

Demaray, John G. *Milton's Theatrical Epic: The Invention and Design of Paradise Lost*. Cambridge: Harvard University Press, 1980.

Depledge, Emma. 'False Dating: The Case of the "1676" *Hamlet* Quartos'. *PBSA* 112 (2018): 183–99.

Depledge, Emma. *Shakespeare's Rise to Cultural Prominence: Print, Politics and Alteration, 1642–1700*. Cambridge: Cambridge University Press, 2018.

Dinshaw, Carolyn. *How Soon is Now? Medieval Texts, Amateur Readers, and the Queerness of Time*. Durham, Duke University Press, 2012.

Dobranski, Stephen B. *Milton, Authorship, and the Book Trade*. Cambridge: Cambridge University Press, 1999.

Dobranski, Stephen B. *Readers and Authorship in Early Modern England*. Cambridge: Cambridge University Press, 2005.

Dobranski, Stephen B. ' Simmons's Shell Game: The Six Title Pages of *Paradise Lost*'. In *Paradise Lost: A Poem Written in Ten Books: Essays on the 1667 First Edition*, ed. Michael Lieb and John T. Shawcross. Pittsburgh: Duquesne University Press, 2007: 57–78.

Dobranski, Stephen B. 'Principle and Politics in Milton's *Areopagitica*'. In *The Oxford Handbook of Literature and the English Revolution*, ed. Laura Lunger Knoppers. Oxford: Oxford University Press, 2013: 190–205.

Dobranski, Stephen B. *Milton's Visual Imagination: Imagery in 'Paradise Lost'*. Cambridge: Cambridge University Press, 2015.

Dobson, Michael. *The Making of the National Poet: Shakespeare, Adaptation and Authorship, 1660–1769*. Oxford: Clarendon Press, 1994.

Donne, John, the Younger. 'To Sr William Davenant'. February 1651 [1652]. BL Thomason 669.f.15 (82) fol. 1.

Donnelly, Phillip J. '"Matter" versus Body: The Character of Milton's Monism'. *Milton Quarterly* 33.3 (1999): 79–85.

Dowsing, William. *The Journal of William Dowsing: Iconoclasm in East Anglia during the English Civil War*. Ed. T. Cooper. Woodbridge: Boydell Press, 2001.

Dryden, John. *The State of Innocence, and Fall of Man: An Opera. Written in Heroique Verse, and Dedicated to Her Royal Highness, the Dutchess. By John Dryden, Servant to His Majesty*. London: for Henry Herringman, 1677.

Dryden, John. 'Portrait Frontispiece'. *Paradise Lost*. London: 1688.

Dryden, John. 'The State of Innocence'. In *The Works of John Dryden, Vol XII*, ed. Vinton A. Dearling. Berkeley: University of California Press, 1994.

Dugas, Don-John. *Marketing the Bard: Shakespeare in Performance and Print, 1660–1740*. Columbia: University of Missouri Press, 2006.

Dulgarian, Robert. 'Milton's "Naturam non pati senium" and "De Idea Platonica" as Cambridge Act Verses: A Reconsideration in Light of Manuscript Evidence'. *Review of English Studies* 70, 297 (November 2019): 847–68.

Duncan-Jones, Katherine, ed. *Shakespeare's Sonnets*. Nashville: Thomas Nelson, 1997.

Duran, Angelica. 'Milton in Puebla, Mexico'. *Battersea Review* 2, no. 6 (2016).

Duran, Angelica. '*Paradise Lost* in Spanish Translation and as World Literature'. In *Milton in Translation*, ed. Angelica Duran, Islam Issa, and Jonathan R. Olson. Oxford: Oxford University Press, 2017: 276–7.

Duran, Angelica. 'Three of Borges's Miltons'. In *Milton Studies* 58, 'Special Issue: Milton in the Americas', ed. Elizabeth Sauer and Angelica Duran. Pittsburgh: Duquesne University Press, 2017: 183–200.

Duran, Angelica. *Milton among Spaniards*. Newark: University of Delaware Press, 2020.

Duran, Angelica, Islam Issa, and Jonathan R. Olson, eds. *Milton in Translation*. Oxford: Oxford University Press, 2017.

Duran, Angelica, and Elizabeth Sauer, eds. 'Milton in the Americas'. *Milton Studies* 58 (September 2017): vii–262.

Dzelzainis, Martin. 'In These Western Parts of the Empire: Milton and Roman Law'. In *Milton and the Terms of Liberty*, ed. Graham Parry and Joad Raymond. Cambridge: Brewer, 2002: 57–68.

Dzelzainis, Martin. 'Conquest and Slavery in Milton's History of Britain'. In *The Oxford Handbook of Milton*, ed. Nicholas McDowell and Nigel Smith. Oxford: Oxford University Press, 2009: 407–23.

Dzelzainis, Martin. 'In Power of Others, Never in My Own: The Meaning of Slavery in *Samson Agonistes*'. In *Milton in the Long Restoration*, ed. Blair Hoxby and Ann Coiro. Oxford: Oxford University Press, 2016: 284–301.

Edmond, Mary. *Rare Sir William Davenant: Poet Laureate, Playwright, Civil War General, Restoration Theatre Man*. Manchester: Manchester University Press, 1987.

Edwards, Jonathan. *Explanatory Notes and Remarks on Milton's 'Paradise Lost'… With the Life of the Author*. In *The Early Lives of John Milton*, ed. Helen Darbishire. London: Constable, 1965.

Edwards, Karen. 'Milton's Reformed Animals: An Early Modern Bestiary: D–F'. *Milton Quarterly* 40.2 (2006): 114–18.

Edwards, Thomas. *Gangraena*, 3 pts. London: T.R. and E.M., 1646.

Erne, Lukas. *Shakespeare as Literary Dramatist*. Cambridge: Cambridge University Press, 2003.

Erne, Lukas. *Shakespeare and the Book Trade*. Cambridge: Cambridge University Press, 2013.

Erne, Lukas. '*Cupids Cabinet Unlockt* (1662), Ostensibly "By W. Shakespeare", in Fact Partly by John Milton'. In *Canonising Shakespeare: Stationers and the Book Trade, 1640–*

1740, ed. Emma Depledge and Peter Kirwan. Cambridge: Cambridge University Press, 2017: 107–29.

Escobedo, Andrew. *Nationalism and Historical Loss in Renaissance England: Foxe, Dee, Spenser, Milton*. Ithaca: Cornell University Press, 2004.

Evans, J. Martin. *Milton's Imperial Epic: Paradise Lost and the Discourse of Colonialism*. Ithaca: Cornell University Press, 1996.

Eyre, G. E. Briscoe, and C. R. Rivington. *A Transcript of the Registers of the Worshipful Company of Stationers of London; from 1640–1708 A. D.* 3 vols. London: Privately printed, 1913–14.

Fadely, Patrick, and Feisal G. Mohamed, eds. *Milton's Modernities: Poetry, Philosophy, and History from the Seventeenth Century to the Present*. Evanston, IL: Northwestern University Press, 2017.

Falcone, Filippo. *Milton's Inward Liberty: A Reading of Christian Liberty from the Prose to Paradise Lost*. Cambridge: James Clarke & Co., 2014.

Fallon, Samuel. 'Milton's Strange God: Theology and Narrative Form in *Paradise Lost*'. *ELH*, 79:1, 2012: 33–57.

Fallon, Stephen M. *Milton among the Philosophers: Poetry and Materialism in Seventeenth-Century England*. Ithaca: Cornell University Press, 1991.

Fallon, Stephen M. *Milton's Peculiar Grace: Self-Representation and Authority*. Ithaca: Cornell University Press, 2007.

Fallon, Stephen M. 'Nascent Republican Theory in Milton's Regicide Prose'. In *The Oxford Handbook of Literature & the English Revolution*, ed. Laura Lunger Knoppers. Oxford: Oxford University Press, 2013: 309–26.

Festa, Thomas. 'Milton's Sensuous Poetics: On the Material Texts of *Paradise Lost*'. *Milton Studies* 59 (2018): 91–124.

Finch, Anne Kingsmill. *Miscellany poems, on several occasions. Written by a lady*. London: printed for John Barber on Lambeth-Hill, 1713; and sold by John Morphew, near Stationers-Hall. *Eighteenth Century Collections Online*.

Finch, Anne Kingsmill. 'The Introduction'. In *The Poems of Anne Countess of Winchilsea*, ed. Myra Reynolds. Chicago: University of Chicago Press, 1903.

Fincham, Kenneth. 'The restoration of the altars in the 1630s'. *Historical Journal* xliv (2001): 919–40.

Fincham, Kenneth, and Peter Lake. 'The Ecclesiastical Policies of James I and Charles I'. In *The Early Stuart Church*, ed. Kenneth Fincham. Basingstoke: Macmillan, 1993.

Fincham, Kenneth, and Nicholas Tyacke. *Altars Restored: The Changing Face of English Religious Worship, 1547–c.1700*. Oxford: Oxford University Press, 2007.

Firth, C. H. 'Sir William Davenant and the Revival of Drama During the Protectorate'. *English Historical Review* 18 (1903): 319–21.

Fish, Stanley. 'With Mortal Voice: Milton Defends against the Muse'. *ELH* 62.3 (1995): 509–27.

Fish, Stanley. *Surprised by Sin: The Reader in Paradise Lost*, 2nd edn. Cambridge: Harvard University Press, 1998.

Flannagan, Roy C., ed. *The Riverside Milton*. Boston: Houghton Mifflin, 1998.

Flannagan, Roy C. *John Milton: A Short Introduction*. Oxford: Blackwell, 2002.

Fletcher, Harris Francis, ed. *John Milton's Complete Poetical Works*, 4 vols. Urbana: University of Illinois Press, 1943–8.

Forsyth, Neil. 'The Seventeenth-Century Separate Printing of Milton's *Epitaphium Damonis*'. *The Journal of English and Germanic Philology* 61 (1962): 788–96.

Forsyth, Neil. 'Homer in Milton'. In *The Satanic Epic*. Princeton, NJ: Princeton University Press, 1997.

Forsyth, Neil. *John Milton: A Biography*. Oxford: Lion, 2013.

Forsyth, Neil. 'Comus Performed at the Wanamaker Theatre in London: Two Views'. *Milton Quarterly* 51 (2017): 67–71.

Foster, Andrew. 'Neile, Richard (1562–1640), Archbishop of York'. In *Oxford Dictionary of National Biography*. Oxford: Oxford University Press, 2004.

Fowler, Alastair. *Time's Purpled Masquers: Stars and the Afterlife in Renaissance English Literature*. Oxford: Clarendon Press, 1996.

Fowler, Alastair, ed. *Milton: Paradise Lost*. New York: Routledge, 2006.

Foxley, Rachel. ' "Due libertie and proportiond equalitie": Milton, democracy, and the republican traditio'. *History of Political Thought*, 34 (2013): 614–39.

Frank, Marcie. 'Staging Criticism, Staging Milton: John Dryden's "The State of Innocence" '. *The Eighteenth Century* 34, no. 1 (1993): 45–64.

Frank, Marcie. *Gender, Theatre, and the Origins of Criticism from Dryden to Manley*. Cambridge: Cambridge University Press, 2003.

French, J. M., ed. *The Life Records of John Milton*, 5 vols. New Brunswick: Rutgers University Press, 1949–58.

Fuchs, Barbara. 'Imperium Studies: Theorizing Early Modern Expansion'. In *Postcolonial Moves: Medieval Through Modern*, ed. Patricia Clare Ingham and Michelle R. Warren. New York: Palgrave Macmillan, 2003: 71–90.

Gardiner, S. R. *Documents relating to the proceedings against William Prynne in 1634 and 1637*. London: Camden Society, 1877.

Garrison, John. 'Plurality and *Amicitia* in Milton's *Epitaphium Damonis*'. *Milton Quarterly* 46.3 (2012): 154–73.

Gay, David. ' "Rapt Spirits": 2 Corinthians 12.2–5 and the Language of Milton's *Comus*'. *Milton Quarterly* 29 (1995): 76–86.

Gilbert, Sandra M., and Susan Gubar. *The Madwoman in the Attic: The Woman Writer and the Nineteenth-Century Literary Imagination*, 2nd edn. New Haven: Yale University Press, 2000.

Gill, Alexander. 'The Preface'. In *The sacred philosophie of the Holy Scripture*. London: Anne Griffin, 1635.

Gillespie, Stuart. 'The Early Years of the Dryden-Tonson Partnership: The Background to their Composite Translations and Miscellanies of the 1680s'. *Restoration: Studies in English Literary Culture, 1660–1700*, 12 (1988): 10–9.

Gilman, E. B. *Iconoclasm and Poetry in the English Reformation: Down Went Dagon*. Chicago: University of Chicago Press, 1986.

Gimelli Martin, Catherine. *Milton Among the Puritans: The Case For Historical Revisionism*. Ashgate: Routledge, 2010.

Goldberg, Jonathan. 'What dost thou in this world?' In *Milton Now: Alternative Approaches and Contexts*, ed. Catharine Gray and Erin Murphy. New York: Palgrave Macmillan, 2014: 51–69.

Goodman, Godfrey. *The Fall of Man, or the Corruption of Nature proved by the light of his Natural Reason*. London: Joseph Browne, 1616.

Graves, Neil D. 'Milton and the Theory of Accommodation', *Studies in Philology*, Vol. 98, No. 2 (Spring, 2001): 251–72.

Gray, Catherine, and Erin Murphy, eds. *Milton Now: Alternative Approaches and Contexts*. New York: Palgrave Macmillan, 2014.

Green, Ian. *The Christian's ABC: Catechisms and Catechizing in England c. 1530–1740*. Oxford: Clarendon Press, 1996.

Green, Mandy. 'Reaching a European Audience: Milton's Neo-Latin Poems for Charles Diodati, 1625–39'. *The European Legacy* 17 (2012): 165–84.

Greenblatt, Stephen. *Renaissance Self-Fashioning: From More to Shakespeare*. Chicago: University of Chicago Press, 1983.

Greenblatt, Stephen. *The Swerve: How the World Became Modern*. New York: W.W. Norton, 2011.

Gregerson, Linda. *The Reformation of the Subject: Spenser, Milton and the English Protestant Epic*. Cambridge: Cambridge University Press, 1995.

Greteman, Blaine. *The Poetics and Politics of Youth in Milton's England*. Cambridge: Cambridge University Press, 2013.

Griffin, Dustin. 'The Bard of Cyder-Land: John Philips and Miltonic Imitation'. *Studies in English Literature* 24.3 (1984): 441.

Griffiths, John, ed. 'Homily against Peril of Idolatry'. In *Book of Homilies*. Vancouver: Regent College Publishing, 2008.

Guibbory, Achsah. *Ceremony and Community from Herbert to Milton: Literature, Religion and Cultural Conflict in Seventeenth-Century England*. Cambridge: Cambridge University Press, 1998.

Guibbory, Achsah. *Christian Identity, Jews, and Israel in Seventeenth-Century England*. Oxford: Oxford University Press, 2010.

Guillory, John. *Poetic Authority: Spenser, Milton and Literary History*. New York: Columbia University Press, 1983.

Gurnay, Edmund. *Towards a Vindication of the Second Commandment*. Cambridge: Thomas Buck, 1639.

Guy-Bray, Stephen. *Homoerotic Space: The Poetics of Loss in Renaissance Literature*. Toronto: University of Toronto Press, 2002.

Guy-Bray, Stephen. '"Fellowships of Joy": Angelic Union in Paradise Lost'. *Early Modern Culture* 10 (2014).

Haan, Estelle. *From Academia to Amicitia: Milton's Latin Writings and the Italian Academies*. Philadelphia: American Philosophical Society, 1998.

Haan, Estelle. *Both English and Latin: Bilingualism and Biculturalism in Milton's Neo-Latin Writings*. American Philosophical Society, 2012.

Hackenbracht, Ryan. *National Reckonings: The Last Judgment and Literature in Milton's England*. Ithaca: Cornell University Press, 2019.

Hakewill, George. *An Apologie of the Power and Providence of God*. Oxford: W. Turner, 1635.

Hale, John K. 'Milton's Self-Presentation in Poems . . . 1645'. *Milton Quarterly* 25.2 (1991): 37.

Hale, John K. *Milton's Languages: The Impact of Multilingualism on Style*. Cambridge: Cambridge University Press, 1997.

Hale, John K. ed. *John Milton: Select Latin Writings*. In *Bibliotheca Novae Latinitatis*, 2. Assen: van Gorcum, also Tempe: MRTS, 1998.

Hale, John K. 'Books and Book-Form in Milton'. *Renaissance and Reformation/Renaissance et Réforme* 4 (1999): 63–77.

Hale, John K. 'Milton on the Style Best for Historiography'. *Prose Studies* 23, no. 3 (2000).

Hale, John K. 'Milton Plays the Fool: The Christ's College Salting, 1628'. *Classical and Modern Literature* 20 (2000): 51–70.

Hale, John K. *Milton as Multilingual: Selected Essays, 1982–2004*. Otago: University of Otago, 2005.

Hale, John K. *Milton's Cambridge Latin: Performing in the Genres, 1625–1632*. Arizona Center for Medieval and Renaissance Studies, 2005.

Hale, John K., and J. Donald Cullington, eds. *The Complete Works of John Milton: Vol. 1*. Oxford: Oxford University Press, 2012.

Hale, John K., J. Donald Cullington, Gordon Campbell, and Thomas N. Corns, eds. *The Complete Works of John Milton: Volume VIII: De Doctrina Christiana*. Oxford University Press, 2012.

Hamilton, Marion H. 'Dryden's *State of Innocence*: An Old-Spelling Edition with a Critical Study of the Early Printed Texts and Manuscripts'. PhD Dissertation, University of Virginia, 1952.

Hamilton, Marion H. 'The Early Editions of Dryden's *State of Innocence*'. *Studies in Bibliography* 5 (1952–3): 163–6.

Hamilton, Marion H. 'The Manuscripts of Dryden's *The State of Innocence* and the Relation of the Harvard Ms to the First Quarto'. *Studies in Bibliography* 6 (1954): 237–46.

Hamling, Tara. *Decorating the Godly Household: Religious Art in Post-Reformation Britain*. New Haven: Yale University Press, 2010.

Hamm, Robert B., Jr 'Rowe's "Shakespeare" (1709) and the Tonson House Style'. *College Literature* 31 (2004): 179–205.

Hammond, Paul. 'Dryden, Milton, and Lucretius'. *Seventeenth Century* 16 (2001): 172–3.

Hammond, Paul. *Milton and the People*. Oxford: Oxford University Press, 2014.

Hammond, Paul, and Blair Worden, eds. *John Milton: Life, Writing, Reputation*. Oxford: Oxford University Press, 2010.

Hampton, Brian Adams. *Fleshly Tabernacles: Milton and the Incarnational Poetics of Revolutionary England*. South Bend, IN: University of Notre Dame Press, 2012.

Hanford, James Holly. 'The Dramatic Element in *Paradise Lost*'. *Studies in Philology* 14 (1927): 178–95.

Hansen, Lara, and Eric Rasmussen. 'Shakespeare Without Rules: The Fifth Shakespeare Folio and Market Demand in the Early 1700s'. In *Canonising Shakespeare: Stationers and the Book Trade, 1640–1740*, ed. Emma Depledge and Peter Kirwan. Cambridge: Cambridge University Press, 2017: 55–62.

Harper, David. 'The First Annotator of *Paradise Lost* and the Makings of English Literary Criticism'. *Studies in English Literature* 112, 3 (Summer 2019): 507–30.

Hart, James S., Jr. 'Noy [Noye], William (1577–1634), lawyer and politician'. In *Oxford Dictionary of National Biography*. Oxford: Oxford University Press, 2004.

Hawkes, David. *John Milton: A Hero of Our Time*. Berkeley: Counterpoint, 2009.

Haydon, Liam. '*Paradise Lost* and the Politics of the Corporation'. *Studies in English Literature* 57 (2017): 135–55.

Heaney, Seamus. *Preoccupations: Selected Prose, 1968–1978*. New York: Farrar, Straus, & Giroux, 1980.

Heath, Jane. *Paul's Visual Piety: The Metamorphosis of the Beholder*. Oxford: Oxford University Press, 2013.

Helgerson, Richard. *Forms of Nationhood*. Chicago: University of Chicago Press, 1992.

Heylyn, Peter. *A Coale from the Altar*. London: Augustine Mathewes, 1637.

Heywood, Thomas. *An apology for actors Containing three briefe treatises. 1 Their antiquity. 2 Their ancient dignity. 3 The true vse of their quality*. London: Nicholas Okes, 1612.

Hill, Christopher. *The Century of Revolution 1603–1714*. Edinburgh: T. Nelson, 1961.

Hill, Christopher. *The Experience of Defeat: Milton and Some Contemporaries*. London: Faber & Faber, 1984.

Hill, Christopher. *Milton and the English Revolution*. London: Faber & Faber; New York: Viking Press, 1997.

Hillier, Russell M. *Milton's Messiah: The Son of God in the Works of John Milton*. Oxford: Oxford University Press, 2011.

Holstun, James. *Ehud's Dagger: Class Struggle in the English Revolution*. London: Verso, 2000.

Homily against Peril of Idolatry. London, 1563.

Hooks, Adam G. *Selling Shakespeare: Biography, Bibliography, and the Book Trade*. Cambridge: Cambridge University Press, 2016.

Hotson, Leslie. *The Commonwealth and Restoration Stage*. Cambridge: Harvard University Press, 1928.

Howard-Hill, T. H. 'Milton and "The Rounded Theatre's Pomp"'. In *Of Poetry and Politics: New Essays on Milton and His World*, ed. P. G. Stanwood. Binghamton: Medieval and Renaissance Texts & Studies, 1995: 95–121.

Howell, Thomas Bayly. 'Proceedings in the Star-Chamber against Henry Sherfield. 1633'. In *Cobbett's Complete Collection of State Trials*, Vol. III. London: R. Bagshaw, 1809: 519–62.

Hoxby, Blair, and Ann Baynes Coiro, eds. *Milton in the Long Restoration*. Oxford: Oxford University Press, 2016.

Hughes, Merritt Y., ed. *John Milton: Complete Poems and Major Prose*. Indianapolis: Hackett, 1957.

Hulley Karl K., and Stanley T. Vandersall, eds. *Ovid's Metamorphosis*. Trans. George Sandys. Lincoln: University of Nebraska Press, 1970.

Hunter, William Bridges, Jr, and Stevie Davies. 'Milton's Urania: "The Meaning, Not the Name I Call"'. In *The Descent of Urania: Studies in Milton, 1946–1988*. Lewisburg: Bucknell University Press, 1989.

Hunter, William Bridges, Jr, C. A. Patrides, and J. H. Adamson, eds. *Bright Essence: Studies in Milton's Theology*. Salt Lake City: University of Utah Press, 1971.

Index librorum prohibitorum Innoc. XI. P. M. jussu editus usque ad annum 1681. Romae: Typis. Rev. Cam. Apost., 1704.

Index librorum prohibitorum Sanctissimi domini nostri Benedicti XIV Pontificis maximi iussu recognitus, atque editus. Romæ: Rev. Cameræ apostolicæ, 1758.

Index librorum prohibitorum usque ad diem 4. Junii Anni MDCCXLIV. Regnante Benedicto XIV. P. O. M. Romae: Rev. Cam. Apost., 1744.

Jacob, James R., and Timothy Raylor. 'Opera and Obedience: Thomas Hobbes and "A Proposition for Advancement of Morality" by Sir William Davenant'. *The Seventeenth Century* 6 (1991): 205–50.

James I. 'A Speech in the Parliament House (1605)'. In *The Workes of the Most High and Mightie Prince, James, by the Grace of God, King of Great Britaine, France and Ireland, Defender of the Faith, &c*. London, 1616.

James I. *The Workes of the Most High and Mightie Prince, James, by the Grace of God, King of Great Britaine, France and Ireland, Defender of the Faith, &c*. London, 1616.

James I. *A Meditation Upon the Lords Prayer, Written by the Kings Maiestie*. London, 1619.

James I. *A Proclamation Against Excesse of lavish and licentious speech of matters of state*. London: Iohn Bill, 1620.

Jardine, Lisa, and Anthony Grafton. '"Studied for Action": How Gabriel Harvey Read His Livy'. *Past & Present* 129 (1990): 30–78.

John, Donald. 'They Became What They Beheld: Theodicy and Regeneration in Milton, Law and Blake'. In *Radicalism in British Literary Culture, 1650–1830: From Revolution to Revolution*, ed. Timothy Morton and Nigel Smith. Cambridge: Cambridge University Press, 2002: 86–100.

John of Damascus. *Three Treatises on the Divine Images*. Trans. Andrew Louth. Crestwood: St Vladimir's Seminary Press, 2003.

Johns, Adrian. *The Nature of the Book*. Chicago and London: University of Chicago Press, 1998.

Johnson, Samuel. *Lives of the English Poets*, ed. Arthur Waugh. Oxford: Oxford University Press, 1952.

Jones, Edward. '"Ere Half My Days": Milton's Life, 1608–1640'. In *The Oxford Handbook of Milton*, ed. Nicholas McDowell and Nigel Smith. Oxford: Oxford University Press, 2009.

Jones, Edward, ed. *Young Milton: The Emerging Author, 1620–1642*. Oxford: Oxford University Press, 2013.

Jonson, Ben. 'An Epistle to Elizabeth, Countess of Rutland'. In *Ben Jonson and the Cavalier Poets*, ed. Hugh Maclean. New York and London: Norton, 1974: 36–8.

Jonson, R. M. 'The Politics of Publication: Misrepresentation in Milton's 1645 *Poems*'. *Criticism* 36.1 (1994): 45–71.

Journal of the House of Commons: Volume 3: 1643–1644. London: His Majesty's Stationary Office, 1802.

Kastan, David. 'Humphrey Moseley and the Invention of English Literature'. In *Agent of Change: Print Culture Studies After Elizabeth L. Eisenstein*, ed. Sabrina Alcorn Baron, Eric N. Lindquist, and Eleanor F. Shevlin. Amherst: University of Massachusetts Press, 2007: 105–24.

Keeble N. H., and Nicholas McDowell, eds. *The Complete Works of John Milton: Volume VI: Vernacular Regicide and Republican Tracts*. Oxford: Oxford University Press, 2014.

Keith, Jennifer, and Claudia Thomas Kairoff, eds. *The Cambridge Edition of the Works of Anne Finch, Countess of Winchilsea*. Cambridge: Cambridge University Press, 2020.

Kenrick, Edward. '*Paradise Lost* and the Index of Prohibited Books'. *Studies in Philology* 53 (1956): 485–500.

Kerr, Jason A. 'Elizabeth Attaway, London preacher and Theologian, 1645–1646,' *The Seventeenth Century*, DOI: 10.1080/0268117X.2020.1825230.

Kerrigan, John. *Archipelagic English: Literature, History, and Politics, 1603–1707*. Oxford: Oxford University Press, 2008.

Kewes, Paulina. '"Give Me the Sociable Pocket-books…": Humphrey Moseley's serial publication of octavo play collections'. *Publishing History* 38 (1995): 5–21.

Kewes, Paulina. *Authorship and Appropriation: Writing for the Stage in England, 1660–1710*. Oxford: Clarendon Press, 1998.

Kezar, Dennis. 'Samson's Death by Theater and Milton's Art of Dying'. *ELH* 66/2 (1999): 295–336.

Kilgour, Maggie. *Milton and the Metamorphosis of Ovid*. Oxford: Oxford University Press, 2012.

King, Bruce. 'The Significance of Dryden's State of Innocence'. *Studies in English Literature, 1500–1900: Restoration and Eighteenth Century* 4, no. 3 (Summer 1964): 371–91.

Knight, Sarah. 'Milton's Student Verses of 1629'. *Notes and Queries* 255 (2010): 37–9.

Knight, Sarah. 'Royal Milton'. *Times Literary Supplement* 5 Feb. 2010: 15.

Knight, Sarah, and Stefan Tilg, eds. *The Oxford Handbook of Neo-Latin*. Oxford: Oxford University Press, 2015.

Knoppers, Laura Lunger. *Historicizing Milton: Spectacle, Power, and Poetry in Restoration England*. Athens: University of Georgia Press, 1994.

Knoppers, Laura Lunger. *The Complete Works of John Milton. Vol. 2, The 1671 Poems: Paradise Regain'd and Samson Agonistes*. Oxford: Oxford University Press, 2008.

Knoppers, Laura Lunger. 'Consuming Nations: Milton and Luxury'. In *Early Modern Nationalism and Milton's England*, ed. David Loewenstein and Paul Stevens. Toronto: University of Toronto Press, 2008.

Knoppers, Laura Lunger, and Greg Colón Semenza, eds. *Milton in Popular Culture*. New York: Palgrave, 2006.

Koerner, Joseph Leo. *The Reformation of the Image*. London: Reaktion Books, 2004.

Kopperman, Paul E. 'Heath, Sir Robert (1575–1649), judge'. In *Oxford Dictionary of National Biography*. Oxford: Oxford University Press, 2004.

Kuzner, James. *English Renaissance Republicans, Modern Selfhoods and the Virtue of Vulnerability*. Edinburgh: Edinburgh University Press, 2011.

Labreche, Ben. '*Areopagitica* and the limits of pluralism'. *Milton Studies* 54 (2013): 139–60, 323–9.

Lafaye, Jacques. *Albores de la imprenta: el libro en España y Portugal y sus posesiones de ultramar (siglos XV–XVI)*. Mexico: Fondo de Cultura Económica, 2004.

Lake, Peter. 'The Laudian Style: Order, Uniformity and the Pursuit of the Beauty of Holiness in the 1630s'. In *The Early Stuart Church, 1603–1642*, ed. Kenneth Fincham. Basingstoke: Houndmills, 1988: 115–37.

Lambert, Sheila. 'State Control of the Press in Theory and Practice: The Role of the Stationers' Company Before 1640'. In *Censorship and the Control of Print in England and France 1600–1910*, ed. Robin Myers and Michael Harris. Winchester: St. Paul's Bibliographies, 1992: 1–32.

Larminie, Vivienne. 'Davenant, John (*bap.* 1572, *d.* 1641), bishop of Salisbury'. In *Oxford Dictionary of National Biography*. Oxford: Oxford University Press, 2004.

Latour, Bruno. *Reassembling the Social*. Oxford: Oxford University Press, 2005.

Laud, William. *A Speech Delivered in the Starr-Chamber, on Wednesday, the XIVth of Iune, MDCXXXVII, at the censure, of Iohn Bastwick, Henry Burton, & William Prinn; concerning pretended innovations in the Church. By the most Reverend Father in God, William, L. Archbishop of Canterbury his Grace*. London: Richard Badger, 1637.

Laud, William. *The History of the Trouble and Tryal of the Most Reverend Father in God and Blessed Martyr, William Laud*. London: Printed for Ri. Chiswell, 1695.

Lawes, H. 'To the Right Honorable John Lord Vicount Bracly'. In *A Maske Presented at Ludlow Castle*. London: 1637.

Le Comte, Edward. '*Areopagitica* as Scenario for *Paradise Lost*'. In *Achievements of the Left Hand*, ed. Michael Lieb and John Shawcross. Amherst: University of Massachusetts Press, 1974: 121–41.

Leo, Russ. 'Milton's Aristotelian Experiments : Tragedy, Lustratio, and "Secret refreshings" in Samson Agonistes (1671)'. *Milton Studies* 52 (2011): 221.52.

Leo, Russ. *Tragedy as Philosophy in the Reformation World*. Oxford: Oxford University Press, 2019.

Leonard, Irving A. *Books of the Brave, Being an Account of Men in the Spanish Conquest and Settlement of the Sixteenth-century New World*. London: Cambridge University Press, 1949.

Leonard, John, ed. *John Milton: The Complete Poems*. Harmondsworth: Penguin, 1998.

Leonard, John, ed. *Faithful Labourers: A Reception History of Paradise Lost, 1667–1970*, 2 vols. Oxford: Oxford University Press, 2013.

Leonard, John. *The Value of John Milton*. Cambridge: Cambridge University Press, 2016.

Lerner, Ross. 'Weak Milton'. *Studies in English Literature* 57 (2017): 111–34.

Lewalski, Barbara. 'Milton's *Comus* and the Politics of Masquing'. In *The Politics of the Stuart Court Masques*, ed. David Bevington and Peter Holbrook. Cambridge: Cambridge University Press, 1998: 296–320.

Lewalski, Barbara. *The Life of John Milton: A Critical Biography*. Oxford: Blackwell, 2000.

Lewalski, Barbara. 'Milton and Idolatry', *Studies in English Literature* 43.1 (2003): 213–32.

Lewalski, Barbara. 'Milton: The Muses, the Prophets, the Spirit, and Prophetic Poetry'. *Milton Studies* 54 (2013): 59–78.

Lewalski, Barbara, and Estelle Haan, eds. *The Complete Works of John Milton: Volume III: The Shorter Poems*. Oxford: Oxford University Press, 2012.

Lewis, C. S. *A Preface to Paradise Lost*. London and New York: Oxford University Press, 1942.

Lewis, Jayne Elizabeth. *The English Fable: Aesop and Literary Culture, 1651–1740*. Cambridge: Cambridge University Press, 1996.

Lieb, Michael. *Poetics of the Holy: A Reading of* Paradise Lost. Chapel Hill: University of North Carolina Press, 1981.

Lieb, Michael. 'Milton's "Dramatick Constitutions": The Celestial Dialogue in *Paradise Lost*, Book III'. *Milton Studies* 23 (1987): 215–40.

Lim, Paul C. H. *Mystery Unveiled: The Crisis of the Trinity in Early Modern England*. New York and Oxford: Oxford University Press, 2012.

Lindenbaum, Peter. 'Milton's Contract'. In *The Construction of Authorship: Textual Appropriation in Law and Literature*, ed. Martha Woodmansee and Peter Jaszi. Durham: Duke University Press, 1994.

Lindenbaum, Peter. 'Rematerializing Milton'. *Publishing History* 41 (1997): 5–22.

Lindenbaum, Peter. 'Sidney's *Arcadia* as Cultural Monument and Proto-Novel'. In *Texts and Cultural Change in Early Modern England*, ed. Cedric C. Brown and Arthur F. Marotti. Basingstoke: Macmillan Press, 1997: 80–94.

Lindenbaum, Peter. 'Authors and Publishers in the Late Seventeenth Century, II: Brabazon Aylmer and the Mysteries of the Trade'. *The Library* 3 (2002): 32–57.

Lindley, David, ed. *Court Masques: Jacobean and Caroline Entertainments, 1605–1640*. Oxford: Clarendon Press, 1995.

Lipking, Lawrence. 'The Genius of the Shore: Lycidas, Adamastor, and the Poetics of Nationalism'. *PMLA* 111:2 (1996), 205–21.

Loewenstein, David. '"Casting down Imaginations": Milton as Iconoclast'. *Criticism: A Quarterly for Literature and the Arts* 31 (1986): 3:253–70.

Loewenstein, David. *Milton and the Drama of History: Historical Vision, Iconoclasm, and the Literary Imagination*. Cambridge: Cambridge University Press, 1990.

Loewenstein, David. *Representing Revolution in Milton and his Contemporaries: Religion, Politics, and Polemics in Radical Puritanism*. Cambridge: Cambridge University Press, 2001.

Loewenstein, David. 'Late Milton: Early Modern Nationalist or Patriot?'. *Milton Studies* 48 (2008): 53–71.

Loewenstein, David. 'Milton's Nationalism and the English Revolution: Strains and Contradictions'. In *Early Modern Nationalism and Milton's England*. Toronto: University of Toronto Press, 2008: 25–50.

Loewenstein, David. 'Radical Politics in *Paradise Lost*'. In Peter C. Herman, ed., *Approaches to Teaching Milton's* Paradise Lost. 2nd edn, New York: Modern Language Association of America, 2012: 68–75.

Loewenstein, David. *Treacherous Faith: The Specter of Heresy in Early Modern English Literature and Culture*. Oxford: Oxford University Press, 2013.

Loewenstein, David, and Paul Stevens, eds. *Early Modern Nationalism and Milton's England*. Toronto: University of Toronto Press, 2008.

Loewenstein, David, and Paul Stevens. 'Introduction'. In *Early Modern Nationalism and Milton's England*. Toronto: University of Toronto Press, 2008: 3–21.

Love, Harold. *Scribal Publication in Seventh-Century England*. Oxford: Clarendon, 1993.

Lowry, Rich. 'Brexit and the Case for Modern Nationalism'. *Politico Magazine* (22 June 2016).

Luck, Georg. 'Introduction to the Latin Love Elegy'. In *Latin Erotic Elegy: An Anthology and Reader*. New York: Routledge, 2002: 307–11.

Lynch, Kathleen. *Jacob Tonson: Kit-Cat Publisher*. Knoxville: University of Tennessee Press, 1971.

MacCallum, Hugh. *Milton and the Sons of God: The Divine Image in Milton's Epic Poetry*. Toronto: University of Toronto Press, 1986.

McCullough, Peter. 'Making Dead Men Speak: Laudianism, Print, and the Works of Lancelot Andrewes, 1626–1642'. *Historical Journal* 41 (1998): 401–24.

McCullough, Peter. 'Lancelot Andrewes's Transforming Passions'. *Huntingdon Library Quarterly* 71.4 (2008): 573–88.

Macdonald, Hugh. *John Dryden: A Bibliography of Early Editions and of Drydeniana*. London: Dawsons, 1967.

McDowell, Nicholas. *The English Radical Imagination: Culture, Religion, and Revolution, 1630–1660*. Oxford: Clarendon Press, 2003.

McDowell, Nicholas. 'Ideas of Creation in the Writings of Richard Overton and the Leveller and Paradise Lost'. *Journal of the History of Ideas* 66 (2005): 59–78.

McDowell, Nicholas. *Poet of Revolution: The Making of John Milton*. Princeton: Princeton University Press, 2020.

Mack, Maynard. *Alexander Pope: A Biography*. New York: W.W. Norton & Co., 1985.

McKenzie, D. F. 'Speech–Manuscript–Print'. In *Making Meaning: 'Printers of the Mind' and Other Essays*, ed. Peter D. McDonald and Michael F. Suarez. Amherst: University of Massachusetts Press, 2002: 237–58.

MacKenzie, Raymond N. 'Tonson, Jacob, the elder (1655/6–1736), bookseller'. In *Oxford Dictionary of National Biography*. Oxford: Oxford University Press, 2004.

MacLennan, Kerry. 'John Milton's Contract for *Paradise Lost*: A Commercial Reading'. *Milton Quarterly* 44 (2010): 221–30.

Mahlberg, Gaby, and Dirk Wiemann, eds. *European Contexts for English Republicanism*. Farnham and Burlington, VT: Ashgate, 2013.

Maley, Willy. *Nation, State and Empire in English Renaissance Literature: Shakespeare to Milton*. Basingstoke: Palgrave Macmillan, 2003.

Maltzahn, Nicholas. 'Milton's Readers'. In *The Cambridge Companion to John Milton*, ed. Dennis Danielson. Cambridge: Cambridge University Press, 1999: 236–52.

Mandelbrote, Giles. 'Richard Bentley's Copies: The Ownership of Copyright in the Late 17th Century'. In *The Book Trade and its Customers, 1450–1900: Historical Essays for Robin Myers*, ed. Robin Myers, Arnold Hunt, Giles Mandelbrote, and Alison Shell. London: St Paul's Bibliographies, 1991.

Mansur, Miriam. 'Machado de Assis and Milton: Possible Dialogues'. In *Milton Studies 58* 'Special Issue: Milton in the Americas', ed. Elizabeth Sauer and Angelica Duran. Pittsburgh: Duquesne University Press, 2017: 167–82.

Mantecón, Carmen Vázquez. *Historia de las bibliotecas en Oaxaca*. Mexico: Dirección general de bibliotecas, 1989.

Marcus, Leah S. *The Politics of Mirth: Jonson, Herrick, Milton, Marvell and the Defense of Old Holiday Pastimes*. Chicago: University of Chicago Press, 1986.

Marcus, Leah S. 'John Milton's *Comus*'. In *A New Companion to Milton*, ed. Thomas N. Corns. Chichester: Wiley, 2016.

Maron, Publio Virgilio. *Traduccion de las obras de el príncipe de los poetas latinos Publio Virgilio Maron a metro castellano*. Ed. and trans. D. Joseph Rafael Larrañaga. Mexico: Herrederos del Lic D. Joseph de Juaregui, 1787.

Marotti, Arthur. *Manuscript, Print, and the English Renaissance Lyric*. Ithaca: Cornell University Press, 1995.

Marquand, David. 'Britain's problem is not with Europe, but with England'. *The Guardian*, 19 Dec. 2017.

Martz, Louis Lohr. *Milton, Poet of Exile*. New Haven: Yale University Press, 1986.

Marvell, Andrew. 'On Mr Milton's *Paradise Lost*'. In *The Poems of Andrew Marvell*, ed. Nigel Smith. Longman: Harlow, 2007: 180–4.

Masson, David. *The Life of John Milton: Narrated in Connection with the Political, Ecclesiastical, and Literary History of his Time*, 6 vols. London: Macmillan, 1877–96.

Medoff, Jeslyn. 'The daughters of Behn and the problem of reputation'. In *Women, Writing, History*, ed. Isobel Grundy and Susan Wiseman. London: B.T. Batsford, 1992.

Menges, Hilary. 'Books and Readers in Milton's Early Poetry and Prose'. *English Literary Renaissance* 42.1 (2012): 119–45.

Mignolo, Walter. *The Darker Side of Western Modernity: Global Futures, Decolonial Options*. Durham: Duke University Press, 2011.

Miller, Christopher R. 'Staying Out Late: Anne Finch's Poetics of Evening'. *Studies in English Literature* 45.3 (2005).

Miller, Christopher R. 'Yet Once More: Milton's Lyric Descendants'. In *Milton in the Long Eighteenth Century*, ed. Blair Hoxby and Ann Baynes Coiro. Oxford: Oxford University Press, 2016.

Miller, Paul Allen. *Subjective Verses: Latin Love Elegy and the Emergence of the Real*. Princeton: Princeton University Press, 2004.

Miller, Shannon. *Engendering the Fall: John Milton and Seventeenth-Century Women Writers*. Philadelphia: University of Pennsylvania Press, 2008.

Milton, Anthony. 'Laud, William (1573–1645), Archbishop of Canterbury'. In *Oxford Dictionary of National Biography*. Oxford: Oxford University Press, 2004.

Milton, John. 'An Epitaph on the admirable Dramaticke Poet, W. Shakespeare'. In *Mr VVilliam Shakespeares comedies, histories, and tragedies Published according to the true originall copies*. London: Tho. Cotes, 1632.

Milton, John. *Justa Edouardo King*. Cambridge, 1638.

Milton, John. 'Upon old Hobson the Carrier of Cambridge'. In *Banquet of Jests*. London, 1640.

Milton, John. *Poems of Mr John Milton*. London: Humphrey Moseley, 1645.

Milton, John. 'Another on the Same' and 'Another'. In *Wit Restor'd*. London, 1658.

Milton, John. 'At a Vacation Exercise'. In *Poems, &c. Upon Several Occasions*. London: 1673.

Milton, John. 'Prolusion VI'. In *Epistolarum familiarium liber*. London, 1674.

Milton, John. *The Digression* (1681). The John Milton Reading Room, Dartmouth College. https://www.dartmouth.edu/~milton/reading_room/britain/digressionms/text.shtml. Accessed 4 March 2018.

Milton, John. *A Complete Collection of the Historical, Political, and Miscellaneous Works of John Milton*. Amsterdam [i.e. London]: *s.n.*, 1698.

Milton, John. *El Paraíso perdido*. Ed. and trans. Francisco Granados Maldonado. Mexico: Ignacio Cumplido, 1858.

Milton, John. *Poems: Reproduced in Facsimile from the Manuscript in Trinity College, Cambridge*. Menston Ilkley: Scholar Press, 1972.

Milton, John. *Political Writings*, ed. Martin Dzelzainis. Cambridge: Cambridge University Press, 1991.

Milton, John. *The Complete Prose Works of John Milton*, Don M. Wolfe, ed. 8 vols. New Haven: Yale University Press, 1953–82.

Milton, John. *Manuscript Writings*, ed. William Poole, *Complete Works*, vol. XI. Oxford: Oxford University Press, 2019.

Miner, Earl Roy, William Moeck, and Steven Edward Jablonski, eds. *Paradise Lost, 1668–1968: Three Centuries of Commentary*. Lewisburg: Bucknell University Press, 2004.

Mintz, Susannah B. 'Anne Finch's "Fair Play"'. *Midwest Quarterly* 45, no. 1 (2003).

Mohamed, Feisal. 'Confronting Religious Violence: Milton's *Samson Agonistes*', *PMLA* 120, 2 (2005): 327–40.

Mohamed, Feisal. *Milton and the Post-Secular Present: Ethics, Politics, Terrorism*. Stanford: Stanford University Press, 2011.

Mohamed, Feisal. 'Milton, Sir Henry Vane, and the Brief but Significant Life of Godly Republicanism', *Huntington Library Quarterly* 76 (2013): 83–104.

Mohamed, Feisal, and Patrick Fadely, eds. *Milton's Modernities: Poetry, Philosophy, and History from the Seventeenth Century to the Present*. Evanston, IL: Northwestern University Press, 2017.

Mohamed, Feisal. *Sovereignty: Seventeenth-Century England and the Making of the Modern Political Imaginary*. Oxford: Oxford University Press, 2020.

More, Thomas. *A Dialogue Concerning Heresies*. In *The Yale Edition of The Complete Works of St. Thomas More*, ed. Thomas M. C. Lawler et al., vol. 6. New Haven: Yale University Press, 1981.

Morrill, John. 'Which World Turned Upside Down?' *Prose Studies* 36 (2014): 231–42.

Morrissey, Lee. 'Milton, Modernity, and the Periodization of Politics'. *Modern Language Quarterly* 78, 3 (2017): 301–19.

Mortimer, Sarah. *Reason and Religion in the English Revolution: The Challenge of Socinianism*. Cambridge: Cambridge University Press, 2010.

Moxon, Joseph. *Mechanick Exercises of the Whole Art of Printing (1683–4)*, 2nd edn. Ed. Herbert Davies and Harry Carter. London: Oxford University Press, 1962.

Moyles, R. G. *The Text of* Paradise Lost: *A Study in Editorial Procedure*. Toronto: University of Toronto Press, 1985.

Mulier, Eco O. G. Haitsma. *The Myth of Venice and Dutch Republican Thought in the Seventeenth Century*. Assen: Van Gorcum, 1980.

Munro, Lucy. *Children of the Queen's Revels: A Jacobean Theatre Repertory*. Cambridge: Cambridge University Press, 2005.

Munro, Lucy. *Archaic Style in English Literature, 1590–1674*. Cambridge: Cambridge University Press, 2013.

Murgia, Mario. 'Either in Prose or Rhyme: Translating Milton (in)to Latin America'. In *Milton in Translation*, ed. Angelica Duran, Islam Issa, and Jonathan R. Olson. Oxford: Oxford University Press, 2017: 279–92.

Murgia, Mario. 'Milton in Revolutionary Hispanoamerica'. In *Milton Studies 58* 'Special Issue: Milton in the Americas', ed. Elizabeth Sauer and Angelica Duran. Pittsburgh: Duquesne University Press, 2018: 203–22.

Mutschmann, Heinrich. *Milton und das Licht: Die Geschichte einer Seelenerkrankung.* Halle: M. Niemeyer, 1920.

Myers, Benjamin. *Milton's Theology of Freedom.* Berlin: de Gruyter, 2006.

Nashe, Thomas. *Strange Newes.* London, 1592.

Neelakanta, Vanita. 'Theatrum Mundi and Milton's Theater of the Blind in *Samson Agonistes*'. *Journal for Early Modern Cultural Studies* 11 (2011): 30–58.

Nelson, Eric. *The Hebrew Republic: Jewish Sources and the Transformation of European Political Thought.* Cambridge: Harvard University Press, 2010.

Nesvig, Martin Austin. *Ideology and Inquisition: The World of the Censors in Early Mexico.* New Haven: Yale University Press, 2009.

Netzley, Ryan. 'Milton Now: Alternative Approaches and Contexts'. *Milton Quarterly* 49 (2015): 190–4.

Nevitt, Marcus. 'The Insults of Defeat: Royalist Responses to William Davenant's *Gondibert* (1651)'. *The Seventeenth Century* 24 (2009): 287–304.

Ngai, Sianne. *Ugly Feelings.* Cambridge, MA: Harvard University Press, 2005.

Norbrook, David. *Writing in the English Republic: Poetry, Rhetoric, and Politics, 1627–1660.* Cambridge: Cambridge University Press, 1999.

Norbrook, David. *Poetry and Politics in the English Renaissance.* Oxford: Oxford University Press, 2002.

Norbrook, David. 'Republican Occasions in *Paradise Regained* and *Samson Agonistes*'. *Milton Studies* 42 (2003): 122–48.

Norbrook, David, Stephen Harrison, and Philip Hardie, eds. *Lucretius and the Early Modern.* Oxford: Oxford University Press, 2016.

Nyquist, Mary. 'Reading the Fall: Discourse and Drama in *Paradise Lost*'. *English Literary Renaissance* 14 (1984): 199–229.

Nyquist, Mary. 'The genesis of gendered subjectivity in the divorce tracts and in *Paradise Lost*'. In *Re-membering Milton: Essays on the Texts and Traditions*, ed. Mary Nyquist and Margaret Ferguson. New York: Methuen, 1987.

Nyquist, Mary. *Arbitrary Rule: Slavery, Tyranny, and the Power of Life and Death.* Chicago: University of Chicago Press, 2013.

O'Keeffe, Timothy. *Milton and the Pauline Tradition: A Study of Theme and Symbolism.* Washington, DC: University Press of America, 1982.

Onela, K. P., et al. 'Structure and Tie Strengths in Mobile Communications Networks'. *Proceedings of the National Academy of Sciences of the United States of America* 104 (2007): 7332–6.

Ong, Walter J. 'Introduction'. In *A Fuller Course in the Art of Logic Conformed to the Method of Peter Ramus (1672), by John Milton*, ed. and trans. Walter J. Ong and Charles J. Ermatinger. In *Complete Prose Works of John Milton*, Vol. 8, ed. Don M. Wolfe. New Haven: Yale University Press, 1982: 144–205.

Orgel, Stephen, and Jonathan Goldberg, eds. *John Milton: The Major Works, including Paradise Lost.* Oxford: Oxford University Press, 2008.

Osborn, James M., ed. *Joseph Spence: Observations, Anecdotes, and Characters of Books and Men, Collected from Conversation*, Vol. 1. Oxford: Oxford University Press, 1966.

Owen, John. *Vindiciae Evangelicae.* Oxford: Leon. Lichfield, 1655.

Owen, John. *Animadversions on a treatise intituled Fiat lux, or A guide in the differences of religion, between papist and Protestant, Presbyterian and independent by a Protestant.* London: E. Cotes, 1662.

Palmer, Herbert. *The Glasse of Gods Providence towards His Faithfull Ones*. London, 1644.

Parker, William R. 'The Trinity Manuscript and Milton's Plans for Tragedy'. *Journal of English and Germanic Philology* 34 (1935): 225–32.

Parker, William R. 'Contributions Toward a Milton Bibliography'. *The Library* 16 (1936): 425–38.

Parry, Graham. *Glory, Laud and Honour: The Arts of the Anglican Counter-Reformation*. Woodbridge: Boydell & Brewer, 2006.

Passannante, Gerard. *The Lucretian Renaissance: Philology and the Afterlife of Tradition*. Chicago: University of Chicago Press, 2011.

Pateman, Carole. *The Sexual Contract*. Stanford: Stanford University Press, 1988.

Patrides, C. A. 'John Donne Methodized; Or, How to Improve Donne's Impossible Text with the Assistance of His Several Editors'. *Modern Philology* 82.4 (1985): 365–73.

Patterson, Annabel. *Early Modern Liberalism*. Cambridge: Cambridge University Press, 1997.

Patterson, Annabel. *Milton's Words*. Oxford: Oxford University Press, 2009.

Patterson, Annabel. 'Say First, What Cause?: The Origins of *Paradise Lost*'. In *The Oxford Handbook of Literature and the English Revolution*, ed. Laura Lunger Knoppers. Oxford: Oxford University Press, 2012: 624–38.

Patterson, Frank Allen, ed. *The Works of John Milton*, 18 vols. New York: Columbia University Press, 1931–8.

Peacey, Jason. *Print and Public Politics in the English Revolution*. Cambridge: Cambridge University Press, 2013.

Peacey, Jason. *Politicians and Pamphleteers: Propaganda during the English Civil Wars and Interregnum*. London and New York: Routledge, 2016.

Pérez-Marchand, Monelisa Lina. *Dos etapas ideológicas del siglo XVIII en México: a través de los papeles de la Inquisición*. Mexico: El Colegio de Mexico, 2005.

Perkins, William. *A Warning against the Idolatrie of the last times*. Cambridge, 1601.

'Petition of Augustine Matthews to Sir John Lambe, Sir Nathaniel Brent, and Dr. Duck, commissioners concerning the printers of London'. *Calendar of State Papers Domestic, Charles I*, July 1637.

Phillips, Edward. 'The Life of Mr. John Milton'. In *The Early Lives of Milton*, ed. Helen Darbishire. London: Constable, 1932: 49–82.

Phillips, Philip E. 'Muses'. In *The Milton Encyclopedia*, ed. Thomas N. Corns, 250. New Haven: Yale University Press, 2012.

Picciotto, Joanna. *Labors of Innocence in Early Modern England*. Cambridge: Harvard University Press, 2010.

Plant, Marjorie. *The English Book Trade: An Economic History of the Making and Sale of Books*, 3rd edn. London: George Allen & Unwin, 1974.

Plato. *Phaedrus*. London: Penguin Classics, 2005.

Plato. *Theaetetus*. London: Penguin Classics, 2014.

Plomer, H. R. *A Transcript of the Registers of the Worshipful Company of Stationers: from 1640–1708*, vol. 1. London: Private printing, 1913.

Pocock, J. G. A. 'British History: A Plea for a New Subject'. *Journal of Modern History* 47 (1975): 601–28.

Pogson, Fiona. 'Cottington, Francis, first Baron Cottington (1579?–1652), diplomat and politician'. In *Oxford Dictionary of National Biography*. Oxford: Oxford University Press, 2004.

Pollard, A.W., and G. R. Redgrave. *The Short-Title Catalogue, 1475–1640*, 3 vols., 2nd edn. Rev. W. A. Jackson, F. S. Ferguson, and Katharine Pantzer. London: Bibliographical Society, 1986–91.

Poole, Kristen. *Radical Religion from Shakespeare to Milton: Figures of Nonconformity in Early Modern England*. Cambridge: Cambridge University Press, 2000.

Poole, William. *Milton and the Idea of the Fall*. Cambridge: Cambridge University Press, 2005.

Poole, William. 'The Genres of Milton's Commonplace Book'. In *The Oxford Handbook of Milton*, ed. Nicholas McDowell and Nigel Smith. Oxford: Oxford University Press, 2009: 367–81.

Poole, William. 'John Milton and Giovanni Boccaccio's *Vita di Dante*'. *Milton Quarterly* 48 (2014): 139–70.

Poole, William. *Milton and the Making of* Paradise Lost. Cambridge, MA: Harvard University Press, 2017.

Poole, William. 'The Literary Remains of Alexander Gil the Elder (1565–1635) and Younger (1596/7–1642?)'. *Milton Quarterly* 51.3 (2018): 163–91.

Poole, William, ed. *The Complete Works of John Milton: Volume XI: Manuscript Writings*. Oxford: Oxford University Press, 2019.

Prawdzik, Brendan. '"Look on Me": Theater, Gender and Poetic Identity Formation in Milton's Maske'. *Studies in Philology* 110 (2013): 812–50.

Prynne, William. *Twelve Considerable Serious Questions touching Church Government*. London: F.L., 1644.

Quilligan, Maureen. *Milton's Spenser: The Politics of Reading*. Ithaca: Cornell University Press, 1983.

Quint, David. 'Milton, Waller, and the Fate of Eden'. *Modern Language Quarterly* 78 (Sept. 2017): 373–93.

Quintrell, Brian. 'Richardson, Sir Thomas (*bap.* 1569, *d.* 1635), judge'. In *Oxford Dictionary of National Biography*. Oxford: Oxford University Press, 2004.

Quitslund, Beth. 'Idologographies: Versions of Miltonic Iconoclasm'. *Milton Quarterly* 33:1 (1999): 22–7.

Rajan, Balachandra, and Elizabeth Sauer, eds. *Milton and the Imperial Vision*. Pittsburgh: Duquesne University Press, 1999.

Raylor, Timothy. *Cavaliers, Clubs, and Literary Culture: Sir John Mennes, James Smith, and the Order of the Fancy*. London and Toronto: Associated University Presses, 1994.

Raylor, Timothy. 'Moseley, Walkley, and the 1645 Editions of Waller'. *Library* 2, no. 3 (2001): 236–65.

Raylor, Timothy. 'Hobbes, Davenant, and Disciplinary Tensions in *The Preface to Gondibert*'. In *Collaboration and Interdisciplinarity in the Republic of Letters*, ed. Paul Scott. Manchester: Manchester University Press, 2010: 59–72.

Raymond, Joad. 'Milton'. In *The Cambridge History of the Book in Britain, Volume 4 1557–1695*, ed. John Barnard and D. F. McKenzie with Maureen Bell. Cambridge: Cambridge University Press, 1999: 376–87.

Raymond, Joad. 'Thomas Margetts: A New Milton Manuscript, and a New Defender of the People of England'. *Milton Quarterly* 50 (2016): 219–40.

Reisner, Noam. 'Obituary and Rapture in Milton's Memorial Latin Poems'. In *Young Milton: The Emerging Author, 1620–1642*, ed. Edward Jones. Oxford: Oxford University Press, 2013: 161–81.

Revard, Stella. *Milton and the Tangles of Neaera's Hair: The Making of the 1645 Poems*. Columbia: University of Missouri Press, 1997.

Reynolds, Myra, ed. *The Poems of Anne Countess of Winchilsea*. Chicago: University of Chicago Press, 1903.

Richardson, Jonathan, Jr and Sr. 'Explanatory Notes and Remarks on Milton's "Paradise Lost" ... With the Life of the Author'. In *The Early Lives of Milton*, ed. Helen Darbishire. London: Constable, 1932: 199–330.

Richek, Roslyn. 'Thomas Randolph's Salting (1627), its Text, and John Milton's Sixth Prolusion as Another Salting'. *English Literary Renaissance* 12 (1982): 102–31.

Rochester, John Wilmot, Earl of. *The Works of the Right Honourable Earls of Rochester and Roscommon*. London: Printed for E. Curll, 1709.

Rogers, Pat. 'Addison, Joseph (1672–1719), writer and politician'. In *Oxford Dictionary of National Biography*. Oxford: Oxford University Press, 2004.

Rosenblatt, Jason. *Torah and Law in* Paradise Lost. Princeton: Princeton University Press, 1994.

Rudd, Niall, ed. and trans. *Odes and Epodes*. Cambridge: Harvard University Press, 2004.

Rumrich, John P. 'The Erotic Milton'. *Texas Studies in Literature and Language* 41.2 (1999): 128–41.

Rutherford, Jonathan. 'The Third Space. Interview with Homi Bhabha'. In *Identity: Community, Culture, Difference*. London: Lawrence & Wishart, 1990.

Sabbadini, Lorenzo. 'Property, Liberty and Self-Ownership in the English Revolution'. Unpublished Ph.D. thesis: University of London, 2013.

Said, Edward. *Culture and Imperialism*. New York: Vintage, 1994.

Salteren, George. *A Treatise against Images and Pictures in Churches: And an Answer to Those Who Object that the Times are Changed*. London: William Lee, 1641.

Sanchez, Melissa. ' "What Hath Night to Do with Sleep?": Biopolitics in Milton's Mask'. *Early Modern Culture* 10.4(2014): https://tigerprints.clemson.edu/emc/vol10/iss1/4/.

Sánchez, Reuben. *Typology and Iconography in Donne, Herbert, and Milton: Fashioning the Self after Jeremiah*. New York: Palgrave Macmillan, 2014.

Sandys, George, trans. *Ovid's Metamorphosis*. London: 1626.

Sano, Hiroko. 'Translating Milton's Poetry into Japanese'. In *Milton in Translation*, ed. Angelica Duran, Islam Issa, and Jonathan R. Olson. Oxford: Oxford University Press, 2017: 470–1.

Sarmiento y Valladeres, Diego, and Vidal Marín. *Novissimus librorum prohibitorvm et expvrgandorvm*, 2 vols. Madrid: Ex Typographia Musicae, 1707.

Sauer, Elizabeth. 'Milton and Dryden on the Restoration Stage'. In *Fault Lines and Controversies in the Study of Seventeenth-Century English Literature*, ed. Claude J. Summers and Ted-Larry Pebworth. Columbia: University of Missouri Press, 2002: 88–110.

Sauer, Elizabeth. *Paper Contestations and Textual Communities in England, 1640–1675*. Toronto: University of Toronto Press, 2005.

Sauer, Elizabeth. *Milton, Toleration, and Nationhood*. Cambridge: Cambridge University Press, 2014.

Sauer, Elizabeth. 'MSA Platinum Jubilee at the 2018 MLA'. *Milton Quarterly* 52 (March 2018).

Saunders, J. W. *The Profession of English Letters*. London: Routledge, 1964.

Scott-Warren, Jason. 'Reconstructing Manuscript Networks: the textual transactions of Sir Stephen Powle'. In *Communities in Early Modern England*, ed. Alexandra Shepard and Phil Withington. Manchester: Manchester University Press, 2000: 18–37.

Scott-Warren, Jason. 'Milton's Shakespeare?' Centre for Material Texts, September 9, 2019 https://www.english.cam.ac.uk/cmt/?p=5751.

Shakespeare, William. *Mr VVilliam Shakespeares comedies, histories, and tragedies Published according to the true originall copies*. London, 1632.

Shakespeare, William. *Poems: Written by Wil. Shake-speare* (London, 1640).

Sharpe, Kevin. *Criticism and Compliment*. Cambridge: Cambridge University Press, 1987.

Sharpe, Kevin. *Image Wars: Promoting Kings and Commonwealths in England, 1603–1660*. New Haven: Yale University Press, 2010.

Shawcross, John T. 'The Date of the Separate Edition of Milton's *Epitaphium Damonis*'. *Studies in Bibliography* 18 (1965): 262–5.

Shawcross, John T. *With Mortal Voice: The Creation of* Paradise Lost. Lexington: University Press of Kentucky, 1982.

Shawcross, John T. *The Development of Milton's Thought: Law, Government, and Religion.* Pittsburgh: Duquesne University Press, 2008.

Shore, Daniel. 'Why Milton Is Not an Iconoclast'. *PMLA* 127.1 (2012): 22–37.

Showerman, Grant, trans. *'Heroides' and 'Amores'*. Cambridge: Harvard University Press, 1963.

Sierhuis, Freya. 'The Idol of the Heart: Liberty, Tyranny, and Idolatry in the Work of Fulke Greville'. *Modern Language Review* 106 (2011): 626–46.

Simpson, D. P. *Cassell's Latin Dictionary*. New York: Macmillan Publishing Company, 1977.

Simpson, James. 'Statues of Liberty: Iconoclasm and Idolatry in the English Revolution'. In *Under the Hammer: Iconoclasm in the Anglo-American Tradition*. Oxford: Oxford University Press, 2010: 85–115.

Simpson, Ken. *Spiritual Architecture and* Paradise Regained: *Milton's Literary Ecclesiology.* Pittsburgh: Duquesne University Press, 2007.

Skinner, Quentin. 'John Milton and the Politics of Slavery'. In *Milton and the Terms of Liberty*, ed. Graham Parry and Joad Raymond. Cambridge: Brewer, 2002: 1–22.

Slack, Paul. 'Religious Protest and Urban Authority: The Case of Henry Sherfield, Iconoclast, 1633'. In *Schism, Heresy and Religious Protest*, ed. Derek Baker. Cambridge: Cambridge University Press, 1972: 295–302.

Slack, Paul. 'The Public Conscience of Henry Sherfield'. In *Public Duty and Private Conscience in Seventeenth-Century England*, ed. John Morrill, Paul Slack, and Daniel Woolf. Oxford: Clarendon Press, 1993: 151–71.

Slack, Paul. 'Sherfield, Henry (*bap.* 1572, *d.* 1634), lawyer and iconoclast'. In *Oxford Dictionary of National Biography*. Oxford: Oxford University Press, 2004.

Smith, David L. 'Catholic, Anglican or Puritan? Edward Sackville, Fourth Earl of Dorset, and the Ambiguities of Religion in Early Stuart England'. *Transactions of the Royal Historical Society* 2 (1992): 105–24.

Smith, Nigel. 'Milton and Popular Republicanism in the 1650s: John Streater's "Heroick Mechanicks"'. In *Milton and Republicanism*, ed. David Armitage, Armand Himy, and Quentin Skinner. Cambridge: Cambridge University Press, 1995: 137–55.

Smith, Nigel. '"And if God was one of us:" Paul Best, John Biddle, and anti-Trinitarian heresy in seventeenth-century England'. In *Heresy in Early Modern England*, ed. David Loewenstein and John Marshall. Cambridge: Cambridge University Press, 2006.

Smith, Nigel. *Is Milton better than Shakespeare?* Cambridge: Harvard University Press, 2008.

Smith, Nigel. 'Retranslating the Bible in the English Revolution'. In *The Oxford Handbook of the Bible in Early Modern England, c. 1530–1700*, ed. Kevin Killeen, Helen Smith, and Rachel Willie. Oxford: Oxford University Press, 2015: 98–110.

Smolenaars, Marja. 'Aylmer, Brabazon (*bap.* 1645, *d.* in or after 1719), bookseller'. In *Oxford Dictionary of National Biography*. Oxford: Oxford University Press, 2004.

Smuts, R. *Culture and Power in England, 1585–1685*. New York: St. Martin's Press, 1999.

Song, Eric B. *Dominion Undeserved: Milton and the Perils of Creation*. Ithaca: Cornell University Press, 2013.

Spenser, Edmund. 'A Letter of the Authors Expounding His Whole Intention in the Course of this Work'. In *The Faerie Queene*, ed. Thomas P. Roche. London: Penguin, 1978.

Spenser, Edmund. 'Sonnet 75'. In *'Amoretti' and 'Epithalamion': A Critical Edition*, ed. Kenneth J. Larsen. Tempe: Medieval and Renaissance Texts and Studies, 1997: 98.

Spink, Ian. *Henry Lawes: Cavalier Songwriter*. Oxford: Oxford University Press, 2000.

Spraggon, Julie. *Puritan Iconoclasm During the English Civil War*. Woodbridge: Boydell Press, 2003.

Stevens, Paul. *Imagination and the Presence of Shakespeare in Paradise Lost*. Madison: University of Wisconsin Press, 1985.

Stevens, Paul. 'Discontinuities in Milton's Early Public Self-Representation'. *The Huntington Library Quarterly* 51.4 (1988): 260–80.

Stevens, Paul. 'Milton's Janus-faced Nationalism: Soliloquy, Subject, and the Modern Nation-State'. *Journal of English and Germanic Philology* 100:2 (2001): 247–68.

Stevens, Paul. 'Milton's Nationalism and the Rights of Memory'. In *Imagining Death in Spenser and Milton*, ed. Elizabeth J. Bellamy, Patrick Cheney, and Michael Schoenfeldt. Basingstoke: Palgrave Macmillan, 2003: 171–84.

Stevens, Paul. 'Milton and the Marginalization of the Humanities'. *Milton Quarterly* 50 (2016): 75–82.

Stevens, Paul, and Patricia Simmons, eds. 'Milton in America'. *University of Toronto Quarterly* 77, no.3 (2008): 761–960.

Straznicky, Marta. 'Introduction'. In *Shakespeare's Stationers: Studies in Cultural Bibliography*, ed. Marta Straznicky. Philadelphia: University of Pennsylvania Press, 2013: 3.

Suckling, John. *The Last Remains of Sr John Suckling*. London, 1659.

Sugimura, N. K. *'Matter of Glorious Trial': Spiritual and Material Substance in* Paradise Lost. New Haven: Yale University Press, 1999.

Taylor, George Coffin. *Milton's Use of Du Bartas*. Cambridge: Harvard University Press, 1934.

Teskey, Gordon. 'From Allegory to Dialectic: Imagining Error in Spenser and Milton'. *PMLA* 101, no. 1 (1986): 9–23.

Teskey, Gordon. *The Poetry of John Milton*. Cambridge: Harvard University Press, 2015.

Thatcher, Margaret. 'Advice to a Superpower'. *The New York Times*, 11 Feb. 2002, s.v. 'Opinion'.

Tournu, Christophe. '"The French Connection" among French Translations of Milton and within Du Bocage's *Paradise terrestre*'. In *Milton in Translation*, ed. Angelica Duran, Islam Issa, and Jonathan R. Olson. Oxford: Oxford University Press, 2017: 139–63.

Trubowitz, Rachel. 'Introduction'. Special issue on 'Milton and the Politics of Periodization'. *Modern Language Quarterly* 78.3 (2017): 291–9.

Turner, James Grantham. *One Flesh: Paradisal Marriage and Sexual Relations in the Age of Milton*. Oxford: Clarendon Press, 1987.

Valdés, Mario J., and Djelal Kadir, eds. *Literary Cultures of Latin America: A Comparative History*. Vols. 1–3. Oxford: Oxford University Press, 2004.

Venuti, Lawrence, ed. *The Translation Studies Reader*. 2nd edn. New York: Routledge, 2004.

Vicars, John. *The Sinfulness and Unlawfulness of making or having the Picture of Christ's Humanity: set Forth in a succinct and plain Discourse, and the main and most vulgar Reasons and Objections against this Truth, clearly evinced and refuted*. London: M.F., 1641.

Virgil. *Aeneid*. London: Penguin Classics, 2003.

von Maltzahn, Nicholas. 'Laureate, Republican, Calvinist: An Early Response to Milton and *Paradise Lost*'. *Milton Studies* 29 (1993): 181–98.

von Maltzahn, Nicholas. 'The Whig Milton, 1667–1700'. In *Milton and Republicanism*, ed. David Armitage, Armand Himy, and Quentin Skinner. Cambridge: Cambridge University Press, 1995: 229–53.

von Maltzahn, Nicholas. 'The First Reception of *Paradise Lost* (1667)'. *The Review of English Studies, New Series* 47, no. 188 (1996): 479–99.

von Maltzahn, Nicholas. 'Dryden's Milton and the Theatre of Imagination'. In *John Dryden: Trecentenary Essays*, ed. Paul Hammond and David Hopkins. Oxford: Clarendon Press, 2000: 32–56.

von Maltzahn, Nicholas. 'L'Estrange's Milton'. In *Roger L'Estrange and the Making of Restoration Culture*, ed. Anne Dunan-Page and Beth Lynch. London: Routledge, 2008: 27–52.

Walker, William. *Paradise Lost and Republican Tradition from Aristotle to Machiavelli.* Turnhout: Brepols, 2009.

Walker, William. *Antiformalist, Unrevolutionary, Illiberal Milton: Political Prose, 1644– 1660.* Farnham: Ashgate, 2014.

Walker, William. 'Milton's "Radicalism" in the Tyrannicide Tracts'. *The European Legacy* 19 (2014): 287–308.

Walsh, Marcus. *Shakespeare, Milton, and Eighteenth-Century Literary Editing: The Beginnings of Interpretative Scholarship.* Cambridge: Cambridge University Press, 1997.

Walsham, Alexandra. 'Angels and Idols in England's Long Reformation'. In *Angels in the Early Modern World*, ed. Peter Marshall and Alexandra Walsham. Cambridge: Cambridge University Press, 2006: 134–67.

Walsham, Alexandra. *The Reformation of the Landscape: Religion, Identity, and Memory in Early Modern Britain and Ireland.* Oxford: Oxford University Press, 2011.

Ward, Charles E., ed. *The Letters of John Dryden, with Letters Addressed to Him.* Durham: Duke University Press, 1942.

Watt, Tessa. 'The Broadside Picture'. In *Cheap Print and Popular Piety: 1550–1640.* Cambridge: Cambridge University Press, 1991: 131–253.

Weiss, Adrian. 'Casting Compositors, Foul Cases, and Skeletons: Printing in Middleton's Age'. In *Thomas Middleton and Early Modern Textual Culture*, ed. Gary Taylor and John Lavagnino. Oxford: Oxford University Press, 2007: 195–225.

Wells-Cole, Anthony. *Art and Decoration in Elizabethan and Jacobean England: The Influence of Continental Prints 1558–1625.* London: Paul Mellon Centre, 1997.

Werlin, Julianne. 'Paper Angels: *Paradise Lost* and the European state system', *Milton Studies*, 61 (2019), 212–38

Westerholm, Stephen. *Perspectives Old and New on Paul: The 'Lutheran' Paul and His Critics.* Grand Rapids: Eerdmans, 2004.

Weststeijn, Arthur. *Commercial Republicanism in the Dutch Golden Age: The Political Thought of Johan & Pieter de la Court.* Leiden and Boston: Brill, 2012.

Whitaker, Curtis. 'Domesticating and Foreignizing the Sublime: *Paradise Lost* in German'. In *Milton in Translation*, ed. Angelica Duran, Islam Issa, and Jonathan R. Olson. Oxford: Oxford University Press, 2017: 115–37.

Wilburn, Reginald A. *Preaching the Gospel of Black Revolt: Appropriating Milton in Early African American Literature.* Philadelphia: Penn State University Press, 2014.

Wilcox, Helen. 'Introduction'. In *The English Poems of George Herbert*, ed. Helen Wilcox. Cambridge: Cambridge University Press, 2007: xxi–xxxvi.

Williams, David. *Milton's Leveller God.* Montreal: McGill-Queen's University Press, 2017.

Willie, Rachel. *Staging the Revolution: Drama, Reinvention and History, 1647–72.* Manchester: Manchester University Press, 2015.

Winstanley, William. *The Lives of the Most Famous English Poets.* London: Samuel Manship, 1687.

Winton, Calhoun. 'Steele, Sir Richard (*bap.* 1672, *d.* 1729), writer and politician'. In *Oxford Dictionary of National Biography*. Oxford: Oxford University Press, 2004.

Wiseman, Susan. *Drama and Politics in the English Civil War*. Cambridge: Cambridge University Press, 1998.

Wither, George. *The Schollers Purgatory discouered in the Stationers common-wealth, and described in a discourse apologeticall, aswell for the publike aduantage of the Church, the state & whole common-wealth of England, as for the remedy of pruate iniuryes.* London: G. Wood, 1624.

Witten-Hannah, Margaret Anne. 'Lady Mary Wroth's Urania: The Work and the Tradition'. PhD dissertation, University of Auckland, 1978.

Wittreich, Joseph A. *Feminist Milton*. Ithaca: Cornell University Press, 1987.

Wittreich, Joseph A. *Why Milton Matters: A New Preface to His Writings*. New York: Palgrave Macmillan, 2006.

Wolfe, Don M., ed. *The Complete Prose Works of John Milton*, 8 vols. New Haven: Yale University Press, 1953–82.

Woodcock, E. C. *A New Latin Syntax*. London: Methuen, 1959.

Woolf, Virginia. *A Room of One's Own*. New York: Harvest Books, 1989.

Worden, Blair. 'Milton, Samson Agonistes, and the Restoration'. In *Culture and Society in the Stuart Restoration*, ed. Gerald MacLean. Cambridge: Cambridge University Press, 1995: 111–36.

Worden, Blair. *Literature and Politics in Cromwellian England: John Milton, Andrew Marvell, Marchamont Nedham.* Oxford: Oxford University Press, 2007.

Wright, Gillian. *Producing Women's Poetry, 1600–1730*. Cambridge: Cambridge University Press, 2013.

Yorke, Peter. 'Iconoclasm, Ecclesiology and "the Beauty of Holiness:" Concepts of Sacrilege and the "Peril of Idolatry" in Early Modern England, Circa 1590–1642'. Unpublished PhD dissertation. University of Kent, 1997.

Young, Elizabeth Marie. *Translation as Muse: Poetic Translation in Catullus's Rome.* Chicago, University of Chicago Press, 2015.

Young, Michael B. 'Coke, Sir John (1563–1644), Politician'. In *Oxford Dictionary of National Biography*. Oxford: Oxford University Press, 2004.

Zwicker, Steven N. 'Milton, Dryden, and the Politics of Literary Controversy'. In *Culture and Society in the Stuart Restoration: Literature, Drama, History*, ed. Gerald Maclean. Cambridge: Cambridge University Press, 1995: 137–58.

Zwicker, Steven N. *Lines of Authority: Politics and English Literary Culture, 1649–1689.* Ithaca: Cornell University Press, 1996.

Zwicker, Steven N. '"On First Looking into Revisionism:" The Literature of Civil War, Revolution, and Restoration', *Huntington Library Quarterly* 78. 4 (Winter 2015): 789–807.

Zwicker, Steven N. 'John Dryden Meets, Rhymes, and Says Farewell to John Milton: A Restoration Drama in Three Acts'. In *Milton in the Long Restoration,* ed. Blair Hoxby and Ann Baynes Coiro. Oxford: Oxford University Press, 2016: 181–90.

Zwingli, Huldrych. *Eine kurze christliche Einleitung* (1523). In *Huldreich Zwinglis sämtliche Werke,* Corpus Reformatorum 89, vol. 2. Leipzig: Heinsius, 1908.

Zwingli, Huldrych. *Eine Antwort, Valentin Compar gegeben* (1525). In *Huldreich Zwinglis sämtliche Werke,* Corpus Reformatorum 91, vol. 4. Leipzig: Heinsius, 1927.

Index